# Victorious Living

E. STANLEY JONES

ABINGDON PRESS
NASHVILLE    NEW YORK

VICTORIOUS LIVING

MANUFACTURED BY THE PARTHENON PRESS AT
NASHVILLE, TENNESSEE, UNITED STATES OF AMERICA

# INTRODUCTION

THREE years ago the Inner Urge came to me to write on Victorious Living. The Voice seemed to sum up what through years of dealing with inquirers has become to me a pressing fact, namely, that the most urgent necessity in human living is to be able to face life victoriously. For many—the number is appalling—are living morally and spiritually defeated. They are inwardly beaten, hence outwardly ineffective. They do not know how to live and to live victoriously. They lack resources. This book is addressed to that need.

I have tried to combine the individual and the social emphases in a living blend, with a devotional spirit running through all. The socially-minded must be patient if I seem in the beginning to stress overmuch the personal emphasis. I think we should begin just there. But we must not end there. The end is the sum total of human relationships.

In the structure of the book I have tried to meet three needs: (1) A book of daily devotions for personal, group, and family devotions. Instead of making it, as usual in devotional books, a book of scattered thoughts, changing from day to day, I have woven the devotions around one theme, VICTORIOUS LIVING. (2) I have gathered these daily studies into groups of seven, so that the book can be used as a weekly study book by classes of various kinds. (3) I have tried to put the subject matter into such a continuous whole that it may be read through as an ordinary book.

I have begun at the lowest rung of the ladder, and have tried to go step by step to the full implications of victorious living. Mature souls must be patient with the first steps, remembering that many are not able to live a victorious life because they do not know how to link up with God's power. I have tried to make the first steps very clear. In doing so I have endeavored to answer this letter: "I am an average young American mother. I have two very small children. I have read your last book, *Christ's Alternative to Communism.* It is great, soul-stirring, ringing with truth, but it leaves me with a terrific thirst —how do you get it? You advised a bored young woman to 'Try Christ, and I give you my word of honor that it will

# INTRODUCTION

work to the degree you work it.' But how? Where to start? Then again in chapter eleven: 'Today so far as I am concerned this program begins'—and, still, how? How to achieve a life evidencing the peace that passes understanding, even in myself, let alone passing it on? How does the kingdom of God start within my unruly, discontented, selfish, ungrateful, impatient, and sullen self, before I can begin to spread it? Your books (I have read several) paint a glorious picture of living life—but you forgot to tell us what brushes and colors to use, and how. I believe there must be thousands like me. Won't you write a book about 'Christ and the Kingdom Within'?"

I am sure that the writer of this letter represents many, and I have written for them as well as for the mature Christian. I mentioned in my last book that I had received a request signed by many prominent Christians of America asking me to write a book on the "Inner Life." I trust that this book fulfills that request—a request which I deeply appreciated. But, as the reader will see, it goes beyond it, for all life is one, the inner and the outer being indissoluble.

The book was written during a three-months' "retreat" in the Himalayas, the mornings being spent in writing and the afternoons and evenings in going through a course of reading —the only vacation—if it can be called one—that I have had for some years. It was the cold season, and these hills were deserted at that time, so that my only companions were an Indian secretary and the wild animals that roamed the estate—the deer, the panther, the tiger, and the wild pig. At noon, after a morning of writing, I would take a walk through these lovely mountain paths to clear my brain, only to return to find that my faithful secretary, who was unused to the mountains, had been spending anxious moments of prayer for me till I got back safely! It was the unknown to him—to me it was the beloved known. Perhaps many of my friends across the seas will share that same anxiety and will be in anxious prayer as we penetrate from the known personal to the jungle of social relationships, and will wonder if we should not stick to the beaten paths of personal religion. But this jungle of social relations must be Christianized, for Christ must claim all life.

At the close of the retreat I had the unspeakable privilege of presenting the manuscript, during May and June, to the Sat Tal Ashram Group, made up of many nationalities, and of receiving their criticisms and suggestions.

# INTRODUCTION

Many in that group were led into victorious living as we made our way through step by step, and now it goes to the larger circle, and it goes out with prayer, that among them too may be many who will find through these pages a clear path from confused and baffled and defeated human living to living that is certain, adequate, and victorious.

E. STANLEY JONES.

Job 11. 7–9   Job 23. 3–9
Job 21. 15   John 14. 8

## THE QUESTION THAT HALTS OUR QUEST

In the beginning God (Genesis 1. 1).

It would be well if, in our quest for "Victorious Living," we could all begin with God. It would put a solid fact beneath our questing feet. It would give meaning and purpose to the whole of life. But, alas, many of us cannot begin there. For God is the vague, the unreal. We wish we could believe in Him, and get hold of Him so that we could live by Him, for life without the Great Companion has a certain emptiness and meaninglessness about it. For many skepticism is not voluntary, but apparently unavoidable. The facts of life are too much for us—the unemployment, the hunger of little children, the underlying strife in modern life, the exploitation of the weak and incapacitated by the strong, the apparently unmerited suffering around us, the heartlessness of nature, the discoveries of science which seem to render the hypothesis of God unnecessary—all these things, and more, seem to shatter our belief in God. We do not reject that belief; it simply fades away and becomes unreal. And we cannot assert what to us is not real. For amid all the losses of our modern day we are trying to save one thing amid the wreckage, namely, the desire for reality. We wish to keep an inner integrity. We loathe all unreality. That leads us to face the fact that our skepticism has gone deeper than the matter of belief in God; we find ourselves questioning life itself. Has life any meaning? Any goal? Is the flame of life within us different from the flame that leaps from the logs in the fireplace—both of them the result of material forces and both destined to die down into a final ash? If it has no ultimate meaning, has it any meaning now as we live it?

———

O God, our Father—if we may call Thee thus—as we begin this quest we are haunted with many a biting fear and hesitation and doubt. Help us to face them all and come out, if possible, on the further side of them into victorious living. Amen.

## SHALL WE FOLLOW A LIFE-NO OR A LIFE-YES?

There are just two elemental philosophies of life: that of Buddha and that of Christ. The rest are compromises between. When H. G. Wells chose the three greatest men of history he selected Christ, then Buddha, then Aristotle—Life-Affirmation, Life-Denial, and the Scientific Method. The two greatest characters of history head up two diametrically different outlooks on life. Both of them looked at the same facts of life and came to opposite conclusions—one to a final Yes, and the other to a final No.

Buddha, pondering under the Bo tree, came to the conclusion that existence and evil are one. The only way to get out of evil is to get out of existence itself. Nirvana is so close to annihilation that scholars are still doubting whether it means annihilation or not. "Is there any existence in Nirvana?" I asked a Buddhist monk in Ceylon. "How could there be?" he replied, "for if there were existence, there would be suffering." "Is it an emptiness, a cipher?" "It is an emptiness, a cipher," he replied with a final and decisive gesture. It is true that this is called "bliss," but it is the bliss of the world-weary. In its revolt against life the soul performs its final "hara-kiri," clothed, it is true, with an air of sanctity and nobility. Buddha would cheat the sufferings and evils of life by getting rid of life itself. He would have us perform a sanctified suicide, not only of the physical, but of personality itself. It is a final "No" to life.

There is much to be said for Buddha's position. Everything seems to be under the process of decay. The blushing bride—then the withered old woman shriveling to fit her narrow final shroud. We grasp the lurid colors of the sunset and find that we have grasped the dark—first the beauty, then the blackness.

———

O God, our Father, we stand confused and dismayed, not knowing if we shall be compelled to adopt the noble pessimism of souls like Buddha. Perhaps there is another way. We hardly dare to believe it. But show us the way—the way to life, if there is such a way. Amen.

## IS LIFE A BUBBLE OR IS IT AN EGG?

A noble missionary drew near in spirit to Buddha when he said with a sigh, "Every new affection brings a new affliction." Bertrand Russell also took his stand with Buddha when he said, "All the loneliness of humanity amid hostile forces is concentrated upon the individual soul which must struggle alone, with what courage it can command, against the whole weight of the universe that cares nothing for his hopes or fears." There are many modern followers of Buddha, unconscious, of course, but driven there by the hard facts of life. They worship with a sigh at the shrine of the "stupa."

Standing in the midst of a Buddhist ruin I asked the learned Indian curator why the stupa was always oval shaped. "Because Buddhism believes that life is a bubble, therefore the stupa is shaped like one," he replied. Life is a bubble—*sunnayavada*—"Nothingness" at its heart! At the very thought I felt the darkness close in upon me and my universe reel. But as I looked at it again light seemed to dawn: "Why, it isn't shaped like a bubble, it is shaped like an egg," I remarked, as I felt the rock beneath my feet.

Is life a bubble or is it an egg? Is it a bubble with nothing in it, or is it an egg filled with infinite possibilities—possibilities of growth and development and perfection? I vote for the egg view of life. I grant that even an egg, if badly handled, can turn rotten, so life can turn rotten if we handle it badly. Nevertheless, I shall have to vote on one side or the other of that question, and I shall tell you why I vote for the egg-view of life.

I follow a Man who saw just as deeply and more deeply than Buddha into the sorrow, the sheer misery of life and yet came out at the other end of it all and affirmed His faith in life. "I am come that they might have life, and that they might have it more abundantly." He affirmed that life was not a bubble, but an egg. Was He right?

O God, our Father, light gilds our darkened horizon as we listen to this Man. But will it be an *ignis fatuus* that leaves us floundering in the swamp of final despair? Help us, we pray. Amen.

## IN WHICH WE LOOK AT THE ALTERNATIVES

Is life a bubble or is it an egg? I must make my choice. On the one side, they tell us that the universe is slowly running down and that one day it will end in ash, carrying with it all things and all life to its final doom. Death shall reign. On the other hand, they tell us that the universe is being renewed by a silent and saving bombardment of life-giving rays, so that the last word is not being spoken by death but by life. Life shall reign. One says the universe is a bubble, the other says it is an egg.

On the one side, they tell us that man is made up of elements which can be purchased in a chemist shop for a few cents, so that life is only mucus and misery. On the other hand, they tell us that man is made in the image of the Divine, that he has infinite possibilities of growth and development before him. One says man is a bundle of futilities, the other says he is a bundle of possibilities.

On the one side, they say that man is just a composite of responses to stimuli from environment, mechanically determined and with no real power of choice. On the other hand, they say that man has sufficient freedom to determine his destiny and that the soul shapes its environment as well as being shaped by it. One says that human freedom is a bubble, the other says it is an egg.

Some say that prayer is an autcsuggesting of oneself into illusory states of mind, that nothing comes back save the echo of one's own voice. Others say that in prayer actual communication takes place, that I link myself with the resources of God, so that my powers and faculties are heightened and life is strengthened and purified at its center. One says prayer is futile, the other says it is fertile.

---

O God, our Father, we want life, but not false life. Show us if there is real life, and if there is, help us to choose it. Amen.

# IN WHICH WE CONTINUE TO LOOK AT THE ALTERNATIVES

On the one side, there are those who tell us that God is an unnecessary hypothesis, that science can explain all, that the interstices and gaps of the universe into which we used to put the working of God are being slowly but surely filled up by science, so that the universe is self-sufficient, law-abiding, and predictable. On the other hand, there are those who tell us that God is not to be found in the gaps and interstices and in an occasional breaking into the process, but He is in the process itself the life of its life; that the universe is dependable because God is dependable; that it works according to law because God's mind is an orderly mind, not whimsical and notional, that since intelligence comes out of the universe and meets my intelligence it must have gone into it, so that according to Jeans "the universe is more like a thought than a machine"; that since the universe seems to work toward purposive ends, we must either endow matter with intelligent purposes (in which case it would not be mere matter), or we must put a purposive creative Intelligence in and back of the process; that since the universe from the tiniest atom to the farthest star is mathematical, we must either believe that matter has sufficient intelligence to be mathematical, or else that "God is a pure mathematician"; it would seem that the purposive matter-hypothesis takes more sheer credulity than that there is an Infinite Spirit, called God, who is within the process working toward intelligent moral ends, inviting our limited spirits to work with Him toward intelligent, redemptive purposes.

One says the idea of God is a bubble, the other says it is an egg. I must make my choice.

———

O God, our Father, shall I rule Thee out and vote for a dead universe—dead because its final goal is death? Or shall I vote for a living universe with Thee as its genesis, with Thee as its perpetual Creator and with Thee as its goal and end? Clarify my mind, my heart, that I may not lose myself and Thee amid the maze of things. Amen.

2 Corinthians 13. 3 (Moffatt)
2 Timothy 2. 8
Hebrews 1. 1–3

## IN WHICH WE STILL CONTINUE TO LOOK AT THE ALTERNATIVES

There are those who tell us that Christ is a spent force in humanity; that Carlyle was right when he stood before the Italian wayside crucifix and slowly shook his head and said, "Poor Fellow, you have had your day"; that His day is over because He spoke to a simple age, but now we face a complicated, scientific age; that He was good, but not good enough—for us.

On the other hand, there are those who feel, with the Carlyle of later years, that His day is just beginning; that what has failed has been a miserable caricature and not the real thing; that even the partial application of His teaching and spirit has been one thing which has kept the soul of humanity alive; that He has been and is the depository and creator of the finest and best in humanity; that when we have hold of Him we have the key to God, to the meaning of the universe and to our own lives; that when we expose ourselves to Him in simplicity and obedience, life is changed, lifted, renewed, that He is the one really unspent force in religion—He faces this age as the Great Contemporary and its Judge. One says that dependence upon Jesus is a bubble, an illusion, the other says it is an egg with untold redemptive possibilities.

There are those who say that conversion is an adolescent phenomenon; coincident with and caused by the awakening of the sex instinct; or that it is the result of mob-suggestion, easily induced and quickly evanescent. On the other hand, many affirm that this change called conversion helps them control and redirect the powers of the sex instinct, and that far from being mob-suggestion it helps them to cut across the purposes of both the mob and the self when they are wrong. One says that conversion is a bubble, the other says that it is an egg.

O God, our Father, hold us steady as we face the issues. May there be no dodging, no turning to irrelevancies, and no excuses. Save us to the real. Amen.

14

## IN WHICH WE MAKE OUR CHOICE

The issues of life are before me, I must vote for or against a view of life which has worth, purpose, goal. If I vote that the universe has no meaning, then I vote that my own life has none. But if my life has no meaning and hence no purpose, it will go to pieces, for psychology tells us that without a strong controlling purpose, which co-ordinates life, the personality disintegrates through its own inner clashes—no purpose, no personality. But that purpose must be high enough to lift me out of myself. If my purposes end with myself, again I disintegrate. They must include God, who gives basis and lasting meaning to my purpose. If I lose God, I lose myself, my universe, everything. I see that Voltaire was right when he said, "If there is no God, we will have to invent one to keep sane."

If I let go of Christ, then God becomes the Distant, the Vague, the Unreal. In Christ I find "the near side of God." In Him God speaks to me a language I can understand, a human language. And as I listen to that Language my universe seems to become a Face—tender, strong, forgiving, redemptive. Law becomes Love.

If I do not sincerely get into touch with Him through the written Word, I neglect the greatest and most redemptive fact of history and I pay the penalty of being unfed at the place of my deepest need. If I do not pray, I shall probably become cynical and shallow. If I do pray, I shall probably get nerve and courage, a sense of adequacy, power over wayward desires and passions. If I undergo a moral and spiritual change called conversion, I shall probably be unified, morally straight, and spiritually adjusted. If I do not, I shall probably become a stunted human soul.

If I must vote, then I do. *I vote for Life.*

———

O God, our Father, I make the choice, I do choose life with all its fullest, deepest implications. Help me to find life and live it—victoriously. Amen.

JANUARY 8

Romans 8. 19–23 (Weymouth)
Matthew 5. 48

## WHY ARE WE RELIGIOUS?

There are a hundred and fifty or more various definitions of religion. One says it is "what we do with our solitariness"; another that it is "how we integrate ourselves socially"; another that "the root of religion is fear," and so on.

The reason that it is so difficult to define is that life is difficult to define. When we define religion in terms of its various manifestations, we get partial, sometimes contradictory definitions. Religion having many forms has one root. That root is in the urge after life, fuller life. In everything, from the lowest cell clear up to the highest man, there is an urge toward completion, toward perfection. "Everything lifts up strong hands toward perfection." The religious urge is found in that urge for completer life. It is that urge tuned toward higher, nobler ends. We feel that we cannot be complete unless this urge for life is fastened upon the highest life, God. Religion is the urge for life turned qualitative. It is not satisfied with life apart from quality. The urge for quantitative life reached its crest in the dinosaurs. That failed—it was a road with a dead end. The huge animals died. In man the life urge turns from being merely big to being better. The qualitative and the moral emerge.

We are religious, then, because we cannot help it. We want to live in the highest, fullest sense, and that qualitative expression of life is called religion. So religion is not a cloak we can put on or off; it is identified with life itself. We are all incurably religious. Even the Communists, though repudiating religion, are deeply religious. They want a better social order. They may be right or wrong in the method of getting it, but the very desire for a better social order is religious. For religion is a cry for life.

————

O God, our Father, who planted this urge for completion within us? Didst Thou? Then, O my God, this urge is not in vain. Thou hast inspired it. Thou shalt satisfy it with Thyself. Amen.

16

## THE DIVINE INITIATIVE

Yesterday we said we are religious because it is the giving vent to the life-urge, the qualitative expression of the life-urge. But this is only half the truth. This upward movement of the spirit of man would not of itself account for the religious spirit of man.

The other side of the truth is that we seem to be pressed upon from above. We do not merely aspire, we are inspired. We feel we are being invaded by the Higher. This pressure from above awakens us, makes us discontented with a divine discontent; makes us pray—sometimes with unwordable longings; makes us revolt, at least inwardly, against things as they are and against what we are. This is the divine initiative—the cosmic Lover wooing His creation to Himself and thus to its own perfection.

Von Hugel speaks of this double movement in religion as the going up of one lift and the coming down of another. Man moves toward God and God moves toward man. The Old Testament is man's search for God, the New Testament is God's search for man. This is true in general but not entirely true, for there would have been no search for God in the Old Testament and in the various religions had not God inspired and initiated that search. So when men began to seek, they had in a sense found Him. God was in the very search for Himself—its author and hence its finisher.

Impossible? Too good to be true? Not if we study the nature of life. Life not only wants more life, but it wants to impart life. The creative urge is within it. God being the perfect life, He would of the very necessities of His being, desire to impart, to share, to create. Hence the divine initiative. We are religious because we long and because He loves. He creates, we crave.

————

My Father, if this be true, I am not far from Thee, for Thou art not far from me. Perhaps this very longing in my bosom is a scent of Thy being, there my heart grows eager, for I would find Thee. Amen.

## IN WHICH RELIGION IS DEFINED FOR US

Yesterday we said that religion resulted from the double movement of our aspirations and God's inspirations. His life impinges upon ours at every point. The result? Something disturbs our clod, we aspire, we pray, we revolt against what we are.

The meeting place of this upward movement and this downward movement is Christ. He is man ascending and God descending—the Son of man, the Son of God. Since He is the meeting place of the two sides of religion He becomes its definition. To the one hundred and fifty definitions we add one more: Christ. This is not a spelled-out, but a lived-out definition. Some things cannot be said, they have to be shown. So it has been shown us what constitutes religion: His spirit of life. His relationships with God and man, His purity, His love, His mastery over environment of men and things, His care for the sinful and the underprivileged, His redemptive purposes for man and society, His overleaping sympathy that wiped out all race and class and bound men into a brotherhood, His final willingness to take all their pain, all their defeat, all their sin into His own heart and die for them, and His offer to them of a new way and program of life—the Kingdom of God on earth—all this, and His sheer victory of spirit amid it all, constitutes religion.

Never was there such a definition of religion as He gives in His own person. It cleanses away all irrelevancies, all magic, all superstition, all controversies about rite and ceremony and superiorities and turns us to the serious business of learning how to live and to live victoriously. When men, therefore, ask me about this rite and that ceremony, this order, that church polity—all marginal—I simply say, I am not interested, for I have seen the Center. This grips me.

————

O God, we have seen what we ought to be, what we must be, if we are to live. Help us from this day to give ourselves to it with a whole-being devotion until it becomes actual within us. In Jesus' name. Amen.

## THE CENTRAL EMPHASIS IN THE DEFINITION

There is one point in this definition of religion which needs emphasis—the Kingdom of God on earth. We need to emphasize it, for He did. It was the one thing around which all else revolved. "And Jesus went about all Galilee, teaching in their synagogues, and preaching the gospel of the kingdom." Just what was this Kingdom?

In another book I said the Kingdom of God is a new Order founded on the Fatherly love of God, redemption, justice, brotherhood, standing at the door of the lower order founded on greed, selfishness, exploitation, unbrotherliness. This Higher Order breaks into, cleanses, renews, redeems the lower order, both within the individual will and the collective will. This is true, but not the full truth. It is an offer from without. It is "at our door." And yet it is within us—"The kingdom of heaven is within you." This Kingdom has been "built from the foundation of the world." Did He mean that this Kingdom has been built within the very foundations of the world and within the very structure of our own mental and moral make-up? Yes, I believe He meant just that. I grant that there is something beyond that—it is "at our doors," and we shall see what that means later. But it does mean that the Kingdom is written, not merely in sacred books, but in the very structure and make-up of the universe and of ourselves and of society. When we study the laws deeply embedded in the universe, in our own mental and moral and physical being, the laws that constitute true sociological living, we discover the laws of the Kingdom. Mind you, not fully, but nevertheless, really and actually. This is important, for when we start with this business of victorious living, we are starting with the solid facts of the laws written within our own being, within the structure of society and the universe around us.

———

Our Father, we are enveloped with Thee. Thy laws are the laws of our being, Thy will has been wrought within the texture of things. Help us to discover Thy kingdom and obey it. Amen.

Romans 2. 14–16
2 Corinthians 3. 1–3
Jeremiah 31. 33

## THE KINGDOM WRITTEN WITHIN

We saw yesterday that we do not begin with something imposed on life when we are beginning with the Kingdom, but with life itself—its laws and its ways of fulfillment.

The moral laws are deeply embedded in the constitution of things—we do not break them, we break ourselves upon them. For instance, many after the War demanded freedom to do as they liked, they revolted against morality as man-made, they would express themselves as they desired. The result? The generation that tried that is sad and disillusioned. It stands abashed and dismayed. At what? At the fact that the thing will not work. "I had thought that faithful marriage was hell, but what have I been living in?" asked a dismayed and disillusioned young woman who had revolted. She found her revolt was not merely against moral codes, but against herself and her own happiness. She was breaking herself upon the laws of the Kingdom.

What does the psychologist mean when he says, "To be frank and honest in all relations, but especially in relations with oneself, is the first law of mental hygiene"? Isn't he saying that the universe and you and I are built for truth, that the universe won't back a lie, that all lies sooner or later break themselves upon the facts of things? Since the Kingdom stands for absolute truth, and our own mental make-up demands the same thing, then are not the laws of the Kingdom written within us?

Again, what does the psychologist mean when he says, "The right thing is always the healthy thing"? Conversely, he could have said that the wrong thing is always the unhealthy thing. Did he not mean thereby that we cannot be healthy, cannot function at our best unless we discover the right and obey it? Is it not true that sin is not only the bad, but the unhealthy, the crippling? That the sinful are the diseased as well as the guilty? This sobers us.

––––––

O God, our Father, the moral law written within makes us tremble like an aspen leaf. But are these laws redemptive? Art thou saving us through hard refusals? Teach us. We listen. Amen.

John 11. 25    John 17. 3
John 14. 6    John 20. 31
John 1. 4

## THE KINGDOM AND LIFE

We said yesterday that life will not work in any way except God's way. When we find the Kingdom, we find ourselves.

Jesus said the same thing—He made the Kingdom and life synonymous, "It is better for thee to enter into life maimed." . . . "It is better for thee to enter into the kingdom of God with one eye" (Mark 9. 43, 47). Here He used the terms "the Kingdom of God" and "life" interchangeably. To Him they were one.

But life to Jesus had to be spelled with a capital "L" to express what He meant. True, it is this life and its laws within ourselves and the universe. But it is more. If that had been all, it would have been a naturalism. Not that we thereby damn it when we call it a naturalism, for nature, human and nonhuman, is God's handiwork. But while God wrote the elemental laws of the Kingdom within us, He did not stop there. The Kingdom is "within us," but it is also "at our doors." Something from without is prepared to invade us, to change us, to complete us. When that happens, we too shall have to spell life with a capital "L." For every fiber of our being will know that this is Life. The two charged electrodes of life, natural and life supernatural, will meet, and when they touch the white light of Life will result.

The Kingdom, then, is life—plus. It is the grafting of a higher Life upon the stock of the lower. The stock will still be there; its roots deeply in the soil of the natural, but we will bud and bloom and fruit with new possibilities. The Kingdom is the Ought-to-be standing over against the Is, challenging it, judging it, changing it and offering it Life itself. It is at our doors. And we are the ones to decide whether we shall live life with a small "l" or a capital "L."

---

O God, our Father, we talk of the Kingdom. But Thou art the Kingdom. Thou art at our doors. We put our trembling fingers to the latch and let Thee in. And when Thou art in, we know that we have let in life. Amen.

## ARE THE RELIGIOUS THE UNNATURAL AND QUEER?

They sometimes are, and this makes many honest souls hesitant, for they do not want to be queer, impossible. Many people feel that religion tries to give human nature a bent that it won't take, that is an imposition on life, something that makes us unnatural and out-of-joint.

A medical student expressed this fear to me when he asked, "Is religion natural?" He feared the unnatural. On the other hand, Tertullian said that "the soul is naturally Christian." My own experience is that Tertullian was right. When I obey Christ, I feel naturalized, at home, universalized, adjusted. When I disobey Him, I feel orphaned, estranged, out-of-joint with myself and the universe. I seem to be made for this Man and His Kingdom.

It is true that when we obey Him we have to break with society in many things. That makes us seem queer and impossible. But may it not be that society, at those points, is queer and impossible? We call a man queer when he is ec-centric—"off the center." Isn't society, insanely bent on its own destruction through its selfishness and its clashes and its lusts, ec-centric, off the center? A great flywheel off its center shakes itself and the building to pieces. On the center it is a thing of construction and production. The center of life is Christ; when we are adjusted to Him, life catches its rhythm, its harmony. When life resolves around something else, it is ec-centric, and thus self-destructive and society-destructive.

Was Christ queer? To the men of His day He was. We now see that His was the only sanity. He moves through those scenes, poised and masterful, at home in the huts of the poor and in the houses of the rich—the one sane One, to whom we must turn or lose our sanity, and ourselves.

———

O God, our Father, we have become so used to the insanities of life around us that we look on the sane as the insane. Give us a clarity of mind and heart, that we may turn from the insanities of selfishness and greed to the sanities of Thy way. For we know that life will not work in any way save Thy way. In Jesus' name. Amen.

## TOILING IN THE DARK

We must get clear this whole matter of whether the Christian way will work before we can go on to "victorious living," for as long as we have the suspicion lurking in our minds that we are about something that cannot be done, that the universe won't back it, there is a paralysis at the center. On the other hand, if we are sure that the sum total of things is behind our acting, then our wills are steeled to do the hitherto impossible.

It was said of the disciples that they were toiling in rowing in the dark and getting nowhere. The wind and the waves were against them and the whole thing was ending in futility. Then Jesus came. They cried out against Him, in fear that He was a ghost. But finally they took Him in, and *"immediately the ship was at the land whither they were going."* Is that the history of our lives? We strive for goals we cannot reach. The whole thing ends in futility—a toiling in rowing and getting nowhere. The sense of meaningless striving is upon us. We are "up against it." And everything is very dark. Life is too much for us. Then Jesus comes and we are afraid of Him—He is ghostly, unnatural, and will demand the unnatural and the impossible. This is our first reaction. But finally we let Him in—and, lo, we are at the very place we were striving to reach—we are at the land whither we were going! This is the very way it works.

But there is no doubt that we are afraid of Jesus. It was said that when Jesus came, Herod, when he heard it, "was troubled, and all Jerusalem with him." Troubled at the coming of the Deliverer! They were naturalized in their own lostness. But should the dynamo be afraid of the coming of electricity? The flower at the coming of the sunshine? The heart at the coming of love? Should life be afraid of the coming of Life?

———

Help me, gentle, redeeming, impinging God, not to keep Thee at a distance through fear. Help me, then, to take Thee into my little troubled boat. Amen.

23

## HOW DO WE GET TO THE GOAL OF SELF-EXPRESSION?

We saw yesterday that we toil in futile striving till Jesus comes. Take the natural things within us; things which are a part of our very make-up, can these instincts be fulfilled, can they reach their goal apart from Him?

Take the instinct of self-expression. Adler says that the instinct of "self" is the strongest of the three major instincts —self, sex, and the herd. Hence self-expression is natural and normal and right. We therefore strive to get to the goal of self-expression. We all do. The smallest member of our Ashram, a three-year-old, after singing at the top of her voice will announce triumphantly at the conclusion of the singing of the grace, "I sang." At which we all laugh. In polite society we do not laugh at sophisticated attempts—we get irritated. Place a dozen people in one situation, all of whom want to express themselves, and you have the stage set for clash and confusion and jealousy. The result is refined strife. The whole thing ends in futility. We thwart each other. We are toiling in rowing and it is getting dark—darker. Then across the troubled waters Jesus comes to us. We cry out in fear against Him, for we suspect what He will ask of us. He will ask that we cease all this and lose ourselves. And that is exactly what we do not want to do—we want to express ourselves. It is unnatural, ghostly, impossible. But as we toil further into our futilities He keeps coming, till at last we let Him in. Then we lose ourselves in His will and purposes. We forget about our self-expression. And, lo, we are at the land whither we were going!

We are never so much ourselves as when we are most His. We have found ourselves. We have arrived. We have obeyed the deepest law of the universe: He that saveth his life shall lose it, and he that loseth it shall find it. It works.

---

O Christ, we feared Thee. The drowning feared the life-line—forgive us. But Thy very coming to us is Thy forgiveness. We thank Thee. Amen.

## HOW DO WE GET TO THE GOAL OF THE RIDDANCE OF ENEMIES?

Take another natural instinct—the instinct to get rid of our enemies. Those who thwart us, who hurt our feelings, who do us harm, become our enemies. So we strive to get to the land of the riddance of enemies. Sometimes we try the crude method of fists; sometimes, if we are more refined, we strive to cut off their heads by the sharpness of our tongues, or socially we "cut them dead." Or we go to the court and hope thus to make them bend the knee. Or collectively we go to war with waving banners, lying propaganda, and with belching cannon. In all these ways, and many others, we strive to get rid of our enemies. But we are soon toiling in rowing and getting nowhere. We are not getting rid of our enemies. We are multiplying them.

For we soon find that harsh words produce harsh words, sharp tongues have a way of sharpening other tongues. "Cutting other people dead" results in isolating—ourselves. Court cases produce court cases. And as for war getting rid of enemies, we find it only produces them—mailed fists, shaken at the world, turn the world into a looking glass from which mailed fists shake in return. We get nowhere. Blank futility.

Then Jesus comes to us across our troubled waters. We are afraid, for we suspect that He will ask us to love our enemies. And we do not want to love them. We want to get rid of them. But He keeps coming, until finally we let Him in. And then something strange happens. As we catch His way we find a positive desire, even a craving, to do good to people, even to our enemies. And lo, we are at the land whither we were going. Our enemies are gone. We have got rid of them in the only possible way of getting rid of them—we have turned them into friends. Even if they do not respond, our enmity has gone and hence our enemies. We have arrived.

———

O Christ, help us today to take Thy way, even toward our enemies. And it may be that at nightfall we shall have no enemies. We too shall arrive. Amen.

## HOW CAN WE ARRIVE AT GREATNESS?

The instinct to be great is another phase of the instinct of self. We all want to be great. The little fellow in the corner and the king on the throne feel the same way about themselves.

Two little boys, children of missionaries, argued over the respective greatness of their fathers, when one little fellow capped it all with this: "My father, why he teaches subjects in the school so hard that he himself doesn't understand them!" That settled the matter—he was greatest, and the son also, by implication!

We laugh at the little ones, but it becomes serious when it gets to us. We try by taking thought to add a cubit to our statures. Many women by expensive clothes try to make their neighbors "green with envy"; many men, by acting the "he-man," try to be forceful and impressive. "Please fine me a decent sum and not four annas. I am no four-anna man. I shall never be able to lift up my head among my people having been fined four annas," said a head man to the missionary in charge of a criminal settlement. He too wanted to be great if only by a great fine! But what difference is there in this and in the man who fines himself the price of a new car each year when he does not need it? He too must keep up appearances—must appear great. Or the student who swaggers because he thinks it will make him great in the eyes of his fellows?

But it doesn't work. It ends in futility. We grow small trying to be great. We toil in rowing, trying to get to the land of greatness, and end nowhere. Then Jesus comes. Again we fear Him, for we fear He will ask us to be servant of all in order to be great. And we do not want to serve, we want to be served. But still He comes. Then we let Him in. We forget greatness as we bend with Him to serve the rest. And, lo, as we bend we rise, the servant of all becomes the greatest of all. We have arrived.

————

O Christ, the Man who came not to be ministered unto but to minister, help me to be like that this day. Amen.

Philippians 3. 1 (Moffatt)
Galatians 5. 22
Acts 5. 41

## HOW DO WE GET TO THE GOAL OF HAPPINESS?

We all want to be happy. And rightly. This is a deep-rooted instinct. God must have planted it there. The God that made sunsets, that painted the rose, that put play into the kitten and the smile on a baby's face and laughter in our souls, is surely not happy when we are unhappy. "Down with the coffeepot face, up with the teapot face."

So we start out to get to the land of happiness. We declare that the world shall show us a good time. But somehow or other it eludes us. It slips through our fingers ere we grasp it. The most miserable and fed-up people I know are the people most bent on being happy. They have to jump from thing to thing in order not to be bored to tears with themselves. They are saying to their souls what the old lady said to the frightened child whom she had taken to the circus, as she shook him till his teeth rattled, "Now, enjoy yourself, do you understand, I brought you here to enjoy yourself—now do it." Thus we try to make our souls enjoy themselves. But the soul weeps within and doesn't know how to enjoy itself. It has missed the way. It is toiling in rowing and getting nowhere. And it is dark, very dark in some people's souls. The land of happiness isn't in sight. Then a Figure across the waters! We are afraid. Is not this "the pale Galilean whose breath has turned the world gray"? We cry out in fear. But this patient insistence overcomes us and we let Him in. We now forget our happiness as we begin to think about the happiness of others. We walk with Him into the saddened homes and strive to lift that sadness, and, lo, our hearts sing with a strange new joy—a deep, fundamental and abiding joy. We have arrived.

------

We have misunderstood Thee, O Christ. We thought because Thy symbol was a cross that Thou art therefore Christ the Sad. Forgive us. We now see that Thou art Christ the Glad. One touch of Thy gladness and our hearts forever sing. We thank Thee. Amen.

# HOW CAN WE ARRIVE AT THE GOAL OF SEX-FULFILLMENT?

Sex is an integral part of human nature and is therefore God-given and in itself is not unclean. It is as natural as the appetite for food. God has given us this strange power through which we share with His creatorship. It is therefore not something to be whispered about in dark corners or brooded over furtively in the mind. It must be faced openly and frankly.

Through this strange power mere femaleness turns to motherhood and mere maleness turns to fatherhood. A home is set up—a child in the midst. Love binds all three. Nothing more beautiful on earth. Heaven bends low and touches that earthly thing into a heavenly thing.

But while sex, under the guidance and restraint of pure love, can be a heavenly thing, used in the wrong way it can turn earth into hell. Sex has produced more happiness and more unhappiness than any one single thing in life. It all depends on what you do with it.

Many try to get to the goal of sex expression through unrestrained freedom. They say they have a right to taste all experience, including sex experience, apart from morality. So they try. They are soon toiling in rowing. It is getting dark. The promised heaven turns to a present hell. They are getting nowhere except into deeper self-loathing. Then Jesus comes. We are afraid of Him. He is unnatural and strict. But since we get nowhere without Him, we let Him in. And, lo, we are at the land whither we were going. Inside the marriage relationship—restraint and dedication to creative ends. Outside marriage—sublimation, the taking of this power of sex and turning its driving force to creative ends on even higher levels—music, art, poetry, religion, serving the weak and underprivileged. In either case we have arrived at sex-fulfillment.

---

O Christ, Thou art shutting to us the gates to lesser life that Thou mightest open them to larger life. Help us not to complain when Thou wilt not let us be swine. For Thou wouldst make us men—men after Thine own image. Help us to arise and follow. Amen.

## HOW CAN WE ARRIVE AT THE GOAL OF INWARD UNITY?

If there is one thing that both modern psychology and the way of Christ agree on, it is this: Apart from inward unity there can be no personal happiness and no effective living.

Jesus said, "Every kingdom divided against itself is brought to desolation." That simple statement has within it all the depths of wisdom that modern psychology has discovered from the facts of the inner life. Divided personality, inward clash— these are the things that bring desolation to human personality.

Many say to a distracted soul, "Pull yourself together." Futile advice when there are mutually exclusive things within us. They won't be pulled together. Experience taught Old-Testament lawgivers the futility of trying to plow with an ox and an ass yoked together. It was forbidden. Experience forbids us from attempting to pull ourselves together when there are conflicting selves.

"Exert your will," counsels another. But suppose the will, which expresses the personality in action, is itself divided? Again futility.

The psychoanalyst, after getting hold of the distracting place in a disordered life, and after relating it to the rest of life, says that to be held together there must be something upon which you can fasten your affections. This will lift you out of yourself and keep you unified. But often he has nothing to offer—except, perhaps, himself, a professional trestle upon which the patient can twine the vines of affection. To say the least—unsatisfactory.

So we toil in rowing, trying to get to the land of inward unity. We are tossed by many a wind and many a wave. And it gets very dark. Then Jesus quietly comes. We more easily let Him in this time, for there seems no other alternative. The soul seems instinctively to feel, "the Master has come." He gathers up the inward distinctions, cleanses away the points of conflict, and unifies life around Himself. We have arrived.

---

O Christ, we need a master, someone to command us. Thou art that law. For thy commandments are our freedom. Help us to accept Thy way, that we may find our own. Amen.

29

## FOURTH WEEK

Acts 17. 23–28

## HOW CAN I FIND GOD?

We have seen that life will work only in one way—God's way. The statement of Augustine is oft repeated because oft corroborated: "Thou hast made us for Thyself, and we are restless until we rest in Thee." Let that fact be burned into our minds. Let it save us from all trifling, all dodging, and bend us to the one business of finding God and His way.

In our quest for God let us look at a few preliminary things. *Hold in mind that the purpose of your very being, the very end of your creation is to find and live in God.* As the eye is fashioned for light, so you are fashioned for God. But many question this. A Hindu student once asked this question, "If there is a God, what d--- motive of His is seen in the creation of this universe, where 'to think is to be full of sorrow'?" At one morning-interview time, five students, one after the other, with no collusion, asked the question, in one form or another, "Why was I created?" It is the haunting question in many minds.

I could only answer thus: Of course we cannot see the whole motive of creation, for we are finite. But why does a parent create? Physical lust? Not in the highest reaches of parenthood. Does not a parent create because of the impulse of love—the impulse that would have an object upon which he can lavish his love and to whom he can impart himself in the development and growth of the child? Is parenthood different in God? Could God, being love, have done otherwise than create objects of that love? And having created us, will He not give Himself to us? If not, then the whole apparent good is stultified. With that thought in mind to think is not "to be full of sorrow," but to be full of hope and expectancy. The creative Lover is at the door.

———

Father God, Thou hast come a long way through creation to the very door of my heart. I hear Thy very footsteps there. I let Thee in. Thrice welcome, Lover of my soul. Amen.

## THE RISK GOD TOOK

Yesterday we left off at the place of God's creative love creating us in order to impart Himself to us and to find that love fulfilled in our growth and development in His own image. We must pursue the thought, for God pursues us.

But we ask, Was it not risky for God to create us as He did, with the awful power of choice and with the possibility that we might go astray and break our hearts and His? Yes, very risky indeed. He might have made us without the power of choice, or with the power to choose only the good. But this would not be choice, for to be able to choose you must be able to choose in two directions, not one. Besides, if we are able to choose only the good, then it isn't the good for us. We would be determined, and the very possibility of goodness is in freedom. "There is nothing in the world, or even out of it, can be called good, except a good will," says Kant. So where there is no will there is no goodness, no badness— in fact, no personality. There was no other way to create personalities except to give them freedom. Risky? Yes.

But parents take that same risk when they bring a child into the world. That child may go astray and crush their lives and his. But parents assume that awful risk. Why? Because they determine that whatever happens they will do their best for the child—they will enter into his very life, until the child's problems become their own, his troubles theirs, his growth and happiness theirs. This will mean a cross! Of course. But parenthood accepts that cross because it cannot do otherwise. So with God. Our creation meant that He would enter into our very lives—our troubles His troubles, our sins His sins, our joy His joy. So creation, then, means a cross for God? Inevitably. But He took it. Love could not do otherwise.

----

God, we stand astounded at Thy courage. But Thou didst create us—it may be, it may be, to re-create us. That is our hope. We clasp it to our bosoms. Amen.

## GOD'S SEARCH FOR ME

If what we learned yesterday is true, then we must accept the thought that God is in a persistent, redemptive search for us. It seems too good to be true. My answer is that it is too good not to be true.

Turn to the pages of the New Testament and read the astonishing parables of the 15th chapter of Luke: the lost sheep, the lost coin, the lost son. Never before did such astonishing truth tremble on human lips. "The author of the universe is hard to find," said Plato. "Why do you trouble God with your austerities so that He cannot sleep?" was said in rebuke to the austere Hindu sage. "In finding God you must have as much patience as a man who sits by the seaside and undertakes to empty the ocean, lifting up one drop of water with a straw," said Mahatma Gandhi to me. But here Jesus flings back the curtains and lets us see the God of the shepherd-heart who seeks and seeks the lost sheep until he finds. And then the woman who sweeps the house for the lost coin—So, says Jesus, God will sweep the universe with the broom of His redeeming grace, until He finds that lost soul. For as the king's image is stamped upon the coin so is the Divine image stamped upon the human soul, lost though it may be amid the dust of degradation. It is true that the father of the prodigal did not go into the far country after the son, but wasn't his love there with him and wasn't that love the line along which he felt his way back to his father's house? Once I saw blind children running a race with a cord in their hands attached to a ring upon a wire which led them to the goal. So this lad got hold of his father's out-reaching love and it led him back to the father's bosom. The Hound of Heaven relentlessly pursuing us a-down the years!

---

O God, I dare not close my heart to Thee. Thou conquerest me with Thy persistence. But how glad, oh how glad, I am to be found! I thank Thee. Amen.

## SOME FURTHER CONSIDERATIONS IN FINDING GOD

We have got hold of one truth, namely, that God is searching for us. But there is the persistent question in many minds: "Very well, but aren't there some souls incapable of finding God by their very mental and spiritual make-up? Some are more mystically inclined—those may find God, but some of us cannot. We are not mystics."

If by "mystically inclined" we mean that some are more emotionally sensitive than others, then we must admit this to be true. But God does not come to us only by the way of the emotions—He comes by the way of the mind and the will as well—He makes a life approach to us, and this includes all three. So if you are a person whose active side is more developed than the emotional, you can receive Him in at the door of the will. The same with the mind—if you lean toward the intellectual, then you have the privilege of accepting Him at the door of the mind. But if He comes in at any of these doors, He possesses the whole person, by whatever door He comes.

The center of the whole relationship will be love, whether the emphasis be on emotional love, intellectual love, or volitional love. Are you sufficiently mystical to love? Everybody is! A man who was very intellectually inclined said he couldn't find God because he wasn't a mystic. But he loved his wife very tenderly. He was mystical enough to love his wife, but not mystical enough to love God! He was wrong and soon found his mistake. Everyone has a capacity to love God. Everyone who is willing to pay the price of finding can find God. Remember this: no one is constitutionally incapable of finding God. If we do not find God, the cause is not in our constitution, but in our consent.

----

O God, Thou who didst fashion us, didst fashion us for Thine own entrance. Our doors may be lowly, but Thy cross has bent Thee so low Thou canst get into the very lowest of doors. Come, Thou gentle Wooer, come. Amen.

## WHO CAN FIND GOD?

Two other things we must look at before we can come
to grips with finding God. Many feel that, since Jesus called
His disciples away from their ordinary occupations, we must
now leave ordinary so-called secular life to find God. This
is a mistake. Jesus did ask His twelve disciples to leave
their occupations and follow Him, but did He not in the very
act of calling them approve their occupation by filling their
boats with fish? And did not one hundred and twenty disciples wait in the upper room for the Holy Spirit, perhaps
only twelve of whom had left their occupations?

"Shall I be a student or shall I be a religious man?" asked
a Hindu youth of me one day. I could only reply that I saw
no conflict; that if he found God, he should be a better student. Before Christ came into my life I was at the bottom of
my classes—afterward I felt that the bottom of the class was
no place for a Christian—and left it. I found myself studying
my lessons on bended knees, praying my way through. No,
any legitimate occupation can be lifted into a sacrament.

There are those, especially in India, who feel that one has to
be mature, even old, to find God. But the Christian way is
different. At question time this question was asked, "Where
is God?" A little fellow of five excitedly whispered to his
mother: "Why, I can answer that. He is in my heart." He
was right! This note was sent up to me written in block
letters: "It works. Wonderfully and well. Thank you for
this. Signed, Jivan Ratman, aged 12 years." It does work,
even for the child, and may I say, especially for the child,
for to find the Kingdom we must catch the childlike attitude
of open frankness and willingness to follow.

————

O Christ, Thou didst hallow every worthy occupation and
didst open the gates of life to the little child. In Thy
Father's house there is the sound of the hammer and the
laughter of little children as well as the quiet oratory for
prayer. We thank Thee. Amen.

## FACING THE ISSUES

The barriers to finding God are not on God's side, but on ours. Since God is seeking us, then the problem is not of our finding God, but of our letting Him find us. We must put ourselves in the way of being found by God. Some of us are not there. There are definite barriers on our side.

Some of them are intellectual. People do have honest doubts, and I have spent many years in meeting those doubts, perhaps too many years, for I now see that the problem is usually deeper. Not always, but usually. For instance, a young man came puzzled about the Trinity. I replied that the emphasis in Christianity was not upon the Trinity but upon the incarnation, that the doctrine of the Trinity was rather overheard than heard in the New Testament, but still I could see reasons why the Trinity is reasonable. The lowest life is the simplest life; the amoeba is a single cell, but as we come up in the scale of existence we find complexity emerging, so that when we come to man we find a very highly complex being made up of body, mind, and spirit—man is a trinity. The movement of life, then, seems to be from the simple to the complex. When we get to the highest of life of all, God, we should expect, not simplicity, but complexity— the Trinity is thus the natural culmination. But the movement of life upward is toward unity amid that complexity. Man is a trinity but he is also a unity. So in God there is a richer unity in the richer Trinity. I waited to see if my answer had any effect. It had none. By a swift insight I saw the young man's problem was not intellectual, but moral. I put my hand on his, and quietly asked if he was pure? His eyes dropped. He was not. His trouble was not honest doubt, but dishonest sin.

———

O God, hold us steady at this point. Help us to be absolutely honest, and it may be that as the barriers go down Thy presence shall strangely warm our hearts. In Jesus' name. Amen.

## WE APPLY THE TESTS

We saw yesterday that moral wrongness makes intellectual blindness. It is easier to live yourself into right thinking than to think yourself into right living. In a moral world the deepest organ of knowledge is moral response. Without that we are blind, however much we may think. So we must look at the moral barriers. They are not the only barriers, but we cannot get on unless we take them down.

I have a friend whose moral and spiritual influence is potent and penetrating. I discovered the secret of it in his relentlessness toward himself. Once a week he goes aside and examines his life in the light of five pointed questions. In the quietness before God, in an air of absolute realism in which there is no equivocation, he examines his life in the light of these five questions:

1. Am I truthful? Are there any conditions under which I will or do tell a lie? Can I be depended on to tell the truth—no matter the cost? Yes or no?

2. Am I honest? Can I be absolutely trusted in money matters? In my work? With other people's reputations? Yes or no?

3. Am I pure? In my relationships with women? In my habits? In my thought life? Yes or no?

4. Am I easily offended or am I loving? Do I lose my temper? Am I quick to sense slights? Or am I taking the attitude of love which refuses to be offended? Yes or no?

5. Am I selfish or am I consecrated? What am I living for —myself, my own position, money, place, power? Or are my powers at the disposal of human need? At the disposal of the Kingdom? Again I ask, what am I living for—myself or others?

As we are about to go on, let us put ourselves before ourselves and look at ourselves. The bravest moment of a man's life is the moment when he looks at himself objectively without wincing, without explaining away.

———

O Christ, it was said that Thou knowest what is in every man. We do not even know what is in ourselves. For we have never looked at ourselves with honest eyes. Help us to do it this day. In Thy name. Amen.

## FIFTH WEEK

## AM I TRUTHFUL?

One of the test questions of a man's character is this: Will that man lie? And yet how easy it is to lie—even for religious people: the willingness to twist a meaning to gain a point; to misquote if the misquotation gains an end; exaggerations to make impressions; a lack of complete truth in making appeals for funds; misrepresentations in presenting goods for sale! What is at the basis of this looseness with the truth? Is it not often in the fact that we think a lie is sometimes justifiable?

I once asked some students whether a lie is ever justifiable and got the answers (1) Yes, in business. (2) In politics. (3) To save a life. (4) In war. One argued (5): That it is all right to tell a little one in behalf of a great cause. She wasn't sure of a big one! They thought to be able to lie well was an asset. They did not see that the ability to lie is a liability and not an asset.

Get hold of the two principles which Doctor Speer lays down: First, God cannot lie. Second, He cannot delegate to you the privilege of lying for Him. Truth is inviolable. The early Christians standing before tribunals, their lives in the balance, could tell the slightest lie and their lives would be saved. They refused. They could die, but not lie. A Hindu doctor asked the compounder why he didn't give the two women before him their slips of paper. He affirmed he had. The women said he hadn't. The doctor turned and said: "Go get those papers. Don't you know who these women are? They are Christians. And Christians never lie." He was right: Christians never lie. When we lie, we are not Christian. The Scripture is unequivocal at this point. "Lie not one to another; seeing that ye have put off the old man with its doings." If lies are still there, no matter how religious we may be, we are still in the old life.

———

O crystal Christ, make me from this moment transparent with nothing covered, nothing which I must conceal from myself or others. I ask for truth in the inward parts. I will do my share. Amen.

## AM I HONEST?

The second question is this: Am I honest?

It is not easy to be absolutely honest with ourselves because of what modern psychology calls the tendency to rationalization. This means that we are seldom objective in our attitudes toward ourselves. We set our minds to work not upon the facts as they are, but upon the business of inventing reasons for our courses of conduct. The man in the parable who was negligent with his talent laid the blame on the hardness of the master. That was rationalization. A man allows himself to fall in love with another man's wife, and then he proceeds to rationalize the whole thing by talking to himself about the sacredness of this feeling of love, until black looks white. The mind has played a trick on him. He is self-deceived.

We need the objectivity and honesty of the youth who said to me: "I cannot keep my degree. It is the badge of my shame. I got help in my examination. I am going to send it back to the University." He did. The vice-chancellor replied: "The end of education is to produce honest character. You now seem to be an honest man. We hope you will keep the degree."

But will not God forgive the sin of dishonesty without this restitution? How can He? He can forgive the sin of the act only as we are willing to restore. We may not be able to restore all at once, but we must be willing. God sometimes has to take us on faith. One of the most honored and loved members of our Ashram put in his budget of need an item to pay back by monthly installments a pre-Christian dishonesty. He is forgiven and happy and useful.

Then am I willing to cut out—ruthlessly to cut out—of my life every dishonest thing no matter how deep the humiliation may be?

———

O Thou relentless Pursuer of our souls, Thou art not content to leave us half-sick, Thou hast Thy finger on our cancers. Help us not to beg off from the surgeon's knife. Cut, O Christ, deeply if need be. But make us well. Amen.

## AM I PURE?

This question of purity is fundamental. The battle of life will probably not rise above the sex battle. If life sags at that place, it will probably sag all down the line.

Obviously, the first thing to do in this matter of purity is to acknowledge the fact of sex. To act as though there are no such things as sex-desires in us is to repress them, and a complex is set up in the subconscious. This brings nervous trouble and probable breakdown. Every normal person has sex-desire. There is no shame in this. It is a part of our make-up. The question is not whether we have sex-desire, but whether sex-desire has us. As a servant of the higher purposes of life it is a wonderful servant giving drive and beauty to the rest of life. As a master—it is hell.

Have we victory or defeat at this place? A young man threw himself into a chair in front of me: "Give me a prescription," he said bluntly. "I'm desperately sick. Everything is wrong with me morally." This seemed encouraging, for he was apparently ready to face the facts of his life. But when I got down to the facts, he wasn't honest. He dodged. Apparently honest in general he was not honest in particulars. When I came to the question of purity, he said, "Well, I do go to women, but I would not consider myself a fallen man. I am not in the gutter." Not in the gutter though the gutter was in him! And yet, because he was a non-Christian I could excuse him in a way, but could not excuse myself or you who have come under the influence of a Master who set the place of guilt not merely in the outer act, but in the inward thought. "Whosoever looketh on a woman to lust after her hath committed adultery with her already in his heart."

Am I committing adultery in act or in thought? If so, will I surrender it? Now? Or will I pray the prayer of the unregenerate Saint Augustine, "Make me pure, but not now."

———

O Thou Man of the pure mind, the pure habit, the pure act, cleanse the festering places of my heart and make me from this hour a man of purity. I consent to have it done. Amen.

## AM I EASILY OFFENDED OR AM I LOVING?

Yesterday we tested our lives at the place of the sins of the flesh. Today we must test them at the place of the sins of the disposition. Drummond has called our attention to the two manifestations of sin in the younger brother and the elder brother in the parable of the prodigal son. The younger son sinned low down in his flesh, in his lusts and appetites. The elder brother sinned high up in his disposition, in his bad temper, in his lack of love, in his smallness of soul, in his unwillingness to co-operate and forgive. Now, the sins of the flesh are despised by us. They are not respectable. But the sins of the disposition are sometimes highly respectable. If a man commits adultery sins in his flesh, we have a church council and we put him out. But if he sins in his disposition—if he is bad-tempered and selfish, we have a church council and we make him a member! And yet it is quite probable that the sins of the disposition do as much harm to the Kingdom of God as the sins of the flesh. Perhaps more. Bad-tempered, touchy and quarrelsome religious people do as much harm to the Kingdom of God as drunkards or adulterers. Suppose the younger brother had met the elder brother on the road to his father's house? One look and he would have turned back to the far country. Driven back by a wrong spirit.

The fact is that psychology says the same thing: "If the psychologist were asked to name the two major sins, from his point of view, he would probably name fear and anger. They form the basis for most of our unhappiness. They are impossible to integrate into a healthy personality" (Ligon, *The Psychology of Christian Personality*, p. 16).

Am I prepared to face the fact of my irritability and bad temper and to consent to have the whole thing taken out—even if it involve a major operation?

---

O Christ of the quiet, disciplined heart, Thou who didst stand poised and unruffled amid the grossest insults and provocations, give to me that loving, disciplined spirit that I may go through life with healing good will. In Thy name. Amen.

## AM I SELFISH OR ARE MY POWERS DEDICATED?

This last test comes to the root of the matter. In the final analysis, what controls my actions—self-interest or Christ-interest? In the deepest citadel of my spirit who gives the final word? Do I or Christ? The answer to that determines whether I am a Christian or not.

And what is the issue? It is this: If I dominate my life, it will disintegrate. I shall lose it. If Christ dominates my life, I shall find it—it will come back to me integrated, happy, useful.

Sat Tal, where I am writing, means "Seven Lakes." The legend says that during a drought a very holy man was dying of thirst by the wayside, and a poor village woman, seeing his distress, ran off and at great trouble brought him seven handfuls of water. These seven handfuls became the seven beautiful lakes. On the other side of the ridge is a lake, really a swamp, the place where the dead are burned. This was the seat of a great Kingdom, but the Rani, the Queen, when the drought came, thought only of herself and cried to the gods for water. They gave her so much that she and her palace were drowned and are now beneath the swamp.

The legend teaches what life teaches: if my desires dominate me, I shall be drowned in my own desires. I shall have my way and then I shall loathe my way. If self is on the throne, its inner subjects are unhappy, discordant. That self may be a very refined self, it may be a very religious self, it may be even an apparently serving self, but if it is on the throne and makes the final decisions, then, as sure as fate, I shall lose my life. My life needs a master, but self is not the master that it needs.

Hush your heart and ask yourself this question: Who has the ultimate say in my life—self or Christ? Am I self-directed or Christ-directed?

———

O Christ, I know in my heart of hearts that when my hand is on the helm my life drifts toward the rocks. I cannot manage my bark. Take Thou the helm. Amen.

## IS CONFESSION NECESSARY?

As you face your life in the light of these five questions, where do you come out? Repeat them to yourself, slowly one by one, and give an honest answer. Your self will want to excuse, to rationalize, to go off to the irrelevant—don't let it. Hold it to the issues.

If you fall down at any or at all of these five places, confess it honestly and straightforwardly. *Confess it?* Yes. Both modern psychology and the teaching of Jesus agree at this point. "When the conscience, acting in the capacity of an observer, condemns the ego for wrong actions, and the feeling of guilt results, there are three possible modes of conduct open to the conscious mind. The consciousness may do nothing whatever about it, allowing the emotion full play; it may repress the feeling; or it may rid itself of the depressing sensation by means of spiritual catharsis, through confession" (*Sin and the New Psychology*, Barbour, p. 215.) The first two methods are obviously unsatisfactory, and more—they are disastrous. To find oneself wrong and to do nothing about it is to condemn oneself to live with oneself when one cannot respect that self. That is incipient hell. To repress it is worse. The new psychology, of all the schools of Freud, Adler, Jung and MacDougall, all unite on this: To drive such a thing as fear and guilt into the subconscious and to shut the door is not to be rid of it. There it festers and sets up an irritation. The life is unhappy, ill at ease, nervous, it scarcely knows why. It is the result of this repression.

And all the schools of modern psychology and all the teachings of Jesus unite on this: That repression must be found, brought up, exposed to the light and resolved through confession. There is no other way out.

———

O Christ, we here take a deep breath, for this confession means humiliation to our inmost selves. We would fain hide our wounds. But we dare not. We open them to Thee —We dare do it to Thee—now. Amen.

## TO WHOM MUST I CONFESS?

We left off yesterday with the conviction that if we are to get rid of the guilt that has gathered about and within our lives, we must confess it, open it up, expose it. But the question arises—to whom?

Obviously, it must be to the one or ones against whom we have done the wrong. That brings in three. When we do wrong, we sin against ourselves, against God, and against society, or, to be more personal, against our brother.

First, we sin against ourselves. We have been false to our highest interest, we have betrayed our ideals, we have sinned against our higher nature. We must then acknowledge it to ourselves. Unless you first acknowledge it to yourself you cannot acknowledge it to God or man. Do you really confess it to yourself? Without equivocation, and fully? The last is important, for you will try to compromise with half-confessions, half-repentances.

Second, we must confess it to God. We have not merely broken a law, we have broken a Heart. You must tell Him so. The approach to God has now been made easy through Jesus. His awful purity condemned sinners, yet invited them. For they saw that His purity was not forbidding, but forgiving. You dare expose your heart to that Heart. You must—to get relief. But, again, it must be wholehearted and without anything held back, for one thing held back spoils it all—cancels the rest.

Third, we must confess it to those whom we have wronged. We do not need to broadcast our sins to everybody. Promiscuous confession to promiscuous gatherings is not healthy. There are some things which God deals with in His private office. But when we have wronged others or others have wronged us, we must both ask forgiveness and offer it.

---

O Christ, Thy knife is going deep. We wince and yet we consent that the whole thing be taken out by the roots. Leave no lingering roots behind. For we do not want to be better only—we want to be well. Amen.

Matthew 5. 9–15
Matthew 5. 23–26
Romans 12. 18

## UNTANGLING OUR LIVES

Yesterday we said we must confess any wrong to our brother or forgive him for any wrong done to us. That cuts deep.

For instance, suppose we have been dishonest. No matter what it does to us or to our positions we must confess it and restore it. A Christian minister laid down four hundred and fifty rupees on the table—the weight that had laid upon his soul for twenty years and the cause of his barrenness. Hard —but an open door.

Take resentment. Whether you have wronged your brother as shown in Matthew 5. 23, 24, where in coming to the altar you remember that your brother has something against you, or as in Matthew 18. 15, where your brother has sinned against you, in either case you are to go and be reconciled. Whether sinned against or sinning, the Christian is under obligations to take the initiative in settling the dispute.

But you say, "I can't forgive." Then may I say it very quietly, but very solemnly: You can never, never be forgiven. "But if you forgive not men their trespasses, neither will your Father forgive your trespasses." Do you not remember that in the Lord's Prayer we pray, "Forgive us of our trespasses, as we forgive those who trespass against us"? So if you do not forgive you ask not to be forgiven. In refusing forgiveness to others you have broken down the bridge over which you yourself must pass, namely, forgiveness.

As I sit in this Ashram I am reminded of one of our group, a government official, who harbored resentment against a subordinate. A wrong had been done and the resentment was deep. And it was not easy to confess that resentment to a subordinate—not in India where rank counts for much. But it was done. Release was found, and now that life is radiant and spiritually contagious. You can do the same. By His grace, you will, won't you?

———

O Christ, Thou Who didst hang on the cross, tortured in every nerve, yet didst pray for Thine enemies, "Father, forgive them," help me this day, now, to forgive those who have wronged me in a lesser way. In Thy name. Amen.

## STILL UNTANGLING OUR LIVES

Yesterday we were in the midst of getting rid of resentments. We must go to the last root.

You say, "Well, I'll forgive, but I cannot forget." You don't really mean that, do you? See how it looks as you pray that prayer again, "Father, forgive me as I forgive others: I forgive that other person, but I won't forget it. You forgive me in the same way: Forgive me, but don't forget my sins, and when I do something wrong bring the whole thing up again." God cannot and does not forgive that way. He blots it out of the book of His remembrance. So must you.

But again you say: "Well, I'll forgive, but I'll have nothing more to do with that person." Now pray that prayer again, "Father, forgive me as I forgive others. I forgive that person, but from henceforth I'll have nothing to do with him. You forgive me in the same way: forgive me, but have nothing more to do with me. I'll get along without you." You see its absurdity, don't you?

Don't try to forget it, don't try to smooth it over, and don't drive it into the subconscious. Get it up and out. A village woman begged the doctor for a plaster to put over an abscess. The doctor said she could have no plaster, for that would heal it over and drive the poison in; it must be lanced. The woman begged for her plaster, pleading that the knife would hurt. When the doctor refused, she went away and in a few days the poison had spread through her whole system and had killed her. Don't ask for the plaster of a half-way measure. Anger and resentment are literally poison. The doctors say so. A child dropped dead on its mother's breast, poisoned by the anger it drank in with its mother's milk. Resentment is physical, mental, and spiritual poison. Get it out!

———

O Thou who didst forgive those who spat in Thy face, help me now to open my heart to the healing of Thy forgiveness and help me to give it as Thou dost give it to me. Amen.

## STILL FURTHER UNTANGLING OUR LIVES

It is not enough to hate our sin, nor even to pray against it—we must surrender it. I say "it," for the temptation will come for us to give up the sins we do not mind in lieu of the central, master-sin. For there is usually a master-sin—a key log in the jam, and unless that is pulled out there is no release.

Take the case of Herod. He was probably earnest in his quest after a new life, he was fascinated by the good. But John, one day, put his finger on the master-sin in Herod's life: "It is not lawful for thee to have her." Herod turned pale. A life struggle was on. The outcome? The revised version says, "And when he heard him, he did many things, and he heard him gladly." "He did many things"—yes, everything except the one thing—give up Herodias. He was willing to give up this thing, that thing, the other thing, but not the woman. That sin was the key log in the jam. Herod was willing to have many another log pulled out. But not this one. There was no release.

The little daughter of a missionary went into a guest's room, took some candy and told her first lie. The broken-hearted mother put her on her lap and told her what it all meant. The little girl wept bitterly, seemed penitent, so the mother said: "I am glad you are penitent. Now take the candy out of your mouth—throw it away to show you are penitent." The little girl looked at her mother through her tears, clamped her teeth shut tight and said, "No." She hated the sin, she wept over it, she did everything except one thing—give it up!

———

O Christ, Thou drivest me into a corner. I would escape but Thou wilt not let me. Nor do I really want to, for I know if I should escape, I should escape from life. And I want to live. Then take, oh take these things from my heart that keep me from Thee and from full life. Amen.

## IN WHICH I MAKE THE SURRENDER

I have now come to the place in my quest for victorious living where I see that I cannot go on until I make the great decision. I must break down every barrier that stands between me and God—and I must do it, withholding no part of the price. But I see I must go further. I must not only give up every barrier—I must give up myself. I need somebody to master me.

I know that something or other will master me. In the shrine of my heart I am bound to bend the knee to something. I may bow before myself and take orders from myself, so that self is my ruler. Or I may let sex-passion or money have the final say. Or I may bow before the fear of society and let it dominate me. Or—and this seems to me my best alternative—I can let Christ master me. I have the decision as to who shall have the final say in my life. I deliberately make that decision: Christ shall have me. There is nothing that is weighed out or measured, nothing that the eye can see, but heart has been given to Heart, will has been given to Will, life has been given to Life. It is done.

As I walked up the aisle of the cathedral in Copenhagen to see the wonderful statue, Thorwaldsen's "Christ," I was almost overcome with awe as I saw the Figure with the soft light upon it dominating the whole cathedral. But as I walked along a Danish friend whispered: "You will not be able to see His face unless you kneel at His feet." It was true, for He was standing with outstretched arms looking at those at His feet. So I knelt at His feet and, lo, His face was looking into mine.

You cannot really see Christ till you bend the knee to Him, till you surrender to Him. Those who stand afar off, surveying Him, never really see His face. So bend the knee. Be conquered by Him.

---

O Christ, at last my heart has said the word. I hold within my trembling palm this will of mine. It is not much, but when Thou hast that Thou hast my all. And I am glad. Amen.

## THRONGING OR TOUCHING?

As Jesus was going along the multitudes thronged Him. A woman in deep need came timidly through the crowd and touched His garment. "Who touched me?" asked Jesus as He felt the power go forth. "The multitudes throng Thee, so why do you say, 'Who touched me?'" said His disciples. "But somebody *touched* me," said Jesus. There is a difference between thronging Jesus and touching Jesus. These who throng Jesus get little, those who touch Jesus get everything.

Never did the thought of the world in East and West so throng Jesus as now. There is more interest in Him than at any time in human history. For other ways of life are breaking down and we turn wistfully to Him. This is true in East and West. And yet I have the feeling that it is more of a thronging of Him than a touching of Him. Inspiration? Yes, but not life.

Sunday after Sunday the multitudes go to church and listen. Their thoughts throng Jesus. But how many of the thronging multitudes really touch Him—set up a connection with Him, and live by Him? How many touch Him so that they go away not merely better, but well?

Some go through our Sunday schools and churches from childhood to old age as mere throngers. My very first convert, my grandmother, did just that, until at eighty-two years of age she really touched Him. Oh, the difference! She knew it and so did we.

Yesterday you said you would surrender to Him. Good, nothing better. But now that you have surrendered to Him, touch Him—touch Him for forgiveness, for power over temptation, over fears, over anxieties, over everything that stands in the way of victorious living. As He threw His life open then so that anyone who had need, might touch Him, provided they touched in faith, so now His life is open—take what you need. Cease thronging Him—touch Him.

---

O Christ, as Thou dost pass by I cease my tentative attitudes, I move up from those who throng to those who boldly touch, and I do it now. By the touch of faith I receive into my inmost being Thy healing and Thy health. Amen.

## WHAT DOES FAITH REALLY MEAN?

Yesterday we talked about touching Christ by faith. What do we really mean by faith?

This woman's faith had a touch of the superstitious in it, for she thought that virtue resided in His garments, and that by a touch she would be made whole. Jesus corrected that and said, "Thy *faith* hath made thee whole; go in peace." What did He mean by "faith"?

Certainly, faith is not an intellectual assent to a fixed creed. I do not decry creeds, for anyone who thinks has to have something which he believes, that is, a creed. Even so, our creeds are never final, for they are our present conceptions of the truth which is forever beyond us. Our creeds must therefore be open to correction as fuller truth dawns. But a man may have an intellectual belief in everything in the creed of the churches and not have faith.

Faith is an adventure of the spirit, a going out of the whole inner life in response to something we believe to be supremely worth while. It is the wagering of the life, and not merely nodding of the head. It is not discussion, it is decision. It is the launching out on the highest hypothesis I know—with my life. I don't believe in a thing unless I act on it. I don't believe in Christ unless I am prepared to wager all to follow Him. That is faith.

Jesus forged an amazing instrument when He made faith the conditioning instrument, for faith is trust in another, and yet it is an adventure and an attitude of our own. It therefore develops self-reliance and Other-reliance at one and the same time. If it were mere passivity, it would not develop self-reliance; if it were mere activity, it would not develop Other-reliance. It is both activity and receptivity. "According to your faith be it done unto you"—you do it and He does it. You are not stifled, and He is Saviour.

———

O amazing Christ, as Thou savest us from ourselves Thou savest ourselves. Thou askest faith, and that very faith makes us well—and makes us. We fling away ourselves to follow Thee and we find Thee—and ourselves. We thank Thee. Amen.

49

## MUST I UNDERSTAND ALL BEFORE I FOLLOW?

Yesterday we said that faith is an adventure. Very little faith is enough to start on, for as we act, it grows. The ten lepers had the word of Christ to show themselves to the priests. They had that and their leprosy. Then that word grew until it possessed them. But they started with very little.

Don't wait to follow Christ until you understand all about Him. None of us really understand electricity. Lord Kelvin, the foremost physicist of his day, declared, "If I were asked what electricity is, actually is, I should have to confess I know nothing about it." But while I do not know all about electricity I am not going to sit in the dark until I do. I know two things about it: I know I need light and electricity supplies that need. That is enough to begin on. I don't know all about digestion—how food turns into blood and bone and tissue, but I'm not going to sit and starve until I do. There are a thousand and one things I don't understand about Christ, but I know this: When I expose my soul to Him in trust and obedience, He meets my deepmost need. That is enough, at least to begin on.

Jesus asked the man with the withered arm to stretch it forth—the one thing he couldn't do. He must have looked at Jesus with helpless astonishment at such a demand—and yet, and yet he responded with the little grain of faith he had, and threw his will in the direction of raising that arm—and, lo, in the very process of obedience the strength came. His arm was well!

As you launch out to follow Christ you will think you are stepping out into a void, but that void will turn to rock beneath your feet. You step out—and He steps in—into your battles, your temptations, your tasks, and then you begin life on the co-operative plan. Faith seals the bond.

———

O Christ, I do not see all, but I see Thee. Let that suffice me. I will take the first steps. I will supply the willingness. You will have to supply the power. Amen.

## FIRST STEPS OUT OF THE OLD LIFE

We ended last week at the place of acting on what little faith we had and it would grow in the process.

A Chinese engineer sat down with me and abruptly said: "What are you going to do with me? I am a man without any religion. The old is dead and I haven't anything new to take its place. In America no church would take me, for I cannot believe in the divinity of Christ." I could almost see him inwardly stiffen to meet my arguments to prove Christ divine. So I used none. Instead I asked: "What do you believe? How far along are you?" "Well," he said, "I believe that Christ was the best of men." "Then let us begin where you can. If He is the best of men, then He is your ideal. Are you prepared to act according to that ideal? To cut out of your life everything that Christ would not approve?" He was startled, and said, "But that is not easy." "I never said the way of Christ is easy. Are you prepared to let go everything He will not approve?" "If I am honest, I must," he quietly replied, "and I will." "Then, whoever Christ turns out to be, man or more than man, wouldn't you be stronger and better if He were living with you, in you, all the time?" "Of course, I would be different." "Then will you let Him into your life?" "I don't know how." "Then pray this prayer after me, sentence by sentence." He did. "This is different," he said as we arose, "for they always told me I had to believe first. Now at least here is something for me to begin on." The next day he came again, his face radiant. "I didn't know a man could be as happy as I have been today. All my questions and doubts as to who Christ is have gone. And, moreover, I have been talking to my wife and she wants it too."

Christ had verified Himself. He does, when we give Him a chance.

---

O soul of mine, full of doubts and fears, arise and take the first steps. Here and now I consent to cut from my life everything Thou canst not approve, O Christ. Amen.

Acts 2. 37, 38   Romans 8. 1, 2
Acts 3. 19   Psalm 86. 11

## WHAT IS CONVERSION?

This young engineer had undergone the change called "conversion." What do we mean by it? Just when the church was allowing conversion to slip into the background through lack of emphasis, modern psychology stepped in and re-emphasized it. Not in the same language, and often not with the same belief in God attached to it. They tell us that the subconscious mind is the place of the driving instincts which have come down through a long racial history. These instincts think only of the pleasure of their own fulfillment, apart from any moral considerations. But in the conscious mind is built up what is called by Freud "the reality principle," or ego ideal, a conscious life-purpose. A conflict between the conscious and the subconscious minds thus ensues. This cleavage at the very center of life brings disturbance, unhappiness.

This conflict can be resolved in one of two ways: either the ideal side is brought down and forgotten and the instinctive side given full play—in which case the personality would be unified—or else the instinctive side is subordinated to and made to contribute to the ideal side of life. This latter process is called sublimation. It unifies the life. The first alternative is impossible for us, for if we take it, we return to the beast where the instinctive rules. Besides, we can never fully forget the ego ideal. The conflict will continue. The second is the only way out. The process by which this is done is called by Freud "re-education"; by Adler, "re-orientation to reality"; by Jung, "re-adaptation"; by McDougall, "reintegration." When Jesus puts within it the content of the moral and spiritual as well as the psychological, he calls it "conversion." All of these are driving toward the same goal, namely, the unifying of the personality and bringing harmony into the center of life. All life says we must undergo a change.

---

O Christ, Thou didst put Thy finger on our need. We must be born again and born different. Help us, we pray, to know this change through a living experience of it. Amen.

## WE CONTINUE TO LOOK AT "CONVERSION"

Jesus said, "Except a man be born from above (Marg.) he cannot see the Kingdom of God." What did He mean by being "born from above"?

According to modern psychology, life can be "born from below." The instincts and drives which reside in the unconscious can control the conscious mind, in which case life is literally "born from below." And let it be remembered that these instincts may not be merely the raw material of human life, they can be warped and twisted by what we may call a "sin-bias"—the nesting place of fears, inhibitions, a sense of guilt. To be born from below would at its best make us animal, at its worst it would make us beastly, and, mind you, *guilty.*

Over against this stands what Tansley calls "the ethical self." The Christian would say that this "ethical self" is the beginnings of the operation of a higher environment, namely, the Kingdom of God. The pressure of a higher Kingdom is producing an "ethical self"—the place where the higher ideals and motives reside.

Now, life depends upon correspondence to environment. To which environment? Shall we make life correspond to the environment which arises from below? In which case we shall have to sacrifice and slay the ethical self at the shrine of the Beast. Or shall we make life correspond to the higher environment, the ultimate order for human living, the Kingdom of God? In which case we shall have to slay our sins, and offer our instincts as a living sacrifice upon the altar of the new man.

The choice is in your hands. In the quietness of your heart, you must make that choice between the high and the low. I said that once to a student and he replied, "I have no quietness of heart." And neither he nor you will ever have quietness of heart in the deepest, fullest sense until you decide that your life shall be born from above.

---

O Christ of the gently pressing Kingdom, we open our hearts to it and to Thee. We cannot go back to the beast, we must go forward to the new man. We do. Amen.

## EMPTY

It may be that some of you do not feel the need of a change because of the uprush of clamoring instincts. The lower-born storms do not drive you to His feet, for you feel no such storms. Life to you is not the Great Struggle, but the Great Emptiness. Your difficulty is not the innate but the inane.

Jesus had a word for that type of person. He told of a house that was swept and garnished—and empty. Modern civilization is "swept." It has banished superstitions which its forefathers held. It is swept—it doesn't believe in this, that, and the other—it is freed from magic and superstition.

It is also "garnished"—garnished with intellectual facts and mechanical toys. Look at our achievements in science and culture and comfort! Our stores and shops are crammed with the mechanical, and we are urged to buy the latest toy which will be sure to bring us final happiness. Yes, modern civilization is "swept" and "garnished." But—and this is the point—it is empty, empty of any constructive philosophy of life. We are all dressed up and don't know where to go! We look with disdain on the barbarous, superstitious ages gone by, we point with pride to our garnished, not to say garish, civilization and its achievements, and yet modern civilization is empty—and it knows it!

> "This pagan magnifies a mindless world
> And searches there for rest,
> He is like an infant tugging at
> A lifeless mother's breast."

But why do I say modern civilization is empty? It comes closer home—perhaps you are empty. You need to be reborn just to know what life is. Moreover, I know this emptiness will not last long. Modern civilization is drawing unto itself the seven devils of unrest, of jazzy pleasure, of exploitation, of materialism, of selfishness, of war, of crime to fill the emptiness. So will you. Nature and the soul both abhor a vacuum. To fill the emptiness you must choose between these, or some other seven devils, and Christ.

---

O Christ, I choose Thee. My house of Man soul is empty. I cannot fill it with other than Thee. I loathe emptiness and I fear devils—but I can trust Thee. I do. Amen.

1 Corinthians 5. 9–11
Galatians 5. 16, 17

## IS CONVERSION A MANIFESTATION OF THE SEX-URGE?

Some modern psychologists trace almost everything to the sex-instinct, including the phenomenon called "conversion." They point out that most conversions take place in adolescence, and as this is the period of the awakening of the sex-instinct conversions are caused by it and are founded on it.

The answer is obvious. Adolescence is not only the period of the awakening of the sex-instinct, it is the period of the awakening of the total personality. The self-instinct, with its restlessness with and revolt against authority, and the herd-instinct, with its tendency to form gangs, are also awakened along with the sex-instinct. It is the period of the awakening of the whole of life.

Now, religion, as we saw, is a cry for life—for complete, fuller, more qualitative life. It is therefore not strange that youth feeling the awakening of life should turn to religion to guide and complete and satisfy that life-urge. That turning to religion often means conversion. It does not come out of the sex-urge, but out of the life-urge. Of course it does come partly out of the sex-urge, which is the creative urge. The sex-urge, sublimated by conversion, creates on higher levels, turns life into higher creative channels. The sex-urge is a part of it, but it is not the whole of it. Moreover, religion holds the sex-urge in restraint. How, then, could it be identified with it? If religion were a manifestation of the sex-urge, then when life ripens into old age and the sex-urge dims, we should expect the religious side of life to dim with it. But does it? Just the opposite. Youth and old age are the most religious periods of life. Why? In youth we want fuller life, in old age lasting life—in each it is the cry for life.

---

O Christ, Thou art creative Life moving upon lesser life and awakening it. Make me into a new person, with a new goal and a new power to move on to that goal. Amen.

## DO CONVERSIONS CONFORM TO ONE PATTERN?

This has bothered a great many souls, for they have seen a type of conversion that greatly moves them, and they are dissatisfied because they cannot find it after that pattern. This is a mistake. No two conversions are exactly alike, for no two persons are exactly alike, and no two persons come up under exactly the same act of circumstance. After God made you He broke the pattern. You are unique. Your conversion will therefore be unique.

Nevertheless, conversions do fall into two great categories— the gradual and the sudden, with shades between. After questioning groups of Christian workers in many lands, I find the usual proportion is about sixty per cent gradual and forty per cent sudden.

The gradual types usually come out of the home, where from childhood they are taught to know and love Christ. They cannot tell where they crossed the line, for they have seen no line. It has always been so. They have opened like a flower to the sun. *That* they do belong to Christ they are sure. *When* they began to belong to Him they are not sure. But their lives are different from the life around them. They belong to the converted.

Then there are others—and I am among them—to whom conversion came all of a sudden. I had come up through a religious childhood with constant attendance at Sunday school and church, but like some vaccinations, it didn't "take." Then there came the Great Change. Nothing after that was the same, except perhaps my name. My wandering planet had swung itself into a new orbit, forever caught by a Love that would not let it go.

Which of these is the valid type? Either one may be. Not the phenomena that surround conversion, but the facts that underlie it and the fruits that come from it make it valid.

---

O Christ, who dost call to Thee the child in its innocence and the older ones in their iniquities, we both come to Thee. To whom else can we go, for Thou hast the words of eternal life? So we come and find Thee satisfying, because saving. Amen.

## THE CENTRAL THING IN CONVERSION

Psychology tells us that there is a master-sentiment around which life is organized. It may fasten itself to one of the instinctive urges: self, sex, or the herd. If the master-sentiment is fastened on the self-urge, then life is egotistical and self-centered. Or it may fasten itself upon the sex-urge and the whole of life becomes sex-centered. Or it may fasten itself upon the herd and life may be lived out under the dominance of what people will say and do—fear of the herd will be the deciding factor. Life is herd-centered. There may be a mixture of all three, but in the end the master-sentiment decides and dominates.

Modern psychology tells us that in curing a patient of inward conflict or complex it is necessary to have the patient transfer his sentiment from himself to some one outside, usually to the psychoanalyst himself. This is called Transference. The patient is thus loosed from himself and his problem by the expulsive power of a new affection.

Now, the central thing in conversion is just that transference. While conversion involves the breaking with this sin, that habit, this relationship, that attitude, yet all these things are the negative side. The real thing that happens is the transference of the master-sentiment from self to Christ. It is the conversion of the master-sentiment. Life is no longer self-centric, sex-centric, or herd-centric, but Christ-centric. He is the master of the master-sentiment.

Jesus quietly said to men long ago, "Follow me"—not follow a set of doctrines, however true; nor a rite or ceremony, however helpful; nor an organization, however beneficial; but "Follow *me*." They did. The transference was made. A strange new word came to their lips, "Saviour," for He was saving them from their complexes, their gloom, their despair, their sins—yes, from their very selves. Conversion was a fact, made so by the conversion of the master-sentiment.

---

O Christ, Thou hast our master-sentiment—and as Thou hast it Thou hast us. We dare not give our love wholly to anyone save the Divine. Take it and us. Amen.

FEBRUARY 19      1 Thessalonians 1. 5    Romans 10. 17
                 Matthew 24. 35      1 John 2. 14

## WHAT IS THE BASIS OF ASSURANCE?

You will ask what is the basis of assurance by which you will know that you are accepted. God assures us from a number of directions, which makes it far stronger than if it were from one direction alone.

First, He assures us through the Word. Nothing could be more explicit than that Christ received sinners. Men did not wait till they were good enough to come to Him. They came as they were, and they were made good in the very coming. That seems a commonplace to us today, but it scandalized the religious then and it does now. A modern Jewish thinker criticizes Jesus at this point, "Jesus was too familiar with God and too familiar with sinners." Celsus, in the second century, debating with Origen says: "Those who invite people to other solemnities make the following proclamation: 'He that hath clean hands and sensible speech may come near, he who is pure from all stain, conscious of no evil in his soul and living a just and honorable life may approach.' But hear what persons these Christians invite: 'Anyone who is a sinner,' they say, 'or foolish, or simple-minded'—in short, any unfortunate will be accepted by the Kingdom of God! And what do they mean by 'a sinner'? By sinner is meant an unjust person, a thief, a burglar, a sacrilegious person, a poisoner, a robber of corpses. Why, if you wanted a band of robbers, these are the very people you would invite." Origen's answer was explicit: "Though we call those whom a robber chieftain would call, we call them for a different purpose. We call them to bind up their wounds with our doctrines, to heal the festering wounds of their souls with the wholesome medicine of faith, nor do we say God calls only sinners." (Origen, Contra Celsus iii, LIX.) We glory in what Celsus conceived to be our shame. The first to enter paradise from the Christian movement was not Peter or James, but a young brigand—the forerunner of the crooked-made-straight.

———

O Christ, Thou didst receive sinners then, and Thou wilt not reject me now. I may have dragged my soul through hell, but Thou wilt wash it—dost wash even now. I thank Thee. Amen.

## THE ASSURANCE OF THE WORD

We saw yesterday that the Word assures us that we are accepted. There are promises there that could not be more explicit: "Come unto me, . . . and I will give you rest." "If we confess our sins, he is faithful and just to forgive us our sins." Does it seem out of date thus to quote passages from Scripture to heal present need? To some it may seem so. But those of us who have been up against raw human need for years know that men need nothing, absolutely nothing, so much as they need the simple assurance that they are reconciled to God. Unhealed at that place, men wear a mortal hurt. The assurance that the grace of God in Christ banishes estrangement and reconciles us to God is the most precious thing that ever sunk into guilty human hearts.

"Please leave India," said a Sadhu who listened to a missionary describe how Christ died for us on the cross, "for we have no such story in our books. The heart of India is very tender, and if it hears that story, it will leave our temples to follow this." We cannot leave India, nor can we leave the world, for this fact of grace is what the world, and India, and you and I need, and need desperately.

He also assures us through the revelation of an act. He says to an adulterous woman, "Neither do I condemn thee; go, and sin no more." He says to a hard, money-loving publican, "Today has salvation come to this house"; to a man with a sin-complex in his life that caused a physical paralysis, "Thy sins are forgiven." This is the eternal Word speaking through the language of act. It is the Spacious speaking through the specific. Then grasp this thought: The love of God shining through those specific acts will not deal differently with me. He forgave and restored them, He forgives and restores me.

———

O Thou whose very healing was a revealing, Thou who didst make timeless truth speak through the facts of time, dost speak to my heart, "Thy sins are forgiven thee!" I take it, for Thy very character is behind those words, and Thou art changeless. Amen.

## THE ASSURANCE OF THE COLLECTIVE WITNESS

God assures us through the Word. But that Word, speaking specifically and fully through words and deeds in the pages of the New Testament, keeps on speaking. The Acts of the Apostles was not completed. It is still going on.

The Chinese cook, hearing that that day was the twenty-fifth anniversary of my sailing to India, brought in a cake with the words on it, "Through the ages one word." It was a quotation from a Confucian classic applied to the fact that through these twenty-five years I had had one word—"Christ." Through the ages the timeless Word speaks the language of time. That Word still speaks through the collective Christian witness.

As I knelt seeking restoration to God, someone knelt beside me and quietly said, "God so loved Stanley Jones that He gave His only begotten Son, that if Stanley Jones will believe in Him, he shall not perish but have everlasting life." Did that Christian have a right thus to assure me? He had. He had once put his own name there in the place of the "whosoever" and it had worked. It was the Church whispering its collective witness into my ear.

Sometimes the collective witness of assurance is given through the absolution of the duly appointed priest. I will not quarrel with those who can get the assurance thus, though I must confess I shrink from the idea of the grace of God being almost mechanically dispensed. But, nevertheless, even this may be a phase of that collective witness where men and women and children have arisen from every tribe and tongue and people, in every walk of life, from the peasant to the professor, from every stage of human development from the ripened sage to the ransomed sinner, and have whispered into the ear of the seeker, "Go on, brother, we give you our collective assurance. We have tried it, and it works."

---

O Thou Christ of the emerging new humanity, we thank Thee that there are millions whose hearts Thou hast touched and lighted and who lay their grateful tribute at Thy feet and ours. We joyfully join their ranks. Amen.

# THE ASSURANCE THAT COMES THROUGH NEW MORAL POWER

We have heard the assurance of two: the Word and the collective witness. There is another—the fact of new moral power over sin. God shows Himself within you in your heightened moral power.

A man came to me one day and said: "I went out of the meeting last night determined to do just what you asked us to do, namely, to take Christ into our lives. I took Him as you asked us to take Him—by faith. I felt no change at the time. But the next day when I went out into the old surroundings, amid the old temptations, I found to my astonishment that the old temptations had lost their hold on me. I simply didn't want them. Then I woke up to the fact that there was a new power in my life. Christ was there." He was—and that new moral power was a sign of His presence.

Another man did much the same thing—took what I said on faith without any consciousness of change. But he said afterward: "I was a bad-tempered man. If anyone crossed me, I easily flew into a temper. But the next day when someone did me a wrong, instead of anger I felt only pity. I was astonished beyond words at myself. Then I knew I was a new man. Christ must be within me." He was.

When we begin to show forth the fruit—"love, joy, peace, forbearance, kindness, benevolence, good faith, meekness, self-restraint," then we know that we are connected with the root, Christ. The new life is at work within us. I do not mean that these things will be there in maturity, nor perhaps even in purity, but I do say that they will be there in the beginnings. Let that fact assure you. The bud is the prophecy of the flower.

---

O Christ, I thank Thee that already I feel within me the stirrings of a new life. I make the first unsure steps, but I make them. I begin this walk with Thee, a walk that will take me down through the years and the centuries—and the ages. I begin it feebly, but I begin it. And as I walk my legs will grow stronger and the moral power now begun within me shall ripen into perfect strength. I thank Thee. Amen.

## THE ASSURANCE OF THE CREATIVE IMPULSE

There is another source of assurance that the new Life is within us. We will be conscious of the impulse to share something, yes, share Christ.

Life manifests itself not merely in a desire for more life for itself, but also for more life for others. Religion is a cry for life—but it is also a cry for life for others. The two sides of religion are love to God and love to man, and the moment we touch God we will have an impulse to touch man. If, therefore, we are not sure of our love to God, we may be assured of it, if we find our love to man increase. If nothing else had assured me that the new life was working within the Chinese engineer, this fact would have assured me, "And, moreover, I have been talking to my wife, and she is wanting it too." Now, the wife had been a nominal Christian and he a Confucianist, but the moment the new life came he wanted to share it apart from the question of labels.

The moment I arose from my knees after surrendering myself to Christ I wanted to put my arms around the world and share this with everybody. There was an almost irresistible impulse to give this precious fact. I felt that everyone should know it and experience it. I feel that way still. It may be that you have no such overwhelming impulse; it may be very feeble, it may be just the timid peeping of the buds through the yet partly frozen ground of your reserves, and yet it is there. Act on it today. You may be rebuffed as I was rebuffed, when the next day I spoke to my companion in the Law Library of what had happened: "What? I'll knock that out of you in two weeks." He didn't—he only knocked it deeper. It is the very life of God within you when you have an impulse to share. Take its assurance.

———

O Christ, Thy love is conquering me—for I would conquer others for Thee. O let this feeble love flame, until I shall rest not, till I have found my brother. Amen.

## THE MOST INTIMATE OF ALL ASSURANCES—THE ASSURANCE OF THE SPIRIT

But, you say, these assurances are good, precious beyond words, but shall I not see Him face to face? You shall.

I cannot feel that God would give the intimations of His presence by giving His gifts, but would withhold Himself. Would you as a father, a mother, do that to your child? Then, "If ye then, being evil, know how to give good gifts unto your children: how much more shall your heavenly Father give the Holy Spirit to them that ask him?" Being love, it would hurt Him as much as us to withhold His very self.

Listen to these words: "The Spirit himself beareth witness with our spirit, that we are children of God." The Spirit—our spirit. They come together. Now, there is nothing between. Hush! He speaks, so gently, so intimately: "Child of mine, you shall never know how far I have come to find you. I came seeking you through a cross. But that is gone now. I have found you. You have thrown down the barriers. That is what I've waited for. Now throw away that lingering doubt and fear. It is I. Be not afraid. When that last fear is gone, then we shall talk together. All you have is mine—you have said it. And now all I have is thine—I say it. Draw on me for what you need. My resources are adequate, inexhaustible. Tell me all your troubles, even the little ones, and I will tell you some of mine. It costs to be God. We shall share together. And as we share together you shall grow, and some day, my son, I want you to be like my other Son. I can think of nothing better for you, and so I can wish for nothing less. You know by my coming that all your sins are forgiven. I blot them out of the book of my remembrance forever. I will not remember them, and you must not."

———

O God, my Father, I bow in speechless adoration. I, the once vile, am now fully accepted. Amazing grace! I bow and kiss Thy feet! But as I do I feel Thy love enfolding me to Thy heart. I thank Thee. Amen.

## IS THIS ASSURANCE BASED ON FEELING?

We now have the fivefold strands of assurance binding themselves about our hearts: the assurance of the Word, the collective witness, the assurance through new moral power, through the creative impulse, and the direct witness of the Spirit to our spirits. Surely, this should give the strongest assurance that can be given to any mortal on any matter whatever. These lines of assurance all converging give not only a spiritual, but an intellectual certainty as well. For the mind, gathering up the facts in experience and the universe around one —facts which seem to approve and work in behalf of the new life—comes to a mental satisfaction from the resultant sense of wholeness.

But is all this dependent on how I feel about the matter? If my feelings change—then?

It depends partly on feeling, but only partly. We should not be afraid of emotions, for they are a part of us—an integral part. They give driving force to the soul. But they are liable to fluctuation, according to the state of physical health and many other things. The spiritual life must use them, but it must not be founded on them. It must be centered in the will. You have made what is called in psychology "a permanent choice." It is one of those choices that do not have to be made over again every day. The lesser choices of life fit into this central permanent choice, not it into them. It organizes life around itself as the Ganges gathers the lesser streams into itself. It remains the permanent abiding fact amid the flow and flux of feeling.

But the decision of the will is not a bare, hard, unfeeling thing. It has its emotional tone, and the more decisive the choice, the deeper the emotional tone. But whether the Ganges is made rough by storms or smooth by calm, it flows on its life-way. So with you. Yours is a permanent life-choice. Don't raise the issue again every time your feelings change.

---

O Christ, Thou changest not, no matter how my feelings change. Thou wilt abide in my heart whether I feel Thee there or not. I thank Thee that, as I make the permanent choice, Thou dost take up Thy permanent abode. Amen.

Acts 9. 17–22   Matthew 17. 20
Galatians 5. 7   Philippians 1. 6

## THE TAKE-OFF

The first days of adjustment after one makes his life decision are the most difficult. Infant mortality in the Kingdom is as devastating as infant mortality is in India. But most of this infant mortality in India is preventable. So too, if there are casualties in the new life in the early days, they are preventable.

But there is no dodging the fact that the first few days and weeks are the crucial days. An expert in aeroplanes told me that it takes twice the power for the machine to rise from the water as it does to fly. The earth and water seem loathe to let it go. It takes twice the power to break with the old life as it does to live the new life after the new habits have been formed.

That need not appall you. This morning in my quiet time I came across this verse, "Who shall roll us away the stone?" . . . "And, lo, the stone is rolled back." We see the difficulties like huge stones before us, and, lo, as we get to them one by one, they are rolled back. Remember the Silent Partner is also at work and He is practiced at rolling back stones.

First of all, let us remember that there are certain laws of the spiritual life as definite as the laws that underlie our physical life. I do not mean that a set of rules is given into your hands for you to obey. The Christian life is not mechanically and minutely obeying a set of rules. It is a love affair. And lovers don't sit down and look at the rules to see what is to be done next. Nevertheless, even in a love affair there are underlying laws of friendship which have to be obeyed or else there will be shipwreck. One of the reasons why so many casualties take place is because we are haphazard. And if we are haphazard, we shall not be happy.

---

O Christ of the disciplined will, teach me to live the life according to Thy way. I come stumblingly, but I come. I am set to obey; teach me. Amen.

## COMMIT YOURSELF

One of the first things to do is to commit yourself. The Christian life is the beginning of a life as different from the ordinary man as the ordinary man is different from the animal. You are different and therefore you will act differently. The temptation will be for you to raise no issues, to upset no life-habits, to take on protective resemblance to your environment and to settle down, hoping that the inward life will somehow or other manifest itself. It won't. You must decide it shall.

Professor William James, speaking from the standpoint of sound psychology, says in regard to any decision: "When once the judgment is decided, let a man commit himself irretrievably. Let him put himself in a position where it will lay on him the necessity of doing more, the necessity of doing all. Let him take a public pledge if the case allows." This is sound psychology and therefore sound Christianity. Note that word "irretrievably." Leave no open door behind you. The mind in a fearful moment may be tempted to take that way of escape. You are no longer a man of an escape-mentality. A business man after the great decision called his employees together the next day and told them what had happened to him. There was not an employee who did not respect him in his heart of hearts.

I was recently called out at night by a servant who told me there was a man waiting to see me in the garden. As I approached this figure in the dark I thought I was being "held up," for he had a handkerchief over his face and his hands in his pockets. But he wanted to find power over habits and to find a new life. I did my best with him, but went away with little hope in my heart for him. He was afraid that I and others might recognize him.

Off with the handkerchief, come out of dark gardens where we hide behind bushes, stand before the world open and unashamed and decisive. Be ashamed of nothing but sin. Commit yourself.

---

O Christ, I offer Thee my resolves. May I take the first bold steps. And help me to take them today. Amen.

## DISCIPLINE YOURSELF

The word "discipline" and the word "disciple" have a close kinship. The fact is they are one—no discipline, no disciple.

One of the needs of the present day is the putting of discipline back into life. We have reacted so strongly against the imposed authority and the taboos of the Victorian age that we have swung into a license, which we thought was a liberty. We are now finding out that it isn't. Teachers have said the child must be left to guide itself, which meant, in large measure, that the teacher did not want to take on himself the discipline involved in the guidance and discipline of youth. He was afraid of youth, so he rationalized his fear. But both teacher and youth need discipline. Otherwise we shall arrive where Henri Frederic Amiel, who spent his life dissecting and debunking his own moods, arrived, when he cried out in his *Journal:* "What a strange creature I am! If I were charged with the education of someone, I should seek what is best everywhere and in everything. But for myself I no longer have the taste to reprimand and direct. I merely examine myself and state my preference. Psychology has replaced morality. That is the effect of this flaccid existence that dispenses with adventures and duties, with work and purpose. I no longer know courage save by name, and hope save by hearsay." He grasped for liberty and found disintegration.

I do not mean that you will have a discipline imposed on you, willy-nilly. You will accept a discipline of your own choosing, under the guidance of God. It will thus be both yours and God's. In our Ashram we accept a discipline which we arrive at after corporate prayer and consultation. It is not handed to us. We accept it from within. Sit down in thought and prayer, asking for guidance as you take on yourself a spiritual discipline. As you accept a discipline then are you a disciple.

---

O Christ, help me this day to find Thy yoke and take it upon me. For Thy discipline is my desire. Amen.

## ESTABLISH THE PRAYER HABIT

Yesterday we suggested that you take on yourself a spiritual discipline, not merely for the sake of the discipline, but because these disciplines gather up the scattered rays and focus them upon the business of finer living.

The first discipline must be to establish the prayer habit. In college I decided how much time I could give to prayer, and I fixed there a prayer habit that has been with me these years. If for some reason I do not keep it—which is very rare —I feel that a chord has dropped out of my symphony. Fix the habit even if you have to get up earlier to do it. The other morning I got up earlier than usual and saw the Great Dipper —and took a drink of the beauty of the silent heavens. If I had slept, I should have missed it. Get up earlier and drink —drink. God's Dippers are full.

A great Christian in England was very sleepy-headed as a youth, and no matter how much he resolved, he slept past his prayer time. He decided on desperate measures—as penalty he would throw a guinea into the river every time he missed his prayer time. He did this for several mornings and sadly paid the penalty—a heavy one for a poor student. But at last the mind responded, the prayer habit was fixed and he became one of the outstanding spiritual men of his generation.

Don't fool yourself into saying that you don't need the particular time and place as you will find God all the time and everywhere. If you are to find God all the time, you must find Him some time; and if you are to find Him everywhere, you will have to find Him somewhere. That some time and some place will be the special prayer time and the special prayer place. Fix them. And as you do you put your feet upon the road that leads to victory. For spiritual prayer and spiritual fare sound alike and are alike—they are one.

———

O Christ of the silent midnight hour, teach me to fix the habit of prayer, that I may find the habit of victory. Help me to begin this day in unhurried talk with Thee. Amen.

MARCH 1

Luke 4. 16    Isaiah 55. 2
Psalm 119. 11   John 6. 27
Matthew 4. 4

## ASSIMILATE THE LIVING WORD

Into the prayer hour, take your Testament and a pen. Had I not written down what came to me through the years in the quiet hour, I should have done myself a wrong. For those notes now seem to have been written by someone else. They seem so fresh and new.

A British government official told how he came out to India with no basis for life. His mother gave him a New Testament which he put in his trunk—at the bottom. But one day out in camp, sick and discouraged, he remembered the Book, fished it out of his trunk, and the first word his eye fell on was the word "Redeemed." That one word was the pivot around which life swung from moral defeat and discouragement to victory and a new life. And no wonder—for what a word!

You will find such words in the Book, and they will meet your need just when you need them. For here life speaks out of life. God has gone into these words, so He comes out of them and meets you there. Sometimes in the rhapsodies of my early Christian life I would find myself pressing my lips to some verse that seemed so living and saving. I do so still. And why not? For through that verse I kiss my Father's cheek—Does His face not shine through those words? And I thus tell Him I am so grateful that I cannot use the language of words.

And sometimes the word seems so personal—almost as if your own name were called through it, as when my Chinese friend, Doctor Lo, homesick and discouraged in America, turned to his New Testament for light and comfort, and the first verse his eye fell on was, "Lo, I am with you alway." It is often just as personal as that!

The Danish children shake hands with their parents at the close of each meal and say, "Thank you for our food." At the close of your prayer hour you will do the same to your Heavenly Father.

---

O Christ, in Thy Word we find the Bread of Thy life and we feed upon it. We thank you for this food. Amen.

## THE HABIT OF SHARING

We have talked about the discipline of prayer and the assimilating of the Word of God. The natural and necessary outcome of those disciplines is the third: the discipline of sharing. The first two have reference to the inflow, and this third has reference to the overflow. There can be no overflow without an inflow, and the inflow will stop—stop dead, if there is no overflow.

I call this the discipline of sharing. We should discipline ourselves as definitely to share by deed and word what we have found, as to pray and read the Word. Many do not do this. They are earnest and regular in their quiet time, but have never disciplined themselves to share. If a happening or a conversation, bumping against them, jolts it out of them, well and good. But sharing seems to depend on accident instead of on choice—it seems to be in the whim instead of the will. Rather it should be the natural flowering of communion with God. A doctor found a little dog by the roadside with a broken leg, took it to his house and attended to it till it was well. It began to run around the house and then it disappeared. The doctor felt himself let down. But the next day there was a scratching at the door, his little dog was back again, and he had another little dog with him— and the other little dog was lame! The impulse in that little dog's heart was natural and right. Has not Christ healed you? And if so, is not the natural normal thing for you to do to find somebody else who needs that healing too?

Someone has defined a Christian as one who says by word and life, "I commend my Saviour to you." No better definition. Will you define your Christian life in those terms? If so, put the discipline of sharing deep down in your life purposes.

---

O Christ, Thy healing is upon our hearts. Help us to bear Thy healing help within our hands. Help us this day that we may find some lamed human spirit and lead him to Thee. Amen.

## THE NEW LIFE AND RECREATION

You must now relate your new life to your recreations. Or, rather, you must relate your recreations to the new life. For recreation must not be the center and the new life fitted into it. If you try that, the new life will die. You must now go over your recreations and see whether they contribute to or dim the new life. They should stay only as they minister to your total fitness.

Some recreations do not re-create—they exhaust one. They leave one morally and spiritually flabby and unfit. They should therefore go or be so controlled that they really do re-create. I find after seeing some films that I have been inspired and lifted. But often a film leaves one with the sense of having been inwardly ravished. The delicacies of life seem to have been invaded, the finest flowers of the spirit trampled upon. You come out drooping. One should never expose himself to such a film—not if he values the higher values. It is like turning pigs into your parlor.

The same can be said of many books. To read books that leave one with a sense of exhausted nerves and emotions is to handicap the spiritual life within one. The idea that you must read everything that comes to hand in order to understand life is a false notion. Does the doctor have to take typhoid germs into his body before he can understand typhoid? Does one have to wallow in a mud hole in order to understand the meaning of faith? To wallow in it is to understand it all the less. Only cleanliness can understand the meaning of filth.

To spend long and exhausting hours over bridge tables with emotions aroused that have no constructive outlet is to leave one spiritually weaker. Ask yourself, therefore, whether your "bridge" is a bridge toward finer and more victorious living, or whether it is a bridge that leads to spiritual anaemia.

Go over your whole life and ask whether your recreations really re-create.

———

O Christ of the fit body and soul, make me fit in every portion of my being and may my recreations contribute to that end. Amen.

Hebrews 10. 25
Acts 2. 43–47
Psalm 133. 1

## THE CORPORATE FELLOWSHIP

"Don't you think I should belong to some church?" asked a lady who has just entered the new life. Was her instinct for corporate fellowship right? It was.

The spiritual life cannot be lived in isolation. Life is intensely personal; it is also intensely corporate, and you cannot separate them. If you should wipe out the Church today, you would have to put something like it in its place tomorrow. For there must be a corporate expression of the spiritual life as well as an individual. Even to separate the social and the personal life in this way is wrong. For the social life is the personal—the personal in its larger relationships.

The idea that it is your duty to support the Church seems to me to be all wrong. The Church is not founded upon a duty imposed on you from without. It is founded on the facts of life. Your very inner nature demands it. Moody, in answer to a man who said he did not need the church, quietly pulled a coal from the hearth and separated it, and together they watched it die. It was a legitimate answer.

I am quite sure that I should not have survived as a young Christian had I not had the corporate life of the church to hold me up. When I rejoiced, they rejoiced with me. When I was weak, they strengthened me, and once when I fell—a rather bad fall—they gathered around me by prayer and love and without blame or censure they lovingly lifted me back to my feet again.

The stupidities and the inanities and the irrelevancies and the formalities of the Church? Yes, I know them all. But nevertheless, the Church is the mother of my spirit, and one loves his mother in spite of weakness and wrinkles. My word, then, to you is that, as you begin this new life you begin it as a member of the Family.

———

O Christ, who didst read our deepest need and who didst gather us together into a Family of which Thou art the Elder Brother and God is our Father, we thank Thee that Thou dost invite us to take our place in the Family circle. We do. Amen.

To Schaal, H. 246

Date_____ Time_____

## WHILE YOU WERE OUT

M_____

of_____

Phone_____
　　　　Area Code　　　Number　　　Extension

| TELEPHONED | | PLEASE CALL | |
| CALLED TO SEE YOU | | WILL CALL AGAIN | |
| WANTS TO SEE YOU | | URGENT | |
| RETURNED YOUR CALL | | | |

Message Aunt Elsie Reich
called. Thinking
about 'you'.

_____
　　　　　　　　　　　Operator

Form 94 - D. P.

246B

To **Rev. Schaal**

Date **9-25** Time _____

## WHILE YOU WERE OUT

M _____

of **Elsie**

Phone _____
Area Code          Number          Extension

| TELEPHONED | | PLEASE CALL | |
| CALLED TO SEE YOU | | WILL CALL AGAIN | |
| WANTS TO SEE YOU | | URGENT | |
| RETURNED YOUR CALL | | | |

Message _____

Not Able to come
& See you - wANted you
to know she thinking
of you _____

Operator

Form 94 - D. P.

246 B

To Pastor Scheal

Date 9-25 _____ Time _____

## WHILE YOU WERE OUT

M _____

of _____

Phone _____
  Area Code     Number     Extension

| TELEPHONED | X | PLEASE CALL | |
| CALLED TO SEE YOU | | WILL CALL AGAIN | |
| WANTS TO SEE YOU | | URGENT | |
| RETURNED YOUR CALL | | | |

Message _____
Elsie Called - that
they are Praying for
you -

_____ MJ
  Operator

Form 94 - D. P.

## IS CHRISTENDOM LIVING VICTORIOUSLY?

It would seem that we might now go straight from the beginning of the new life to the social order and talk about our relationships to it. But we cannot—not yet.

For to do that would mean that we have passed by the problem of victorious living within the ranks of the Christians themselves, within the ranks of the converted and the semiconverted and—shall I add?—the unconverted inside the Church. For we have all three. Even the most enthusiastic would scarcely claim that the characteristic of the rank and file of the churches is victorious living. Here and there one sees it, but the chief thing that strikes me in looking at Christendom is the lack of it. A strange sadness, which we mistake for solemnity, has come over us. What is its root?

I had asked a congregation in India to express this desire for a new life, and many had done so. The pastor was translating my prayer in which I said, "O God, we do not know what these people need, but Thou knowest." He translated, "O God, Thou knowest what these people need, and so do we"! He could not let that pass! And many a pastor in the quietness of his own heart would have to say, "O God, Thou knowest what I need, and so do I!" It is victorious living.

Spiritually we seem to have turned gray. The vivacity, the sparkle, the spontaneity, the joy, the radiancy which should characterize people called Christians seem to have faded out. Moreover, there seems a lack of moral dynamic, a paralysis that makes us limp and helpless in the face of rampant wrong. We protest, but seem to have little power to change.

There is nothing—absolutely nothing needed so much among Christians today as the discovery of the secret of victorious living. If we can find that, then anything can happen. Without that nothing will happen—except staleness, tastelessness, and bitter disappointment with religion.

---

O Christ, art Thou putting Thy finger on our need? Then help us not to rest till we know this secret, and use it in our living. Amen.

## THE SPIRIT OF NONEXPECTANCY

Yesterday we said that the chief characteristic of modern Christianity is not victorious living. This would not be so serious if we expected something else—if we were pushing upon the gates of abundant life to have them open. But many have settled down to a spirit of nonexpectancy. They do not expect anything beyond spiritually muddling through. This is serious.

For I have watched what the awful power of fatalism can do when it falls upon a civilization. Have I not seen these lovely people of the East paralyzed at the center by a strange fatalism that makes them turn over their hands in helpless resignation? Across the world that danger is at our doors. It has slowly crept into many a heart and we are resigned to moral and spiritual defeat—take it for granted, in fact. Doctor Worcester, who has labored for years in clinics for people troubled in body and soul, can say these astonishing words: "Most Christians do not expect their religion to do them any great or immediate good." When one tells them that this condition of moral and spiritual defeat need not last for a single hour, that we can find victory and adequacy and buoyancy in living, they look at you as one who announces strange doctrine. For they have become naturalized in defeat. John Macmurray (*Reason and Emotion*, p. 86) quotes Mathias Alexander, who tells the story of a little girl who was permanently lop-sided and who was brought to him for treatment. After working with her for some time he managed to get her to stand quite straight. Then he asked her to walk across to her mother. She walked perfectly straight for the first time in her life and then, bursting into tears, threw herself into her mother's arms, crying, "Oh, Mummy, I'm all crooked." We too think of being spiritually straight and upstanding and adequate as something strange and unnatural.

---

O Christ, speak to our dead desires and bid them rise. We know we cannot live unless, first of all, we desire to live. We do desire to live—to live fully and adequately. Thy pressure awakens us. Our eyes open. Amen.

## IS FORGIVENESS THE BEST WE CAN EXPECT?

Many Christians do not expect anything beyond repeated forgiveness for constantly repeated sins. They do not expect victory over sins. Thus in Christianity the most beautiful thing, namely the forgiving grace of God, is turned into the most baneful, for it actually turns out to be something that encourages evil. What a cross that must be on the heart of God! And what a travesty it is on our Christian faith!

This expectancy of constant forgiveness for constantly repeated sin is weakening to character, and is one reason for so much weak character within the Christian Church. Under this idea, life turns flabby.

The Hindu believes that he will have to suffer for his sins—the law of Karma will exact the last jot of retribution. There is no forgiveness. Stokes, a famous American missionary, who turned Hindu, told me that one reason he did so was that he wanted his "children to be brought up under Karma, rather than under redemption." I could see his point if redemption meant constant forgiveness for constantly repeated sins. And if I had to choose between a cheap, easy forgiveness on the one hand, and the law of Karma on the other hand, I should choose the law of Karma.

But I do not have to make that choice, for a cheap, easy forgiveness does not represent the gospel. The gospel does offer forgiveness for sins, but along with it, and as a part of it, offers power over the sins forgiven. Forgiveness and power are the indissolvable parts of the grace of God. We cannot take one without the other. If we should try to take the forgiveness without the power, it would mean that moral weakness would remain, and if we should try to take the power without the forgiveness, it would mean that moral guilt would remain. God does not give one without the other. We must take both or neither.

———

O Christ, we thank Thee for redemption. This redemption that comes out of the cross we have twisted and have made into a further cross for Thee. Forgive us—and give us power to do so no more. Power—power, we need. Amen.

1 John 1. 7–10
Romans 7. 24, 25 ; 8. 1, 2
Mark 5. 15

## WHAT DOES THE GOSPEL OFFER?

There are two dangers at this point. One is to make the standard too low, and the other is to make it too high. In either case it paralyzes us—one because it demands no change, and the other because it demands such a change that we simply feel helpless before it and give up the struggle. We must avoid this double danger.

It is interesting that both modern psychology and the gospel unite in being pessimistic about man. They both say that "we are less perfect than we might be; that there are great possibilities for idealistic progress which we universally reject." Freud says: "Psychoanalysis here confirms what the pious were wont to say—that we are miserable sinners" (Barbour, *Sin and the New Psychology*, p. 136). But while they are both pessimistic about man, they are both amazingly optimistic. Both modern psychology and the teaching of the gospel unite in saying that this divided state must not continue, man and his ideals must come together if human happiness is to result. Sin is no necessary part of our make-up. It is an intrusion. It is no more necessary to give spice to life than sand in the eye is necessary for sight.

The first thing, then, to get hold of is this: *the gospel offers freedom and release from every single sin.* There is no compromise at that point, for compromise would be deadly! It sweeps the horizon and says, "Sin shall have no longer dominion over you." "The law of the Spirit of life in Christ Jesus hath made me free from the law of sin and death."

We have repeated these words until they are, to many of us, threadbare. But to some of us they are not threadbare words; they are the astonishing offer of God to give us release from the tyranny of evil.

———

O Christ, we thank Thee for what this opens up to us. It is the open door—the one open door out of our inner divisions, our inner strifes and confusions to harmony, to just what we want. We thank Thee. Amen.

## WHAT THE VICTORIOUS LIFE IS NOT

In order that we may see what the victorious life is we must first see what it is not.

*It is not freedom from temptation.* Sin results from the using of a good thing in a wrong way. As dirt is misplaced matter, so sin is misplaced good. Sex is natural and right— adultery is sin. Self-respect pushed too far becomes pride, hence sin. Self-love is normal; pushed beyond limits it becomes selfishness. The herd instinct is right, but when against our ideals, we make the herd the final arbiter, it is sin. James says, "Let no man say when he is tempted, I am tempted of God. . . . Every man is tempted when he is drawn out of his own desires and enticed." Note the phrase "drawn out"—the natural is drawn out—pushed too far into the sinful.

Now, the natural is always with us. Every moment it will be pressing upon the boundaries we set up for it. Every moment, therefore, we shall be tempted. But temptation is not sin. It is only when we yield that it becomes sin. "You cannot help the birds flying over your head, but you can help them building nests in your hair." You cannot help the suggestion of evil coming, but you can help holding it, har- boring it, and allowing it to rest in your mind till it hatches its brood. Dismissed at once it leaves no stain. Thoughts of evil only become evil thoughts when we invite them in and offer them a chair, and entertain them.

Moreover, temptation is the place where a tension is set up between the lower and the higher, and when we throw our will on the right side of that tension, we actually become stronger. Temptation, therefore, can be the ladder to the higher life. We sublimate the moral tension into a moral triumph.

Constant temptation may be consistent with victorious living.

----

O Christ of the wilderness struggle, we thank Thee that Thou art in our struggles, lifting, saving, and turning the tide of the battle. Thou wilt go with me today as I go to turn temptation into character. I thank Thee. Amen.

77

## WHAT THE VICTORIOUS LIFE IS NOT—Continued

Yesterday we saw that victorious living does not mean freedom from temptation.

*Nor does it mean freedom from mistakes.* We are personalities in the making, limited and grappling with things too high for us. Obviously, we, at very best, will make many mistakes. But these mistakes need not be sins. Our actions are the result of our intentions and our intelligence. Our intentions may be very good, but because the intelligence is limited the action may turn out to be a mistake—a mistake, but not necessarily a sin. For sin comes out of a wrong intention. Therefore the action carries a sense of incompleteness and frustration, but not of guilt. Victorious living does not mean perfect living in the sense of living without flaw, but it does mean adequate living, and that can be consistent with many mistakes.

*Nor does it mean maturity.* It does mean a cleansing away of things that keep from growth, but it is not full growth. In addition to many mistakes in our lives, there will be many immaturities. Purity is not maturity. This gospel of ours is called the Way. Our feet are on that Way, but only on that Way, we have not arrived at the goal.

*Nor does it mean that we may not occasionally lapse into a wrong act, which may be called a sin.* At that point we may have lost a skirmish, but it doesn't mean we may not still win the battle. We may even lose a battle and still win the war. One of the differences between a sheep and a swine is that when a sheep falls into a mudhole it bleats to get out, while the swine loves it and wallows in it. In saying that an occasional lapse is consistent with victorious living I am possibly opening the door to provide for such lapses. This is dangerous and weakening. There must be no such provision in the mind. There must be an absoluteness about the whole thing. But nevertheless victorious living can be consistent with occasional failure.

O Christ, we thank Thee that Thou knowest our frame. And yet we know that Thou canst remake that frame after Thy likeness. We put ourselves under its processes. Gladly we do so. Amen.

Acts 15. 37–41
Philippians 4. 2, 3
Romans 12. 18

MARCH 11

## WHAT THE VICTORIOUS LIFE IS NOT—Continued

*Victorious living does not mean the ability to get on with everybody.* There are certain people whose outlook and interests are so different from ours that when we are thrown into close contact, we shall find it practically impossible to get on with them. And they may be very good people. Nevertheless, we find ourselves incompatibles. John Wesley was married to one such. Others are. But who shall say that John Wesley was not a victorious soul? He was, and yet he found it practically impossible to get on with his wife. However, he used that thorn in the flesh to make him a better, a more patient, victorious man.

If you are Christian workers and find you are incompatibles, the best thing to do is to talk the matter over frankly and honestly. And if there is no other way out, get a transfer.

But—and this is the point—as you talk the matter over calmly and honestly you will probably find that what you thought were incompatibilities are misunderstandings. You will see the other person's point of view, and seeing it will probably sympathize with it. It is not at all necessary to agree with another person to get along with him. Some of the greatest of fellowship come out of the most opposite temperaments.

In our Ashram we bring together people of differing outlooks and temperaments and races and theological beliefs and we undertake to make a brotherhood out of these differences. And we do! So far I cannot say we have had any real incompatibles. What we thought at first were incompatibilities have usually yielded to understanding—and sometimes spiritual surgery. We shall see very often the difficulties are not rooted in our real nature, but in complexes, in hidden sin, in wrong attitudes, which when brought out and corrected lead to an amazing depth of fellowship. There are some incompatibles—but they are very, very few.

---

O Christ of the patient heart, we thank Thee for the possibility of bridging gulfs through love. Teach us to love even those whom we find hardest to love and give us victorious living in all our relationships. Amen.

## WHAT IS THE VICTORIOUS LIFE?

We have seen what the victorious life is not, we must now see what it is: It is the life of Christ reigning victoriously in every portion of our being and in every one of our relationships.

First, in every portion of our being. There are many Christians who have certain areas of their lives in which Christ functions, feebly perhaps, but there is a functioning. But there are areas withheld. There are "reserved subjects" in the government of the soul. Over these reserved areas we rule, we make the decisions there. Thus a principle of duality is introduced into the life. When the British reserved certain subjects after turning over other subjects to Indians, that kind of government was called "Dyarchy." It was a failure. The attempt to have a spiritual dyarchy within Man-Soul is also bound to be a failure. Yet millions of Christians attempt it and wonder why the spiritual life is so unsatisfactory. It is bound to be. For we cannot be happy and effective with an inner division. We must be unified. You must make your choice: either you must dismiss Christ entirely from your life and forget Him, and take over the entire control into your own hands, in which case you will be unified under the control of self; or you must make a complete surrender of every withheld area into the control of Christ, in which case the life will be Christ-controlled and therefore unified.

There is no third way. And yet millions are trying the third way—the way of compromise between. It won't work. We have just enough of the love of Christ in our hearts to make us miserable. A war is set up between opposing ideas of life and we live in that war and call it being Christian. As pure unadulterated pagans we might be happy. "Might be"— note that, for the attempt has so far not succeeded. But as compromised Christians we *cannot* be.

* * *

O Christ, forgive us that we have thought to make Thee a half-King, leaving other half-gods in our hearts. We cannot bow at a double shrine. Forgive us. Amen.

## WHAT IS THE VICTORIOUS LIFE?—Continued

Yesterday we saw that the life of Christ must reign victoriously in every portion of our being, and now we must look at the second part—in every one of our relationships.

Duality cannot be introduced within the soul without disaster. But there is another point of duality which is just as disastrous—it is the point between the individual and the social. If duality is introduced at that point, there will also be defeat—the life of Christ must rule in every one of our relationships.

Now, many try to introduce duality at that point—Christ shall function in their personal lives, but the social and economic life is something else. There other ideas and ideals must be applied.

Of these two dualities I am not certain which is the more disastrous—possibly the latter. For if an amazing amount of unhappiness comes out of inner division, then a greater amount of unhappiness comes out of this division which applies one rulership on the inside—Christ, and another rulership on the outside—mammon. This is the point where the house of present-day civilization is divided against itself, and it cannot stand. With this duality at its heart our present-day life is unhappy and paralyzed.

For it is bad psychology. This division between the personal and the social is artificial. It is not rooted in the facts. The personal exists in relationships with others. My relationships with others are just as much a part of my personal life as my so-called inner life. Think of how much of your personal life is made up with relationships with others, and how much is made up of relationships with yourself alone, and you will see at once that they cannot be divided. It is all personal.

Victorious living must include both, for it takes in life, and life takes in both.

———

O Christ, we thank Thee that Thou art claiming the whole of life—the whole. For we can tolerate no longer these paralyzing divisions. Help us to end them by bringing everything under Thy sway. Amen.

## DOES CONVERSION GIVE US VICTORIOUS LIVING?

We have our definition of victorious living, and now let us step back a bit. Does the victorious life take place in what we call conversion, or is a further crisis or a number of crises necessary to bring about this complete sway of the life of Christ?

Conversion is certainly the beginning of victorious living. Here life is lifted to a permanently higher level. Things are changed. "Do you know me?" eagerly asked a Hindu youth. "I am sure you don't, for I am not the same person who saw you yesterday. Last evening as I sat on the hilltop looking at the sunset, Christ came into my life. I am strangely new today." He was, we all are, when the new life is introduced within us. Life is permanently changed. But not fully changed.

Most of us experience a rapid climb to a new height in conversion, but after that there ensues a tableland of alternate defeat and victory. It is up and down. In one of my books I quoted a very radiant soul as saying in one of our Round Table Conferences that religion meant to him three things: Victory, Victory, Victory. It did. But to some of us it means no such thing. On the lowest scale it means defeat, defeat, defeat. A little higher it means an alternation—defeat, victory, defeat. Or, better still, it may mean victory, defeat, victory. But it certainly does not mean Victory, Victory, Victory. And yet religion should mean just that. And when it doesn't, we feel disappointed and aggrieved. We expected more.

Conversion introduced new life, but not full life. As the first flush of the new life ebbs a bit we find things within us we did not dream could survive the inrush of the new. But they have. The rank growth has been cut down, but roots have remained. And we are uneasy with old roots alongside of new life, and cry out for full deliverance.

--------

O Christ, Thou Who hast begun a new work within us, wilt Thou not complete it? Our very uneasiness is a sign of Thy redemptive love at work, gently pointing out that we ail here and ail there. Heal us where we ail, and heal us completely. Amen.

## THE INNER CONFLICT

I found after my conversion a strange conflict ensuing. For weeks I did not think there could be any conflict—life was one glad, unified, and universal day. But I soon found something rather strange for me—I began to be bad-tempered with a tendency to be morose. I was usually sunny-tempered, so this periodical inner conflict, producing a tendency to get out of patience, startled me. I could not account for it, for I was never more earnest and Christ was never more precious. But I was startled to find myself divided. I think I now see what happened.

Modern psychology tells us that down in the subconscious lie the instincts, holding within them the race habits and tendencies. These instincts have gathered up within themselves the race experience running back through a long history. They, therefore, have certain leanings, certain drives, which unrestrained tend toward evil. This all sounds strangely like the almost forgotten doctrine of original sin. But there it is. These instincts control the conscious mind in very large measure. It is true that the mind builds up ideals which try to hold them in check.

Now, in conversion there is a sweeping out of the conscious mind all that conflicts with the love of Christ and the establishing of His reign there. For weeks perhaps no conflict ensues, the new life reigns supreme. These instincts in the subconscious are cowed—they are cowed, but hardly converted. They soon demand recognition and expression. They knock at the door of the conscious. We are startled and alarmed that there are voices in the cellar. To change the figure, these suppressed instincts are like the Chinese pirates who hide in the hold of the vessel and then rise up while the ship is on her voyage and try to capture the bridge and with it the ship. A fight ensues.

With the introduction of new life within me by conversion a conflict began between this new life and the old life found in the instincts. I was divided.

---

O Christ, Thou knowest what is in man. I open it all to thee! Cleanse Thou me in the secret places, the hidden depths. I would be unified. Amen.

## CAN THE SUBCONSCIOUS BE CONVERTED?

Doctor Flew ends up his scholarly study of *Christian Perfection* with this rather startling question: "Is salvation possible for the subconscious? This is the real question for the seeker after holiness in our time." He has raised a most important issue.

These instincts cannot be eradicated. Weatherhead says: "The instinctive forces cannot, by any known process, be eradicated, and the method of evasion and pretense simply means that these forces function at the depth of the personality at which they cannot be controlled" (*Psychology and Life*). India has tried the eradication of these instincts. Her holy men try by every possible device to root them out. But put out of the door they come back by the window. I saw naked Sadhus, who had renounced the world and themselves, very touchy about getting the proper place and prestige in the processions going to bathe in the sacred Ganges. These instincts still showed through the ashes! You cannot eradicate them.

Nor must you repress them. If they are repressed, then they are driven below and form what is called a complex. "A complex is a system of emotionally toned ideas ranged around one central idea." They are festering places in the subconscious mind. Repression of the instincts is dangerous.

Then, if they cannot be eradicated, and they must not be repressed, and in the interests of the new life we cannot allow them to be expressed, is there no way out? Psychology says they can be sublimated—that is turned into expression in a higher form. In the language of religion they can be converted. We cannot put them out, nor put them under, but we can put them behind the central purposes of our lives and they can become the driving force. Our former enemies now become the allies of the new life. The wild horses are now tamed and harnessed to the tasks of the Kingdom.

The instincts can be converted and dedicated.

---

O Christ, we thank Thee that in Thy life every power, conscious and subconscious, was dedicated to the Kingdom. We want that oneness within us. Amen.

Luke 24. 48, 49
Acts 1. 8
Acts 2. 4, 33

## MUST WE FACE ANOTHER SPIRITUAL CRISIS?

Of course we shall face many spiritual crises along the way, for the soul gets on by a series of crises. But I mean, another decisive crisis like conversion. Yes, I think that usually we must. For we cannot go on changed in our conscious mind and unchanged, or only partially changed, in the subconscious. The instincts must be brought into line. We must be inwardly unanimous or we shall be outwardly defeated. We cannot carry on a civil war and a foreign war at the same time.

It is instructive to find many different types of movements —the Holiness movement, the Pentecostal, the Wesleyan, the Keswick, the Oxford Group, and many others—all converging on this one fact, namely, that there is a necessity of bringing the whole of life into line with the will of God. There must be an absoluteness about the whole thing. And they all converge on this: that while conversion began this process, a further crisis in some form or other is necessary to bring everything into line. Are they all wrong about this? That they are wrong in many things I grant, for many stupidities have been built up around these movements. But in the central thing I believe they are profoundly right. At least I have found it so in my own experience and in the lives of thousands of others whom I have dealt with intimately.

I have seen hundreds of missionaries come out to India and the dedication to mission work carries them through for a year, perhaps longer. But the changed environment sooner or later strips them bare to the inmost spirit. India finds them. They are then driven to a deeper and completer self-giving and thus go into victory, or they sink back into being very mediocre Christians—serving Christ, but not like Him. They develop tempers and superiority complexes and attitudes of patronage, and thus they come to a working compromise between Christ and the old instincts. The result is not a clear-cut Christian impression, but a spiritual blur.

---

O Christ of the united will, we bring ours to Thee. They are not united, but we want them to be. We consent for them to be. Amen.

85

## THE OLD AND THE NEW SIDE BY SIDE

This fact of the old and the new side by side and unrelated to each other can be seen in the case of the disciples. As we study them we may see ourselves. Read carefully Luke 9. 18-62.

Jesus took them to Caesarea Philippi, where there was a white rock with a grotto and temple in which the image of Caesar was worshiped as God in the flesh. He came here to ask them the great question, Who am I? Here the great battle was joined: Is Caesar God manifest in the flesh? Is might the final word? Or is Jesus God manifest in the flesh? Is love the final word?

When Jesus asked the question, upon the lips of Peter trembled the great confession: "Thou art the Christ the Son of the living God." At last the great revelation had dawned. It was a great moment. We would have thought that from this moment on to the end everything in their lives would have adjusted itself to that fact, and that their spiritual lives would have taken on harmony and power as they organized themselves around it. On the contrary, there is nothing done right in the rest of the chapter. Everything seemed out of harmony. Jesus did nothing in the rest of the chapter but correct their mistakes. What is wrong? Had they not seen this glorious fact of Christ, the Son of the living God? Yes, the conscious mind had accepted that fact, but the subconscious mind had not. They had been converted, but their instincts had not. Particularly the instinct of self. It was at the place of the self-instinct that the battle had to be fought and won if they were to be Christian. Jesus immediately took the task in hand. He says to them, "If any man would come after me, let him deny himself." He launched a dart straight at the self.

---

O Christ, we come to Thee. Thou hast Thy finger upon our problem—it is this inmost self. Heal us there and we are healed everywhere. Then heal us there. Amen.

## THE REVELATION OF THE CENTRAL DIFFICULTY

Yesterday we saw that the central problem in the lives of the disciples before Pentecost was the fact of the unconverted instincts. Particularly the self. Jesus undertook to let them see it. He showed, first of all, that He Himself was going to the cross to lay down Himself, but that self would rise again. And He taught them that they too must do the same—they must go through spiritually what He was going through physically. The central thing in their being sons of God must be a self-losing. But in losing themselves they would find themselves.

They did not catch this profoundest of spiritual lessons. So He took them to the mountain to show them the same thing in a kindergarten way. As He looked out toward the cross and talked with Moses and Elijah about His death His face began to shine. The lesson? It was this: Life would only shine as it faces its cross. The self would shine with higher light as it surrendered to higher life.

They did not get the meaning. At the foot of the mountain the disciples were fumbling. Divided in inner allegiance, they were defeated in outer attempts. Jesus cast out the evil spirit with a word. They "all marveled at the majesty of God." But as they did so Jesus said to His disciples, "Let these words sink into your ears: The Son of man is to be delivered into the hands of men." You think my "majesty" is in performing miracles of healing, but my "majesty" lies in the miracle of self-losing. That is the central thing I have come to do in myself—and you.

"But they understood not this saying." They understood not this saying because they understood not this attitude. We really think more with our emotions than with our minds, and the emotions still fastened themselves about the self. They were not surrendered.

---

O Christ, we thank Thee that Thou hast blazed the way for us. We see Thy amazing self-losing turn into an amazing self-finding. We would follow Thee. Amen.

## THE CONSEQUENCES OF THIS ATTITUDE

This attitude of the unchanged self-instinct began to show itself in social consequences. The clashes began. For where there is a group of people who have unsurrendered, and therefore unsocialized selves, the stage is set for clash and strife. If the self is supreme within, it will try to be supreme without. It may try to do it in subtle, refined, even religious ways, but it will do it. The clashes began; "Then there arose a reasoning among them, which of them should be greatest."

Here was Christian disciple clashing with Christian disciple, and all were clashing with the whole outlook of the Master. And, moreover, each was inwardly clashing with himself. The conscious mind must have been ashamed, but the unregenerate self-instincts demanded that "number one" be looked after. Of course they all fought for principle! For the self soon learns that it cannot get its way in the presence of religious scruples unless its assertions are clothed with religious principles. Each convinced himself that the interests of the Kingdom demanded that he be first. "I am the oldest," said Peter, "and, besides, I made the great confession of His Messiahship —the interests of the Kingdom demand that age and insight be first." "But who brought you here?" demanded Andrew. "First here, first in authority." "But I belong to the best family," replied John. "After all, if we are to influence these big people for the Kingdom, I must lead, for I am known to the high priest." "But the Kingdom depends on solid financial sense, and I am treasurer and therefore first," said Judas with an air of finality. And thus probably it went. The Kingdom was in their words, but self was in their intentions.

Nine tenths of the difficulties in Christian service come out of clashes between Christian workers, and nine tenths of these clashes come out of the unregenerate self-instinct of otherwise converted people.

---

O Christ, Thou who didst show the nature of the Kingdom through a little child, make me a child again. I must be reborn deeper this time. Amen.

## GROUP CONSEQUENCES OF THE ATTITUDE

We saw yesterday that the first clash was the clash between individuals. The clashes have just begun, for the unregenerate self-instinct dropped into human relationships sends out waves of clash in widening circles to the far shores of society.

As Jesus was dealing with His disciples over this matter, John felt the sting of it and was constrained to bring up another: "Master, we saw one casting out devils in thy name; and we forbade him, because he followeth not with us." Here was the second clash—one group of workers with another group of workers. The unregenerate self-instinct may want to fight with individual members of its own group for place and power, but it is quite ready to combine with them in standing against the encroachments of another group. For the self sees in the threatened position of the group a threat to its own self. It is ready to stand up and fight—for principle, of course! The interests of the Kingdom are endangered. "Who are these unauthorized people? They are dangerous. They are not in the proper line. Besides, did they say the formula for casting out devils properly as we do? It must be stopped."

The unregenerate self-instinct is back of religious party spirit, and it is at the basis of a great deal of denominational refusal to unite with other Christians.

I was trying to heal a breach within a church, a breach that had resulted in spending the equivalent of two hundred thousand dollars in court cases for the right to manage an endowment of four thousand dollars. Said a high ecclesiastic, one of the leaders of the parties concerned, "We must defend the faith." I think he really thought he was defending the faith, for the self often stands concealed in the shadows of the unconscious. But anyone could see that the defense of the faith meant only that the self was defending and asserting itself into power through group supremacy. The faith was really in the mud.

———

O Christ, how our narrowness and bigotry must recrucify Thee, for Thy heart is Kingdom-wide, and beyond! Make us like that. Amen.

## RACIAL CONSEQUENCES OF THIS ATTITUDE

Yesterday we saw the group consequences of the unchanged self-instinct. I am persuaded that a part of the opposition to the Group Movements, such as the "Oxford Group" movement, is sheer jealousy that an upstart movement like this can get the devils of gloom and defeat out of people, when we of the regular Christian churches cannot and do not. Search your heart and see.

But we must go on. The clashes do not end here. Jesus sent His disciples to a Samaritan village to prepare for Him. The Samaritans refused to accept them because His face was set in the direction of Jerusalem. John was furious. "Lord, wilt thou that we command fire to come down from heaven, and consume them, even as Elias?" The self is ready to assert itself through one race against another race. Again, it does religiously. "Lord . . . from heaven . . . even as Elias." But underneath all this religious verbiage was the stark fact that the inner Jewish self hated Samaritans, for they were in a struggle for position and power. We dress up our prejudices in religious garments in order to conceal the naked selfishness beneath.

But these race prejudices are not inborn. The self learns it from the social heredity. Missionary children, born in other lands, grow up among children of another race and know no racial prejudices. Deep and abiding friendships are formed. If, later, they absorb race prejudice, it is from surroundings, and is not inherited. With all of us they are dropped into the subconscious and the self-instinct absorbs them there. We wonder why we are critical about other races, easily find their faults, rather glory in their weaknesses. The reason i that the subconscious mind has absorbed the prejudices, and the subconscious mind is still unregenerate. The self-instinct has never bowed to the yoke of the Kingdom.

---

O Father, who madest every man of every race, forgive me that I do not love every man, of every race. But I cannot do it unless this self within bends its head and accepts Thy yoke. Help me to do it. Amen.

## THE CONTRAST

We have seen how the unchanged self-instinct is at the base of most of our difficulties of adjustment with ourselves and others. We agree with Adler that, "the unsublimated ego stands in the way of the individual's attainment of a happy adjustment to life and to his fellows."

We must remind ourselves that these disciples were changed men in very large measure. Most of the conscious mind was under the sway of Christ, most of the unconscious was not.

Now note these contrasts. We saw in Luke 9 that the recognition of Christ as the Son of God solved very few of their spiritual problems. It left the problems of inner adjustment, adjustment of individual with individual, of group with group and of race with race, untouched. But those four problems were later solved so easily and majestically that we scarcely see that they were solved. Now look at Acts 2. 46: "They took their meals with great happiness and single-heartedness." That solved problem number one—they were no longer at war with themselves in the inner life—they were "single-hearted," no longer double-hearted. Now Acts 2. 14: "Peter stood up with the eleven." That was their attitude with each other—they stood together. That solved problem number two—they were no longer competitive, they were co-operative. Now Acts 2. 44: "And all the believers kept together"—this brought together all groups of believers and made them into a living brotherhood, where they rejoiced in each other's successes. That solved problem number three—there was no longer suspicion among groups of believers. Now look at Acts 8. 14–17: "Then the Apostles placed their hands on them [the Samaritans], and they received the Holy Spirit." Instead of calling down fire from heaven to consume Samaritans they tenderly lay hands on their heads, that they might receive the Holy Spirit. That solved problem number four—their race prejudices had vanished.

All four of their problems had vanished. How? It can be answered in one phrase: The Holy Spirit!

---

O God, our Father, we thank Thee that Thou hast provided for the depths. Thou art not leaving us unhealed there. We thank Thee. Amen.

## THE SECRET

We saw yesterday that the coming of the Holy Spirit into the lives of the disciples solved their fourfold problem. Most of Christendom stands with the disciples and confesses that Jesus Christ is the Son of God but is appalled and dismayed that this does not solve their spiritual problems. It leaves practically all their great problems intact. To recognize Christ as the Son of God is a more or less outer thing, a matter of the perceptive intelligence, a matter of our conscious mind. This may not touch the subconscious at all. But the Holy Spirit does.

For the area of the work of the Spirit is in the subconscious as well as the conscious. This is important, for it brings salvation where we need it. The subconscious can be cleansed, converted, controlled, and united with the purposes of the conscious mind by, and only by, the Holy Spirit. Following Christ as an example will not do it, for this is more or less outer. It has to be deeply inward and permanently inward. Even seeing the Holy Spirit as an influence coming now and again into the life will not do it. The Holy Spirit as a living Person must permanently abide in the depths of our being, assuming full control, and cleansing, directing, and co-ordinating the powers of the instincts to the purposes of the Kingdom of God. The disciples after Pentecost were not mechanically trying to copy Christ in their actions, they were joyously expressing a new life that welled up from within. The Christian life was not a force pump, but an artesian well.

Therefore their lives were not mechanically and jerkily trying to copy an Example, they are rhythmically and harmoniously giving vent to an inner Life. Nothing, absolutely nothing, was left out of the control of the Divine. Therefore they were no longer double-minded—conscious and subconscious warring with each other—they were single-minded, because single-controlled. They were Spirit-filled men.

———

O God our Father, we thank Thee that we need not go through life with an inner contradiction. Thou canst bring everything under Thy sway. Then there will be no part dark. Amen.

## STUNTED LIVES

Spiritual freedom is not a characteristic of present-day Christianity. We are stiff, stilted, inwardly tied-up Christians. Unified spontaneity is not the thing we think about when we think of ourselves. "People in this place will insist on talking about God outside of Church," said a horrified English lady. God should be spoken about in churches, but the door should be closed in on Him when we leave. But God as the thought of our thought, the joy of our joy, the will of our will, and the life of our life—well, that isn't our experience. Yes, but that is normal Christianity.

"I came to India as a medical missionary, so I would not have to speak about God," said a lady describing her inwardly tied-up condition. She was free in her hands, but not in her heart. She could minister to the body, but deeper than that she was out of her depth. Later, when she was inwardly released, she joyously said, "I do believe I am getting vocal about God."

The Japanese have a way of stunting forest trees so that they never grow higher than a couple of feet. They become potted plants, instead of forest giants. This is done by tying up the taproot, so that the tree lives off the surface roots. It remains a stunted thing.

Many of our lives are like that. We live off the surface roots, not from the depths. The surface roots go out into the cultural, the educational, the economic, the social, the political, perhaps also into the thin religious life of our churches, and they draw sustenance from these, but it leaves the life stunted, for the taproot has not gone deep into God. Only as the taproot goes into the depths of the Divine and draws every moment its sustenance from those depths do we fully and truly live.

Are you a stunted spiritual being?

* * *

O Christ, Who didst come to give us life and to give it abundantly, we pray Thee to help us to put our taproot into Thy resources and draw power and life and victory from Thee. Amen.

## ARRESTED GROWTH

Is there anything more pitiful than a child that never grows up? The body is that of a man or a woman, the mind that of a child. We are deeply touched by that tragedy. But are we as deeply moved by the sight of people who grow up in mind and body and remain absolutely undeveloped in soul? Moral and spiritual dwarfs.

What are some of the things that inwardly tie up the taproot and arrest our growth as spiritual beings? I should name first of all, *possessiveness*. In a competitive order the mark of success is the amount of possessions we can accumulate around us. The Hindu who said the order of life is this, "Get on, get honor, get honest," was speaking from the outlook of many. The first thing is to "Get on," and that means get possessions. In an acquisitive society "honor" comes as a result of this getting on. To "get honest" is often an after-thought when we are compelled to make peace with God and our souls—souls now so stunted that we can hardly find them amid the accumulation of things.

We have become so intent on putting our surface roots into the economic life around us that we forget that they are only surface roots. True, they are necessary roots and are quite in place if the taproot goes deeper. But life fed upon them alone becomes a very shallow thing. When Jesus said, "A man's life consisteth not in the abundance of things he possesseth," He was not moralizing, but announcing simple fact.

We speak of "frozen assets." The most real "frozen assets" are the neglected spiritual resources, the real sources of power in life.

Many a man finds that in gaining the outer world he has tied up his inner world. He has gained all, and lost a greater all. Often possessiveness turns into inner powerlessness. The taproot is tied up.

---

O God our Father, Thou knowest we have need of these things, and yet we allow these things to be first things. Save us from the secondary. Unloose our spiritual lives. Amen.

## TIED UP THROUGH FEAR

Is anything quite as prevalently paralyzing as fear in human life? Of course there is a fear that is biological and which tends to efficiency. The other night in going through these Himalayan jungles I surprised a deer feeding behind a great rock. Up across the mountain it bounded in great leaps —the Great Fear was upon it. But it was a fear that tended to efficiency and fleetness.

As I came up the steps to an operating room the famous surgeon asked, "Are you afraid?" The question might have been turned toward him, for if he was not healthily afraid, I should hardly let him operate on me. The fear of cutting into wrong places would make him surgically efficient. I have a fear of hurting my inner spiritual life without which I would be careless. One must also have a fear of letting other people down spiritually. So when a temptation is presented, it is right to say: "I am afraid to do that—I would let other people down. Moreover, what would happen to my work?" This is a fear tending to spiritual survival and fitness.

But there are fears that paralyze. The wild chickens of the Himalayas are the progenitors of all the chickens of the world, so the scientists tell us. One of these was seen crouching in fear before a cobra's overarching hood. Fear had paralyzed it.

Some of our fears may be outer things which seem to stand over us like a cobra's hood and make us afraid, or they may be vague inward fears of poverty, of sickness, of death, of failure, of what people will say, of attempting anything new, of certain people, of being laughed at—all these, and many more, tie up the inner life.

How to deal with these fears must come later, but now we simply note that unless we can unbind the cords of fear from the taproot of our lives, we shall remain stunted beings.

———

O God, our Father, these fears infest the inner life and keep us little. Release us from them. And help us to stand up unafraid because Thy hand is upon the center of our lives. Amen.

## TIED UP THROUGH MENTAL PRIDE

The outer movements of life leave their influence upon our inner life. The scientific movement has captured the minds of many and has left the inner life tied up. We have made terms with the natural world and with natural law to such an extent that we have become naturalized in nature. We are afraid that there are no other roots of life save these surface roots that go into the natural order. Is there a taproot and is there a Deeper Soil?

We are afraid to unbind the taproot completely and let it go into God, lest we seem to be unscientific. And we fear that. We cannot be mentally out of fashion.

But surely it is scientific to live and to live abundantly. When Steinmetz, the wizard of electricity, was asked what he thought would be the greatest discovery of the future, he unhesitatingly replied, "In the realm of the moral and social and spiritual." He was right, for having turned to the outer laws, we must now turn to the inner.

Modern religious liberal thought has gained its altitudes; it must now find its depths. Much of it is shallow, feeding on the surface roots of modern culture. It cannot go further till it goes deeper.

It will mean a wrench for some of us to lay down our mental pride and confess to needs deeper than the mind, but we must do it if the inner life is to be freed. The laying down of the pride of the mind will be the symbol of the laying down of the self. There must be a crucifixion of mental pride in order to attain to a resurrection of the spiritual life. You must become a little child—and that is scientific as well as Christian. In doing so you will find an inner release that will astonish you. You will then know you are truly alive—alive at the center.

---

O Christ, Thou hast said that we should know the truth and the truth should make us free. Help us to lay down our mental pride, that we may gain life. Amen.

## TIED UP THROUGH MORAL DEFEAT

It would be nice, more respectable, to say that we are inwardly tied up through mental difficulties, rather than through moral defeats. But respectable or not, this is where many of us will have to hold our attention if we get release. For to many the problem is just plain sin.

It is not easy to confess that to ourselves, especially if we are religious persons. It is easier to keep up pretenses. Easier —and more deadly. Suppose we gossip about others, tear their reputations to pieces (doing it, of course, in the interests of the Kingdom), suppose we are jealous and make light of the ability and work of a rival, suppose we hold resentments in the heart, suppose impure thoughts are allowed to gather in the mind, suppose we are dishonest in our dealings with others and ourselves, and suppose we exaggerate till it means lying, and twist things till it is untruth, will it be of any use to pretend that we are inwardly free? We know that we are not free—and others know it. An evangelist put his Bible on top of things in his trunk so that the customs inspector might see that he was religious and would not search for undeclared, dutiable articles. Thereafter, when he spoke, his audience knew that he was inwardly bound, no matter how free he might try to be.

The first thing to do is to acknowledge to ourselves just what we are. If we have been Bible-plus-hidden-dutiable-articles-type of Christian, we must say so to ourselves. We must "exteriorate our rottenness," first to ourselves, and then, if necessary, to others. For an editor of a respectable paper to publish in his paper that they had published false circulation figures was not easy, but it unbound the cords about his inner life. Now he is a free man. His taproot is in God!

---

O God, help us not to wriggle or excuse, but in Thy sight confess our need and have these cords of defeat cut from our inner lives. For we would be free. Amen.

2 Timothy 1. 3, 7, 8
Luke 1. 74
Jeremiah 1. 6

## TIED UP THROUGH SHYNESS AND SELF-CONSCIOUSNESS

The spiritual life should be contagious. It should be winsome and winning. But many find it impossible to share their inner lives with others because of shyness and self-consciousness. I put these two things together, for shyness is a species of self-consciousness. When it ties up the inner life and inhibits us from being natural as Christians, it must be looked on as bondage, as sin.

For shyness and self-consciousness mean that when an issue is raised, we refer it to ourselves—there is the constant state of self-reference, in other words, of self-centeredness. This is a hard saying, but it must be said. We must look on shyness and self-consciousness as bondage from which we are to find deliverance.

For it is bondage. The speaker who becomes conscious of himself and of what he is saying will probably stumble and lack grip on his audiences. Only as he forgets himself, becomes lost in his message, will his words come with power and effect. I have often said to an interpreter: "Lose yourself in the message—don't become word-conscious, or self-conscious, and the words will flow." Self-consciousness ties up the flow of thoughts and words. It is profoundly true in speaking that he who saveth his life by thinking about it shall lose it, and he that loseth it shall find it. I was once introduced by the principal of a Hindu college thus: "Now, students pay close attention to his gestures." I could have thrown a book at him! It was a full five minutes before I could forget that introduction and get lost in my message. When the center of life is shifted from oneself to Christ, this bondage of shyness drops away. Instead of a constant self-reference there is a constant Christ-reference. Instead of asking, "How will this affect me?" the question will be, How will this affect Christ and His Kingdom? We are then delivered from these inner cords. The taproot goes into God.

———

O Christ, we thank Thee that we can be delivered from shyness and self-consciousness—this is a deliverance we need. Amen.

## TIED UP BY SHEER EMPTINESS

Many of us are tied up, not so much by positive sins, but by the lack of anything spiritual to give. The cords that bind the inner life are just a consciousness that we have nothing to contribute—at that level.

The innate politeness of the Indian people makes them begin each letter with the assurance that everything is all right and going on beautifully. After that comes the recital of what sometimes are amazing troubles, accidents, quarrels, deaths, and what not. So I seldom read carefully the first paragraph of a letter, but look for the words, "Digar hal yih hai"—"The other condition is this." In the same way I am now spiritually habituated to say to myself and others, "After the preliminary word is over, what are the real facts? What is at the center? Stripped of all words and habitual phrases, what do we find?" Often a central emptiness.

Around this emptiness we build up vast activities to atone for that central lack. As Bowie puts it, "A dizzy whirl around a central emptiness." But life cannot long resolve around emptiness. I once saw a sign on a railway engine, "Boiler Empty." It was at a railway station—it could go no further till the boiler was filled. So we.

No amount of mere stirring of our emotions by sermons will do. To stir emptiness is futile. A little lass, having received her tea from her mother, began to stir it. She alternately stirred and sipped her tea. Presently, with tears of disappointment in her eyes, she said, "Mother, it won't come sweet." Her mother smilingly said, "I'm sorry, I must have forgotten the sugar." No amount of stirring will ever make it sweet until the sugar is in it!

Our lives do not need stirring—they need filling. If Christ is not in the depths of our being, no amount of stirring will make life come sweet and victorious. With Him there it does so, naturally and inevitably.

---

O Christ, Thou hast come to give us not merely life, but to give it abundantly. We need that "abundantly." For life is not enough—we want full life. Amen.

Romans 6. 6, 7
Romans 12. 2, 3
Romans 13. 14

## RESULTS OF THE VICTORIOUS LIFE

We have now seen some of the things that inwardly bind us. We must now see some of the positive fruits that result if we find the victory at the center.

*The first thing will be that we will be released from ourselves and our own problems.* Many never get beyond their own problems. They seem constantly tied up with them. When any occasion arises where help could be given to someone, there is the inhibition that comes from within: "But how about your own self?" That stops dead the processes of helping others. We haven't release from ourselves and our own difficulties.

On my way back to India I came through Persia, on the worst roads of the world, in a sputtering, protesting, broken-down car. It would run thirty or forty miles and then sputter, protest, and die. We would tinker with it a bit and it would start again, and the same process would be repeated. At the end of the day I was worn out, and one night after such a day, when I had to give an address, my head began to whirl and I had to stop. A badly functioning car engine did it. How I wanted to look at the scenery as we went by, for I had never been in Persia before, and i wanted to be effective at the close of the day. I could do neither. All my attention was absorbed in that badly functioning engine. Had the engine been normal, I could have forgotten it.

Many of us have our strength and attention absorbed by badly functioning inner lives. We haven't hearts at leisure from themselves to enjoy God's world and to soothe and sympathize with others. And at the end of the day we are worn out with ourselves. And when life presents its opportunity for service, our minds are too much in a whirl to meet it.

The victorious life would release us from our own problems and our own selves.

---

O Christ, Thine own problems never inhibited Thee from helping the needy that crowded around Thee. Thou wast always free, full, and available. Make me like that. Amen.

## THE LEISURED HEART

Yesterday we said that many are absorbed with themselves and their own problems. They haven't the leisured heart. But some have. Jesus had. He was never in a hurry, never ran, was never fussed and worried, was always busy—so much so that often there was no time even to eat. But He always had time for that next person and that next need. And at the end of the day He was fresh and adequate. Why? He was not worn out by inner conflicts. He was inwardly adjusted to the will of God. That adjustment meant adequacy.

Many of His followers have found the same secret. Many such instances leap to the mind. I lived in a home while attending college in which the mother, surrounded by a dozen young people, most of them growing boys of her own, and with a multiplicity of interests outside the home, was never seen ruffled, never angry, and always leisured. She always had time for your problems. She was inwardly adjusted to the will of God. That will operated as peace, power, poise, and adequacy.

When Livingstone came back from Africa, after spending years there for his beloved Africans, someone asked him about his soul. "My soul, my soul, I almost forgot I had a soul," replied Livingstone. He was so interested and absorbed in other people's souls that he had almost forgotten about his own soul. Healthy condition. Much more healthy than a great deal of modern spiritual advice which sets one to too much introspection, too much absorption with oneself. It tends to morbidity. It is true that we must perhaps periodically look at ourselves with one long, searching self-examination which will result in a complete surrender, a complete adjustment—and then a dismissing of ourselves from the focus of attention, and get on with the work. That will bring us the leisured heart.

---

O Christ of the adjusted will, give us that inner adjustment, that we too may move quietly through our tasks with our heads high, our hearts adequate, and our hands full. Amen.

## THE POWER TO LIVE IN SPITE OF

The second thing that will come to us with the coming of the victorious life will be *the power to live in spite of*.

Many of us know the power to live on account of, but not in spite of. When our surroundings are favorable and life is with us, we go on. But life is not like that always. It often turns rough. And then we are tested to the depths. If our faith is but an echo of our surroundings, then it will fade out. But if it is real, it will then speak from the depths.

Before finding the victorious life the disciples were at the mercy of many of their circumstances. Afterward they were the masters of them. They learned how to mold life instead of being molded by it. There are three kinds of Christians: the rowboat type, the sailboat type, and the steamboat type. The rowboat type is the type that is humanistic, self-dependent, trying to get on with its own resources. But as those resources are limited, the progress is limited. The sailboat type depends on the winds. They are the people who are dependent on circumstances—the other-dependent ones. If the winds are with them, if people are constantly complimenting and encouraging them, they get on. But if the patting on the back stops, they stop. They are circumstance-conditioned. Not very dependable Christians. Then there is the steamboat type—those who have power on the inside, and they go on whether winds are favorable or unfavorable. It is true they go on faster when there is a helping wind, but nevertheless they go on, wind or no wind. They have an inner adequacy. They are not self-dependent, nor circumstance-dependent, but Christ-dependent. They are dependable.

This power to go on when life is dead against us is the deepest necessity of our lives. In victorious living this becomes a working fact.

---

O Christ, Who didst go on when life turned to such roughness that it meant a cross, help us to find that same power of going on—in spite of. Amen.

## THE STRAIN TAKEN OUT

The third thing that the victorious life means is that *the strain is taken out of our lives*. Many are living strained spiritual lives. They are trying, and trying hard to be good. Their fists are clenched, their teeth set, their backs to the wall—they are fighting, fighting. It is all very earnest, but not very inviting, for the type of piety thus produced is a strained piety. And a strained piety is not contagious. Moreover, it is wearing on the person concerned. For all strain means drain. We are inwardly screwed up so tight that we snap under things.

I was once in a tin-plate factory and was told that in one of the processes the inner strain was taken out of the plates by subjecting them to the very severe heat of seventeen hundred degrees. By this process the molecules were so harmonized that thereafter when the tin plates were bent they would not break. Without this fiery process the bending meant a breaking.

Do we not need something like that to take place within the soul—a fiery baptism that will set every molecule of our souls in right relation to each other, so that when the strain comes we shall not break but only bend?

Jesus bent in Gethsemane, for the weight upon Him was very, very heavy. But, thank God, He did not break! Why? Because that prayer, "Not my will but Thy will be done," set every fiber of His spirit in right relations with the indwelling will of the Father. Thereafter life might bend, but it would not break, for there was no inner strain.

Life is often not broken from without but from within. The victorious life takes away the inner strain, and makes life so harmonized that it can stand anything, anything that can outwardly happen to it.

———

O Christ, we thank Thee that Thou didst not break! For hadst Thou broken, we should have broken too. Put us through Thy fiery baptism till all strain is taken out! We consent to the Fire. For we know it means freedom. Amen.

## POWER OVER EVERY SIN

One of the greatest difficulties in evangelism, particularly in the East, is the moral fatalism that says in regard to one's own personal sin: "What could I do? I am a man." The implication is that sin is an integral part of human nature and as long as we remain human we remain sinful. The tyranny of that fatalism must be broken if we are going to live the victorious life. In the depths of our being—note I say "the depths," for a mere surface acceptance will not do—we must get hold of the idea that sin is unnatural, an invasion, an intruder, and is thus no necessary part of human nature. When a man sins, he is not a normal human, he is subhuman, or antihuman. There are three unnatural things which have invaded life: Sin is the unnatural evil of the soul, error is the unnatural evil of the mind, disease is the unnatural evil of the body.

Jesus said that salvation is health. Wherever He uses the term "Be saved," it can be literally translated, "Be whole." The health of the soul is goodness, the health of the mind is truth, the health of the body is freedom from disease. Is a mind more of a mind when it has error in it? Is a man more of a man when he has evil in him? He is less and other.

Every sin, then, can be conquered. Hold that within the mind. Do not allow the mind to admit of any exception. That exception will be the loose bolt that lets the bridge down. "Put ye on the Lord Jesus Christ, and make not provision for the flesh, to fulfill the lusts thereof." In other words, do not provide for any failure; provide for victory. There must be an absoluteness about the whole thing.

I know the dangers of hypocrisy involved in this absoluteness. But of the two dangers, the greater is in mentally providing for sin in the life.

---

O Christ, we thank Thee that no word of Thine ever fell upon human ears except a complete offer of complete release from all sin. Help us to accept that deliverance. Amen.

## SIMPLICITY AND STRAIGHTFORWARDNESS

A Hindu sent up this comment: "I am not enamoured by your dramatic gestures. If you have found Christ, tell us simply and straightforwardly." I could only reply that my gestures were a natural part of me, and that I was not conscious of them, but that I was deeply impressed by his demand that we be simple and straightforward. He was right. *The victorious life should and does reduce life to inward unity, and, therefore, to outward simplicity and straightforwardness.*

We need to be cleansed from all double purposes in word and attitude. Our speech should become "chaste" in the sense of expressing a single thing.

See what the coming of the Spirit into Peter's life did for him. Note the contrast. At the Denial Peter says: "Man, I know not what thou sayest." Here was Peter double-minded and double-worded. Now: "Peter was filled with the Holy Spirit, and he replied, 'Rulers and Elders of the people, if we today are under examination concerning the benefit conferred on a man helplessly lame, as to how this man has been cured; be it known to you all, and to all the people of Israel, that through the name of Jesus the Anointed, the Nazarene, whom *you* crucified, but whom *God* has raised from among the dead—through that name this man stands here before you in perfect health. This Jesus is the STONE, TREATED WITH CONTEMPT BY YOU THE BUILDERS, BUT IT HAS BEEN MADE THE CORNERSTONE. . . . And in no other is the great salvation to be found; for, in fact, there is no second name under Heaven that has been given among men through which we are to be saved'" (Acts 4. 8–12, Weymouth). Note the straightforwardness, the directness, the chaste simplicity of his words. The Holy Spirit, who is the Spirit of Truth—the Spirit of Simplicity and Directness, brought this revolution into his life. He will bring it into ours. Weasel-words and weasel-attitudes will give way to words that flow in simplicity out of the depths of unified life.

---

O Christ of the simple speech and of the direct attitude, give to us of Thy likeness in this. For we too would be saved from complexities and diplomacies and double-meanings. Amen.

105

## LIFE CREATIVE

The last thing we shall mention as being a sign of the victorious life is the fact that *life now becomes spiritually creative*. The victorious life is life organized around love. But as love is creative, life now becomes creative.

When there is love there is always a plus, a margin for somebody else. We have enough and to spare. A woman, who became one of the great missionaries of the world, was being taken in a sedan chair through the dirty, narrow, crowded streets of a Chinese city just after her first arrival. Everything in her revolted against the strangeness and the dirt. "O God," she cried, "how can I live among these people without love in my heart?" An immediate answer came in the flooding of her heart with what was nothing less than divine love. From that moment on she forgot dirt and narrow streets and strangeness; she saw only people for whom Christ died. Instead of being driven back upon herself love drew her out of herself into an amazingly creative service for her beloved people. There was a plus now.

In Bengal when the wedding ceremony is taking place, a child is placed in the arms of the bride as a symbol of her fruitfulness. When the soul is inwardly wedded to Christ in complete surrender, then there are put within our arms tasks and responsibilities and opportunities, for love can and will be creative.

The victorious life means the heightening of all the powers of the personality. The mind becomes keener and more creative, the emotions become broader and more sensitive, and the will more active and decisive. The whole of life is outreaching. Lives begin to be changed, movements begin to be launched, a creative impact is made upon life. "I used to pick and choose my friends," said a recently changed society lady, "but now since the great change has taken place I take everybody into my heart." Love had begun to be creative.

———

O Christ, we thank Thee for the creative impact of Thy love in our hearts. Make us creative this day as we come into contact with dull, dead life. Amen.

## HOW SHALL I ENTER?

The most delicate moment for many of us now comes as we approach the question of how we may enter the victorious life. We must approach it with a prayer upon our lips and in our hearts.

First of all, there is a difference now in your coming. When you first come, you come as a stranger and a penitent rebel knocking at the door for admission. Now you are a child within that Home, but seeking a deeper and fuller correspondence to the spirit of the Home. You are not asking for admission, but for adjustment. You are asking that everything may be taken out of you which clashes with the spirit of the Home. You can now come with a sense of confidence and assurance, born out of contact with the Father, that if you meet the conditions, He will meet you more than half way. The barriers are all within us—not in Him.

But the first thing we must look at is what we are not to do. *Don't undertake to gain the victorious life by fighting your individual sins.* The way into victory is not in that direction. And yet that is the first thing many people think about—"I'll put up a stiff fight against my sins." Don't; you'll lose. For when you fight your individual sins, you are compelled to center your attention on those sins. Now, it is a law of the mind that whatever gets your attention gets you. If, therefore, your sins get your attention, even though it may be a fighting attention which you give, then your sins will get you. We fall into the very sins we are fighting. Many a man is astonished to find that while praying against his sins, and earnestly fighting those sins, he succumbs to them. "Why did God let me down when I was fighting so hard against my sins?" asked a perplexed soul. Later she found the way and her perplexity vanished. She had been on the wrong track.

---

O Christ, take us by the hand and lead us at this hour, for without Thy guidance we stumble and lose the way. For we must find the way—simply must. For we can live no longer without perfect adjustment to Thee. Amen.

## THINGS TO AVOID IN SEEKING

Yesterday we said that the first mistake we must avoid in seeking to enter the victorious life is not to try to enter by fighting our individual sins. We must pursue this a little further. Suppose you are fighting sin at the place of sex. In fighting that sin you have to concentrate your attention upon it. The result is the imagination is aroused. A battle then ensues between the imagination and the will. Now, modern psychologists tell us that in any battle between the imagination and the will, the imagination always wins. So we go where imagination goes. We fall into sex sin.

The imagination must be called away from our sins and centered elsewhere. In other words, the imagination must be centered on Christ. But the imagination cannot and will not be centered there unless we make a complete surrender to Him. For the imagination goes where its supreme treasure is. "Where the treasure is there will your heart be also." Your treasure must be in Christ—wholly and supremely there. If so, your imagination will be there also. So the problem is not merely the shifting of the imagination—it is the shifting of the place of your supreme treasure, the shifting of your very life. You must surrender.

There can be no love between persons unless there is a natural inward surrender. When one withholds his inmost being from the other, there is no love. So there can be no complete love between you and Christ until there is a complete surrender to Him. When the complete surrender takes place, then love springs up. It begins to burn. The imagination follows. Since love is centered here, the imagination is also centered here. It now fights with the will and not against it. There is victory.

The problem, then, is to shift that imagination. That can only be done by shifting the center of life itself from self to Christ.

———

O Christ, I would have Thee as the home of my imagination. I would always be centered on Thee. In order to do so I will surrender to Thee. Amen.

## FURTHER THINGS TO AVOID

As we have seen the futility in trying to fight with our individual sins, we must now look at another mistake. Don't try to forget your sins. This is to invite defeat again. For the very effort made in trying to forget will call the matter back into mind. To try to forget is to remember.

A fakir came to an Indian village, declaring he could make gold. The villagers gathered around him as he poured water in a tub, and then putting some coloring matter into it, began to stir it with a stick and to repeat "mantrams." When their attention was diverted, he let some gold nuggets slip down the stick. He poured off the water and there was the gold at the bottom! The villagers eyes bulged. The money-lender offered five hundred rupees for the formula. The fakir explained minutely how to make it, and then added, "But you must not think of a red-faced monkey as you stir, or the gold won't come." The money-lender promised to remember that he was to forget. But, try as hard as he would, the red-faced monkey was there before him, spoiling everything. The gold would not come!

As you try to forget your sins they will be before you all the more. The only way to forget your sins is to have your attention centered elsewhere. But, again, your attention cannot go unless you go. This, again, points to self-surrender. This will produce "the expulsive power of a new affection." Your sins will be fully forgotten, because Christ is fully remembered.

Perhaps one word of possible correction is necessary. Sometimes we do succeed by effort to get sins out of the mind, but this means that they have gone into the subconscious mind, where they work havoc in the life. Whether we succeed in forgetting, or call the sin more vividly back into the mind, in either case there is defeat and disaster.

---

O Christ, as we clear these things from the pathway that leads to Thee, our hearts become the more eager to arrive at perfect victory. Lead us, we follow. Amen.

## WHIPPING UP THE WILL

There is one more thing we must look at before we get to grips with the center of our problem. There are many who feel that the problem will be solved and they will go into victorious living if they only try a little harder. So they proceed to whip up the will.

Much of our present-day Christianity is founded on this idea. So our preaching partakes of that note. We lay a demand on the souls of our people—our gospel is a demand. But somehow after a few days the will relaxes and we are where we were. It doesn't work. Why? The reason is that when we say, "I'll try," we are still on the basis of self. It is self-effort. But before the self can put forth any real effort it must be released from its inner conflicting desires. On the other hand, when a man says, "I'll trust," then he shifts the basis from self to Christ. His attitude is no longer self-centered, but Christ-centered. Niebuhr rightly says, "The moral fruits of religion are not the result of conscious effort to achieve them. . . . Merely taking thought cannot strengthen their will. . . . What men are able to will depends not upon the strength of their willing but upon the strength which enters their will. . . . Deeds of love are not the specific acts of the will" (*An Interpretation of Christian Ethics*, p. 220).

Since the will is the self as it is organized at that particular moment acting against recalcitrant impulses, the strength of the will is in direct proportion to the strength of the self. This strength depends upon the unity of the self.

But if the self is divided? Then the will is weak. The problem, then, is not the whipping up of the will, but the unifying of the self. But that self cannot be unified until it comes under the control—the complete control of the power of Christ.

---

O Christ, we have tried to reach our goals by urging our wills forward, but our wills are weak because we are weak. Unite and strengthen us at the center of our being. Then we shall reach our goals. Amen.

110

## THE CRUX OF THE PROBLEM

We have seen that we cannot merely try to fight our sins, or forget our sins, or to whip up our wills—we must go deeper. For our outer sins are rooted in something deeper. Just as my fingers are rooted in the palm of my hand, so my individual sins are rooted in the unsurrendered self. It is the thought of self-advantage in some form or other that lies at the root of our sins. Why do we lie and steal? We think the self will be protected or advantaged. Why do we quarrel with others? Because the self has been crossed. Why are we envious? Because we are afraid that someone will get ahead of the self. Why do we give way to sex passion? Because we think the self will thereby find pleasure. Adler is profoundly right when he says the ego-urge is our prime difficulty in life and is at the basis of most of our unhappiness. The problem of victorious living centers, then, in one thing chiefly: self-surrender.

But, you ask, didn't I do that in conversion? Yes, you did in a measure. But not wholly. Now you see deeper depths that must be surrendered. The conscious mind was given to Him in conversion, now the subconscious mind, the center of our divisions and inner clashes, must be laid at His feet as well. These basic instincts must come under His control—and they must be cleansed. The self we now give is a fuller self, both conscious and subconscious, for we want a fuller salvation—a complete salvation.

The difference between a quack and a real doctor is this: a quack doctor treats symptoms, a real doctor treats diseases. Christ now asks that we allow Him not merely to treat the individual sins, the symptoms of a deeper malady, but the very root, the self.

That self must be crucified in order to rise again. His finger is on our problem.

O Christ, Thou hast touched the seat of my disease. I know it. Help me not to wince or be afraid, or ask for halfway measures. Help me to surrender all. Amen.

## LETTING THAT LAST THING GO

The last thing we want to let go is just ourselves. It is the one and only thing we really own. And now Christ with imperious demand asks for that last one thing. It is at this place that the real battle is joined. All else have been skirmishes.

Jesus said with awful decisiveness, "If any man cometh unto me, and hateth not his own father, and mother, and wife, and children, and brethren, and sisters, yea, and his own life also, he cannot be my disciple" (Luke 14. 26). The family and ourselves must be placed on the altar. This does not mean that we should necessarily leave the family. To "hate" means to "love less" according to the parallel passage in Matthew 10. 37. A lighted candle when it is put before a high-power electric light casts a shadow. Thus the lesser loves, while really light, cast a shadow when this all-consuming Love makes its demand upon the human spirit. These loves are not to be abandoned. They are to be surrendered. You still live with yourself even after you surrender yourself, so you may still live with your family after you surrender them.

Now, the interesting thing to note is that the "life," or the self, was the last thing mentioned—"yea, and his own life also." Why did He put that last? Because it is the last thing we ever give up. The missionary gives up his home and loved ones to come to another land—he gives up everything except himself. He finds his inner self touchy over position, place, and power. The minister sacrifices a great deal to go into the ministry—everything except the minister. He finds himself preaching the gospel with a great deal of vanity and personal ambition mixed up in it. The layman gives up much to follow Christ, but he finds himself easily offended in the very following of Christ. In each case the self is still there. It must be surrendered.

---

O Christ, I come to Thee to help me in this central thing. I am hardly willing to let go that last thing, but I am willing to be made willing. Amen.

## COMPROMISES

We saw yesterday that we were up against the demand for self-surrender. This is the first step, and it must be taken. But here we do not let go without a struggle. The whole of the biological urge is against this. For this demand reverses the process of nature. It is an invasion of the rights of self-assertion. It is true that this demand means the possibility of self-assertion on a higher level, but the lower urges do not understand this and will resist it. The urges of the ages will fight this hour. They will rise up like the elemental Peter and say: "Be it far from thee. This shall never be unto thee." This is to think as "man" thinks, said Jesus. When you are about to take the step that will make you a man "plus," then the old, elemental man of the ages will rise up within you and try to pull you back into elemental desires and urges and will plead for the *status quo*. Or he will suggest compromises. If he cannot conquer by denial, he will try to conquer by dividing. Compromises ensue.

A patriot was making a speech, and glowing with patriotic feeling, said: "For the sake of my country I am willing to sacrifice my old mother—yes, I am willing to sacrifice my children, and, if necessary, I am willing to sacrifice my own self." He was last! He was willing to let the old mother and the children go first! We smile at the "patriot," but in him we see ourselves. The self presents compromises, not quite so baldly, but it presents compromises to save itself. When Jacob was about to meet the angered Esau, he sent presents before him, hoping thereby to save himself. There is much of the Jacob in us!

That recalcitrant Jacob within us must be subdued and changed into Israel, even if it means wrestling till the breaking of the day.

---

O Christ, I come to Thee. Help me not to blur this hour by compromises and by a patched-up truce between the old and the new. I would be new, entirely new. Amen.

## FURTHER COMPROMISE

Last week I said that the self lets go reluctantly and that compromise will be asked for. This old Pharaoh, who has been used to ruling for ages, when asked to let you go into freedom will say, "No," and then, "Yes—no." But you must insist that "not a hoof shall be left behind."

The "Yes-no" attitude at this place is subtle and sometimes covered. I gave up my mattress to someone at the Ashram and felt virtuous for doing so. Then I remembered where there was another, and got it for myself. I thus satisfied two things within me—one the desire to get the approval of my higher life and of my fellows by giving up the mattress, and the other the desire for comfort for myself by getting another.

Many Chinese offer to their gods, what to them is one of the most precious things they have—the pig. It used to be that the whole was offered. Now they offer the severed head with the severed tail in its mouth—and keep the body for themselves! With us there is a good deal of offering of that kind—we offer the more or less useless remnants and keep the essential self intact. We offer our service and withhold the self. We offer our talents on occasions to Christ and reserve to ourselves the right to decide the really big things of our lives. Thus religion becomes the window-dressing that hides our essential motives. We are not necessarily hypocrites, for many of these motives are hid from us—we are just halfway givers. Or we are what we boys used to call, "Indian givers"—a reference to the custom of some American Indians which meant a giving that gave and then took back. This exactly expresses what we try to do with God. We pass a resolution of complete surrender, and then nullify it by "riders." And then we wonder why there is no liberty in the life.

———

O Christ, search our hearts relentlessly to find the hidden stowaway. We want everything, everything to come under Thy sway. For we want everything to express Thy freedom. Amen.

## WE SEARCH RELENTLESSLY

I must not seem to labor the matter of compromises too much, lest you become vexed with me. But this is so important that I must hold myself and you to this point. It may be that your very vexation with me is a sign that I am on uncomfortable ground, and that you would prefer that I change the subject.

One can often see a Hindu Swami on the small raised platform while the faithful lay at his feet their offerings. He seems to be indifferent to it all—in fact, treats the whole thing with contempt—does it not belong to the world which he has renounced? He gets up and leaves the whole thing with an air of utter indifference and goes into the rear. As the curtains close behind him the servants deftly garner up the rich offerings and follow him. It goes into the treasury. The Swami is wealthy beyond words. He is probably not a conscious hypocrite, at least not now, for he has lived so long in the illusion of renunciation that he really believes he has renounced all—and others believe it—hence their offerings. The essential self underneath it all is covered so that one hardly sees that it occupies the throne in the rear.

When you come to offer this inmost self, you will be strongly drawn to do what the Hindu does when he offers a water buffalo to his god. The long knife falls toward the neck of the buffalo, but just as it is about to strike, the executioner deftly turns it and it cuts off the tip of the ear instead. The sacrifice is finished and everyone is satisfied.

When you are about to lay low your essential self, the temptation will be very strong to cut off the tip of some self-indulgence instead, and leave the matter at that—the essential self untouched.

O Christ, Thou seest how we hesitate to strike the blow that would seem to slay our most precious possession. But nerve our hearts and our arms that we may not divert the blow into irrelevancies. Amen.

## TWO WELCOMES

Perhaps we can see ourselves in one of the other of these welcomes. Jesus was invited into the house at Bethany, and there Mary "sat at his feet and heard his Word." A Pharisee also "desired him that he should eat with him. And he went into the Pharisee's house, and sat down to meat." Then follows the story of the woman who anointed His feet. The Pharisee said within himself, "This man"—note the attitude —"if he were a prophet, would have perceived who and what manner of woman this is which touched him, that she is a sinner." "Is a sinner"—to men like the Pharisee, there is never a "was a sinner"—it is always an "is." A sinner always a sinner. They never forgive and forget. To Jesus she "was a sinner"—she is not one now. But to go on: Jesus says, "Simon, . . . I entered into thine house, thou gavest me no water for my feet; . . . thou gavest me no kiss: . . . My head with oil thou didst not anoint." In other words, Simon, "I have come into your house, part way, at the door. You gave me food—and reserved your heart. You gave me a welcome—with reservations. I am in, and yet not in. This woman has sinned in her flesh. You are sinning in your spirit. I can release her. But I cannot release you. You won't let me. For you want to retain your pride—and me. You would like to have me—and not have me. You are divided—and therefore self-damned."

But Mary welcomed Him and gave Him food—and her heart. She sat at His feet. He was at home there. For the welcome was complete.

Is your heart a Bethany to Christ, or a Pharisee's house?

Self-surrender will turn that proud, barren, critical, aloof, self-righteous Pharisee's house into a Bethany.

---

O Christ, I fling open the door to my house and to my heart to Thee. Thou shalt be to me no longer the threshold-Christ, but the throne-Christ. Take the very throne of my divided heart. Take it now. For I give it. Amen.

## ALL I KNOW AND ALL I DON'T KNOW

There may be the lingering fear that your giving may not be complete. But if you are completely honest in giving what you know, then you can lump all the other unknown things and future contingencies in the words, "I give all I know, and all I don't know."

"All I don't know" has within it the future as it unfolds. It means that in your giving there is about it an absoluteness and yet a relativity. There is an absoluteness in that it is once and for all, and yet a relativity in that you will have to keep offering things to God as they come up day by day. But you need not be anxious now about those things which will come up in the future—let them be met as they come. If there is no Inner Voice telling you that you are withholding, then you have a right to believe that all has been given, for if there were something left behind, the Spirit would let you know.

The absoluteness and the relativity in full self-giving can be seen in real marriage. There is a once-and-for-allness about self-giving in real marriage, but there is a relativity in that there are continuous adjustments and continuous unfoldings of pledges of self-giving. Marriage is over in an hour, and yet it takes a lifetime to be really married.

The "all" that you use is a small word, but it has within it an amazing capacity for unfolding. It holds within it pleasure and pain, struggle and battle, joy and peace, glorious relationships and difficult adjustments. It is well that the curtain shrouds all that it holds. For we do not need to live all of life at once—that would exhaust us. We can live it a day at a time. What the future holds is not for me to ask, but whatever it may be, He has that too.

---

O God, I thank Thee that I need not worry about the to-morrow. Thou hast today, and Thou hast me. Let that suffice me. Amen.

117

## ALL I DON'T KNOW—Continued

We saw yesterday that "All I don't know" covers the unfolding future. But it covers something else: it covers the hidden depths of the unconscious mind. Its reach is not only in length into the future, it is in depths within us.

The unconscious mind is now a well-established psychological fact. Long before modern psychology began its description of it sincere religious people had felt the fact within them. It has been variously described as **another law** working within "my members," "Evil is present with me," "the old man," "inherited evil," "original sin," and so on. All these point to a realm which seems to be working against the conscious purposes of the life and over which we have little control. It is unconscious—the place of inherited instincts, instincts polluted by the streams of racial tendencies which have poured into them for ages.

We do not know the subconscious mind except indirectly, nor can we control it except indirectly. That control must come from God. We can surrender it to Him. He takes over charge of the depths. They become cleansed and Christianized. How do I know this? I do not know it except indirectly. But look at the disciples after Pentecost. They do not seem to be men sitting on the lid of an inner volcano. They seem to be unified to the very depths of their being. The new life came out of them like perfume from a flower—it seemed the natural expression of their unified lives.

The life that is controlled at the depths of the subconscious mind by the Spirit seems tensionless, not between itself and its ideals, for that tension will always remain, but tensionless in regard to itself. The conscious and the subconscious are both dedicated to the same purposes and working toward the same ends.

---

O God, I thank Thee that Thou art about to give me healing at the very center of my being; Thou wilt make conscious mind and unconscious, now according well, beat out music vaster than before. I give both to Thee. Amen.

## THE ACCEPTANCE

We now come to the place where we are prepared to take the step that will mean full deliverance. It is the step of faith. Faith is an adventure in acceptance. It banks on the *bona fides* of God. It believes that the character of God and the moral stability of the universe are behind this offer of full deliverance. There is an element of quiet aggressiveness in our reaching out and taking this pearl of great price, inward freedom, for we have paid the ultimate price, our all, and now we have the moral right to accept all. It is a step in mutual confidence.

But some stand, having paid all, hesitating to take all. I once saw a lady who, about to go into the Chicago Exposition, having dropped her coin into the turnstile slot, stood waiting for the turnstile to open for her. But it did not open, even though she had paid the price. It needed the aggressive push of faith against it, and when she made that push, it opened.

You have paid the price, now press, literally press against the promises held out to you and you will walk through them into freedom. A few days ago a doctor, who had found life turning sour, walked out into freedom through these words, "Whatsoever things ye desire when you pray, believe that ye have received them, and ye shall have them." "Have received them," not "will receive them," for it is already done. It only awaits your acceptance. You cannot trust yourself, you cannot trust your own resources, but you can trust Him. He will never let you down.

I have stood alongside of thousands of people at this hour of acceptance, and whenever people have made the step in simplicity and aggressive sincerity, God has never let them down. Not once. He will not let you down. Try it.

---

**O God, my Father, I come to the moment of the test of my love to Thee. For I know if I love Thee, I will trust Thee for this gift of full release. I do love Thee and I do trust Thee now. Amen.**

## A PERSONAL WORD

Perhaps a personal word might help. I was a Christian for a year or more when one day I looked at a library shelf and was struck with the title of a book, *The Christian's Secret of a Happy Life.*

As I read it my heart was set on fire to find this life of freedom and fullness. I reached page forty-two when the Inner Voice said very distinctly, "Now is the time to find." I pleaded that I did not know what I wanted, that when I finished it, I would seek. But the Inner Voice was imperious, "Now is the time to seek." I tried to read on, but the words seemed blurred. I was up against a divine insistence, so closed the book, dropped on my knees and asked, "What shall I do?" The Voice replied, "Will you give me your all—your very all?" After a moment's hesitation I replied, "I will." "Then take my all, you are cleansed," the Voice said with a strange, inviting firmness. "I believe it," I said and arose from my knees. I walked around the room affirming it over and over, and pushing my hands away from me as if to push away my doubt. This I did for ten minutes, when suddenly I was filled with a strange refining fire that seemed to course through every portion of my being in cleansing waves. It was all very quiet and I had hold of myself—and yet the divine waves could be felt from the inmost center of my being to my fingertips. My whole being was being fused into one, and through the whole there was a sense of sacredness and awe—and the most exquisite joy.

Very emotional? So be it! But I knew then, and I know now, that I was not being merely emotionally stirred, but the very sources of my life were being cleansed and were taken possession of by Life itself. My will was just as much involved as my emotion. The fact is the whole of life was on a permanently higher level.

---

O God, I too take Thee in this simple way. If Thou art looking for a heart to refine and dwell in, Thou hast mine, completely and forever. I accept the Gift. Amen.

APRIL 22

Romans 5. 1–5
1 Peter 1. 8, 9
1 Corinthians 5. 7

## A FURTHER CLARIFICATION

I hesitated to write what I did yesterday, for there may be those who feel that they must find exactly that experience or else they are not united and released and filled. This is a mistake. I have never known two experiences exactly alike in emotional tone. They differ widely, and yet there is the same sense of inner release and unity, and thereby heightened power to live creatively. Don't seek the experience of another, seek Christ, and let Him give you the kind of experience suited to you and which will make you more useful.

Christ said to a friend of mine who is really alive with God, "I won't stir your emotions, but I will give you mine." He did. And His emotions were for her exactly right. His emotions were always healthy and always under the control of the purposes of the Kingdom.

I know the modern reaction against emotion in religion. But it often takes a real emotional upheaval to shift the center of life from self to Christ, and when emotion does that, it is redemptive and releasing and not merely for selfish enjoyment.

That such a profound change could take place without emotion is unthinkable. And yet the emotion is a by-product of the facts that are taking place. We do not depend on them. We depend on Him. And He comes in to abide permanently amid the flux and change of emotion. But if my soul takes its tambourine and dances at His coming, don't be astonished. I should be astonished at myself if I didn't do just that! Such a Guest, bearing such a Gift, into such a heart—the wonder is not that one has emotion, but the wonder is that one can be so restrained!

When Archimedes, after coming suddenly on a mathematical solution, ran out into the street crying, "Eureka, I've got it," we understand him. Then it is just as easily understandable, and more so, if we cry out in the same way, not over a mathematical solution, but over a life solution. Life is untangled—we've found the Way!

O God, my Father, I thank Thee that I have put my feet upon this way of complete victory. I do not depend on anything extraneous, but I do depend on Thee. Amen.

## FEAR OF NOT HAVING EMOTION

But there are many who are not afraid of emotion, they are afraid that they will not have any. To such I would say that the emotion will come, if you keep your eyes on the right place. If you look in, you will be discouraged; if you look around, you will be distracted; but if you look at Christ, you will have peace.

But it may be that you will have to launch out and steer by what the mariners call "dead reckoning," a steering by obedience to instruments without any sight of the stars. You may have to act on obedience without any stars in your sky. The stars are there, but you don't see them. But act on faith. Keep affirming in your heart, "I have paid the price and I accept the Gift—it is done." Talk faith to God—and to yourself. The answer comes back to you, "My grace is sufficient for you." That is not a promise, it is a fact. You can bank on it to cover your need—and more. "Thanks be unto God which *giveth* us the victory through our Lord Jesus Christ." Victory is a gift. Empty your hands and take the gift. The manifestation will come.

A father, absent from home for a long time, was expected by the eager and excited family at a certain time. But he did not come, and the children and the mother went to bed disappointed and dejected. The next morning they sat at the breakfast table in silence through sadness, when, lo, the father walked in from upstairs! He had come in late and had gone to bed without arousing them. But he was just as much there the night before as when he was manifested in the morning.

So when you pay the price and accept the gift, then He is there—there to protect and save you, even though the manifestation of His presence has not come. That will come. And when it comes to you, it will be morning!

------

O Christ, whether I sail under "dead reckoning" or under the clear stars, I sail—with Thy hand on the helm of my life and everything under Thy control. Amen.

## TALK FAITH TO PEOPLE

We said yesterday that in taking this step we should talk faith to God and to ourselves. If talking faith to ourselves seems like autosuggestion, we have no apologies to make, for we all practice autosuggestion in everything. It is a process of all thought. The question is, Just what do you suggest to yourself? If it is a suggesting to oneself the highest hypothesis that one knows, then it is legitimate autosuggestion and most necessary. You are suggesting to yourself what you honestly believe to be the highest truth you know, namely, that the character of God demands that if you do your part, God will do His part. You are suggesting to yourself that you launch out upon that. You cannot do otherwise. Therefore talk faith to yourself.

But you should probably talk faith to others. It might help you, probably will, to confess your faith. You need not tell of something that has not happened, but you can tell where you stand, and where you are going, and what your faith is on the way. This turns the whole attitude of the life toward faith and affirmation. It cuts the channels through which the new life comes to you. It establishes new habits of thought, it commits you to the highest.

The acceptance of the gift by faith drives in the nail. The confession of that faith to others clinches the nail on the other side. It gives the soul a push in the direction you want to go. That push may be decisive. It may be the opening of the door into conscious freedom and victory.

It is not unreality. It is a confession of faith, not of accomplished fact. That faith will turn into fact, and the fact into feeling. In truth the faith is a part of the fact—it is the fact begun. The redemption is now in operation in the very fact of the faith.

———

O God, my Father, I cannot confess to my worthiness, nor to my conscious finding, but I do confess to my faith in Thy utter trustworthiness. Thou wilt see me through. Amen.

## CLEAN THROUGH THE WORD

Jesus uttered these remarkable words, "Already ye are clean because of the word which I have spoken unto you" (John 15. 3). What was this "word" that gave them cleanness? Why did He use "word" instead of "words"?

The reason seems to be that His words gathered themselves into such a living body of truth and insight, into such a coherency and oneness, that they were no longer words, they were "the word." The three stages seem to be "words," "His word," "the word." But He also "shared with us His silence," and His silence also became a part of "the word."

Laotze in the seventh century said, "The way that can be expressed is not the Eternal Way. The name that can be named is not the Eternal name." But he did not see Christ—had he, he would have seen the Eternal Way and Name walking the ways of time and speaking our names. The Word became flesh! Someone has said:

> "Lo! Thy vast Self we name, but do not know,
> And in the naming break the mystic spell,
> O Lord, if the silence is Thy hymn,
> Teach us to sing it well."

In the naming of Christ we do not break the mystic spell of Eternity—we interpret it, and more, are cleansed by it. For the alabaster box of the Eternal must be broken, that the perfume may fill our hearts, and with the filling cleanse them.

But the cleansing He had been performing through the impact upon His disciples for three years was more than a personal cleansing. He was cleansing them *and their universe.* It was a cluttered-up world they faced, and Jesus left them, as far as they were concerned, with a world of things and relationships, cleansed.

---

O Christ, help us to let that Word be spoken in every portion of our being and in all our relationships, that they may be cleansed, and that we may be cleansed. Amen.

## THE CLEANSING OF THEIR WORLD

Yesterday we said that the disciples had come to Jesus with a very cluttered-up universe. Superstitions and magic and wrong notions and practices filled their world. It is true that the prophets had cleansed away many things by their cutting words, and we cannot know how much they did till we see it in contrast, say with India, where religion, lacking this prophetic cleansing note, is still cluttered up with magic and superstitions and wrong notions.

First of all, Jesus cleansed God, or, rather, our ideas about God. He cleansed away the gods and half-gods, the national and local deities, and took away an autocratic, irresponsible God and left us with God, our Father, who does not ask you and me to do anything that He Himself will not do. "Anything," except one thing—repent for sin committed.

Beyond that He shares everything with us. I wonder if in the cross He did not do that too. Is the cross His repenting for our sins?

Dr. Shailer Mathews says that the future idea of God will be in terms of pervasive life-force within the universe, instead of in terms of God as Father. I feel he is wrong. If your eyes are on nature as the place to see God interpreted, then it will be in terms of life-force. But if they are on Jesus, you will interpret that life-force in terms of the Father. You have looked into the face of the Son. And that one look makes you feel that, whatever else is to be unfolded in the interpretation, this is the interpretation. This is what Jesus meant when He said, "No man cometh unto *the Father*, but by me." The emphasis is on "the Father," you cannot see the Father unless you look on the face of the Son. There you see His likeness. And what a likeness!

He has forever cleansed our ideas of God through the Word which He has spoken unto us.

---

**O God, how can we ever cease to love such a God. Our hearts bend in deepest gratitude that such a God fills our universe—and us. Amen.**

## THE CLEANSING OF THE KINGDOM

But He not only cleansed our ideas of God, He went further. He cleansed our ideas of the Kingdom of God. The Kingdom of God was to the Jewish mind a setting up of a world State with God as ruler and the Jewish people as the viceregent of God. Jesus took this idea and cleansed it from national elements and universalized it, and made the Kingdom to be ruled by a new dynasty of viceregents—the Servant-Kings. God as the chief Servant is the greatest of all, and power will now be distributed to us according to service rendered. This will be beyond all thought of race and birth and color, and will be given to man as man.

Upon this Kingdom all the Hitlers and Mussolinis will ultimately break themselves, for we cannot ultimately tolerate the recrudescence of a nationally Messianic people ruling the world. We have seen a vision, the Kingdom of God has been forever cleansed for us, and we cannot rest this side of it. The Kingdom is the ultimate order.

But He also cleansed the material. We have alternated between the idea of matter as God and matter as bad. The materialist takes the one side, and Hinduism, on the whole, the other side. Jesus cleansed away both ideas and gave us a world of matter which God looked upon and saw it was "good." My body is not an enemy, but the handiwork of God and as such is to be kept fit and well and used in the purposes of the Kingdom of God. This is my Father's world and should be enjoyed and used and dedicated. Since I have seen the Word become "flesh" I can no longer be afraid of "flesh," the material, for it has within it the possibility of expressing the Divine. He cleansed the material. I never really saw the material until I saw Him. Then my world was new. And an amazingly worth-while world is the scene of the coming Kingdom.

————

O God, we thank Thee that we live in a world of matter. Help us not to fear it, but to use it—in Thy Kingdom. Amen.

## FURTHER CLEANSING

He goes further: He cleansed the family. The home was the one and only institution He defended. But He not only defended it—He cleansed it. He cleansed it from polygamy on the one side and polyandry on the other, and founded it on the life partnership of one man and one woman on the basis of an utter equality. This is an ultimate conception, and modern looseness and promiscuity will fail, for it will break itself upon this ultimate rock. Hindu and Moslem women are now advocating social boycott of any man who has more than one wife, and in the end the conscience of the world will approve a boycott of all promiscuity.

But Jesus went further and cleansed love. He found it as lust and left it as love. That love can be between those of the same sex, and between those of the opposite sex, married or unmarried. It is possible truly to love a married man or a married woman of the opposite sex—and that without lust. Jesus has cleansed love.

He also cleansed prayer. He found it as magic and mere petition and left it as communion. Prayer was no longer getting something out of God, but God getting something out of us. It was a pulling of ourselves to God that, through this higher contact with higher power, higher purpose might be achieved.

He cleansed religion. He made Himself the definition of religion. To be religious is to be Christlike, and that definition forever cleanses our minds from unworthy and lesser conceptions. "But don't you shield unworthy religion behind your definition when you give such a definition of religion?" asked a Hindu. No, I do not shield it; I cleanse it. We have looked into a Face, and we can no longer think of religion except in terms of this Life.

Finally, Jesus cleansed them—cleansed them to the depths of their being through the Word spoken unto them. What a cleansing—themselves and their universe!

----

O God, our Father, we thank Thee for the breadth of this cleansing and for its depth! Help us to accept both. Amen.

APRIL 29

Matthew 4. 19
Luke 22. 31, 32
Matthew 28. 18–20

## HIS DECLARATION OF FAITH

We saw last week that Jesus cleansed the disciples and their world through the word spoken unto them. It was a bold thing for Jesus to say to them, for He was declaring a faith, rather than a completed fact. It is true that they were cleansed from many things, but it was not true just then that they were "clean." Were they not quarreling over first places, proposing to call down fire from heaven, and asking other disciples to stop their work because they did not belong to their party? This is hardly being "clean," and yet Jesus was right.

As far as He was concerned, they were clean. The power which they needed for perfect cleanness was all available. It seemed to Jesus so actual that He declared it already done. This statement was the expression of His consciousness that this was all provided for in His word, and also the expression of His faith that they would connect up with that word and take the cleanness. It took about sixty days before it was actually accomplished. This cleanness was accomplished at Pentecost, so this statement is made with about sixty "days of grace" attached to it. But at the first moment they were prepared to pay the price and take it, it was theirs. In other words, Jesus gave them a check which they could cash any time they needed it. All they had to do was to endorse it and take the cash. A minister, living in the backwoods and denied many things, was sent a check which was seemingly too good to be true. He went to the city, tremblingly presented it to the bank, and was told to endorse it; which he did by writing on the back, "I endorse this with all my heart!" That is what the disciples did—at Pentecost they endorsed with all their hearts the check that gave them cleanness.

———

O Christ, we thank Thee for the consciousness of Thy adequacy and of Thy faith in us. We will not disappoint that faith, for we will take that adequacy. Amen.

## OVERCOMING THE WORLD

Among the most penetrating and hope-bringing words Jesus ever gave us were these, "In the world ye shall have tribulation: but be of good cheer; I have overcome the world" (John 16. 33).

"Ah, yes," you say, "He did overcome the world, but that was two thousand years ago—and I am living now. What has this to do with me, now?" In answer we would say that two ideas belong together—the announcement that Jesus was identified with the hunger and the sickness and the imprisonment of people—"Inasmuch as ye have done it unto one of the least of these, my brethren, ye have done it unto me," and this verse telling us that "in me ye shall have peace," for "I have overcome the world." In other words, as He is identified with us in our defeats and sicknesses and hunger, so we are also identified with Him in His victory—His overcoming the world is our overcoming the world, provided, of course, that we enter into it and relate ourselves to it and make it our very own.

This opens up to me an amazing possibility—I can make every one of His victories my very own. I can so relate my life to His in complete adjustment that when He overcomes, I overcome. I live actually by the life and victories of Another.

A missionary couple, married rather late in life, were deeply in love with each other. The husband at the breakfast table was telling guests of a dream he had the night before. The wife broke in, "Why, F—, did you dream that dream, or did I?" They were so identified that they couldn't tell which one dreamed the dream!

We smile at the naïveté of these married lovers, but in very fact one can say to Christ, "Why, Master, did you overcome the world or did I?" and hear Him gently answer, "Why we both did, for my victory is your victory."

---

O Christ, I thank Thee that I, poor unworthy I, partake of the most magnificent thing this planet ever saw—Thy overcoming. Help me to relate myself to it completely and make it mine. Amen.

## OVERCOMING THE WORLD OF THE COMMON-PLACE

Jesus overcame the world of the commonplace. To live in a village for thirty years amid dull humanity and work at a carpenter's bench, to support a widowed mother and the family, is not difficult if you see nothing beyond that. But if you feel the call of the living God upon you, and know in your heart of hearts that you have the one thing this sad world needs, and then to be compelled to stay in these cramping surroundings, and to do commonplace work for ninety per cent of your life in order to live the remaining ten per cent in fulfilling your real life purpose—if you do all this happily, then that is victory.

A French writer says: "Do you know what makes man the most suffering of all creatures? It is that he has one foot in the finite and the other in the infinite, and he is torn between two worlds." But Jesus had one foot in the hard commonplace facts of Nazareth and another in the center of the world's needs. Two terribly conflicting worlds—was He not torn between them? And therefore unhappy? No, for He made these worlds one. He brought the infinite into the finite and the finite into the infinite. The making of the plow had within it the remaking of the world, so He would make that plow well, and worthy of a world's Redeemer. Someone has said, "If you do a small thing as though it were a great thing, God will let you do the great thing as though it were a small thing." So day by day in commonplace Nazareth He wove with infinite patience the seamless robe which He would wear before the world.

Someone asked a woman of the Balkans if she did not tire of the awful task of sewing such minute stitches day after day. "Oh, no," she replied; "this is my wedding dress." These stitches were no longer commonplace—they were related to something big.

---

**O Christ, Thou didst overcome dull tasks and dull hours, for Thou didst relate them to the infinite. Help me to do the same. Amen.**

# OVERCOMING THE HANDICAP OF A MEDIOCRE FAMILY

Jesus overcame two handicaps—He had no formal education and He did not belong to a foremost family. "How knoweth this man letters, having never learned?" He suffered in the eyes of the educated and cultured because He had no learning which would correspond to our college degree. But He overcame that, and made what He had so real and worth while that the people who followed Him saw that He knew life and could give it. You and I can enter into that victory.

Then, again, there was victory over a commonplace family tradition. He came from a peasant family, from a despised place. And when you look at His family history as seen in the genealogy you see some streams of rather evil blood poured into that family tradition. Many of us have to gain victory at this point, for we come, not from "the best families," but from very common stock. But that very handicap can make us start a new tradition. We are reminded by Fosdick that Shakespeare was the son of a bankrupt butcher and a woman who could not write her name. Beethoven was the son of a consumptive mother and a father who was a drunkard. Schubert was the son of a peasant father and a mother in domestic service. Michael Faraday was born in a stable, his father an invalid blacksmith, his mother a common drudge.

When the people objected to a lady marrying Matthew Henry because of his lowly birth, she replied, "I don't care where he came from, I'm only interested in where he is going to, and I want to go with him."

We too can enter into that victory which Jesus gained and make people forget where we have come from as they watch us going on—with Him.

----

O Christ, we thank Thee that Thou didst overcome these two things, help us that we may begin in Thee a new learning and a new heredity. Amen.

## OVERCOMING THE WORLD OF THE SPEC-
## TACULAR

Jesus was fiercely tempted at the place of being spectacular. He had the power, could it not be used to impress people? Of course it would all be in the furtherance of the Kingdom, and would it not therefore be right? But He turned down very decisively this temptation. He overcame the world of the spectacular. He would win by worth and service alone. Everything else was of the devil. He was right. Had He advertised Himself, we should have forgotten Him. His reticences are more vocal than His self-display would have been. He did not go to the pinnacle of the Temple, but we put Him on the throne of the universe for this very reason. He refused a miracle before Herod and we denounce the asking and remember the refusal.

Today the man who is to live victoriously must find victory at this place, for we live in an age of advertising, sometimes leather-lunged. It is easy for the Christian to allow this psychology of advertising of goods to run over into self-advertising. One shudders to see the light of the church turned off, all except the stream of light pouring upon the pastor as he prays, the audience thereby tacitly invited to keep its eyes open to watch the display.

A beautiful tower is dedicated to the people of a state and charming music comes from "the Singing Tower." It was a lovely thing to do, but the donor spoiled it all by having his own grave at the foot of the Tower. Had he put it in some secluded place in the garden, we should have gone to it to pay our respects, but somehow I instinctively turned my back when I saw the grave with the great Tower as its monument. The "Singing Tower" had lost its music.

Christ kept His music, for He refused to blow His own horn. And millions now sing His praises!

We too can enter into this victory and make it our very own.

---

O Christ of the reticent heart, teach us Thy lowly ways, for we see they lead to the heights. Amen.

## OVERCOMING THE WORLD OF HASTE

The Man who had most to do seemed never to be in a hurry. He was launching a Kingdom which would turn out to be the ultimate order for all men, and yet in the launching of it He seemed to be in no feverish, fussy haste. Not that He was idle, far from it. He never wasted a moment, and yet He was never fussily busy.

The Hindus worship the great god Hari (pronounced Hurry). The West also worships at the shrine of the great god Hurry! This is the god that dispenses fevers and strained hearts and unlovely lives, too busy to live. Jesus said to Martha, "Thou art careful and anxious about many things." Martha probably said beneath her breath, "Yes, but if I am not careful and anxious, you'll go hungry." But Martha with all her rush and haste fell down in her supposedly strong point. Note this passage: "And on the morrow, when they were come out from Bethany, he hungered." Why did she let Him go from Bethany without anything to eat? She fell down where she thought she was strongest. This fussy haste of the modern day has also fallen down in its strongest point. We speeded up our machines and our civilization and then left millions upon park benches unemployed, idle, and hungry. We failed where we thought ourselves strong.

We must regain victory at the place of the unhurried heart. We have put up this motto in our Ashram, taken from a Greek writer, with our addition: "Whirl is king, having driven out Zeus—but not here!" With the decay of religion (Zeus) they turned to "Whirl!" as king. But in our Ashram we say that, "Calm is king, having brought in Christ." So both in our Ashram and in our hearts we must enthrone the unhasting Christ, that the benediction of His quiet might spread to every portion of our being.

---

O Christ, we thank Thee for Thy victory over unresting haste. Give to us too that victory of the quiet, assured heart that knows that in the end God's victory is certain. Amen.

## OVERCOMING IMPATIENCE WITH BUNGLING INSTRUMENTS

The Kingdom which Jesus launched required delicate handling. Its virtues might very easily turn into vices by the slightest twist. Its light might turn into darkness. In such circumstances He would have tremendous temptation to be out of patience with the bungling instruments of His Kingdom. It is a wonder He didn't dismiss His disciples at a number of places along the way. When they twisted His highest into something else, why didn't He let them go and try it with another group? He didn't, for He would make this group! That would be victory!

Often we face the same temptation—dismiss this group of employees and try another; get rid of the trouble—some wife or husband—and start all over again; dismiss these Christian workers and try to bring in the Kingdom through a fresh group; get rid of our pastor and try for a better one; change congregations—the next may be more convertible, and so on. All of this is in its essence a running away from the problem— an escape mentality. It is not victory—it is an attempt at escape.

After all, the next group we have to deal with will probably have the same streaky human nature. The new brooms will sweep clean for a few days—and then the dust! That second wife will not be an angel! The fact that she was willing to take a man who got rid of one to take her is prima facie evidence that she is pretty poor stuff at best. And leaps from the frying pan into the fire are often very short and easy.

Jesus overcame this impatience with bungling instruments and made those instruments into changed men, who changed the world. That was victory.

We must learn how to refashion people—the ordinary, streaky people around us, remembering that as we put up with them Christ has to put up with us. Even if we do our best we may not succeed. But we are all convertible!

O Christ, we thank Thee for Thy patience and for Thy persistence with us. Help us to deal with others in the same patient, redemptive way. Amen.

**MAY 6**

Colossians 3. 12–15
Luke 23. 34
Acts 7. 59, 60

## OVERCOMING THE WORLD OF RESENTMENT

A man who is a man of faith is usually a man of sensitive, eager disposition. He sees beyond the *status quo* and wants something different and sets about getting it. Almost immediately he will run across oppositions, for people do not easily give up the "is" for the "ought-to-be." He will be tempted to be resentful against people who do not see what he sees. The man of faith must have victory over the world of resentment.

It is interesting that Jesus linked faith in God and forgiveness to others. In Mark 11. 22-25, "Jesus answering, said unto them, Have faith in God. Verily I say unto you, whosoever shall say unto this mountain, Be thou taken up and cast into the sea; and shall not doubt in his heart, but shall believe that what he saith cometh to pass; he shall have it. Therefore I say unto you, all things whatsoever ye pray and ask for, believe that ye have received them, and ye shall have them. And whensoever ye stand praying, forgive, if ye have ought against anyone." He put faith in God and forgiveness to people together, for they belong together. Faith without forgiveness makes religion hard, fanatical. Forgiveness without faith makes religion soft, nonprogressive. But faith and forgiveness makes religion Christian. This forgiveness element puts love in faith, so that now "faith worketh by love."

The man of faith forgives those who lash back at him because they do not see what he sees. He follows a Man who saw His attempts at a new world end up in a cross, deserted by the multitudes whom He would save and by the disciples who professed allegiance to Him, and seemingly by the Father who sent Him, and yet at the last with a prayer of forgiveness upon His lips. This was victory.

We too can enter into that victory and make it our very own. So that resentment has no place within us.

---

O Christ of the unresentful heart, make us like that. Make us full of faith toward God and full of tenderness toward others who do not agree with us. Amen.

## OVERCOMING THE WORLD OF THE IRRELEVANT

If one is to live a victorious life, he must live in the relevant. Many do not—they live in a lot of irrelevancies which
occupy and absorb their time.

A friend of mine was in a terrible train wreck. Many
were killed outright and many wounded were groaning
under the wreckage. The few unhurt were trying desperately to rescue the wounded and attend to them. In the midst
of all this, a woman sat beside her suit case which had been
torn open and kept repeating, "Oh, my sixteen dollar pair
of shoes!" This she repeated over and over again, and
mingled it with the cries of the wounded. A pair of shoes
was the center of her attention with a wreck around her!
This portrays vividly what we often do: we become absorbed
with personal irrelevancies and miss the big issues of life.

We should go over everything that has a place in our lives
and ask this question: "Are you relevant to the really big
issues? Do you keep me from the really worth-while things?
You may not be bad, but are you relevant?" If anything in
our lives cannot answer that call for relevancy, then out it
should go.

Someone asked, "What is the first necessity for a college
president?" and received the reply, "A wastebasket." The
Christian must have a wastebasket, not only for the bad but
for the irrelevant.

Jesus has a sifted mind. He never once was led into a
subordinate issue, never once missed the real point, never
got into a bypath, was always on the relevant. He overcame
sin and also the unimportant.

We must cut out not only what isn't good, but also what
isn't good enough. He did that, and we can share His overcoming and enter a world of relevancies.

---

O Christ, we thank Thee that Thou dost want to save us
both from iniquity and from irrelevancy. We expose our
minds to the searching of Thy mind and we consent to let
go the trivial and irrelevant. Prune us. Amen.

## OVERCOMING THE WORLD OF ANXIETIES

"In nothing be anxious; but in everything by prayer and supplication . . . let your requests be made known unto God." In nothing be anxious! Was there ever a message so deeply needed as now? Anxieties fill the air—and they fill us. Jesus conquered the world of anxieties.

There are three things that become the center of our anxieties: food, shelter, and future security. Then Jesus must have been the man most filled with anxiety, for not one of these was assured to Him. He had no food except what was given to Him day by day. He had no assured home. Ofttimes He slept under the open heavens, huddled beneath a tree. As for future security—He knew there was none, for His road would end in a cross. The three things we are most anxious about were utterly missing in His life. He shared our disabilities—minus our anxieties. How did He do it?

His prescription was simple: Obey God, trust God. Those four words were the four cornerstones of His life. And when the storm broke, the foundation stood. Note He puts them together. You cannot really trust God unless you obey Him. For if you do not obey God at the place of your conduct, you cannot trust Him at the place of your clothing. A lady told me of the loss of her faith: "The Bible says, 'Ye shall ask what ye will,' and I prayed for my father's recovery, but he died. So my faith is gone." But she did not quote the whole: "If ye abide in me, and my words abide in you, ye shall ask what ye will, and it shall be done unto you." Obey God, trust God!

MacDonald wrote to Keith Falconer, a young missionary: "This is a practical working faith: first, it is man's business to do the will of God; second, God takes on Himself the special care of that man; third, that man should be afraid of nothing."

---

O Christ, there was no corroding care in Thy heart. Give me a heart like that. I pay the price of freedom from anxiety—the price of obedience. Amen.

## OVERCOMING THE SPIRIT OF WITHDRAWAL

There is a real tendency in religion to try to win victory by withdrawal. We encase ourselves with the hard shell of refusal to face any issue, withdraw within ourselves, and thus hope for victory. We try to maintain peace by dodging the battle. A missionary tried to maintain a high spirituality by never coming to grips with any issue, never taking sides, never crossing anyone—he made for himself a desert and called it victory.

Of another Westerner in India someone said, "His face is peaceful, he has gained unity." "By withdrawal," I remarked. He had no cares, for he didn't care. He had no burdens, for he took none. It seemed to me to be not the unification but the nullification of life.

Jesus overcame this tendency to try to find victory by withdrawal. He found His victory not by getting out but by getting in. One of the most important verses in the history of religion is this, "He steadfastly set his face to go to Jerusalem." That meant that He would face issues, would precipitate crises and see the whole thing through to the bitter-glorious end. But in setting His face in that direction He set the face of religion in that direction too. We can never be true to Him now unless we are true to Him at this point. All withdrawal from real issues is withdrawal from Jesus.

One of the saddest verses in literature is this, "And Pilate, wishing to content the multitude, . . . delivered Jesus." And for us one of the saddest days in life is the day we allow the herd-fear to conquer the highest judgments and instincts of the soul. Sometimes we content the multitude, when we should contend with the multitude. "Pilate took water"—a baptism into irresponsibility. Pilate took water to get out from the responsibility of Jesus' death; Jesus was taking a baptism of responsibility for every man. One was crawling out, the Other was marching in!

———

O Christ, I too need this power to come to grips with issues as they arise. Give me Thy decisiveness. Amen.

## OVERCOMING THE UNWILLINGNESS TO BE IN A MINORITY

It is a truism to say that truth in the beginning is usually found in a minority. A stricken lad in a faint lay on the ground before Jesus. The account says, "The more part said, He is dead." Had a majority vote been taken there, they would have decided that the boy was dead and should be buried. But the truth was in the minority of One. Jesus called the boy back from collapse to restored health.

"The more part" often decides that a cause is dead. Twenty years ago in a conference in India a proposal for reconstruction was presented that would give India local self-government in church matters. It went "on the table" with a bang. "The more part" decided it was dead. Twenty years later I saw that idea taken from "the table" and adopted by the Church, not only in India, but throughout the world. "The more part" was wrong.

"The more part" decided that Prohibition was dead. That majority was wrong. It will arise, purified, and will be adopted again. "The more part" now decides again and again in its elections that any new order, which will replace the present world-order with its injustices and wrongs, is dead. But again "the more part" is wrong. For the idea of a just social order, in which every man shall have an equal opportunity, is God's idea, and will not down.

We cannot get spiritual victory unless we are willing to be in "the less part," if necessary. If you look at the Gethsemane scene, you will see the relative size of the crowds: Jesus alone, then the three, then the eight, and then the Jerusalem multitude. If you desire the multitude you will probably find yourself in a crowd furthest from Jesus.

The victorious life means that you are released from an itching to be on the popular side—you become willing to stand alone if necessary. But alone—you may be with Him!

---

O Christ, I would rather be alone with Thee than be in a multitude without Thee. I want to be with Thee, wherever Thou art, with many or with few. Amen.

## OVERCOMING THE WORLD OF SIN

One of the things most necessary in living victoriously is to realize that when we are fighting evil we are fighting a conquered foe. Jesus met every sin and conquered it. Many do not realize this, so develop an inferiority complex before evil. They allow evil to bully them, to make them feel that it is a permanent part of things and cannot be eradicated. Hence they are defeated in mind even before the battle begins. We must get hold of the idea that sin has been conquered—every sin has been conquered, both within the individual and the social order. We have now to accept the gift of complete victory and then proceed to make it actual in us and in the order around us.

So when sin begins to bully me, I quietly ask it to bend its neck and let me see. When it does, I quietly but joyfully point to the footprints of the Son of God on the neck of sin. My inferiority complex is gone. I am on the winning side. I shall meet not one single sin today that has not been defeated. I walk the earth amid conquered foes. A story runs that in the ancient days in Central India a leading warrior during a battle had his head cut off, but so bent was he upon fighting that he fought on even with his head gone. This headless warrior killed many. But he collapsed when a woman saw him and cried out, "But your head is off—you're dead!" So he fell down and died!

When evil seems strong and invincible and is about to overcome, I point and say, "But look, your head is gone! Did not my Master conquer you by meeting you in life? And did He not sever the head of evil by the sword of the cross? Begone! You're headless!"

Evil fights on. But it is brainless. It depends on prejudices, old habits, and unreasoning emotions. Reason is on the side of good. We fight a fierce but brainless foe.

---

O Christ, I thank Thee that Thou didst not succumb to a single temptation. Show me how to accept and enter into this completed victory. Amen.

## THE SECRET OF THE OVERCOMING

In these last few days we have been thinking together on the amazing statement, "Be of good cheer; I have overcome the world." You say, "Well and good, wonderful, but how do I get hold of His victory and make it mine?"

The whole verse reads this way, "These things have I spoken unto you, that in me ye may have peace. In the world ye have tribulation: but be of good cheer; I have overcome the world." "In the world"—tribulation. "In me"—peace. What does this "in me" mean?

It surely means being identified with Him, merged into Him, so at one with Him that His victories become ours and hence His peace becomes ours. Surrender of yourself means identification with His self. Life flows into life, Mind into mind, and we share a common life.

In the Old Testament it says, "Where is he that . . . caused his glorious arm to go at the right hand of Moses?" God's power and Moses' efforts coincided. When he raised his right hand, God's right hand was going alongside of it. God's arm didn't do everything, for that would have kept Moses from developing. Moses' arm had to go too, but when he tried, God triumphed.

Say this to yourself today: "Why, I am in Christ, and so His power is identified with every single thing in my life. Today His glorious arm will go at my right hand. As I take hold of my tasks there will be an unwonted strength within me. As I face perplexities there will be unexpected solutions. As I face relationships with others there will be a love beyond my own, making those relations sweet and beautiful, nothing will meet me today that He will not be in, and together we will go through with it. He will cause His glorious arm to go at my right hand. That is enough."

"Round my incompleteness flows His completeness,
Round my restlessness, His rest."

---

O Christ, I thank Thee that I am "in" Thee. Help me to accept the full meaning of that "inness" and live by it— today and forever. Amen.

**MAY 13**

2 Corinthians 5. 16, 17
Romans 6. 13
1 Corinthians 15. 9, 10

## SUBLIMATION OF THE INSTINCTS

Last week we ended with the idea of being "in Christ," and we saw that meant identification with His purposes so that His victories become our victories. We must now see some of the results of being "in Christ." Paul says, "If any man is in Christ, he is a new creature: the old things are passed away; behold, they are become new." This translation says, "old things are passed away," and yet they have not passed away; they (the old things) "are become new."

There was a sense in which old things had completely passed away, and yet there was a sense in which they had come back again completely transformed and new. This "new creature" is entirely different from the old creature, and yet he is fundamentally the same, only new. The modern peach was once used in ancient Persia from which to get poison to tip arrows. The modern peach once poisonous! The modern peach is a new creature, old things have passed away, behold, they have become new. It is new—the poison has been eliminated, but the fundamental life of the tree remains, only now, instead of being used to bring forth poison, it brings forth luscious, health-giving fruit. That is sublimation.

Paul saw that the poison of the old instincts had been eliminated, but the instincts themselves had now come back again, sublimated. Whereas they had been used in purposes that ended in death, they were being used in purposes that ended in life. He found he was the same Paul with his fundamental Jewish human nature intact, and yet he was so fundamentally changed that he had to change his name to express a new fact. There was discontinuity with the past and yet a continuity. Conversion had meant a cutting and a conservation. The driving forces of his spirit were under a new control, directed toward a new end—sublimation had taken place.

----

O Christ, I thank Thee that Thou dost take this raw material of human life and dost cleanse and refashion it, and dost make it serve other ends—Thy ends. I put it all at Thy disposal. Make out of me what Thou canst. Amen.

## SUBLIMATION OF THE INSTINCTS—Continued

The instincts are the driving life-forces. The stream of life energy flowing through us breaks into three instinctive channels: self, sex, and the herd. Minor instincts can be tabulated, but they usually turn out to be phases of the above dominant instincts. Concerning these instincts there are these possibilities: biological expression, perversion, repression, suppression or self-control, and sublimation.

The Christian way of life would eliminate perversion and repression and would use biological expression, suppression or self-control, and sublimation. The distinction between repression and suppression seems to be that in repression the instinct is pushed down into the subconscious and the lid closed. There it works havoc. As Hadfield says, "Repressed instincts are like bad boys who, when put out of the class, begin to throw stones at the windows." But in suppression the instincts are kept within the conscious mind and are suppressed at certain places in order to be sublimated at others. In other words, the bad boys are kept in the class, under observation and direction, and taught to direct their energies to constructive ends. But suppression without sublimation may end in repression and is therefore dangerous to handle.

Christianity believes in biological expression. It believes in the individual, in the family, and in society. It is not at war with human nature. Some religions are: "I never mention my family—I am a religious Sadhu," said a Hindu to me one day. Buddha was at war with the self-instinct when he would finally wipe out the human personality. The Christian way uses the biological expression, but always under the control of its ideals. That means expression at certain places and suppression at others. But the suppressed can always be sublimated—the turning of the instinctive forces to higher expressions. That opens the door—upward.

---

O Christ, we thank Thee, that Thou hast made it possible that we should be wholly dedicated to Thy purposes and that human nature is not to be eliminated, but redeemed. Redeem me. Amen.

## SOME OLD THINGS NEW

Paul says that "old things are passed away; behold, all things are become new." We are now discovering how old these "old things" are. The instincts are very old. They stretch back to untold ages, race tendencies have gone into them. They have become grooved and set in certain directions. And yet they can be abruptly changed and redeemed.

Take a phase of self-instinct, the pugnacious instinct in Paul. Before his conversion he was very pugnacious; he breathed out slaughter against the Christians. Then the change. After his conversion he was still pugnacious. But now this pugnacious energy was directed against the kingdom of evil. Sometimes it was on the verge of becoming directed against his associates. But on the whole and in the main, this pugnacious instinct was bridled and harnessed to the chariot of God's purposes, and Paul drove it toward Kingdom-ends. The pugnacious instinct was sublimated and made constructive.

I saw a Sadhu who had a tame lion with him, and when I asked him why he kept him, he said: "To teach the people how human nature can be changed. If this lion can become so meek, men can also tame their passions." But I felt the lion had been de-lionized and had become a lazy dog, led about by a chain. As a psychologist said that he had cured a man of thinking he was a dog, but unfortunately he now thought himself a water-rat; so I felt the magnificent energy of the lion should be tamed and harnessed to constructive tasks if it was to be a real symbol of conversion. Have you a pugnacious spirit? Don't try to get rid of it. Let Christ cleanse from it the selfish pugnacity that stands up for its own ends and ways, and then let them harness it to the task of fighting disease, wrong conditions, inequalities, hate, and evil of every kind. Then you can say, "My old pugnacity has passed away; behold, it has become new."

---

O Christ, take this pugnacity of mine. I lay it upon Thy altar. I ask Thee to use it. But it needs harnessing. Harness it, sublimate it, and use it. Amen.

1 Corinthians 11. 1    John 15. 16
John 18. 20—23    Philippians 4. 9

## SUBLIMATING THE SELF INSTINCT

The ego instinct is probably the most imperious of all. It is at the basis of most of our actions. We must face that fact. To talk about a person being "a selfless man" makes me inwardly squirm. Christ was not selfless, nor was Paul, nor should any Christian be. I once asked a Sadhu where he was going. "Rama, Rama," he replied, naming his god. No matter what I asked him he answered the same words. He was selfless—Rama had taken the place of the self. But had he? Not at all. The self was still there asserting itself into prominence by saying it wasn't there!

It simply makes for hypocrisy to say the self isn't there. It is bound to be there and should be there. But the question is, What kind of a self is it?

The self was sublimated in Jesus, the meekest of men and the most self-assertive. He renounced power, refusing to be made a king, and yet the self was satisfied by gaining the most amazing power ever exercised. Paul became the servant of the churches—their troubles his troubles, their weaknesses his weaknesses. As you look at him you say, "The man has lost his own ego." Not at all. That ego instinct was sublimated, and therefore satisfied by having an authority over people by the very fact of his renunciation. He did not renounce for that purpose; had he done so, it would have spoiled it all, but the power over others was a by-product of the losing of himself. The self was not lost—it was loosed. Mahatma Gandhi lost the smaller, lawyer self and found a larger servant-of-India self, and with it an astonishing authority. He is not selfless, he is imperious.

Your old ego must die, be crucified. Then it will come back and you can say, "The old ego has passed away; behold, it has become new."

---

O Christ, take this ego of mine and cleanse it from all egoism, and harness it to Thy purposes, so that I may be able to live with it. And perhaps rejoice in it. Amen.

145

Matthew 23. 37-39
Matthew 2. 11, 12
Galatians 4. 18, 19

## SUBLIMATING SEX

"Life is heavily loaded at the place of sex," too heavily loaded, some would say, for the purposes of the propagation of the species. But whether it is overemphasized or rightly emphasized in our make up, it is an integral part of us, and as such must be dealt with frankly, sanely.

To confess sex-desire to oneself is no more shameful than to confess desire for food. Both are integral parts of us. Where it is functioning biologically for the purposes of procreation, the problem is normally solved. Even there it must be under the restraint of the rest of the ideals of the life. For if one part of the nature demands satisfaction at the expense and sacrifices of the rest of oneself, then the result is not satisfaction but inner division and hence unhappiness. But the problem becomes more acute at the place where the sex instinct is denied biological expression. In that case it may be repressed, which is dangerous, setting up a complex, or it may be sublimated.

The sex instinct was sublimated in Jesus. He was creative at the place of the mind and spirit. He was bringing into being a new race, a higher type of humanity. He was mothering and fathering the family of God. "O Jerusalem, . . . how often would I have gathered thy children together, even as a hen gathereth her chickens under her wings!" That is sublimation. Paul, denied a family life, was not unhappy, because he was sublimating his sex-life, by being procreative in the higher reaches of life, the mind and spirit. Wherever he went he saw the new birth take place. He was a spiritual Father. For twenty-eight years I have been able to say that I have never known of a single moral lapse among the thousands of single lady missionaries in India. Why? Largely because they have been sublimating the sex instinct by mothering the unfortunate and the orphans.

If any man be in Christ, he is a new creature, the old sex instinct has passed away; behold, it has become new.

O Christ, I thank Thee for release from inner bondages. Loose my soul in creative activity. Amen.

# SUBLIMATING THE INSTINCTS OF CURIOSITY AND PRIDE

The instinct of curiosity is early shown in the child as it asks concerning everything, "What's that?" In grown-up people it may manifest itself in ugly ways of prying into other people's affairs and meddling with their private business. On the other hand, the instinct of curiosity may be a decided help in furthering the spiritual life. The Christian should sublimate it from lower ways to higher.

He belongs to a Kingdom to which there are no frontiers. He, therefore, is under the sway of an Ideal which is always ahead of him, always receding, a flying goal. He accordingly has the possibility of an infinite curiosity. His mind and spirit should grow as they stretch forth to know. The instinct of curiosity is sublimated from useless, pointless prying to the purposes of infinite growth.

The instinct of pride can also be converted, can be sublimated. We near people say, "My pride has been killed." I hope not. If so, *we* are killed. Of course there is the sense in which the silly pride, which thinks in terms of bedecking itself to attract attention, needs to die. But pride can be harnessed to the Kingdom. Paul could say, "For what is our hope or joy, or the crown of which we boast? Is it not you yourselves? . . . Yes, you are our glory and our joy" (1 Thessalonians 2. 19, Weymouth). Here was the old Pharisaical pride turned redemptive. He was not glorying in his ancestry and his learning, but glorying in this new creation taking place before him—proud of this new humanity. The instinct of pride was loosed from pettiness and was glorying in the worth-while work of his own hands.

A sublimated pride would save us from slovenly sermons, from skimped work, from spiritual half-heartedness, from not being at our best for Him.

So we should be able to say, "The old curiosity and pride have passed away; behold, they have become new."

---

O Christ, kill within me foolish pride and then raise up within me a nobler pride that will tolerate nothing less than the highest. Amen.

## SUBLIMATING THE ACQUISITIVE AND THE HERD INSTINCTS

The acquisitive instinct is the driving force in many lives. It is at the basis of many of our world difficulties, individual and collective. It drives men to bow at the shrine of "grubby thing-worship." It needs converting. Can it be done?

Jesus pointed the way when He said, "Lay not up for yourselves treasures upon earth, . . . but lay up for yourselves treasures in heaven." You are still to "lay up," the acquisitive instinct is still operative, but now toward higher values. In other words, we invest in people instead of in things. We are now as eager for this new treasure of changed people and changed society as we were for the treasure through exchange. The old instinct of acquisitiveness has passed away; behold, it has become new.

The herd or the social instinct can be used for narrow, partisan, nationalistic ends. It can eventuate in a bombastic nationalism, asserting itself against its neighbors and pushing the world into war. Or it can be converted, sublimated. In Christianity it is. The herd instinct is fastened upon the ultimate conception in human relationships, namely, the Kingdom of God on earth. Then one can say, "Who is my mother, my brother, and my sister? They that do the will of God the same are my mothers, my brethren and my sisters." The herd instinct is not done away with, it is enlarged, enlightened, enlivened. It has now its real home. The lesser loyalties of home, country, and church take their meaning from the highest loyalty—the loyalty to the Beloved Community, the Kingdom of God.

Every power of our lives is to be purged and presented as instruments of the new life. "No longer lend your faculties as unrighteous weapons of wickedness for Sin to use. On the contrary, surrender your very selves to God as living men who have risen from the dead" (Romans 6. 15, Weymouth). Paul taught sublimation before modern psychology named it.

--------

**O** Christ, I thank Thee that my faculties are all at Thy service. Take hold of me, not at the surface but at the depths. Amen.

148

John 3. 3
Matthew 18. 3
Matthew 15. 19, 20

## VICTORIOUS LIVING AND THE SOCIAL ENVIRONMENT

So far in our quest for the victorious life we have centered upon the causes of evil within ourselves. It is well to begin there, for many are like a man with fever, tossing on his bed to find a cool spot, when all the time the fever is within him. You cannot cure him by giving him a cool spot on new sheets as long as the germs of the fever are within. This modern age, intent upon social change as the cure-all for human ills, must not lose sight of this fact. We have a way of brushing past our own inner problems and fastening our attention upon outer difficulties.

As William Adams Brown says, "It is not so much that this modern age has lost its sense of sin as that we have developed a technique by which we are able to fasten it upon those we dislike and whom we disapprove—big business men, for example, wicked imperialists, or corrupt labor leaders." This transference of guilt to others is essentially dishonest. Whitehead says, "Religion is a force of belief cleansing the inner parts, therefore the primary religious virtue is sincerity, a penetrating sincerity."

That sincerity must begin with ourselves. Beginning any other place is insincerity. It is an escape mentality. No man is in any fit state of mind to face the problems of the world unless he is prepared to face honestly his own life and right it. George Arliss in his reminiscences, in telling of a fellow actor, John Mason, whose work Arliss greatly admired, makes this comment: "John Mason would, in my opinion, have been the greatest actor in America if his private character had been as well balanced as his public performance."

Public performance in social reconstruction is out of balance if the private character is left unattended to.

We have rightly begun with ourselves. But we dare not stop there.

_____

**O Christ, we thank Thee that Thou hast put Thy hand upon our own hearts first of all, now help us to follow Thee as far as Thou goest. Amen.**

## ADAPTIVE ORGANISM AND SUITABLE ENVIRONMENT

Yesterday we said that the first emphasis in our quest for victorious living should be on ourselves. But while it may be the first, it must not be the last. We said that to go to environment, passing over the personal, is an escape mentality, but to stay at the personal and to refuse to go to the environmental is also an escape mentality.

Many of the hindrances to victorious living are within us. But there are many hindrances to victorious living which are not within us. They are within the social order. It will not do to counter this by saying that the social order is made up of individuals. It is and it isn't. The social order is not entirely the product of the individuals now living. It is made up of accumulated attitudes and customs passed on from generation to generation and may be only modified slightly by existing individuals as individuals. It can therefore be very impersonal. The question is, Does this social order help or hinder the new life?

For life depends on two factors: an adaptive organism and a suitable environment. The organism may be very adaptive, but if there is no suitable environment, it will die. On the other hand, if the environment is suitable and the organism not healthy and adaptive, it will also die. If life depends upon response to environment, the question arises, Does the present social order provide an environment to which the Christian can respond? Does it feed him, or poison him? If it feeds him, it must be preserved at all costs. But if it poisons him, then he must either convert it from poison to food, as in the case of the Persian peach, or if it cannot be converted, then it must be replaced by something that will feed him. For live he must, and live victoriously.

---

O Christ, as we pass over into the question of the order about us take from our hearts the blinding prejudices that keep us from seeing things as they are. Make us open-eyed and open-hearted. Amen.

## IS A PRIVATE ENVIRONMENT SUFFICIENT?

We saw yesterday that life depends on a suitable environment. No matter how healthy the palm may be in itself, if transferred to a northern climate, it will die. "But," the objection is made, "the analogy doesn't hold, for the Christian has his own private favorable environment—the Kingdom of God. As the diver down in the sea has the air-pipe leading to the surface, so the Christian has his personal contact with a higher world, the Kingdom of God." But the diver cannot stay down very long and is restricted at every point by the hostility of his environment. That we can exist in this world-order as Christians, I do not deny. But we are restricted at every point. And it is not our native air, so that unless we periodically rise to the atmosphere of a co-operative society, a Christian Church, and take off our helmets and breathe freely, we shall probably suffocate. And what about those who are compelled to live in this world-order without any contacts with the Kingdom? How shall they live who have to breathe one atmosphere and one alone—the poisoned atmosphere of the modern social order?

We must have an environment that will minister to the spiritual life, one in which we can live freely and fully. Now we have to live a Christian life in spite of our environment. Is it not possible to have one in which we shall live Christianly, not in spite of it but on account of it?

Besides, did Jesus intend that we should have a private favorable environment and not a collective one? Did He not ask us to pray that the Kingdom might come on earth as it is in heaven? Do they in heaven have only a private and personal Kingdom-of-God environment, or is it built into the collective order? To ask it is to answer it. If there, then here.

---

O Christ, we pray again, "Our Father, may Thy Kingdom come and may Thy will be done on earth as it is in heaven." Help us to put that into our plans as well as into our prayers. Amen.

## ALL CAUSES OF SIN

In Matthew 13. 41 there is this remarkable statement: "The Son of Man . . . will gather out of His Kingdom all causes of sin and all who violate His laws" (Weymouth). Note the two emphases: "All causes of sin and all who violate His laws"— the latter refers to personal, individual transgression, the former to the impersonal causes of sin. One kind of sin was in the individual will and the other in the social order. We have been dealing throughout our quest with sin in the individual will; we must now look at the causes of sin in the social order.

For the social order may cause sin and it may cause good. It may positively cause people to do evil, for they cannot survive under that order without doing evil.

It is not easy for us to see the causes of evil in the society to which we belong, especially if we are in a favored position in that order. Man thinks emotionally; his reason tries to make rational his emotional attachments. This fact of emotional thinking will put us on our guard about the validity of our social attitudes.

A man recently died who was called, "The Excise Monarch of Sind," for he controlled nearly all the liquor shops of the province of Sind. Government gave him the title of "Rai Bahadur," because of his "cleverness in the detection of crime." But he never detected his own liquor shops as the cause of most of the crime! He probably prided himself on his righteousness as shown in his zeal against crime, for his reason always skirted around one of the most prolific causes of crime— his own system. He was probably not a conscious hypocrite— he didn't see it, for he thought emotionally. We all do. We shall therefore need open-eyed wisdom as we look at the causes of sin in our Society.

---

O Christ, Thou didst pierce beneath the seeming to the real and bared the hearts of men and didst put Thy finger on festering sores in the Temple system, give us Thy clear-eyed vision and courage. Amen.

## SOME CAUSES OF SIN

In searching for causes of sin in modern society we are compelled to brush aside the lesser causes and go straight to the central one—selfish competition. The competitively acquisitive spirit in modern society is probably the most prolific cause of sin. It sets the stage for evil. It becomes easier under a competitive order to be hard and ruthless than to be loving and generous. It loads the dice against goodness.

When I say that, there probably arises in your mind an objection which is a real one: If competition is taken out of life, will there not be the loss of individual initiative, and will life not then sag and become nonprogressive? This is a real fear to many. But note that I said "selfish competition." There is a higher competition which is not selfish. In a co-operative order there would still be competition, we should still compete as to who could give most to the collective good. But this friendly competition would be constructive and not destructive. As the individual self-instinct must be redeemed and turned toward constructive ends, so the collective ego-instinct must be redeemed and made to serve the public good. In either case you cannot eradicate the ego, you must harness it to the making of a better order. It must be sublimated. But competition there will be—now Christianized and harnessed to the purpose of the Kingdom.

However, this selfish competition which holds the center of our total life is a very different thing. It has been softened and civilized, but underneath that softness and civilization is a ruthlessness, just as hidden under the soft pads of a tiger are flesh-tearing claws. If you don't believe it, ask the ten million victims that walk our streets unemployed, to show you their wounds of soul and body. They know. We all know. For civilization is bleeding from a thousand wounds—bled white by a competitive struggle. The selfish competitive order is the chief cause of sin.

---

O Christ, we ask Thee to help us to face this matter calmly and courageously and right it. In Thy name. Amen.

## SELFISH COMPETITION—THE CHIEF CAUSE

Yesterday we said that selfish competition was the chief cause of sin. We must pursue it.

Here are boys brought up in a refined and loving home. The basis of life in that home is co-operation—it is in any good home. That is what makes it a home. But suppose when meal time came the stronger boy would snatch as much as he could from the younger and weaker and pile it around his plate, whether he could eat it or not, would not the family be outraged? And would not such unsocial conduct be severely dealt with? Good families are simply not built that way. Each meal is not a scramble to get all we can get. Each gets his proper share of whatever there is, and the older and stronger ones look after the younger and weaker. The whole family attitude and mind-set makes it easier for the children to be co-operative and helpful. A family life is built on co-operation. So is our best education.

But the moment one of those boys steps out of that home or out of that school to go into the business world most of his values are reversed. In order to be a good family member he had to develop in sympathy and mutual helpfulness and service. Now, in order to be successful in a competitive order, that must be trained out of him. He must drive hard bargains, without too much looking into detail as to the results in the ruination of others in that bargain. Blinkers have to be put on the eyes so that he looks straight ahead at what he wants. He would be shocked to find that around this table of business he is grabbing all he can from the weaker members and piling it up around his own plate regardless of whether he can eat it or not. And yet that is exactly what he is doing. The family spirit is dying in him. The competitive order is a cause of sin to him.

---

O Christ, Thou who didst come to make us one family, forgive us that we have not put that family spirit into our total life. Help us yet to do it. Amen.

154

## LOVING YOUR NEIGHBOR IN A COMPETITIVE ORDER

When that young man who is slowly becoming hardened and is losing his ideals, takes his hat and goes back from business to the family circle, he looks at his father in a puzzled way and says: "Dad, this is different. I am unlearning everything you taught me in the home. Why this difference?" His father, remembering with a sigh the reversal of his own ideals, helplessly replies, "Son, business is business." They are both caught in a system which is a cause of sin to them. Wells is right—"Human society is the limited and legalized struggle of men and women to get the better of one another."

I received this question: "Isn't the very center of Jesus' teaching that we are to love our neighbor as we love ourselves, and if we did that, wouldn't we have a new world?" I happened to turn the paper over and saw the printed announcement on the other side that a new printing press had been opened in that city, and asking for people to come and "give it their blessing." Now, there were already sixty-eight printing presses in that small city, and the oldest and best was going out of business because of the ruthlessness of the competition. One more participant enters the struggle. On the back of his announcement is the statement that the only way out of the world's difficulties is to love your neighbor as you love yourself. Can he apply that in the struggle he is entering? It isn't impossible, but it is highly improbable. The dice are loaded against him. One side of the paper says, "Love your neighbor as you love yourself." And the other side says, "Get all the business you can, no matter if your neighbor goes to the wall." Which side of the paper will be his history? He will probably try to compromise. The competitive order will become a cause of sin to him.

---

O Christ, help us to make a world in which the light that is in us will not be snuffed out. Thou art calling us to make that order. Help us to come. Amen.

---

### FAMINE NEEDED!

---

Last week we were dealing with selfish competition as a cause of sin. We must look at it again until this fact burns itself into our souls.

India is the poorest-richest country of the world. Here we have the world's richest man and the world's poorest side by side. A man will say to you, "Sahib, that wage means only half a stomach for me and my family." Wages not in terms of the possibility of the latest car, but of half a stomachful. In the midst of this kind of an India I sat and talked with an able missionary, devoted and hardworking. He said: "What we need is another famine to get rid of surplus stocks. That will raise the prices and will bring back prosperity." I felt as though I had been struck, for the statement was serious and thoughtful. Now, here was a man of most gentle, loving disposition talking about the necessity—mark the word—of another famine. Look at that word "famine" until it is no longer a word but a fact—the fact of living skeletons, of babies, thin and scrawny, sucking in vain at the dry breasts of famished mothers—but you can't look any longer, for you're sick at the thought. And yet a missionary, a Christian, a father of little children, said we needed that—that! It horrifies you? Yes. But the thing that horrifies me most is, not that he said it, but that what he said was true—*under this order*. In a competitive order you have to produce scarcity, in other words, a famine, to keep up prices, to bring back prosperity. There is something wrong here. And the thing that is wrong is the system itself. It must be changed.

"Hush don't say that—you'll lose some of your friends." My answer is simple and final: If I don't say it, I'll lose my own soul. For I cannot tolerate an order that causes my gentle friend to sin by saying we need a famine. Can you?

---

O Christ, we ask Thee to give us a burning sense of shame that we have tolerated and still tolerate an order where famine is our suggested remedy. Forgive us. Amen.

## EMPLOYER AND EMPLOYEE

A phase of this competitive system works out in relations between employer and employee. Does it there become a cause of sin—on both sides? It does.

Here is an employer who is a gentle, kindly man and desires to be a Christian. His Christianity tells him that he should do unto others as he would like to be done by, were he an employee. If he were an employee, he would like as high a wage as possible under the circumstances. But he has to compete with others, so he hires men at the lowest wage he can get them. The competitive order loads the situation against his being a Christian—causes him to sin.

Some of these employees may be young girls, and because of the insufficiency of their wages they are tempted, yes, pushed to sell their virtues to feed their bodies. The employer's forcing down wages becomes a cause of sin.

Or the employees may not go that far, but may simply take it out in resentment. To harbor resentment, according to the gospel, is sin. The system causes that sin too.

Or because the employee feels himself wronged his resentment may be shown in poor work done, loafing on the job. Skimped work is not honest—it is sin. The order caused that sin.

Or it may be that he is getting a decent wage but knows that if he speeds up, there will be an end of his job the sooner. What incentive is there to a man to work harder if in the working harder he is working himself out of a job into unemployment? The pressure is to string out as long as possible. This is not honest, hence sin. The system caused the sin.

Then the employer finding his employees lying down on a job reacts in anger. He tightens the screws. More resentment. The situation goes from bad to worse—a strike, a lockout. Hate.

The system was a cause of sin to both.

———

**O Christ, we have been caught in the meshes of an impossible situation. Our souls are ground by the very machines we have produced. Help us to a way out. Amen.**

## WORSHIPING THE MACHINE

We ended up yesterday by showing how the system runs both employee and employer into a clash. Two pack ponies trudging wearily up those steep Himalayan mountainsides, loaded with too heavy burdens, jostled one another on the narrow pathway. One kicked and broke the other's leg. Their burdens made them bad-tempered. This system lays too heavy a burden on both employer and employee. The kick of the lockout or the strike is the result. Somebody is always crippled.

"But what are you going to do, if you see new machinery introduced that sends half of us to the bread lines? 'Labor-saving machinery' indeed—'labor-sacrificing' would be a better name," someone retorts. I agree. This system causes the employer to shut his eyes, tighten his lips, and install the machinery and let the man go—to the bread line and the park bench. It causes him to sin.

Once a year the Hindus worship their tools—did they not provide them bread that year and should they not be grateful? But I was in a great steel mill on that day and saw them decorating the huge machines with flowers and plantain leaves and palms and making merry, bowing to the machines in worship.

I think I too could have bowed to the machine—not in worship, but in gratitude—if I knew that the machine were harnessed to a co-operative order and used for the collective good. But I knew those machines were in the hands of a competitive order, and because of the fierceness of competition they would be replaced by "labor-saving" machines, and many of the laborers would be thrown into unemployment. Poor wretches, I thought, "If they only knew! Worshiping that which will send many of them to the scrap heap!"

No, I cannot worship the machine. Not now. Some day, I hope to bow to it in gratitude because it is in the hands of co-operation. Now the spirit back of it causes men to sin.

---

**O** Christ, Thy best gifts to us become to us a curse because we do not know how to use them. Forgive us and help us to find a new way—Thy way. Amen.

## ANOTHER CAUSE OF SIN—WAR

Another phase of selfish competition is war. Selfish competition works out into international relationships and then—war!

Even with the clouds of war in the sky and the world filled with increasing armaments, I am not hopeless about getting rid of war. Look where we have come from! The Old Testament says, "It came to pass, at the time that kings go out to battle, . . . David tarried at Jerusalem." Kings went out to battle when the springtime came exactly as a man went to his spring plowing—and as regularly. *It was news when David stayed at home.* And then the Bhagavad Gita, the very cream of India's philosophy, is a philosophical defense of war. We have come a long way since then. Practically every nation on earth has signed a Pact renouncing war. War is now sin. Not ready to live up to it? No—not yet. But a conscience is being created. Fifty years ago had Italy attacked Abyssinia, we should have shrugged our shoulders. Now we are profoundly stirred. A conscience is forming. And a conscience is a terrible thing when it does form. Conscience banished slavery and conscience will banish war.

The world was never so near to war and never so near to getting rid of war. We are not more warlike than we used to be. We are far less. But science has thrown us together as a world by its rapid communications, and it has at the same time put into our hands terrible instruments of destruction. The result? Fear. It is fear, not warlikeness, that is driving us to war.

If the very center of life could be changed from competition to co-operation, then war would drop off like a dead leaf. But war is almost inevitable in a world based on competition.

Selfish competition makes men sin the chief of collective sins—war. I therefore want a co-operative world.

---

**O** Christ, we stand before this appalling fact of war. If ever we needed Thy help, we need it here. And if ever we needed to follow Thee, it is at this place. Help us to do it. Amen.

## MY ATTITUDE TOWARD WAR

During the World War I preached on these two texts: "And Herod and his soldiers set Jesus at naught," and "When they saw the soldiers, they stopped beating Paul." Militarism sets Jesus at naught, but then it does defend the weak and defenseless—that was my theme. Of course German militarism was setting Jesus at naught, and we were on the defensive protecting the defenseless. How blinded I was! Every nation felt the same.

The distinction between the offensive and defensive war has for all practical purposes broken down. There is nothing left to do but to renounce all war. And that I do. And I'll tell you why. My chief reason is that war causes men to sin. Men caught in the war spirit do things they would not dream of doing otherwise. It causes man to sin in the following ways:

1. It poisons the air with lies. The first casualty in war is Truth. You cannot fight your enemy unless you make him out a devil. Lying propaganda attends to that.

2. It poisons the air with hate. If the first casualty is Truth, the second casualty is Love. Bitter, burning hate settles into the breasts of millions. The very air becomes poisonous with it. You cannot breathe without breathing it. Hellish hate.

3. It makes men sin economically. A shot from a big gun costs $500, the equivalent of 20,000 loaves of bread. The economic cost of the World War is estimated at $337,000,000,-000, so that if we had had paid $20 an hour since the birth of Christ we would not have finished paying for it. And yet we wonder why the world is hungry! War is economic sin—a sin against hunger.

4. It causes men to sin against persons. Professor Hirsch, of Switzerland, estimates that the war cost directly and indirectly 40,000,000 lives, so that if these dead could march past us 10 abreast, it would take 184 days for them to pass. And they the flower of our race!

———

O Christ, how can we stand indifferent before this collective madness? We do not. We hate it. We renounce it. Amen.

## MY ATTITUDE TOWARD WAR—Continued

Yesterday I began to tell why I renounce war. I must continue. War causes men to sin—

5. By killing the conscience. Here is the portion of an address delivered July 19, 1918, by a drill sergeant drilling boys in the use of the bayonet: "You've got to get down and hook them out with a bayonet; you will enjoy that I assure you. Get sympathy out of your head. If you see a wounded German, shove him out and have no nonsense about it. . . . Kill them, every mother's son of them. Remember your job is to kill them, exterminate the vile creatures. . . . I remember a corporal saying to me, pointing to some German prisoners close by, 'Can I do these blokes in, sir?' I said, 'Please yourself.' He did. When the corporal came back, he said, 'I felt something that I never felt before. . . . I felt what it was like to kill; but it's d—d hard to get it out, he had a belly like iron!'" War does that to a man. That!

6. It lays hold of the finest virtues and prostitutes them. It lays hold on patriotism, heroism, self-sacrifice, idealism, and turns them toward destruction. It takes this fine gold and turns it into the very coin of hell.

7. It sins against the helpless. War protects? When? Where? Did it protect millions of little children from starving? And millions of mothers and widows from weeping beside their dead? Protect the helpless? It produced them.

8. It stands against everything that Christ stands for. It sins against Christ. If war is right, Christ is wrong; and if Christ is right, war is wrong. If Christ stays in this world, war must go. If war stays, Christ must go. Or if He does stay, He must be blown to pieces on a thousand battlefields.

Christ and war are irreconcilables. They are not "compossible." If I must make my choice, I choose Him. Therefore I renounce war.

---

O Christ, we pray Thee to help us to make the break complete. And help us to help others to see the light until we shall have a warless world. Amen.

## THE WAR GOD'S END

I once saw the Hindus worshiping their two war gods. They worshiped them with the deepest reverence and most passionate loyalty, and then a strange thing happened—immediately after the ceremony the tension seemed to relax, the spirit of reverence left, and they put their war gods on a platform and carried them to the river and dumped them in most unceremoniously. When I asked the reason for this sudden change of attitude, they replied, "After the worshiping has taken place, the spirit goes out of them, and they are only common clay."

I thought I saw light. We have been worshiping the war gods for centuries—ardently we have sacrificed the finest of our youth, and the noblest of our virtues upon that altar. We thought something was there—protection, chivalry, duty, love of country, perhaps God Himself was there. But now we are disillusioned. The spirit has gone out of the thing for us. There is nothing there except lies and blood and mud and hate and hunger and death and desolation. We cannot worship *that*—not now. Yes, the real spirit has gone out of the thing. It is just clay. No more.

The painted mustaches of the Hindu war gods were still there after the departure of the spirit, turned up still in triumph. But it was only painted. There was no spirit in it. Mussolini and Hitler and Araki may repaint those mustaches, but it is the painting of the dead. True, we shall still carry these dead gods through our civilization, and we shall try to make the people think they still live and can do something for them. It will not do. Our eyes are open.

I tell you: *They are dead the moment you cease worshiping them.* Never, never again shall I bow at their shrine. They are only clay.

The next step is—to the river bank! We shall do it some day.

———

O Christ, Thy hand, Thy terrible hand, is on our consciences. Help us to put these strange gods away. They belong to our ignorant, barbarous past. Help us to begin anew—without war. Amen.

Amos 9. 7     Acts 10. 34, 35
Colossians 3. 11    Luke 4. 22–29

## ANOTHER CAUSE OF SIN—RACE PREJUDICE

We have looked at two causes of sin in the social order—selfish competition and war. We must now look at a third, race prejudice. H. G. Wells says that it causes more sin than anything he knows: "I am convinced myself that there is no more evil thing in this present world than race prejudice, none at all. I write deliberately—it is the worst single thing in life now. It justifies and holds together more baseness, cruelty, and abomination than any other sort of error in the world." This is literally being proved true.

Race prejudice is self-starvation. An American lady said, "Oh, can't we have an American doctor instead of this Dutch doctor?" Why? This Dutch doctor had more than the average medical training, was an artist of very rare ability and a musician of high attainment, and withal a Christian gentleman. But this lady would shut herself off from all that culture and skill because of one thing—race prejudice. She was practicing self-starvation through race prejudice. Race prejudice caused her to sin—against herself and against the doctor.

I had volunteered to go to Africa as a missionary. I was in a streetcar in my home city when a Negro woman got into the crowded car, and as there was no seat for her, I got up and gave her mine. I heard a titter run through the crowd behind me. "Getting up and giving a Negro woman your seat! He doesn't know what he is letting himself in for!" Hence the laugh. But the laugh is now on the other side. I opened the door of my heart to the people of another race and of a different color of skin, and outside of the influence of Christ it has proved to be the most enriching experience of my life. What love, what friendships, what wisdom, what Christlikeness, what nobility have come to me during these years through that open door! They closed their door with a bang of superiority. But they starved themselves.

---

O Christ, open my heart wide to the people of every race, and perhaps Thou too shalt come through that open door. Amen.

## RACE PREJUDICE AND SNOBBERY

Yesterday we talked about opening our hearts to the people of another race. But if you open the door, you must really open it, for the people will sense whether it is really open or not.

Some new missionaries were studying the language on board ship going out to India. An English lady who had been in India before listened to them trying to get the proper pronunciation. She broke in with this: "Of course I believe in getting the language, but I don't believe in pronouncing it like the native." I suppose she still wonders why the "native" (perish the word!) is so hard to understand! She would go back from this land pinched and starved, having denied herself many enriching friendships.

A Hindu youth told me how he rescued an outcaste boy from drowning and how his parents scolded him, saying he should have let him drown rather than touch an outcaste. But if that youth had let him die, something would have died in him. He flung away his Brahminhood and found a brotherhood.

Peter came near keeping his Jewish Brahminhood, "Lord, I have never touched anything common or unclean," but he flung it away, went unto the Gentiles and found a brotherhood. Had he refused to open his heart, he would have shriveled and died. We should have heard little or nothing of him. You and I will shrivel and inwardly die if we refuse to open our hearts to every person, of every race, of every class.

The members of the Ashram were asked to volunteer to do the outcaste sweeper's work and give him a holiday. For the first time in his life did a people of another "caste" do that for him! When at eventime I looked out of my window, I saw the sweeper back from his holiday, standing before my window with folded hands, his face wreathed in smiles! It was worth it all! Race and class prejudice would have shut me out from that!

---

**O Christ, I pray Thee give me victory at this place—the place of my prejudices. For if I do not gain victory here, I shall be poor and I would be rich. Amen.**

## ECONOMIC INEQUALITY—A CAUSE OF SIN

In tracing back the various causes of sin we come across the fact that the unequal distribution of wealth is a cause of a great deal of sin. This inequality works in several directions in causing sin. First, it works harm to the man who has more than his legitimate share. It often produces in him the feeling that he must in some way deserve all this, and that God must be very pleased with him, when the fact of the matter is that he may have been only clever enough to choose his parents! Inequalities produce superiority complexes. We often think that because we have more we are worth more, which doesn't necessarily follow. It might make us decidedly worthless. Without it we might give a great contribution to life, with it we give only contributions. It also sets the stage for lack of ambition, parasitism, selfish hedonism, and wasted time in general.

Again, it creates the mentality which tries to justify this condition of inequality. Rationalization sets in and with it an unconscious hypocrisy. Moreover, it keeps men from fellowship. How can you have fellowship across these chasms? One of the severest indictments that can be drawn up against unequal distribution of wealth is that it sends cleavages through life everywhere and separates man from man. And the deepest need of the world at the present time is fellowship. The Christian must question everything that makes fellowship more difficult.

At a certain function in England there were tables for "ladies" and tables for the "working girls." At the one table butter was served, and at the other margarine. It is difficult for butter-table people to associate with margarine-table people!

In India one can see on railway quarters these words painted, "Menial quarters." The difference in wages makes one belong to the "Menial." Fellowship with "menials" is difficult. The inequality puts up a barrier.

---

O Christ, Thou who didst come to break down barriers, forgive us that we have set up barriers between us and our fellow man. And forgive us that we have thought these barriers were blessings from Thee. Amen.

## CAUSES SIN TO THE UNDERPRIVILEGED

Unequal distribution of wealth causes hurt to those who have more than their share, but it also causes hurt to those who have less than their share. It tends to create in the one a superiority complex and in the other an inferiority complex. In an acquisitive society where men are judged as to their "worth" by their wealth, not to have wealth brands one as inferior. This is a positive sin against personality.

Moreover, from the Christian standpoint it loads the dice against inward peace and harmony. Sullenness and positive bitterness are engendered. A fine lady came out of her castle to give charity to the poor. A workman saw it, spat on the ground, and said bitterly: "Their charity! Let them be just and we shall not want their charity." It is not enough to preach to that man that such bitterness is unchristian. We must strike at the causes that produce that bitterness.

Among the Zulus there is the saying, "The full-belly child says to the empty-belly child, 'Be of good cheer.'" Our preaching of contentment and cheer to the poor, while leaving untouched the causes of their gloom and lack of contentment, is to add insult to injury. "An optimist is one who is hopeful about other people's troubles." No man today has any message to that gloom and misery unless he has in his hand an ax to strike at the root of that misery. And what is the root? Professor Frank A. Fetter, of Princeton, in *Facing the Facts, an Economic Diagnosis*, puts his finger on the root: "We are living in a society which is financially controlled to intercept the gains of economic progress, by means of higher prices to consumers and financial rewards to insiders, thus keeping the fruits of science and technology from passing on to the people." Note the phrase: "To intercept the gains." When men become alive to *that*, will bitterness not be engendered and will that bitterness not continue till the cause is removed?

———

O Christ, we pray Thee to teach us to hold steady at this point and not to excuse or explain away, but in Thy name to be straightforward and courageous. Amen.

## NATIONALISM—ANOTHER CAUSE OF SIN

One of the greatest dangers to the peace of the world is the rise of modern nationalism, as seen in the totalitarian State. It has taken that lovely sentiment called patriotism and has turned it into the deadliest enemy to our modern world. It causes men to sin where they otherwise would not. The common people of one nation usually have no reason to hate the common people of another nation. But nationalism takes hold of these common people, subjects them to propaganda, instills fears, inspires hates, puts bayonets into their hating, frightened hands and flings them against the common people of another country. Why? Who knows? The grinning devil that inspires this mad business is nationalism.

This nationalism, becoming preposterous beyond words, reaches in and puts its dominating, determining hand on the one thing that is sacred between me and God, my conscience, and says that it is sovereign in there. God is secondary, nationalism is primary.

This nationalism sees that Christianity is a brotherhood stretching across all barriers and is bent on the brotherhood of man, and hence it looks on it as its most deadly foe. So it produces a new paganism that would oust Christianity, or it proceeds to render Christianity innocuous, which amounts to the same thing.

Listen to this official declaration of how nationalism, where it cannot oust, will proceed to render innocuous: "The new Church leadership fully agrees that, in accordance with the fundamental principles necessary to safeguard the national existence of Germany, 'The National Socialist work of nation-building on the basis of Race, Blood, and Soil,' must be recognized and supported, while at the same time the Church will preach the gospel of 'The Saviour and Redeemer of all nations and races,' which gospel bridges over all temporal and human changes."

The gospel "bridges" these gulfs, but nationalism rules at the two ends of the bridge. And Christianity rules over what? The gulfs—emptiness!

---

O Christ, we are asked to follow another god, nationalism. How can we? We love our native land. But we love Thee more and supremely. Amen.

## A CAUSE OF SIN—SUBJECTION

Another cause of sin—the subjection of one people by another.

I know that imperialism in general has been the cause of an amazing amount of advancement to undeveloped peoples. And of all imperialisms I look on the British as the most beneficent that has ever existed. Nevertheless, I am persuaded that the subjection of a people over a long period of time against their will is a cause of sin on both sides. When Sir John Seeley said that "deterioration sets in in any subject race," he was simply recording fact. Life is weakened, loses initiative, is driven underground, loses frankness, becomes sycophantic, untruthful and undependable. Not always of course. But that is the tendency and the trend.

Moreover, it causes inner deterioration in the rulers. For they believe in freedom for themselves, but being compelled by the system to deny it to others an inner contradiction takes place. A defense mechanism is built up which wars against their own finest ideals. Deterioration is bound to become a fact under these circumstances.

Young men come out of the universities of Britain, nourished upon great traditions of liberty, and when they arrive in India are eager to serve and to share their traditions. Then the system begins to tame those impulses, and they who came out to be brothers, end up by being bureaucrats.

One of my chairmen, a British official, once said, "I have a quarrel with the speaker. He began by saying, 'Mr. Chairman, Brothers and Sisters'! He left me out of the brotherhood and I refuse to be left out." It was said so sincerely that the Indian crowd roared its appreciation. For he was a fine type of Christian gentleman. But the next day when I saw him on a matter connected with India, he was a different man. He stood within the framework of the system. The system made him, not a brother, but a bureaucrat.

---

O God, our Father, help us to share our liberties with everyone, everywhere, for we know that if we do not share them, we cannot keep them. Help us, then, to share them. Amen.

# ANOTHER CAUSE OF SIN—INADEQUATE HOUSING

We have crowded the weakest and most unfortunate members of society into that blot on human civilization called slums. Here many families are compelled to live in one room. In this one room they have to eat, sleep, and breed. At every moment of their lives that most sacred shrine, human personality, is invaded. There is no privacy. Now, preach to that group of human beings that modesty is a virtue, and purity is a necessity and quarrelsomeness is bad, and your words sound hollow. Why? Because the whole situation is loaded against purity and against modesty and against good temper. The very physical basis of life works against your preaching. Young people growing up in such surroundings are handicapped in their battle for purity. Their very surroundings take away fifty per cent of their chances for success.

Obviously, our message must have two sides—a demand for purity and amity and a demand for proper housing.

A picture haunts my imagination: In the Anti-Religious Museum at Leningrad is the picture of a large two-storied mission bungalow and beside it a tiny African grass hut. The suggestion is that religion is doing "spiritual" work for the people of that grass hut, but that the disparity between the hut and the bungalow will remain. That indictment must be disproved. That disparity must go; for as long as that disparity persists there will be an undertone of resentment as soon as the people come to self-consciousness. That disparity causes sin. Mission bungalows, on the whole, have been too large, and the huts around them are too small. There must come a closer approximation—the hut should come up a long way and the bungalow should come down some. The cells in which most of us live in the Lucknow Ashram are about six by eight. And we are happy and brotherly. But the point is—our cells, however small, give us privacy, and a slum does not.

---

O Christ, we bring to Thee those who are crowded into slums. Forgive us that we have these blots of our shame still unchanged, and help us to change them. Amen.

Deuteronomy 14, 15
Matthew 20. 7

## OTHER CAUSES OF SIN—LOW WAGES AND UNEMPLOYMENT

If bad housing sets the stage for sin, so do low wages. The temptation to dishonesty is very great when wages are very small. As I sit here writing, a letter comes to my desk from one of the ablest missionaries in India telling how when she was a little girl, reared in a poor home, she went to a wealthier home where there were dolls in abundance—and she had none. She felt she had a right to one, so stole one, and for many years suffered untold tortures from a sensitive conscience. Her poverty made it easier for her to take that doll and suffer those years of torture. This happens on a larger scale when wages are low.

But if low wages cause sin, unemployment is worse still. It causes deterioration—to be an unwanted and unneeded man in human society is enough to take the light out of any eye and make any set of strong shoulders droop. The amazing thing to me is that so often the light still shines in the eye and the shoulders are still square after years of fruitless knocking at doors. I salute unconquered human nature! But I cannot salute the system that causes these unemployed. It is all so unnecessary. In a competitive order it seems necessary and inevitable, but in a co-operative order it would not be. I therefore stand for a co-operative order, and will give what strength and influence I have to bring it into being—these hot tears that unbidden fall upon the paper as I write being witness. For an unemployed man breaks my heart. Did it not strike home to me very early when I saw my own father unemployed and I had to watch the deterioration set in day by day?

Unemployment causes sin in the victims, and in those who allow it to continue, because they selfishly refuse to co-operate in ending it. We are all guilty.

———

O God, our Father, forgive us that we have tolerated so long this inhumanity, and give us, we pray Thee, the strength and wisdom and courage to end it. Amen.

## THE EXISTENCE OF CLASS

Another cause of sin in society is the existence of class. As long as society is based on class, causes of sin are in the social structure.

For the consciousness of class produces the consciousness of those who are not of that class. That produces a cleavage. Across that cleavage, misunderstandings arise. On board ship I looked at a film which made me boil with indignation— everyone interested in bettering labor conditions was a rotter, every labor-leader a demagogue. It was class speaking to class. On the other hand, I boil again when I hear every capitalist made out to be a bloated exploiter of the poor. It just isn't so. There are capitalists who are the salt of the earth. Class speaks to class and calls names.

Moreover, these class cleavages cause us to feel class-pain and class-disabilities, but not human pain and human disabilities. It thus causes us to sin the sin of callousness to people of another class. It tends to dry up our sympathy in certain directions. Therefore these class distinctions turn the situation in an unchristian direction and make it easy for people to sin against their brethren of another class.

We must get rid of the notion that these class cleavages are rooted either in nature or in the will of God. They are rooted in the will of man. They are nothing less than artificial barriers placed by the wrong organization of human society between man and man. Sir Algernon Sydney is right when he says, "The mass of mankind have not been born with saddles on their backs, nor a favored few booted and spurred ready to ride them legitimately by the grace of God." That attitude must die.

This conception of class on both sides is a cause of sin, and its roots must be cut if we are to live victoriously in the fullest sense.

O Christ, whose heart went out across these barriers and gathered men of all classes into a new living brotherhood where there was no class, give us, we pray Thee, that same spirit. Amen.

171

## ANOTHER CAUSE OF SIN—ATTITUDES TOWARD WOMEN

The economic and political order is largely the result of man's organizing. And in the organizing, woman has been fitted into it largely on the basis of a sex-being, and she is supposed to be treated and to act as such. Woman has, in general, accepted this false mentality and has given herself to the petty business of being attractive to the male. This has been the cause of much sin in human society.

The position of women is changing throughout the world. Some years ago when about to speak to the ladies of a palace in India, I wondered where my audience was as I came into a large room with a screen across it. I soon saw the bejeweled feet of my audience under the screen and talked to those lotus feet! Now, however, this is changing rapidly. A young woman of that very palace group was recently killed driving her own motor car. Alas, there will be many casualties in the transition from woman as a sex-being to woman as a person with equal rights and duties. The fact is we are now rather appalled at the number of those casualties. Woman, in driving this new force called freedom, is making a wreck of many a fine reticence, many a strong trait. But we cannot stop until woman arrives at the place where Jesus placed her as a human personality and not a mere sex-being. She must be given an equal place and an equal task in the reconstruction of the world. As I crossed the borderland into Russia, a uniformed young woman with men soldiers at her back with fixed bayonets came into the train to inspect it. When I saw her, I knew I was in a new civilization. But I do not want women to step into our systems and take over our guns and with them our spirit. I want this new freedom to lead women to do what one woman did when she suggested that cannon of both Chile and Argentine be melted and cast into the "Christ of the Andes"—symbol of perpetual peace between these two nations.

O Christ, help us to treat women as equal persons and help women to set up a Christ of peace on every dividing line in human life. Amen.

## ECONOMIC INSECURITY

I mention this cause of sin last, for in many ways it is the most prolific cause of sin in human society. Under the doctrine of *laissez faire*, or unrestricted competition, economic security is at the lowest ebb both for the employer and the employee. For both of them, economic security has almost reached the vanishing point. Under unrestricted competition three quarters of all business ventures fail. How can the business man be sure that he belongs to the fortunate one quarter? And if he is sure that he does belong to it, then is he quite sure of his inner moral position, for in a competitive order his success has caused the failure of others? If he gets more than he needs, somebody will have less than he needs. His success makes him morally uncomfortable, or should do so. Moreover, because of the fear of insecurity in old age and disability he is driven to pile up far beyond his actual needs in hope of meeting that insecurity. This creates an enlightened greed that is appalling.

And the wage earner? His economic destiny is not in his own hands, nor in the hands of his fellow laborers, but in the hands of the man who owns the capital. He therefore lives in constant dread of joining the ragged ranks of the unemployed. That haunting fear is one of the most desperate things in human life at the present time and it may disrupt society in an awful explosion. If it does not cause an explosion, it will drive men to a sycophancy, a subserviency, a denial of their own manhood that will be just as disruptive of society as an explosion.

Thus economic insecurity causes the sin of fear—the employer is afraid if he gives better wages, his competitor will undercut him and he will go on the rocks; the laborer is afraid of losing his job.

———

O Christ, Thou who didst come to take all fear from our hearts, help us to produce an order in which fear will have no place. We could do it if we knew how to love. Then help us to love. Amen.

## WHAT IS TO BE DONE ABOUT IT?

We have seen that certain things in the social structure set the stage for sin, cause sin: selfish competition, the wage system under competition, war, race prejudice, economic inequality, the existence of classes, unemployment, subjection of one race by another, nationalism, wrong attitudes toward women, and economic insecurity. These things deeply rooted in the structure of society block victorious living at every turn. They do not render victorious living impossible, but certainly render it very difficult, and often under the pressure of these things victorious life in the individual is crushed out.

If religion has no message at this point, if it undertakes to live victoriously without facing these issues, then the method used is a method of evasion, and this violates two fundamental principles of victorious living, namely, mental honesty and courage to face the facts. To attempt to win by strategic retreat is to run into the pitfall of mental insincerity and without mental sincerity no victorious living is possible. The process of evasion is therefore self-defeating.

Obviously, the first thing to be done is to look at these things as causes of sin and therefore an evil in human society —something to be eradicated and not tolerated. At this point our greatest difficulty lies. Many think these things are an ineradicable part of society's structure. They accept them fatalistically. This defeatest mentality is our greatest problem. It must be broken. Just as the individual, in order to have personal victory over personal sins, must have the faith that it can be done, so we must gain the attitude of faith that these social sins are disease, and as such are no normal part of human living and can be eradicated. The health of society demands it.

---

O Christ, we need to be reborn mentally and spiritually at this place, we need to come into a faith that believes that anything is possible with Thee. Give us this faith for our society is very, very sick. Amen.

## FACING SOME HALF-TRUTHS

We said yesterday that one of the first things to be done is to get the faith that these social evils can be overcome. In order to get this faith we must rid our minds of certain half-truths, for if we get caught in these half-truths, we shall not go on to full faith.

Professor Bennett, in *Social Salvation*, says there are these three half-truths: (1) That individuals can rise above any combination of social circumstances. (2) That, since individuals control institutions and systems, it is enough to change individuals. (3) That you can change society without changed individuals.

To these we would add three more: (4) That society is relatively immoral and man is relatively moral. (5) That the method of the coming of the Kingdom is only gradual. (6) That it is only apocalyptic and catastrophic.

Half-truths can become more dangerous than whole lies. For there is nothing in the whole lie to hold good people to its allegiance, but a half-truth often gains the allegiance of good people, and with their eyes fastened on that half-truth they are oblivious of the lurking evil. Jesus was crucified on half-truths. Religious people, seeing those half-truths, were blind to the other side and allowed themselves to commit the worst deed in human history. They did it clinging to half-truths as justification. He did say that He was a king. He did say if they destroyed this temple, He would rebuild it. He said almost everything they accused Him of—minus their twists. Half-truths.

Today He and His Kingdom are being crucified on half-truths. Wrong ideas are causing as much damage as wrong wills. And the wrong ideas are usually half-right ideas. Again it is the fatal twist that sends the whole thing in a wrong direction.

———

O Christ, Thou who didst suffer and art suffering from half-truths, open our eyes, that we might see whether we hold any half-truth that keeps us from seeing things as they are. Amen.

175

## INDIVIDUALS AND THEIR CIRCUMSTANCES

The first half-truth we must notice is this: That individuals can rise above any combination of social circumstances.

Sometimes they do, and this book is stressing that possibility. The possibility of using one's very adverse circumstances and sufferings for the furtherance of the spiritual life must not be dimmed. This has been my contention in *Christ and Human Suffering*. But I was struck with a criticism made by a class of Indian college girls using that book as a study book: "This is all right for the spiritually developed, for the exceptional person, but for the rank and file of ordinary Christians it is too high. And if it is difficult for ordinary Christians, what about the great masses who have no Christian faith? Can they use pain and sorrow?" In spite of this criticism I still maintain that the use of suffering is the privilege of the ordinary Christian. Nevertheless, there is real point to this criticism. We cannot blink at the fact that the majority of people do not change their circumstances, but are changed by them. Somebody has said that if a letter were sent to that most influential person called "Circumstances," most of us could end it by saying, "I am, Sir, your most obedient servant." For the most of us are the obedient servants of our circumstances. We must think in terms of the weaker members and produce a society in which it will be easier for them to grow. All of us are weak during the first fifteen years of life, and it is at that weakest period of life that we are most conditioned by environment and influenced by it. For the sake of each succeeding generation we must produce a society that will work with and not against the total growth of youth.

For in those years most of us are not self-contained, but environment-conditioned.

---

O Christ, Thou who didst pronounce woes on those who become causes of stumbling, especially to little ones, forgive us that we have produced a society in which this is literally a fact. And help us to right it, for their sakes and ours. Amen.

Luke 11. 42
Luke 24. 52, 53
Acts 17. 6

## WILL CONVERTED MEN NECESSARILY CONVERT SOCIETY?

That society is made up of individuals there is no doubt. That if you change a sufficient number of individuals, you can change society there is also no doubt. Changed men have changed society.

But these are only half-truths. It is not wholly true that individuals make up society. Society is made up of individuals, but it is also made up of inherited customs and attitudes which have become a part of the social structure and which exist apart from the will of the individual. To change the individual will may leave entirely intact this inherited social structure. To change individual slave owners did not get rid of the slave system. That could only be accomplished by what Bennett calls "a wide-scale frontal attack." Both in England and America slavery was ousted by the frontal attack of legislation. It is true that the converted Wilberforce was a big factor in the getting rid of it, but it was only after he had persuaded sufficient people to attack it on a Parliamentary front that it was abolished. An attack on a personal front alone would have left the slavery system to this day. Parliamentary coercion for recalcitrants had to supplement personal change.

Even where the converted individual will is directed toward the change of a system, that change will not take place unless you have this wide-scale, concerted, frontal attack. But, suppose, instead of this converted will being directed toward social change, it stops at the half-way house of contentment in the fact of its own change, then the case is still worse. This it often does. Conversion instead of becoming the life of social change often becomes in lieu of social change. It often makes our attention glance off either toward ourselves or toward heaven, and leaves the essential problems of life untouched. Half-conversions may become whole perversions. Conversion must be fully converted.

O Christ, I pray Thee to convert my conversion into the wide sweep of Thy purposes for myself and all men. Put the content of social change into my individual change. Amen.

# CAN YOU CHANGE SOCIETY WITHOUT CHANGED INDIVIDUALS

Another half-truth is that you can change society without changed individuals. The individually-minded say that the greatest necessity is for changed individuals, and the society-minded say the greatest necessity is for a changed society. Each contains a half-truth, but only a half-truth. It is only a half-truth to say that you can change society and neglect individual change.

For a changed society needs changed individuals to sustain it. The whole of the outer structure of life rests on that imponderable and subtle thing called character. If the character breaks, the confidence breaks, and if the confidence breaks, the society breaks. Marxian Communism, if it fails, will probably fail at this place—there will not be enough dynamic in it to change individuals, so that those changed individuals will undergird and support the structure of society resting on them. The best of schemes need changed men to make them work. "For the remaking of the province I need two things," said a Chinese governor to a friend of mine; "I need money, and I need men who will honestly expend that money. I can get the first, but I cannot get the second. If you can produce the men, we can remake the province." He put the situation in a nutshell, not only in China, but everywhere.

Today I came on a motor, belonging to a former motor syndicate—a syndicate which was obviously in the interests of all those in it, but the syndicate broke down on account of one simple thing—a lack of character in the people who made it up. Whenever individual members saw a smaller immediate advantage as against a larger long-term advantage, they didn't have enough character to resist the immediate in behalf of the more remote. A changed society needs changed men to keep it changed.

---

O Christ, it is here that we need Thy power. For how can we go into the new day with the old life? Cleanse us at the heart, that we may cleanse society to its utmost limits. Amen.

## A CORRECTION

Yesterday we insisted that you cannot change society without changed individuals to sustain those changes. But a correction to restore a balance needs to be made at this point—a changed society would tend to change individuals. That is a point which the evangelicals have largely missed. They should welcome these wide-scale basic changes in the structure of society in the very interests of individual conversion.

We now know the power of environment in the making of the individual. Many things which we think to be innate are socially conditioned at a very early stage in life, so early that we mistake them for the innate. This can be seen in India very vividly where caste lines are sharply drawn. Take a child out of an outcaste sweeper home at birth, and let it be subjected to a new social heredity in which it would know nothing of its so-called inferior birth, and let it be given the privileges of education and culture of other children, and in nine cases out of ten you can make an almost entirely new personality out of it, whereas had it stayed in the sweeper home in nine cases out of ten it would have taken on the likeness of its surroundings and would have caught the average outlook and conformed to it.

A competitive order works against individual conversion at every point; a co-operative order would work toward individual conversion at every point. For you cannot make a co-operative order work except by the very things inherent in spiritually changed character, namely, a change from the ego-centric to the Kingdom-centric, from self to God and others. In preaching conversion in such an order you would be working, not against the grain of the social order as now, but with it.

---

O Christ, we pray Thee to help us to have a changed society, that we may more easily have changed individuals. For we want men to be changed—and so dost Thou. Amen.

Exodus 23. 1–8
Leviticus 19. 13–15

# THE HALF-TRUTH OF MORAL MAN AND IMMORAL SOCIETY

The insistence that man as an individual is comparatively more moral than society has a truth within it. For man as an individual is not prepared to do many things which as a member of society he is prepared to do: for instance, ruthlessly compete to the ruination of others, and collectively butcher in war. This is a truth, but is only a half-truth.

For the matter might be reversed. In a co-operative order the very reverse would be the case—society would be the comparatively moral and the individual comparatively immoral. In our Ashram this can be seen in miniature. There the organization is on the basis of a sharing brotherhood—to each according to his need and from each according to his ability. The collective order in its organization is just and brotherly, but now and again individuals break this justice and brotherhood by individually wrong moral acts. They are judged by the spirit and organization of the Ashram. They are less moral than the collective order. It would be the same on a wider scale when society comes to a co-operative order—it would be moral society and immoral man.

The insistence by Doctor Niebuhr that because society is immoral this is all rooted in nature, and must be dealt with as such, is again only a half-truth. What seems rooted in nature may be rooted in a wrong social organization, namely, a competitive collective order. Change that order to a co-operative one and many things which now appear rooted in nature will be seen to be rooted in a wrong social organization and are not inherent, but collectively imposed. Much that seems to be nature is nurture under an order which produces wrong attitudes. This gives us a basis of hope rather than a basis of pessimism, for we can change what we have made, namely, a wrong social organization.

----

O Christ, we come to Thee for strength and nerve and clear-sighted love, that we may not sink back into the pessimisms of nature, but that we may rise to the optimisms of Thy redemptive grace and power. Amen.

# THE HALF-TRUTH OF THE COMING OF THE KINGDOM AS ONLY GRADUAL

Modern liberalism has insisted that the coming of the Kingdom will be by gradual changes. It has drawn its inspiration from two sources: from modern democracy and from certain teachings of the New Testament which teach a gradualism. Modern democracy has committed itself to a faith in democratic processes of change according to constitutions. This means by vote instead of by sudden, catastrophic revolution. Liberalism has felt that the processes of the Kingdom would be the same.

In this they have been supported by passages in the New Testament—the leaven that leavens the whole lump, the Kingdom like the growth of the corn—first the blade, then the ear, then the full corn in the ear. These passages seemed to fit in with the spirit of democratic, evolutionary change. But with the recent decay of faith in democratic government much of this faith of liberalism in gradualism has decayed with it. The spirit of these last few years is that changes in government should come suddenly and by compulsion from above. Dictatorships, veiled and overt, have arisen. Now liberalism is partaking of that changed outlook. It is saying in many quarters that change can only come suddenly and in a catastrophic manner. This volte-face shows how liberalism is dependent on modern culture; in fact, liberalism is modern culture turned religious. It is most unstable.

It should hold to its principle of gradualism. For that lets the responsibility rest where it should rest, namely, on us, to bring in that Kingdom by individual and collective endeavor co-operating with the redemptive God. This outlook holds us from flying off at tangents of various short cuts and keeps us with our souls against the task. For gradualism is in the New Testament as a living part of the outlook of the gospel. It is ineradicable.

But it is only a half-truth—we should remember that. There is another side.

---

O Christ, keep us from evading responsibility by throwing it on Thee, on future circumstances, and help us to take our tasks like men. Amen.

## THE HALF-TRUTH OF THE COMING OF THE KINGDOM AS ONLY SUDDEN

Modern fundamentalism in many cases has rejected the principle of gradualism and has said that in the Second Coming of Christ the Kingdom will in fact be set up. This coming will be sudden and catastrophic.

In this they have been supported by passages in the New Testament which teach His coming as a thief in the night, by the nobleman who went into a far country to receive a Kingdom and to return to set it up, and so on. That the New Testament does teach this sudden and catastrophic phase of the coming of the Kingdom there is no doubt whatever.

But it is a fact that the holding of this phase alone has produced a mentality that has withdrawn interest from social change by gradual processes, has made those who hold it discount those changes, and has made them look for a worsening of things in order to a final, sudden triumph at the coming of Christ. This has been a moral and social drain.

Christian thought has moved by the dialectic from the catastrophic to the gradual and back again—thesis producing antithesis. It is now time for us to come to the synthesis. And the synthesis is this: there is in the pages of the New Testament both the teaching of gradualism and the teaching of the apocalyptic. Both are there and are integral parts of the account. They cannot be explained away. And in the interests of the Kingdom itself they must not be explained away, for we need both phases of the Kingdom. Each is a half-truth that needs the other to complete it. We need to understand that the task is ours and must be assumed as such, and we must also see that it is God's and that He will complete it, perhaps even when we least expect it.

--------

O Christ, we thank Thee that Thou hast taught us that the task is ours and the consummation is Thine, and the task is Thine and the consummation ours. We shall work it out together, and together we shall triumph. Amen.

## THE SYNTHESIS

From many angles we have been working toward a synthesis. Modern liberal emphasis on gradualism by the endeavors of men has produced its Barthianism with its demand that we cease this humanism and humbly accept the Kingdom as a gift of grace. We have felt the truth in each contention, but each is only a half-truth. The Christian world is working through these half-truths to a synthesis, a larger truth.

That larger truth is that the New Testament teaches both. Modern minds have hesitated to take the apocalyptic at its face value. They have thought it was something read into the account, but the extracting of it has been impossible. It is an integral part. Schweitzer says the New Testament taught a future Kingdom only, that Jesus died mistaken, believing to the last that the Kingdom would come by catastrophic intervention. We feel the half-truth in this position. Why not say that He was mistaken as to the *time?* He Himself said concerning that hour no one knows, "neither the Son, but the Father." And was He not right even in being mistaken as to the time? Are we not to look on every hour as the possible hour? And while mistaken so far in human history, would it not have been a mistake if we had not looked on every hour as the possible hour?

But will He finally be right in the fact of His catastrophic intervention? Why not? History has not proved Him to be wrong, for history is not exhausted as yet. He was so right in everything else, will He not be right in this also?

To accept this synthesis of gradualism and apocalyptic would leave us just where we should be as Christians—within the stream of human history and yet above it, within the world process to suffer and bleed and thus remake it and yet above the process as its judges through Him who is to be its final Judge.

———

O Christ, Thou art leading us into the larger truth of the Kingdom. We accept it, for the Kingdom is our one hope. Amen.

## TWENTY-SIXTH WEEK

JUNE 24

Matthew 23. 4
James 2. 12, 13
Revelation 2. 23

Romans 14. 10, 11
John 12. 31, 32

# IS THE CHURCH TO TAKE THE RÔLE OF JUDGE?

We must look at one more partial emphasis. There are those who would tell us that the function of the Church is to stand aloof from all these movements of social reconstruction, to commit herself to none of them, but to be the constant judge of all. I have the feeling that this counsel is an escape-mentality.

Isn't this getting out of the problem by assuming the rôle of a judge, instead of being in it as a participant, suffering along with it, and thus saving it from within? If we assume the rôle of judge in the struggle ahead of us, would we not turn out the perfect Pharisee, instead of the perfect Christian? Did not Jesus reject all the methods of trying to save the world by standing outside the process? Did He not accept the way of standing within it, making its sorrows, its problems, its sins His very own, the cross thus becoming inevitable?

In the early days of the Salvation Army in Britain a Salvation Army lassie was brought before a judge to be tried for the sin of seeking the lost in these scandalous ways. The judge deliberately left the judgment seat and stood alongside of her as the proceedings went on. He identified himself with her and would be tried along with her. In doing so he revealed the Christian attitude: "For God sent not his Son into the world to judge the world; but that the world should be saved through him." Jesus rejects the rôle of judge. But a strange thing happens. Through this very identification He becomes the Judge. The Christian Church today can only become the judge of movements of social reconstruction to the degree that she is in them and suffers vicariously. Then she gains a moral authority which makes her a judge. Not otherwise. To take the attitude of an aloof judge is to assume an unchristian attitude.

---

O Christ, Thou judgest us from a cross. Help us to gain our moral authority over the world from the same place—the place of our own suffering for men. Amen.

## VISITED AND REDEEMED

We saw yesterday that the only way of redemption is for the Christian to get into these movements and save from within. It will not do to assume the rôle of judge and leave it at that. As this is fundamental to the whole Christian attitude we must look at it more steadily. Zacharias said a penetrating thing in Luke 1. 68, "Blessed be the Lord God of Israel; for he hath visited and redeemed his people." Note the phrase, "visited and redeemed." He probably had little notion of how amazing in its sweep that redemption was, and how deep the visitation.

For in the redeeming of the world God might have issued orders from heaven or He might have been incarnate as a Teacher, an Example, or He might have done just what He did, namely, become One with us, and let everything that falls on us fall on Himself—plus. This was visitation.

The Church must follow in His steps at this point. It dare not merely issue condemnations of the social order from its sheltered sanctuaries; it dare not be a detached spectator of the world going through its struggles after a new order; it dare not merely take the rôle of teacher—it must visit, and that visitation must mean in its case what it meant in His —a visitation that means identification.

And this identification must not be a generality—it must be specific enough to cause it to suffer. As Dr. Wade Crawford Barclay says, "The question is whether the Church can become specific enough to save itself." Jesus' visitation was specific— ours must be too. It must be sufficiently specific to gain a specific cross. Dealing in pious generalities is usually evasion of issues. We must find the places where the real issues are being joined and take sides.

If we refuse the visitation, we shall renounce the redemption. We cannot have one without the other.

---

O Christ, we pray Thee to save us from the spirit that would save ourselves by various subterfuges. For we know if we save ourselves, we shall not save others. Give us courage to be specific. Amen.

## THE BLENDING OF TWO EMPHASES

We have now come in our quest to the place where we can see the necessity of blending the individual and social emphases into a living whole. Jesus did just that. Of Him it was said:

"A bruised reed shall he not break,
And smoking flax shall he not quench,
Till he send forth judgment unto victory,
And in his name shall the Gentiles hope."
(Matthew 12. 20, 21.)

Here we find this blend—a tenderness toward individuals, a refusal to break the bruised reed or quench the smoking flax and a demand for social justice. For "judgment" was not a deciding of legal points, but a giving of a fair, equal opportunity to all—the words "social justice" express it.

First, there was a tenderness toward individuals—the bruised reeds which have been bruised by the storms of nature, or by the trampling feet of men. The gospel comes as an infinite tenderness to those who are hurt by the awful powers of unconscious nature, or by the conscious inhumanities of man to man, or bruised by their own follies and sins. Also to those who are smoking flax, those in whom life and hope are very dim, in whom the fires are about to go out, the gospel comes as an inspiration, hope, life. We must never fail the stricken individual by withholding this message of tender healing and life-healing hope, for this is a badly stricken world.

But just because we are so interested in individuals we must pass on to that "judgment" that would end social injustices through which many lives are being bruised, and many made to burn dimly. Just because we are passionately interested in individuals we must be passionately interested in social justice. You are really not interested in either in the fullest sense unless you are interested in both. For neither can be fully effective without the other.

———

O Christ, to whom these two worlds of individual and social were one, help us to cease our divisions at this point and to make them one. Amen.

186

# THE MEANING OF JUDGMENT

The blending which we saw yesterday was that of a tenderness toward the individual and a stern demand for a social justice—the bruised reed was not to be broken, and judgment was to be sent forth to victory. These two are integral parts of the work of Christ, so the account says. If so, then we must look more steadily at the meaning of "judgment." It has a history. It came down through the Hebrew tradition, where the individual and the social emphases were one. The Jewish people in their corporate life were to express the will of God. The idea of religion being a private affair between the soul and God is unthinkable to the Old-Testament prophets. The nation as a nation were the chosen people of God, and as such were to express the mind of God in their total life. So the word "judgment" came to express equality, fairness, divine law and divine love operating in the sphere of the collective life.

Jesus took this same attitude. He expected the nation to embody the Kingdom. When they refused, He said, "The Kingdom of God shall be taken from you and given to *a nation* bringing forth the fruits thereof." Note, it was to "a nation." His final appeal was to Jerusalem, representing the nation, "O Jerusalem, Jerusalem, . . . how often would I have gathered thy children together" to embody this Divine will, "and you would not." He also demanded of the cities of Capernaum and Bethsaida a corporate repentance because He had expected a corporate obedience. We forget that note in the gospel and because we forget it, the world is corporately adrift, without guidance.

We have allowed this note of the corporate expression of the will of God to largely drop out of Christianity, to its own impoverishment, and to the worse than impoverishment of the corporate life. We must rediscover it—or allow humanity to perish through internal discord.

---

O Christ, who didst come to send forth judgment unto victory, help us to catch anew that note and fearlessly apply it to our total living. If we do not, we perish. Amen.

## THE WISDOM OF THE JUST

We saw that the deepest need was to set judgment, or social justice, into human affairs. This passage concerning John the Baptist emphasizes the same: "He shall . . . turn the hearts of the fathers to the children, and the disobedient to walk in the wisdom of the just; to make ready for the Lord a people prepared" (Luke 1. 17). Note: "*a people*" prepared, a nation was to stand ready to do the will of God. And how were they to be prepared? By two things—by turning the hearts of the fathers to the children; in other words, by making the generation now in power to cease from its own selfishness and to think in terms of the betterment of the rising generation; this to be done by embodying "the wisdom of the just."

Note that phrase—"the wisdom of the just." It is a truism to say that what the poor and the dispossessed need is not charity but justice, but it needs to be said again and again. We have seen the unwisdom of injustice. We have built a society in which those in control have intercepted the gains brought by science and technology and have kept them from passing on to the people. The result—economic disaster to everybody. The unwisdom of the unjust. Each nation tried to grab all the raw materials and advantages it could for itself regardless of what happens to others. The result? International anarchy, fear—and war! The unwisdom of the unjust. Talk about the Kingdom of God not being practical and workable? Let those who have not made a mess of things by injustice bring that criticism! This generation is disqualified.

A basic, thoroughgoing justice for everybody would be social wisdom. If we will not listen to this word from the sacred Book, then we must listen to it spoken by the fiery tongues of a world in flames. For God speaks! And the wisdom of the just is His message.

---

O Christ, we pray Thee to save us from our own follies, and help us to be lovingly just in the whole of our relationships. And help us to begin now. Amen.

## JUDGMENT UNTO VICTORY

Yesterday we saw that God speaks, and His word is that we should learn the wisdom of the just. But we are afraid of it for two reasons: it will cause loss to us, and it won't work.

I do not say that it will cost nothing to be just. You will have to have the seifish self knocked out before you can become fundamentally just and willing to give everybody an equal opportunity. It will mean a real renunciation—a brotherhood of sharing. When the master in the parable said to the grumblers at his equality, where the last hired got as much as the first, "Friend, I do thee no wrong," he spoke to a common fear. We are afraid that an equal justice will do us a wrong. To this privileged, unsocial self it will. But a new, just, brotherly self will be born, and to that man it can be said, "Friend, I do thee no wrong; in fact, I do thee a supreme good."

But we are afraid it won't work. The verse concerning Jesus says, "He shall send judgment unto victory." Will He, can He do it? He is doing it! Today He is breaking down this unjust and therefore decaying social order. His hammer is smiting it. It is crumbling to dust at our feet. Its injustices are breaking it down. It is the hour of judgment—judgment in the sense of condemnation, in order that the hour of judgment in the sense of social justice might come. The condemnation falls on us that the construction might begin through us. He is sending forth judgment unto victory! The eternal God will not fail in His redemptive purpose and His redemptive purpose includes the total life.

---

O Christ, we thank Thee that this whole redemptive process is unto victory. It shall not fail by the way. In the end there shall be one word upon our lips—"Victory!" Help us to take up that word now and make it our own. Amen.

## OUR ONE HOPE

This age needs a renewing of hope. Cynicism and despair have bitten deep into our souls. And this is serious, for God says, according to Francis Thompson, "I shall forgive thee all—save thy despair." Despair closes the gates against the redemptive purposes of God. But where shall we find a renewal of our hope?

The passage we have been studying says, "In his name shall the Gentiles hope." The hope lies in Him who will not break the bruised reed, and will send forth judgment unto victory. In other words, the hope lies in One who blends in His message to mankind a tender redemptiveness to the individual and a stern demand for social justice. These two together will be unto victory. This is our hope.

But one without the other will not be unto victory. Our hope does not lie in changed individuals, alone. It may leave untouched the social problems. As Herbert Gray says: "Conversion has often meant going through a process of personal readjustment which has left the men and women concerned still dominated in mind by the received ideas about money, and war, and the claims of the dispossessed." The content of social justice must be put into conversion. Nor will social reconstruction without individual conversion be unto victory. I have just been attending to a very sick man suffering from appendicitis, who in his agony begs me to send him back to his village where it is warmer and all will be well. But a change of climate will not cure a suppurating appendix! It needs an operation. A change of the social climate will leave untouched many of our inward maladjustments which would persist in any climate. We need a personal spiritual operation.

No, our hope lies neither in one, nor in the other, but in both. In Christ and His Kingdom they are one, so in Him is our hope.

----

O Christ, whether we take the road of personal need or the road of a social reconstruction, they both lead us to Thy feet. We are there, for Thou art the one hope of our stricken world—and of us. Amen.

## THE HALF-WAY HOUSE

We have now completed half our journey in our quest for victorious living. One note running through these pages, which will continue in the pages to come, is this—if there is to be victorious living, there must be no paralyzing divisions, there must be unity. This is psychologically and spiritually sound.

But we have only begun to see how wide this demand for unity will be. It must take in everything. We saw that there must be no clashing division between the conscious and the subconscious mind. Freud says that the process of mental harmony is brought about by "making the unconscious conscious." In other words, there should be no hidden strife between the conscious and the subconscious minds. We also saw that there must be no clashing division in the conscious mind itself. When we try to give ourselves to mutually competing ends, we find defeat. There are some things that are not "compossible"—they cannot exist side by side without causing spiritual paralysis. If we are going to have victory, we must decide between them. Again, there must be nothing between us and God. Every barrier must go down between His will and ours.

And now we see the necessity of a further unity—the unity between the individual and the social. If we allow a division to grow up between these two through lack of emphasis on either side, there will be spiritual defeat. The social without the personal is a body without a soul, and the personal without the social is a soul without a body—one is a corpse and the other a ghost. But together they make a living person. This division between the individual and the social has been the root cause of the major defeats of religion in modern life. The hope of the world is in the healing of this breach.

In order to get victory are you prepared to heal that breach as far as you are concerned?

O Christ, Thou art leading us to unity. Help us to hold back at no point, but to go on to complete unity. Amen.

## THE UNITY OF THE IDEAL AND THE REAL

We said yesterday that we were beginning to see how wide the demand for unity will be. This demand will confront us at the place of the ideal and the real, of theory and practice.

While in Russia an intelligent woman said to me, "I suppose you are an idealist?" I replied that I was. She waved her hand and said, "Au revoir, I'm a realist." I smiled then and rather pitied her for her contempt of idealism, but since then my smile has worn off and there has come a sense of concern that she might be right.

Will it prejudice a truth in our eyes if it comes by way of Karl Marx? Well, we shall have to get over those prejudices if we are going to discover reality and through it victory. Marx propounded the idea of the unity of theory and practice. This means that you have only one theory and that is what you put into operation, at least in its beginnings. The only thing you really believe in is the thing you believe in sufficiently to put into operation—at least, in its beginnings. This unity of theory and practice searches to the depths and should prove a cleansing cathartic to Christendom.

Professor Macmurray says that the next great step forward for Christianity is to get rid of its idealism. As an earnest Christian he means it. Just what does he mean by it? His contention is that we have built up idealism as mental compensation for low practice. The very fact that we hold these high ideals gives us comfort that we are such persons as could be so lofty, at least, in ideal. This compensates for the real, and excuses us, or lets us down easy. This mental world becomes a world of phantasy while something else holds us in fact, because it holds at the place of act.

Is Professor Macmurray right? Must idealism go and realism take its place? Or can they be unified?

---

O Christ, we come needing guidance at this place. Help us to be willing to let go even our ideals if they interfere with reality. For we must be real. Amen.

## LOSING OUR IDEALS TO FIND THEM AGAIN

Yesterday we said that one of the first steps toward unity of life is to break down divorces between idealism and realism. One or the other must go, or they must come together. Macmurray says that idealism must go: "But the first step of all, on which everything else turns, is the total rejection of idealism." . . . "For idealism is profoundly irreligious, because it is the perversion of religion into unreality." . . . "The idealism of pseudo-Christianity consists in the divorce between hunger and love, through which love becomes an ideal, and hunger is left to control and determine action. Love becomes a sentiment or a feeling or the exaltation that accompanies the contemplation of an idea" (*Creative Society*, pp. 149, 151, 152).

If we lose idealism, does it mean that we should have no ideals? On the contrary, I think if we should lose idealism as something built up above and apart from life, if we should sow it into the soil of the real, our ideals would spring up again and flower into renewed beauty. We should lose them and find them again. Now we haven't them, for they stand apart from life; then we would have them, for they would be deeply rooted in life itself. Now they are castles in the air to be realized in some future age or future world; then they would become houses here and now for us to live in.

In suggesting this we find ourselves very, very close to Christ in our thought and spirit. For He had no idealism apart from realism. He says, "The words that I say unto you I speak not from myself: But the Father abiding in me doeth his works." Here "words" and "works" were used synonymously—His words were works. They were one.

They must become one in your life and mine. But how?

---

O Christ, Thou art searching us with Thy realism. Thou art calling us to overhaul and throw overboard useless thinking that we do not intend to put into operation. Help us not to ask for compromises. Help us to be true. Amen.

## THE APPLICATION OF THIS PRINCIPLE

Yesterday we ended by asking the question of how we could make our idealism and our realism one. Here we shall have to walk softly and ask for light and a transparent honesty.

First of all, we should take an inventory of our ideals which we think are now being used in our lives as mental compensation—things which are held to comfort us mentally, but not to guide us morally. We shall probably come across things like this: A little girl of three not wanting to go to bed, was hiding from her mother. She said to someone sitting near, "If my mother asks where I am, tell her I am not here, but don't tell a lie." That last phrase was idealism used as mental compensation for what she was doing. We will find many such things in our lives. At the close of a question period someone overheard a member of the audience saying as he passed out, "It is our business to ask questions, and it is his business to answer them, but none of us expect to do anything about it." This was searching. It showed that he believed that religion was idealism and not realism. We must end this hiatus.

As we go over our lives in the quietness before God and come across such things, we must renounce this idealism in the name of Christianity. It will hurt us to the very core to renounce our idealism, for it will mean that we will appear in our own eyes less good than we had led ourselves to believe. But at the very least there will be this gain—there will be a mental honesty. And that is the beginning of a fresh approach. So,

> "Down with every barrier,
> Off with every mask,
> Out with every sin, and,
> Away with every sterile ideal."

O Christ of the kindly searching eye, we open our lives to Thy gaze, and we open our wills to Thy full obedience. Help us to be completely honest and completely responsive. Then we can go forward. Amen.

## THE APPLICATION OF THIS PRINCIPLE TO THE SOCIAL ORDER

When we come to apply this principle of the unity of theory and practice to the social order, we shall find ourselves in difficulties, for here the realization of our ideals does not depend entirely on us. Other people are involved and social change must await their co-operation. What, then, can we as individuals do?

We can ask ourselves two questions: First, In what direction is my face turned? Is my attitude straight in regard to doing away with a competitive order in favor of a co-operative one? Am I really inwardly set against ghastly in-equalities between man and man? Am I inwardly committed to the wiping out of distinctions based on class and color? Have I inwardly renounced war? Am I inwardly free from the dominance of narrow nationalism? Am I inwardly set against all exploitation of man by man? Do I want to see all people free? Do I really want a brotherhood?

Second, what steps am I taking toward the making real of these inner attitudes in outer life? As far as it depends on me and on the circumstances which I control, am I, here and now, taking steps to end the things that are wrong? Am I going as far as I can in realizing the things that are right? I may not be at the goal, but am I on the way, with the con-sent of my whole being? Now?

This "now" is important. For without it, even the inten-tion to do it some time or other becomes a mental compensa-tion and therefore an opiate. "Of course we've got to do away with these injustices and inequalities, but then I don't suppose, at least I hope not, that it will be in my time," said a large landowner to me in India. There is no reality that hasn't a "now" in it. Am I prepared to put a "now" in all these intentions?

---

O Thou Who art the Alpha—the Christ of the beginnings —help me to begin here and now to take the right attitudes and to take the first steps. Used to living in two worlds, it will not be easy to begin in one. But help me to do it. Amen.

## THE UNITY OF THE SECULAR AND THE SACRED

One of the most disastrous divorces that ever took place in Christendom was the divorce between the sacred and the secular. In early Christianity they were one. When the disciples wanted men to look after the food arrangements, they said they must get men "of honest report, full of the Holy Ghost and wisdom," to look after this matter. Wisdom and the Holy Ghost were to be carried into the so-called secular and were to make it sacramental. All life was to be saved.

Now we have divided life into the sacred and secular, sacred callings and secular callings, sacred days and secular days, sacred buildings and secular buildings, sacred books and secular books. We thought thus to preserve both. In doing so we have impoverished both. The secular has become materialized, and the sacred etherialized, with the emphasis on the "ether." It has been the very devil's strategy thus to divide and rule. And he does rule where they are divided. We can never live victoriously as long as we try to live a compartmentalized life. They must be brought together. They need each other.

Wrote an earnest missionary: "When you write, show us how to live victoriously in such dull commonplaces as the keeping of books, attending to uninteresting details such as a missionary has to do. Can we not make the whole thing vicarious by the thought, that, if I do these things someone else will be spared the drudgery of them?" Very beautiful. And yet was there not still the lurking thought that the material was less and other than the spiritual, and that one goes into it as one takes up a cross? Instead, should it not be looked on as a part of one's spiritual life—that the spiritual life cannot be manifested except in and through the material? The word must become flesh or die as a word.

---

O Christ, in whom everything became one and in whom the commonplace was no longer the commonplace, but glowing with meaning and purpose, help us to make them one this day. Amen.

Exodus 31. 1–6
Romans 12. 1
1 Corinthians 6. 19, 20

# THE SACRED AND THE SECULAR LOOKED AT AGAIN

We cannot leave this cleavage between the sacred and the secular without pausing another day, for if we still keep them divided, then we are defeated indeed, and defeated where it counts most.

We often quote with approval the man who said that he made shoes to pay expenses while he served God. But should he not have thought of serving God through the making of the shoes? Was not that material thing itself to become the manifestation of the spiritual? Is not the thing that attracts us to Brother Lawrence the fact that he practiced the presence of God in and through the washing of his pans and the scrubbing of his floors? The Old Testament says that every pot in Jerusalem shall have "holiness unto the Lord" written upon it. And was not this the thing that Brother Lawrence fulfilled? His pans had just that written on them.

The business man must be able to handle his ledgers with the same sense of sacredness and mission as the minister handles the sacred Book in the pulpit. Of course that would mean the scrapping of many a business, for you cannot handle crookedness with sacredness. But it would be far better to scrap the business than to scrap one's soul. But legitimate business can be made a sacrament. "The extension of the incarnation" should mean just this: here today I stand in this business, in this workshop, in this schoolroom, to become the embodiment of the spirit of Christ in this situation. I shall work out His mind and spirit in my relationship with things and persons. As Peter offered his boat to Jesus to teach the multitudes from, so I offer to Him my boat, my business, my life from which He may teach in this situation the meaning of the Kingdom. I am an extension of the incarnation.

---

O Christ, we thank Thee that Thou canst make life glow with meaning when we take Thee into the whole of it. Help me this day to do that very thing. I shall need power. But I know I can bank on Thee. Amen.

Hebrews 10. 5—7     Romans 6. 13
1 Timothy 4. 8      Romans 12. 1

## THE UNITY OF BODY AND SOUL

We have been taking up one by one the places where there have been divisions, trying to see the possibility of bringing unity, and hence, power, into the total life. We now come to the division between the body and the soul.

The body has been looked upon as the enemy of the soul. It must be suppressed, sometimes mutilated, and finally laid aside with a sigh of relief for the freedom. Of someone it was said, "He seemed to be ashamed that he inhabited his body." Religion has often intensified this war between soul and body.

But not so in Jesus. There is not one word in the Gospels of this morbid idea concerning the body. Jesus accepted His body as He accepted His soul—gifts from God. "A body Thou hast prepared me." His body and His soul were attuned. He did not neglect His body, nor pamper it, nor suppress it—He offered it as the vehicle of God's will and purpose. And He kept it fit for God. There is no mention of His ever having been sick. Tired—yes, but never ill.

He, and not anaemic saints, must be our pattern for the way we are to act toward our bodies. Just enough food to keep us fit, and a little less than that which would keep us fat. Why carry excess luggage anyway? We may sometimes become ill, but we have no business to be more ill than we should be. For many of our ills are self-induced. They come from wrong mental attitudes. Just enough sleep to make us fresh, and a little less than that which would make us lazy. Enough exercise for fitness, with an eye on the fact that too much attention to sport may drain higher interests.

We must keep our bodies fit like a well-tuned violin, and then the music of God will come from every fiber of our being.

———

O Christ, we thank Thee that Thy body and Thy soul were not at cross purposes, so the ages bend low to catch the rhythm of that harmony. Help us to be the same. Amen.

## THIS IS MY BODY

One of the most astonishing things Jesus ever said was this: "Take, eat; this is my body." He offered His body for humanity to feed upon. It is an astonishing offer.

I would not dim the idea of the atonement in these words. That idea is there and we are grateful. But is this idea not there too: that He offered to feed men on the way He treated His body, the way He made his bodily appetites subserve the purposes of the Kingdom, the way He sublimated His sex impulses, and the way He kept pure in act and in thought—in short, does He not offer to men His whole bodily victory? Feed upon that fact, He says. And we do.

If we can say the same thing to others, then we are really knowing victory. Are we able to feed people at the place of our victories which we have in and through our bodies? Can we say to tempted and harassed people, "Take, eat of this victory I am gaining with my bodily appetites"? If so, we are in line of the succession of His spirit. We are an extension of the incarnation.

So when tempted today to indulge our passions in thought or in deed, we shall say: "No, this cannot be. For, if I do that, my lips will be sealed when someone comes to me to feed upon the fact of my victory. I shall have nothing to set before him. I cannot offer him the possibility of his feeding upon my soul, unless I can offer him the possibility of feeding upon my bodily triumphs. They both go together. I shall keep myself pure today, by feeding upon His victory, that some might feed upon mine. I cannot offer to people to feed upon the bitterness of my defeat. It must be victory."

O Christ of the pure body, make me like that. May no impure thought or deed this day incapacitate me for offering at eventide my victory to tempted souls. Keep me pure at the place of earth contacts. Amen.

## THIS IS MY BLOOD

Jesus said another astounding thing: "Drink ye all of it; for this is my blood." Again we repeat that the idea and the fact of the atonement are in those words. But is not this idea also there? He was beginning a new blood stream, a new heredity of a higher race, and that now we can have the source of our blood heredity, not in the tainted, contaminated past of which we are the unwilling inheritors, but in a new, pure, untainted source of inherited life.

My ancestry may be a poor, contaminated, streaky human line—whose isn't? So be it! But now I step into a new line from a new Ancestor. I am not a victim of the past—I begin a new line—in Him! "Christ is in my very blood," said a joyous Indian to me one day. Why not? More—He is my very blood! He becomes Life of my life, Blood of my blood when I assimilate Him in obedience and trust.

But this has another side to it. You and I must be able to say the same thing to others: "This is my blood—drink it. You will find coursing within my blood a new victory and a new purity—drink of that victory and of that newness." If this be so, then we must let no impurity, no disease get within our blood stream—it must be kept pure and healthy that the present and future generations may inherit from us a new heredity. So when tempted today you must say, "No, that would make me unfit at eventide to say to anyone, 'Drink of my life and of my new line.' No, for their sakes I sanctify myself—yea, my very blood, that I may be able to feed, not poison, this and coming generations."

"Christ is in my very blood." Is He? Then rejoice—and give it!

———

O Christ, I thank Thee that Thou canst offer to me Thy blood and that I belong to that new heredity. Help me to be worthy of such a line. And help me to hold within me the dignity of the life to which I belong. May a new humble pride possess me. Amen.

## BODILY SICKNESS—WHAT ATTITUDE?

Our victory should extend to our bodies. Our bodies should be as fit as possible. I say "as possible," for some are handicapped with a poor physical frame. Even so, it can be made better, perhaps well.

First of all, get rid of the idea that your sickness is God-sent. It isn't. God is fighting against disease. Christ never said sickness was the will of God—He cured it. The Kingdom of God is an offensive against everything that cripples life, including disease. Doctor Burnett Rao was right when he said, "If you believe that it is the will of God that you should be anything but well and healthy, that your sickness is God-sent, then obviously, however much you may develop the spiritual life, its power does not get through to the physical: you have put out the clutch." The *British Medical Journal* says that "there is not a tissue of the human body wholly removed from the influence of spirit." If so, we must let the power of our spiritual lives pour into the physical. "The Spirit . . . that . . . dwelleth in you . . . shall quicken also your mortal bodies." Other things being equal, the Christian should be healthier than the man who is not a Christian, for he has tapped a source of power for the body.

The greatest source of power for physical health is the absence of inward clash and strife in the spirit. Many people would be well physically if they were spiritually.

Hold, then, to these two things—your sickness is not the will of God, and it may depend on the state of your soul. Of course it may not. But if it does, the first step to physical health is to get rid of all inward clashes and complexes.

---

O Christ of the healthy soul and body, make us like that. May we pass on to our bodies no weariness of soul. May we be as healthy as Thou dost will us to be. Amen.

## ARE YOU TIRED?

Weatherhead quotes an African proverb which says, "Don't be tired tomorrow." Many of us are for we pass on mental states to the body.

A famous physician, who has cured thousands in her Sanitarium, says that nature balances up the accounts about every twenty-four hours. That is, if you are tired and will give nature twenty-four hours of rest, it will throw off the fatigue toxins within that time. She says that you do not lay up fatigue toxins for weeks and months, that if you did, you would not be a tired man, you would be a dead man. Beyond the twenty-four hours the tiredness is in the mind. Up to that time there is a physical basis for the tiredness, after that it is mental and spiritual. She therefore pooh-poohs the idea of lying up for weeks and months for bodily rest. Twenty-four hours will do the trick, provided the soul is adjusted and harmonious. It is amazing what the body can stand if the soul is unified. Most people do not wear out from overwork, but from under-being.

"How do you do it?" asked a colleague as we started on a speaking tour. "Well," I replied, "there are two ways to do it—one is the way the railway engines get their water in India: they stop at the station, take time off and thus get their water tanks filled; the other is the way the engines get water in America—they scoop it up as they run." "All right," she said, "I'll do it. I'll scoop it up—I'll take the power and victory of Christ as I go along." She did, and it worked. Say to yourself, not merely as you fall asleep at night, but again and again throughout the day, "I can do all things through Christ which strengtheneth me." Its balm will soothe your nerves and will quicken every fiber of your being.

---

O Thou Who didst go through the strain of the day without strain, give us that inward sense of Thy healing quiet upon our spirits, that we may be ready for anything. Amen.

Exodus 23. 25    Proverbs 17. 22
Psalm 105. 3     Matthew 8. 7
JULY 13            Matthew 9. 12

## HOW DOES GOD HEAL?

The healing of God does not flow in one channel only. He heals in many ways. He heals by physicians, by surgeons, by climate, by mental suggestion, by the direct touch of the Spirit upon our bodies, and by common sense.

By "common sense" I mean that, while God gives grace to undertake greater tasks than we are normally fitted for, nevertheless He may be saying to us through this sickness: "Lighten up. You are carrying too heavy a load." You cannot do everything, and, it may be that by doing less, you can do the worth-while thing better. There is the positive duty of sometimes refusing to do good. If we find that we have "too much on our plate," then we must take less—take only as much as we can digest. We must go to the limit of our strength, but then we must watch our margins, and not to go beyond them.

Common sense told me years ago that if I was to get exercise in the kind of work I was doing, I should have to get it at night just before going to bed, for it was the one time I was sure of. I found that it not only gave me exercise, but it took the blood out of my brain, distributed it through the system, and my mind thus relaxed went off to sleep at once. Whereas, if I lay there with brain congested, it continued active—and sleepless. Common sense will tell us many other things about the physical bodies we live with, and we must obey that common sense. It is one of God's methods of healing. It is not a spectacular method, but often God comes along some very lowly, dusty roads to us. And we must not despise His coming because He came to us along a lowly road.

---

O Christ, Thou didst call Thy disciples aside to rest from the many things and the many people; help us not to despise this call of Thine as Thou dost call us to Thy side for rest, and perhaps the letting go of the many things that we may do the one thing well. Amen.

## HOW DOES GOD HEAL?—Continued

Christian people have often brought discredit on Christian healing by choosing one way alone, perhaps healing by the method of prayer, and treating lightly or rejecting the other methods. This is a mistake. Nor should doctors despise the method of prayer, but lay hold on it and use it.

For God does sometimes touch the body directly through prayer. When asked to pray for a lady who was in the last stages of tuberculosis, I replied that I could not pray for her physical healing unless she were willing for Christ to heal her soul. I am not sure I was right in demanding that condition, for Jesus did not make such a demand in His healing. Anyway, she was more than ready to meet that demand and did, so I prayed for her healing. In two months she had gained twenty pounds, and became the mother of a lovely family.

A girl had a cancer on her tongue which had been cut out and burnt out ten times. After she had just given herself to Christ, and as we were still in prayer, I had an intuition that God would heal her. I leaned over and asked if she didn't believe God would heal her. "Why, He has," she said in glad astonishment. And He had! I called in a doctor who had known the case in the hospital, and telling him nothing that had happened, asked him to examine her. After examination, he turned to us and said, "She's well." "What would you say, doctor, if we told you that God had healed her?" we asked. "Well," he said very thoughtfully, "I couldn't say anything against it."

But science should go further: it should say something in favor of it, and use it. And Christians in turn should look on the ways of healing through science as God's ways—and use them. For God wills health.

---

O Christ, whose seamless robe is by our beds of pain, we pray Thee to help us to touch it in faith and rise into health. Amen.

## TWENTY-NINTH WEEK

**JULY 15**

Philippians 4. 6    1 Peter 5. 7
Psalm 127. 2    Psalm 37. 8 (R. V.)

## LIVING RELAXED

In our quest after victorious living one of the most important things to learn is to live inwardly relaxed. This age seems against it. Its whole demand is high tension, high pressure. So we do not die of the diseases our forefathers died of—we go at high pressure until the boiler bursts. Nervous diseases and heart failure are the outcomes of inner tensions. And all this destroys not only the body but the mind and soul as well. For freedom and efficiency depend upon relaxation.

A bee was beating itself upon my windowpane in a frantic endeavor to get out to freedom. I tried in vain to rescue it, but the more I tried, the more it beat its head against the windowpane. Finally it fell to the windowsill exhausted. And, lo, as the window was raised a bit, it crawled out and immediately flew away to freedom. Until it relaxed and let go, it could find no freedom. Some of us are all inwardly tight, screwed up and frantically beating ourselves against the windowpanes of our circumstances and tasks, and vainly trying to find freedom and power. We shall never get it till we let go. So the phrase, "Let go, let God," is more than a catch-phrase, it has sound wisdom in it. A missionary came to our Ashram with a serious, drawn countenance. He did so want to be good and effective as a missionary, but both goodness and effectiveness eluded him the more earnestly he pursued them. He was getting nowhere. I saw at a glance where the difficulty lay, got him to relax and trust—which, of course, meant a self-surrender—and, lo, goodness and effectiveness are now his. He is a relaxed soul!

Relaxation means that you have ceased to worry. You are trusting, and trusting means drawing on the inexhaustible resources of God.

---

O Christ, we thank Thee that amid all the strain of things Thou didst have the relaxed spirit. Give that to us, that we too may fully live. Amen.

JULY 16

Psalm 112. 7
Isaiah 26. 3
Isaiah 30. 15

Romans 15. 13
Philippians 4. 7
Mark 4. 38

## MORE ABOUT LIVING RELAXED

I once had a new stenographer, an Indian youth, who was so eager to do well that he pressed so hard upon his pencil that the whole table shook. I watched the pathetic performance for some time, stopped him, and said: "You'll never be a good stenographer unless you cease trying so hard. Now, let go, and relax, and believe that you can do it, and let the pencil glide smoothly and naturally across the paper." We laughed together, and that laugh helped to let go the tension, and in a little while he had improved amazingly.

Someone has said, "Watch a young lady trying hard not to blush, or a speaker without experience trying to address a meeting, or a novice trying to hit a golf ball, or a patient trying to go to sleep, or a person trying to remember a name —the secret of mastery is not in the flogging of the will." In each of these cases relaxation would have brought release.

Jesus said, "Which of you by taking thought can add one cubit unto his stature?" He had probably seen little boys, who wanted to be big, trying with bursting cheeks and bulging eyes, to grow taller, so through it He talked to us grown-ups about the folly of it all. Live relaxed, He said.

A very able musician told me that her teacher insisted that every muscle must be relaxed, so that her very soul could come into her fingertips. Then there was mastery. Some live spiritually that way. They let the very power of Christ into every portion of their being—and it is all done so easily. But, oh, how effective!

Jesus was so relaxed that the power of God had an unhindered channel within Him. Spiritual relaxation meant spiritual release. The machinery of life can be oiled by the peace of God, so runs without friction.

----

O Christ, I come to Thee for strength to be weak, for courage to let go, and through it find Thy power in every portion of my being. Amen.

JULY 17

2 Samuel 23. 5
Psalm 3. 3–6
Psalm 16. 1, 8, 11

2 Timothy 1. 12
Psalm 18. 32

## RELAXED IN OUR WORK

I was once asked to give an address on the technique of my work among the educated non-Christians. I was puzzled, for I really did not know I had a technique! But it made me think, and I suppose the center of the technique is just this relaxed spirit. When I began my work, this word was given me: "And ye shall be brought before governors and kings for a . . . testimony against them; . . . take no thought how or what ye shall speak; for it shall be given you in that same hour what ye shall speak. For it is not you that speak, but the spirit of your Father which speaketh in you." I felt that I could utterly bank on that—and have. And I cannot remember a single situation in these years where this verse has not proven true. As I walked home from a tense meeting in which I had spoken for an hour, and very keen non-Christians, especially militant there, had cross-examined me in no gentle way for two more hours, a lady missionary said to me: "I'm physically exhausted from that meeting tonight. I didn't know what they were going to ask next, and I didn't know what you were going to answer, so I have been sitting up in the gallery holding on to the bench with all my might for two solid hours, and I'm physically exhausted." I could reply: "Why, my sister, I was having the time of my life. I had no fears or worries whatever. I knew my verse would hold true." And it did! My chief opponent said at the close, "You may be able to answer his arguments, but what are you going to do with this calm confidence, this unruffled assurance and peace? Only the power of Christ can give that." He was right! Amid the rough-and-tumble of things, by His grace I had learned something—it was inward relaxation, in other words, faith.

---

O Christ, give to me more and more this day this assurance that will take away all worry, all strain, all clash, and make me at Thy best. Amen.

## RELAXED AMID OPPOSITION

It is comparatively easy to be relaxed in one's work, but amid opposition, sometimes unfair, it is not so easy. I have often fallen down at this place, but where I have been able to retain it, it has worked amazingly.

A missionary who always felt that he must steady the ark lest the whole thing fall to pieces if he didn't, said at the close of a meeting: "I do not see how he can stand to have the chairman at the close pick to pieces everything he says and kill the whole thing. I would not tolerate it." But I could tolerate it simply because I knew he couldn't "kill" it. My brother thought he had to defend the faith, but the fact is that he didn't have faith in the faith! Had he, he would not have fretted and worried. Across the years I have watched hostile chairmen try to take advantage of their position and spike everything I had to say, and just as often have they broken their own necks before the audience. In the very audience mentioned above the reaction was so strong against the college principal who took unfair advantage that the non-Christians themselves said he was no longer fit to be their college principal. There is an innate fairness in every heart, however smothered it may be, and we can depend on that to give its verdict.

I could not be relaxed amid this opposition if the message were my own, for there I could not be sure. But where one is proclaiming the message of Christ, however poor and partial his interpretation may be, he knows that he has at the core of that message something eternal, something standing within Time and yet above Time, something that does not need to be defended, but to be proclaimed and lived, something that is self-verifying. Therefore he can be relaxed even amid opposition.

———

O Christ, Thou who didst stand amid the crowd at the judgment hall, the only calm one amid that howling crowd, give me this day a touch of that assurance, that calm. Amen.

## SHALL WE LET DOWN TENSIONS?

But, someone objects, this talk of living relaxed is liable to let down tensions between us and our ideals. Are not the tension points the growing points? If, therefore, we let down tensions, shall we not cease to grow and become flabby? Is not the ideal of strenuous endeavor better than that of inward relaxation?

Our objector is right in saying that we must keep up places of tension in the moral life. Without them we do not grow and ours is an ideal of ceaseless and eternal growth. But Jesus emphasized this very thing when He said, "Consider the lilies of the field, how they grow." The emphasis was on the method of their growth—"how they grow." They do not grow by trying to grow by working themselves up into a frenzy of endeavor, by anxiety and worry—they grow by obeying the laws of their own nature and by absorption from without. Do the same, says Jesus; obey the laws of the Kingdom now within you, draw sustenance—and calm. The fact is that you cannot draw sustenance unless there is relaxation and trust. The agitated soul is the poverty-stricken soul.

We must remember that it is the calm and relaxed people who are the strenuous people. Strenuous, but not strained. They tell us that at the very center of a twisting cyclone is a place of absolute calm. It is the place where the resident forces of the cyclone reside. Out of that calm comes the power of the cyclone. Out of the relaxed, co-ordinated spirit comes the power that reshapes the world.

Jesus was never so powerful, never so consonant with His call, never so gripping as He stood before Pilate calm and silent. That calmness, that silence is not flabby—it is dynamic. Out of it come the resident forces that reshape the world.

---

O Christ, I know that if I am fussy in my endeavors today, I shall not reshape the world around me. Give me Thy calm—and Thy dynamic. I shall be weak with only one. I must have both. Amen.

## RELAXED UNDER BURDENS

Years afterward I looked up the forty-second page of the book, *The Christian's Secret of a Happy Life*, to see what was on it, for it was at that page that life began anew for me. I found it saying that if you should go to bed and should lie there with all your muscles taut and strained because you were afraid the bed would break down under you, you would not rest, but would get up in the morning exhausted. You have to trust to rest. Some people are still holding themselves inwardly taut, afraid that if they let go, the grace of God won't sustain them. So they live exhausted lives, worn out from within.

An old woman trudged along the road with a heavy pack upon her back, when a man in a wagon overtook her and offered her a lift. Grateful beyond words she climbed in, but sat there still holding her burden on her back. When the man suggested that she put it in the back of the wagon, she replied, "Oh, but it is so kind of you to carry me, I don't want to make you carry my burden too. I'll carry that." We smile at the old lady, and yet how many of us do just as she did! We believe that the grace of God can save our souls, but we do not trust that same grace to carry our daily burdens, our daily cares and anxieties, the worries of business and of the home—these we still continue to keep on our own backs. Exhausted souls! From out of childhood days I can only remember this one quotation spoken from the Bible by my mother, "Casting all your care upon him; for he careth for you." That was enough to remember, for I saw her do that very thing—she did cast all her care upon Him, else how would she have gone through it all?

---

O Christ, Thou dost offer to carry us and our burdens. Help us to surrender our burdens as well as ourselves. For Thou wilt carry both! We thank Thee. Amen.

## DISTRESSED AND SCATTERED

We have been saying that there is no possibility of victorious living unless we are inwardly unified, no longer at inward strain but relaxed. This verse of Jesus diagnoses our condition and suggests the remedy: "But when he saw the multitudes, he was moved with compassion for them, because they were distressed and scattered, as sheep not having a shepherd" (Matthew 9. 36, 37). "Distressed"—inwardly at strain, literally, "drawn in different directions"—no inward unity. "Scattered"—no outer unity.

Here are the two things lacking in mankind: inner and outer unity, at peace with oneself, and at peace with one's fellow men. And the reason for this condition then was and now is: "No shepherd," the lack of a center around which life can find its inner and outer unity. Until we can absolutely center in some perfect Life we shall lack unity. That center can only be Christ.

Even the religious world of the West is distressed and scattered because it is often missing this center. Religious men jump from issue to issue, from emphasis to emphasis, from doctrine to doctrine, and the whole thing lacks coherency, unity. If they would take their stand at Christ and work out from Him to these issues, emphases and doctrines, then there would be coherency, because there would be a center. Put one point of the compass on the cross and let the other point take as wide a sweep as you will, then you will be coherent and vital and inclusive.

Moreover, life needs a personal, enduring Friendship to keep it centered and immovably fixed. Christ offers Himself as that Friend. When our love is completely and utterly fastened on Him, we are no longer lonely, no longer drawn in different directions, no longer at war with ourselves. We have found a center—a center of unity. And I see no center for outer unity in the world save as the sons of men find it around the Son of man.

---

O Christ, Thou art our Center as Thy power alone can hold the centrifugal forces of our souls from breaking our unity. Hold us, and we are held. Amen.

Isaiah 8. 11–13
Proverbs 1. 33
1 John 4. 18

## FEAR—THE DESTROYER OF INNER UNITY

Of all the things that destroy inner unity fear is perhaps the most devastating and the most prevailing. We saw that there was a biological fear which tended to efficiency, but there are other fears which paralyze. The victory over fear is an essential part of our victory in victorious living. Without it there is no victorious living, for fears divide us and paralyze us.

As I was speaking before an audience a very intelligent and beautiful Parsee lady on the front bench fainted away. I wondered what I had said to cause her thus to faint, but on inquiry found it was this: as she sat there the face of a woman, whom she greatly feared, came before her, and as a result she fainted away. All her culture, all her intelligence, all the spiritual atmosphere of that meeting were nothing before that fear. Nature retreated into a faint.

A very able American doctor in Ceylon told me of one of his patients, a wealthy man upon whom he had operated and who was ready to be discharged from the hospital as cured. But his astrologer, whom he had with him, said the crisis would come the following week and therefore he should not leave the hospital. The next week he died—died from no other apparent reason except fear. Fear had snapped the will to live within him and killed him. A man accosted the Cholera who was returning from a devastating visit to a city: "How many died?" he asked. "Eighty thousand," Cholera replied, "but I touched only twenty thousand." "And the rest?" "Oh, they died from fear."

There is no doubt that fear is the most paralyzing thing in human life. "I was afraid, and I went and hid my talent." Fear paralyzes us and paralyzes our endeavors.

We must gain victory over all fears—can it be done? Yes, thank God—yes!

***

O Christ, I thank Thee that I need not be the victim of any fear. But teach me the clear road to that victory and I shall walk in it. Amen.

## FEARS FROM EARLY SHOCKS

Some of our fears come from early shocks. The mind, always wishing to forget the unpleasant, drops the incident that caused the shock down into the subconscious mind and closes the door upon it. There it works its silent havoc, causing nervousness and general upset.

Weatherhead tells of an officer who during the war would stand on the parapet of the trench rather than get down into the dugout. Some thought it bravery, but it was really fear —fear of a closed place. He found the reason: when a child he met in a narrow alleyway a fierce dog which attacked him. That attack in a narrow alley left a fear of closed places upon him.

Now, what is to be done with a fear like that? Repress it? Try to forget it? Nothing worse. It must be brought up to the surface and faced. The incident must be gently and quietly looked at. That bringing it up and looking at it will draw its sting. It will be seen as a childhood incident, with no right to being the basis of a lifelong fear. The complex is dissolved. The incident is related to the rest of the life.

A lady missionary seeking the victorious life was found to have a dread of deep water, and therefore never learned to swim. On inquiry I found that in early childhood she came near drowning, and it had left a shock and with it a fear. Obviously, there could be no fully victorious life until that fear complex was dissolved. And the only way to dissolve it was by learning to swim and by going into deep water, which she did. So she dropped her fear into the deep, deep lake! And it has never troubled her again.

---

O Christ, I come to Thee to take from my inner consciousness all basis of fear, for I know I have no business to be afraid of anything—of anything if Thou art my Redeemer. Amen.

## THE FEAR OF THE HERD

The fear of the herd suppresses Christians and makes them conform to the average, and the average is always below Christ's way. We take on "protective resemblance" to our environment and fit in, become mediocre, and are slowly de-Christianized. We are afraid of being queer. And yet it is just that queerness that may be necessary to save you and the herd. For often the herd survives only when some member becomes different and shows a higher method of survival.

Nevertheless, the herd demands conformity, and it will persecute those who depart from its standards. Fall below its standards and it will punish you, rise above them and it will persecute you. Or it may ridicule you. And sometimes that is worse. A French officer, riding in front of his lines inspecting his troops, was thrown off his restive horse in an ungainly fashion. The troops laughed. The officer went and resigned his commission. He could not stand ridicule. But a simple laugh on his part would have saved the situation.

And that suggests the remedy—when ridiculed, simply laugh back, knowing that in the end you will laugh longest and perhaps loudest. You have a better basis for laughter. But deeper still, to get rid of the fear of the herd we must surrender the herd, we must acknowledge in our inmost spirit no dominance save that of Jesus Christ. After I had become a Christian I went past the crowd on the street with whom I had associated and one of them called out in derision, "Hello, Stanley, going down to see Jesus?" "Yes, I am," I quietly replied, to their astonishment and my own. But I knew in my heart of hearts that by that defiance the fear of the herd was broken. I was free—not only from them, but to come back to them with what I had.

---

O Christ, deliver me from the fear of what the herd will say, and give me a deeper susceptibility to what Thou shalt say. For I must be delivered from all fear. Amen.

214

## THE FEAR OF FAILURE

Like the one-talented man, many do not attempt anything with their talents because they are afraid of failure if they did. So, like this man, who went off and "dug a hole in the ground," they too end in emptiness and futility—a hole in the ground. Fear produces the very failure that we fear. Many do not start the Christian life because they are afraid they would fail if they did. So they never start. Fear feeds on failure and failure feeds on fear.

To know victorious living we must conquer this fear of failure. But how? First of all by looking at it at its worst. Suppose you should fail, would you be any worse off than now? Hardly. Because in a world of this kind by doing nothing you are now failing, for to do nothing is failure. By doing nothing you are living in a constant state of failure. Again, suppose you did fail in obeying what you felt was the call of God, would you really fail? Hardly, for your very obedience is success. It is not your business whether you succeed or fail—it is your business to be true to the call of God as you know it. Results are in His hands. Besides, God has a way of turning even failure into ultimate victory. The cross is the world's supreme failure. When He dropped His head on His pulseless bosom and died, everything had crashed. But had it? Ask your own heart! If it is like mine, it clings to that Failure as the one hope of the race. So God has a way of turning the cross of your failure into supreme success. The seed sown fails and dies, but in its failure a new life springs up.

Therefore away with fear and forward with Christ! Where? Anywhere, provided it be forward!

---

O Thou who didst see Thy Kingdom crash about Thee on the cross and still didst hold Thy heart above the crash of things, give us the power this day to be unafraid of fear. Amen.

215

## THE FEAR OF DESTITUTION IN OLD AGE

In a competitive order fear of destitution in old age is real. Almost all of this fear could be cured by collective action. In a world of plenty no one has a right to be haunted by the fear of what will happen to him in old age. One day we shall provide for honest destitution in old age and banish it, and with it the fear that accompanies it. But in the meantime, what shall we do?

Feverishly pile up to provide against it, is the world's answer. Hardly the Christian answer, for by my having more than I need, someone has less than he needs. The Christian conscience can scarcely stand for that. Jesus said, "Seek ye first the kingdom of God, and his righteousness; and all these things shall be added unto you." What were "these things"? Food and clothing. He guarantees you those two things—not motor cars and fine houses—if you put His Kingdom first. Aren't these two things enough for life? Listen to Epictetus: "Is it possible for a man who is naked and homeless, without a wife, without a country, to be happy? See, God has sent such a man to Rome to teach you that it is possible. I possess nothing but heaven and earth and this old cloak. But what do I want? Do any of you see me going about with a sad countenance?" If a pre-Christian can say that, then how much more a Christian? Will you starve? I have lived in the poorest country on earth for twenty-nine years, and while there may have been people dying of starvation during that time, I haven't seen one. How much possibility is there that I shall see you as that one? Besides, if you should die of starvation in serving God, haven't others died for Him a martyr's death? Then why not a martyr's death by starvation? Even at its worst, it might be glorious! Then away with fear! Your Father lives.

---

O Christ, I thank Thee that I can live, as Thou didst live, a happy, trustful child of the Father, without fear. Help me to begin it today. Amen.

## THE FEAR OF BEING DEPENDENT ON OTHERS

There are many who, while not afraid for themselves, are afraid that their actions in obeying God will cause suffering to those whom they love. I saw a man in a crisis decide his whole life course on the basis of the fear that to take the higher course might cause inconvenience to his family. It was a tragic mistake. Our obedience to Christ is bound to cause suffering to those whom we love. We are all bound up in a bundle of life together, and we cannot wait to act till we can be sure that we alone will get the consequences. If we did, we should never act.

Jesus' acting on the will of God involved His whole family in a cross—and also in a resurrection! It will work both ways.

A part of this fear of hurting others is the fear of being dependent on others in old age. Some of this springs from a false pride. We don't want to be dependent. Nonsense. We are all dependent, every moment of our lives, both on God and man. To act as if we weren't is silly, superficial pride. If we honestly contribute to others during our earning period, why shouldn't others contribute to us when we need it? Besides, you took care of this younger generation when it was helpless, why shouldn't this younger generation take care of you when you are old and helpless? It will probably do them good to have this responsibility; may save them from selfish isolation. So the crucifixion of your pride may turn out for their redemption. Moreover, if you accept the situation joyously and sweetly, you may be the kind of person they will delight to take care of—and would miss you if they didn't have the opportunity.

Then away with all fear of being dependent—be dependent on God and man, and do it joyously.

---

O Christ, we thank Thee that Thou hast shown us the way. Thou didst break the heart of Thy mother—and didst make it well again. Help us to launch out with Thee, no matter the cost—and to whom. Amen.

## NEGATIVISM

Another form of fear which modern psychology describes is Negativism. People with inner conflicts find it hard to be positive in their attitudes and decisions, so they retreat into the negative. When a proposition or opportunity is presented to them, their first impulse is to reject it. Almost everything comes to them difficulty—foremost. As a consequence they live in an almost chronic state of "No." They cannot gather up the forces of the soul within themselves sufficiently to say, "Yes." They are negative natures.

Such negative natures cannot lead others. It is the positive, hopeful, affirmative type that becomes a leader of others. Besides, to be negative is to be unchristian. The Christian is positive, affirmative, hopeful. Sometimes he does say, "No," but only to say a greater, "Yes." Paul felt the sheer hopefulness, the sheer affirmative nature of the gospel and said, "In Him is the yes," or, as Moffatt puts it, "In Him the Divine Yes has sounded." To be in Him, then, is to take a positive attitude toward life.

This morning in my daily reading I read this: "Judas then, having received the band of soldiers, and officers from the chief priests and the Pharisees, cometh thither with lanterns and torches and weapons. Jesus therefore, knowing all the things that were coming upon him, went forth." "Jesus . . . knowing all the things that were coming upon him"—did what? Prepared to compromise? to escape? to soften the blow? No, "went forth" to meet it! At the moment of the great "No," the betrayal, He was positive. Be positive even in the face of impending calamity. Wring out of it a victory. Keep affirming to yourself, "I can do all things through Christ which strength neth me." Then your negative fears will drop off before the rising sap of a new, abundant, affirmative life. For the Christian belongs to the great affirmation.

O Christ, I thank Thee that in Thy company my negative fears are dissolved and I feel that anything—anything is possible. Help me to catch this spirit this day—from Thee. Amen.

1 Timothy 1. 5
Psalm 119. 45
2 Corinthians 3. 17, 18 ; 4. 1, 2

## THE BASIS OF THESE FEARS

All of the fears we have been looking at are rooted in one thing—inward division. The inwardly united soul has no fears. What is the basic remedy proposed?

There are two great modern answers which are strangely alike: One comes from Walter Lippmann and the other from Mahatma Gandhi. Lippmann says, School your desires, don't expect too much, contract the area of your expectations and hopes, and then life won't hit you on too wide a front, and your fears will thus be lessened. His remedy is, Pull in. Mahatma Gandhi, on the other hand, following the Gita, says, Stand inwardly aloof, without desire for the fruit of action. His remedy for fear is, Pull apart.

The answer of the gospel? It is this: "Love has in it no element of fear; but perfect love drives away fear, . . . and if a man gives way to fear, there is something imperfect in his love" (1 John 4. 18, Weymouth). Perfect love drives away fear! The answer is not Pull in, or Pull apart, but Pull out all the stops! Expand through perfect love. That expansion drives out all fear. The answer of the gospel is in line with its own nature—it is positive, affirmative, expansive.

But first it contracts. It narrows its love down to one Person—that Person, God, through Christ. "The love of Christ narrows me," says Paul. We become single-pointed, with one consuming passion that eats up the lesser passions in the life. This love of Christ fuses the divisions of the soul into a burning unity. There is no room for inner fear, for there is no room for inner division. Division confuses, love fuses. Fear cannot live in this fire of love—this love that wants nothing and is therefore afraid of nothing. Wants nothing—except Him. Bowing before Him, we now bow before nothing else. Unafraid.

———

O Thou, who hast conquered our inmost being, we thank Thee that no fear can now make us afraid. For nothing can separate us from the love of Christ—nothing. Amen.

## FEARS AND DIVIDED LOYALTY

There is no deliverance from fears unless there is an undivided loyalty to Christ. Perfect love literally does cast out fear, and, vice versa, imperfect love admits fear into the heart. This is vividly brought home to us in the Transfiguration scene. The Jewish heart of Peter was divided in its loyalty, wanting to keep Moses, representing the law; Elijah, representing the Prophets; and Jesus, representing the new Revelation, all on the same level—"Let us build three tabernacles." This was serious, for the whole of the future was bound up with the question of whether Jesus was final and whether supreme allegiance should be given to Him.

The moment that division came a cloud overshadowed them, "and they feared as they entered the cloud." That inner division brought clouds and fears. Then God speaks out of the cloud.

Where there is division there will be clouds and fears. Take the international situation today. Why are we so overshadowed with war clouds and why do we fear as we enter those clouds? The answer is simple—division. Each nation is thinking in terms of itself, is losing a sense of the collective unity, selfish nationalism emerges and controls, and hence world division. The result? Clouds come over us and we fear as we enter those clouds. And no wonder! But out of those clouds comes a Voice. God speaks! And because we would not listen to the voice of God as it spoke through intelligent reason, now we must listen to His voice as He speaks to us through the roaring of the cannon and the crash of our civilization. The Voice is one of judgment and invitation. It is this: "This is my beloved Son, . . . hear ye him." And those clouds will never lift and those fears will never depart until we do listen to Christ.

———

O God, Thou art speaking out of the clouds today. We tremble at Thy voice of judgment. Help us not merely to tremble but to obey. Save us from our divisions. Amen.

## THE CLOUDS OVER THE ECONOMIC LIFE

Today clouds hang over our economic life—unemployment, glutted markets, scarcity, depression, fears. Why? The reason is simple: division. Those in control of the organization of our economic structure, thinking they held the whip hand, intercepted too much of the gains that science and technique had brought and kept them from passing on to the people. A cleavage went clear through society between "the haves" and "the have-nots." The result? A cloud of depression hangs over our economic life and the brooding fears underneath that cloud are terrifying. And now God speaks out of this cloud of depression. Let Doctor Horton interpret that Voice: "Is it tenable, one may ask, that God should be at once a God of wrath and a God of love? Has He two hands, one iron-gloved, the other warm and human? Is it conceivable that He should alternately woo us with the one and strike us with the other? Could we believe this, we might hear Him saying to this generation in tones of mingled sorrow and anger, 'You must and shall have deeper fellowship in your social order. You may take it *this* way (stretching out the right hand), or you may take it this way (clenching the left fist). If you will hear my word, you may make the great soulless machine of your industrial civilization an instrument for the common good and a bond of fellowship between you; but if not, then I will smash your civilization, and reduce you to a primitive level of existence, where you *must* recover the art of fellowship, which your pioneering forefathers knew and you have lost'" (*Realistic Theology*, p. 112). In other words, God is speaking out of the cloud of this depression: "This is my Son; hear ye Him." And unless we do, that cloud will never lift and those fears will never depart.

———

**O God, why cannot we listen to Thy still small voice? Why must we have to listen to Thy voice of wrath as it speaks through our calamities? Forgive us. Amen.**

## THE CLOUD OVER OUR CHURCHES

No one has to argue that there is a cloud over the church life of Christendom. Our vague uneasiness has grown into a fear that all is not well. Why? Again, divided loyalty, inner division.

The divided loyalty is this: In each nation, instead of keeping the gospel of Christ in a framework of universal reference, we have more and more identified it with national cultures. The conquest of the gospel of Christ by local national cultures is going on apace, and this process means the slow de-Christianization of our churches. On the "Antioch Cup," which is claimed by some to be the original Holy Grail, the figure of Christ is seen sitting above the Roman eagle. That was the position Christ occupied in those early centuries— He was first and the nation was second. Today the nation is using the national culture for its own ends, and because the Church has become so domesticated, so identified with that national culture, it is using the Church too for its nationalistic ends. "A process which began with a culture molded by religious faith has ended with a religious faith molded by a national culture." Dr. Francis Miller puts it this way: "The irony of the situation is that Protestants now find themselves in exactly the same position as the Catholics four hundred years ago. The Catholics mistook static ecclesiastic forms for the content of their faith. The Protestants are mistaking dynamic cultured forms for the content of their faith. And the triumph of cultural forms over the religious content is even more deadly than the triumph of ecclesiastic forms." We are divided between Christ and national culture. Which is supreme?

Again the clouds come over us and again the Voice speaks: "This is my Son; hear Him." And until we do the clouds will not lift and our fear will not depart. For Christ must be first.

---

O God, Caesar comes again, clothed in national culture, and demands our supreme allegiance. Help us not to bend the knee. Amen.

## THE CLOUD OVER OUR CHURCHES—Continued

But the division within Christendom is not merely between allegiance to the national culture and the allegiance to Christ, there is division between the churches themselves. The household of Christ is divided against itself. And as a result of our family divisions a cloud has come over us, and under that cloud we are fearful, and for good reason, for a divided Church has little moral authority in a divided world. We must adjust our differences or abdicate our moral leadership.

I asked a missionary how they ever got hold of such a lovely piece of property and received this reply: "The man who owned it built such high and expensive walls around it that he went bankrupt building the walls and had to sell the property." "Bankrupt building the walls"! Is that not dangerously near the history of the Christian churches today?

We have so exhausted our resources in putting up ecclesiastical walls between ourselves and others, and in keeping them in repair, that we have little left to use in helping redeem a world. If the time and intelligence and soul-force which we have expended in proving that we were right as against our brethren had been expended in united action against the problems that now confront the world, they would not now be so far from solution. And we would be leading the procession of events instead of being led by them.

These divisions have brought a cloud over our religious life—dark, rainless clouds, clouds that presage storms of revolt, clouds that produce fear. God is today speaking out of that cloud and His voice is as of old: "This is my Son, hear Him." And what does that Son say: "Father, I will that they may be one." When we become one, the clouds will lift. But not till then.

----

O God, our Father, forgive us that we Thy children have set up walls against each other. Help us to feel and act upon the solidarity of Thy family. Amen.

## CLOUDS OVER THE PERSONAL LIFE

We have looked at the clouds over the collective life; we must now look within and see if there are any cloud-producing divisions left within ourselves.

It may be that you have started to pay the full price of victory and then have drawn back. That hesitation has meant a division, and that division has meant a cloud, and that cloud has meant a fear.

In South India the temples are usually in the form of a hollow square with high, beautiful ornate tower-gates on the four sides. I noticed that one of those tower gates was closed and apparently never used. The reason was that the rich man who was presenting the tower gate to the god sat down in the midst of the building of it and began to count how much it was costing him. This offended the god—the idea that anyone should ever count the cost of a gift to him! So he refused to be taken out in procession through that gate, and since it was deserted by the god, it is now deserted by man. A cloud of uselessness and decay is upon it.

Perhaps you have felt that same cloud of spiritual uselessness and decay over your inner life, and perhaps you realize it is there for the same reason—you have counted the cost and have hesitated to pay the full price. You are willing to give, but not to give up. You have prayed very hard that the cloud might lift, but it doesn't, and it won't. But there is one saving factor—God is speaking to you out of that cloud, and His voice is this: "This is my Son; hear ye Him." And if we cease our hesitations and listen to that voice, we shall lift up our eyes and see no man save Jesus only. He will then have our complete allegiance. And there will be neither clouds nor fears.

———

O Christ, we know that Thou wilt only fill our horizons when Thou dost fill our hearts. Help me to let Thee fill my heart undividedly. Amen.

## THE UNDIVIDED IN HEART SEE GOD

"Blessed are the pure in heart: for they shall see God."
The word "pure" literally means "the undivided." When the
disciples listened to the voice of God, became united in their
inner allegiance, then their uplifted eyes saw Jesus and Him
alone. But many of us refuse to listen to that Voice, and so
the cloud lingers and the fears cling. The reason we don't
listen is because we are listening to something else—something closer by.

I paused in writing the above paragraph to call down to a
workman who was carrying some old tin sheets upon his head,
but no matter how loudly I and others who joined me called
he did not hear, for the sound of the near rattling of the tin
was in his ears. Some closer thing, as insignificant perhaps
as old tin sheets, fills our ears with its din—some personal
hurt or loss, some slight, some resentment, some clamoring
habit, some foolish ambition, some infatuation, some love of
money—these fill our ears and God's voice is drowned out.
And that Voice was calling us to something big.

The harbor at Galle, Ceylon, is a beautiful one, and it was
the original harbor of the island, but now it is comparatively
deserted in favor of newer Colombo. The reason was this:
When the sailing ships came the harbor was perfect for them,
but to make it fit for the big ocean liners they would have to
blast out a huge rock at the center. It would cost a hundred
thousand pounds or more. Lesser voices of fear and hesitation prevailed, they refused to pay the price, and the city now
is a dead city, a shell of its former greatness. Had they
listened to the voice of faith and courage, they would now be
a growing city, but the lesser voices filled their ears and
prevailed.

---

O God, save me from these lesser things that incapacitate
me from hearing Thy call, and help me to pay the full price,
that I may have full deliverance from fear, and the full
vision of Thee. Amen.

## THE CONQUEST OF ANGER

Doctor Ligon says: "If the psychologist were asked to name the two major sins, from his point of view, he would probably name fear and anger. They form the basis of most of our unhappiness. They are impossible to integrate into a healthy personality" (*Psychology of the Christian Personality*, p. 16).

We have looked at fear and now we must look at anger and its conquest. First of all, we must note that there is a form of anger which is biologically helpful. Anger is often a protection against evil. The soul rises up and resists evil with deep indignation. Nietzsche was probably right when he said, "Your virtue is of no use unless it can be lashed into a rage." If we were incapable of anger, we should become "moral cows in our plump comfortableness."

Jesus was angry: "He had looked round about on them with anger, being grieved at the hardening of their heart." But note that in His anger was grief—He was "grieved." That determines the legitimate from the illegitimate type of anger. Where there is a sense of moral hurt, of moral grief, and not mere personal resentment in the anger, then it is right and worthy and helpful. But note again that it was anger at something done against another. He was indignant that they had no sympathy for the stricken man. That too is a test of whether it is legitimate anger. We must be suspicious of all angers that come from hurts to ourselves. They probably have in them less moral indignation than of personal resentment.

Paul says, "Be ye angry, and sin not." But if we are to be angry and sin not, then we must be angry only at sin, and that sin not against ourselves but others. Even this kind of anger Paul suggests should not be kept overnight, "Let not the sun go down upon your wrath." If kept overnight, it might fester.

-----

O Christ of the whip and the flashing eye, give us an inward hurt at the wrong done to others, but save us from personal resentments, for they destroy us. Amen.

Colossians 3. 8
Hebrews 12. 14–17
James 4. 1–3

## THE ROOT OF ANGER

Yesterday we saw that anger could be Christian when it had moral grief in it, and only when it was anger because of hurts to others. But we usually dress up our personal resentments in the clothes of moral indignation and try to make them respectable and Christian. This process of rationalization allows many Christians to tolerate unchristian anger. A clergyman thought he was fighting for principle, but when he honestly looked at himself, he saw that the fight had in it more personal pique than principle. He acknowledged it and got rid of it.

Those words "personal pique" point us to the root of anger. It is in the self. The self has its pride, and when that pride is wounded, it boils with anger.

It is therefore of no use to say, "I'll try not to be angry." You will almost certainly fail by this sort of trying. You cannot kill anger in your life, but you can consent for Him to do it. And how will He do it? By striking at the root—the self. You remember when Jesus withered the fig tree, the disciples saw it "withered away *from the roots.*" That is the way He withers things—from the roots. And how will He wither anger from the roots? By asking us to consent to the crucifixion of the self, in other words, its surrender. The self undergoes by that surrender its supreme mortification. It anticipates all the wounds that people can inflict upon it by deliberately wounding itself unto death. Having undergone that central death wound, what can marginal wounds now do? Having been torpedoed in midocean, and survived, are we now afraid of being drowned in a duck pond? But after that central death we still survive. There is a resurrection—a new man arises. And he is too great and too glad to be angered by petty annoyances.

---

O Christ, make me too glad and too great to be angered by petty things this day. Amen.

227

Ephesians 4. 31, 32
James 1. 19–21
James 3. 6

## THE ANGER REMAINS

Ofttimes the anger remains to plague us after the surrender. Why? Because of two things: either the surrender has been partial or the cultivation of the life after the surrender has been neglected. Ninety per cent of the germs that fall upon a healthy skin die in ten minutes. Health kills them. The way to kill many of these sin germs is to strengthen the organism upon which they feed. To neglect cultivation is to let our spirits get below par; and when that happens, our resistance is weakened, and the disease germs get a footing, and cause havoc. After cure there must be cultivation or collapse.

But sometimes the surrender is only partial—what an Indian youth called "a feeble surrender." That partial surrender sets up a dualism in the nature, and the dualism turns into a duel. There is a struggle for the mastery of the spirit. Anger results. We are still touchy.

The Jains of India do not take life if they can help it. But dogs fill the streets in such numbers that they become an overwhelming nuisance and then something must be done. So they are caught and taken out about ten miles from the city and loosed. They then make their way back to the city, fighting their way through the intervening villages—for the dogs there will not allow them to stay—and they arrive back more lean and hungry and therefore more bad-tempered than ever. Thus our tempers come back to us again, sometimes worse than ever, because we made a compromised effort to get rid of them. We try to please God and the self life. We put self out a little distance. We do not deal with it decisively. And the temper based in the self, like hungry dogs, comes back.

O Christ, we pray Thee to help us to consent that this self may "lay in dust life's glory dead," that from the ground there might "blossom red life that shall endless be"—and angerless. Amen.

## MEETING CRITICISM

Perhaps I am drawn to write this morning on the meeting of criticism, not only because it comes in line with our thought of overcoming anger, but because yesterday I received three letters of severe criticism and I analyzed my reactions. One of them was a very fair criticism and the other two were not. One of the two unjust criticisms was based on partial knowledge and the other apparently based on spleen. All three of these criticisms were about different things, and yet all were in regard to what one considered his finest efforts.

What is one to do when criticism comes? First of all, I have accustomed myself to ask, Is it true? And I had to acknowledge to myself and to this friend that the criticism was a fair one. I would profit by it and use it. I would right the thing which I had overlooked. In this way my critics become my helpers. They become the unpaid watchmen of my soul. They keep me straight. I need them. One of the greatest helps to the spiritual life is healthy criticism. If you have no friend or friends to do this for you, then you are the poorer for it. And that saving criticism may come from those whom we consider more undeveloped than we. A convert of a few weeks, a Sikh staying at our Ashram, said this to me before the group: "Whenever we put difficult questions to you, you make us forget the question by going off the point and talking about something else that is very interesting. You thus dodge our questions. It isn't honest." We all laughed, but in opening my mouth to laugh I swallowed the lesson! He was right. I can never forget it. And now when I don't know the answer I say so, instead of trying, perhaps unconsciously, to save face by going off to something else. Our critics can become the very hammers of God to beat us into shape. And all of us need to be beaten into shape, for we are only Christians in the making.

———

O God, help me not to resent criticism, but to take it as from Thy shaping hand—Thy efforts to save me and make me. Amen.

## MEETING UNJUST CRITICISM

Some of our criticisms are unjust and unfair. They may come out of partial knowledge, or out of willful misrepresentation. What is one, then, to do?

First of all, quickly breathe a prayer for your critics and for yourself. It is harder to hate a man after you have prayed for him. After you have asked God to bless him, it is harder for you to curse him. Prayer pulls the sting of resentment. Your attitude toward him becomes redemptive instead of resentful. You want to cure his ignorance and help him get rid of his spleen. Keep your thought bathed in prayer as you think of him. A prayerless thought will become a resentful thought.

Second, keep saying to yourself with Luther, "My soul is too glad and too great to be the enemy of any man." Keep an inner spiritual dignity that will keep you from descending to his level.

Third, begin to contrive ways to do him good. Steal a march on him. He will have his armor up awaiting your return blow. Strike him where he is unguarded—at the heart. Overcome evil with good. Buddha says: "If a wicked man foolishly do me wrong, I will return to him the protection of my ungrudging love. The more evil comes from him, the more good shall come from me. The poison of the slanderer's word always returning to him, the perfume of my good deed returning to us." In loving one's enemy, in turning the other cheek, as Jesus commanded and illustrated, we rise above our enemy, become superior to him—and we may win him. But if not, we have won our own souls. In either case we win.

———

O Christ of the smitten cheek and of the still loving heart, help us to follow Thee at this point. These criticisms make us writhe in pain. But may that pain drive us to Thee. If we are smitten by the rod of criticism, may we take it as a schoolmaster that shall lead to Thee. For we would come to Thee even if it be by the road of pain. Amen.

## ANSWERING CRITICS

Sometimes we shall have to answer those who wrong us. We owe it to ourselves and to them to clear up things by an explanation. But if you do write, then write that letter upon your knees, as it were. Don't give them a piece of your mind —you will lose your own peace of mind if you do! And don't think that Satan can cast out Satan, that you by acting like the devil can get the devil out of people. Write the kind of a letter to them that you would like to receive. And after you have written it, don't send it off. Not that day. Sleep over it. Your subconscious mind may give you light. It will, if the Spirit of Christ is in that subconscious mind.

Or perhaps you shouldn't answer at all. Let Jesus answer for you. In Luke 5. 30 it says, "But their scribes and Pharisees murmured against his disciples, saying, Why do ye eat and drink with publicans and sinners? and Jesus, answering, said unto them, They that are whole need not a physician, but they that are sick." They murmured against the disciples and Jesus answered for them. He often answers for me! It is safer to have Him answer. His answer was deathless and redemptive, the disciples' answer would probably have been very evasive and unreal. Let Jesus answer for you!

I once wrote to a man a letter which was devastating, for he had opened his armour. He deserved it. But I submitted it to the Ashram group before sending it. Their verdict was, "Not sufficiently redemptive." They were right. Instead of writing an answer I decided to let Christ reply for me. He did! Some months later I got a letter from the man asking forgiveness for what he had written. My reply would never have produced that apology. Christ's did. Then let Him do it for you.

———

O Jesus, I do not know the way to men's hearts. I bungle. But Thou dost come in as softly as light, and oh, how redemptively! Help me to win where I cannot win. Amen.

## DON'T WORRY ABOUT YOUR REPUTATION

"Oh," but you say, "if I don't answer, then what will become of my reputation? I will have to look after that." No, you don't. One who is living victoriously has gained victory over nervous concern about his reputation. You don't have to look after it. Look after your character and your reputation can look after itself. Be the kind of person about whom people won't believe things.

Besides, Jesus says: "If they have called the master of the house Beelzebub, how much more shall they call them of his household? Fear not: . . . there is nothing covered" (Matthew 10. 25, 26). In other words, don't be afraid of your reputation, if they call you Beelzebub, there is nothing covered—the truth will out in the end. It is a moral universe, and in the end it will be just. You can wait.

The most loved man that America has produced is Lincoln. Most loved and most slandered. Nothing was too vile to print about him. And yet no one believes it now. "There is nothing covered." His slanderers slandered themselves. When Wesley's wife accused him of a certain sin, he exclaimed: "There! The record is complete now, I've been accused of every sin in the catalogue." But his wife only succeeded in burying herself beneath her own slanders. "There is nothing covered."

"People do talk about me so," bitterly complained a particularly loose-tongued slanderer. "Yes," I replied, "but honestly, haven't you sown most of those slanders, and aren't you now reaping them?" She acknowledged she had. "There is nothing covered." When a fellow Christian, who did not agree with my theology, printed a pamphlet saying that I was "the most dangerous devil in China," I felt rather assured that I belonged to the household of Him who was called Beelzebub. At least He seemed very, very near to me at that time. I was in wonderful company! Besides, "there is nothing covered."

---

O Jesus Christ, purest of souls and yet called Beelzebub, "the lord of filth." Help me not to be nervous about my reputation. Help me to have faith at this point too. Amen.

## VICTORY THROUGH SUFFERING

We come now to the question of pain and suffering. We shall meet them on the pathway to victorious living; it may be that they will be our constant companions on that way. The question is, What shall we do with them, and what will they do with us?

First of all, we must note that pain has probably saved the race from physical extermination. Had there been no such thing as pain, we should probably not have survived as a race. For if we did not know that fire would cause pain to us if we thrust our fingers into it, we should probably let our fingers be withered by fire. If disease did not cause us pain, we should probably think little about it, and we should succumb to disease, because unwarned by pain. Pain says, "There is something wrong—attend to it." So pain turns out to be our friendly watchman guarding us against dangers to life. Pain is God's preventive grace, built into the structure of our physical life, to keep us from committing individual and collective suicide.

Nevertheless, there is much needless pain—it is in the world far beyond its biological uses in survival. For we inflict it on ourselves and others needlessly. Much of this pain is curable and should be cured by individual and collective action.

Suffering is a wider term. It may be caused by pain, but it has other and deeper causes. Suffering may be intensely mental and spiritual. Suffering too may be a part of God's preventive grace. It may be God's danger signal that something is wrong. Were there no mental and spiritual suffering, we should probably as a race have committed mental and spiritual suicide long ago.

Our first step, then, is to look on pain and suffering not entirely as enemies—they may become our allies in gaining fuller life.

———

**O Christ, we thank Thee that here at this place of pain and suffering Thou hast an authentic word to speak to us. For Thou dost *know*. Amen.**

## ARE CHRISTIANS EXEMPT?

Pain and suffering are the common lot of all. We are environed by nature, by other human beings, by our own physical bodies, and through these avenues pain and suffering come to us. Nor will the fact of our being Christians exempt us from their coming.

A young man was stunned by his failing in his examination. He said: "I cannot understand. I prayed very hard before the examination and I lived a very good life. Then why, oh, why, should I have failed in my examination? My faith in God has gone." He felt that if he only lived a good life, and prayed hard enough, he would be sure to pass examinations. When he was not exempt from suffering through failure, he felt that his religion did not work—it should have exempted him. Now, suppose it had exempted him and others like him, what would happen to the human race? If it could be proved that if you lived a good life and prayed hard enough, you would be bound to get through your examination, then our classrooms would be deserted before examination, and students would flock to the hillsides for prayer and meditation, and in the process their minds would dry up. Mental suffering through failure, because of slovenliness in studying or incapacity, is one of God's methods of keeping the human race mentally alive. It is a hard spur, but it is mentally redemptive.

I grant you that real Christians are exempt from sufferings which come from within, from their own wrong moral choices. This does save them from an enormous amount of suffering which comes upon those who sin, and suffer as a consequence of those sins. But it does not save them from sufferings which come through nature, through other human beings, and through their physical bodies. Nor does it exempt them from the suffering that comes from the very fact that they are a new moral and spiritual departure from the world. That departure itself brings suffering.

———

O Christ, Thou art our way out. Help us to learn Thy secret. Amen.

## WHAT ATTITUDES ARE WE TAKING?

We said yesterday that sufferings happen to us all—the good man included. But while the same things happen to us all they do not have the same effect upon us all. The same thing happening to two different people may have an entirely different effect upon them. It all depends upon inner attitudes. As someone has said, "What life does to us in the long run depends upon what life finds in us."

Sorrow and suffering makes some people querulous and bitter, others it sweetens and refines. Same event, but with opposite effects. "What happens to us from without does not determine the consequence." That depends on what life finds in us.

There were three crosses that day on a Judean hill. The same event was happening to three people. But it had three different effects upon them. One thief complained and railed on Jesus for not saving Himself and them; another saw this tragedy as a result of his sins, repented, and through it saw an open door into paradise; the third through that cross redeemed a race. The same event, but with three entirely different results. So the thing that matters is not what happens to you, but what you do with it after it does happen to you. Your cross can become the bitterest of unrelieved agonies, or it may become to you the most blessed of unlimited opportunities. The same sunshine falling on two branches of a tree —in one it causes decay, in the other it causes growth. It all depends on the responses the branches gave. One meets the sunshine with inner life and more life results. The other meets it with inner death and more death results.

So we find life choosing one and rejecting another. Not arbitrarily, but according to inward response. Suffering leaves some people writhing in helpless agony, others it leaves stronger and more capable of meeting more suffering, capable of meeting anything.

----

O Christ, give us such inner attitudes this day that we shall transmute the base metal of ordinary happenings into the gold of victorious living. Amen.

## DO YOU KNOW WHAT TO DO?

In *Christ and Human Suffering* I took the position that we were not to escape suffering, nor merely to bear it, but to use it. We can take it up into the purpose of our lives and make it contribute to the ends for which we really live. The raw materials of human life, the things that come on us day by day, can be woven into garments of character.

All of this depends on what inner attitudes we take. Two women in a certain city in India, both intelligent and refined, are suffering from practically the same illness. One it is making bitter and querulous and hopeless, the other it is making radiant. She will emerge from it pure gold. And her very attitudes are helping her to emerge. For nothing tones up the body as a peaceful, hopeful, victorious spirit. The other may not emerge, for she is handicapping her body in its fight with disease by dragging her body down by her despairing spirit. The difference is that one inner life is adjusted to the will of God, and the other is not. Same circumstances, two results.

Two families each lost an only son, one the family of a minister and the other a worldly family. A little boy of twelve years, talking to his mother about it, said, "Mother, it isn't so hard on the minister and his wife, for they know what to do. But these other people don't know what to do." The little fellow had put his finger on the crux of the matter. He saw the same event falling on two families, each with a different result. Because in the one case *they knew what to do*. And what is the Christian to do? He can say to himself: "I cannot determine what happens to me, but I can determine what it shall do to me after it does happen. It shall make me a better man and more useful." That is victory.

––––––––

O Christ, help me this day not to be determined by my circumstances, but to determine them in that I use them. Amen.

## THE PAIN GOD IS ALLOWED TO GUIDE

In Moffatt's translation of 2 Corinthians 7. 10, 11, Paul says, "The pain God is allowed to guide ends in a saving repentance." He saw that some pain leads to life and some leads to death. And the difference was this: In one case one kept his pains in his own hands and dealt with them on an entirely human level. This makes men bitter and cynical and full of complaints. It leads to death. On the other hand, a man takes God into his pains and allows Him to guide them. God then turns what would have been senseless suffering into a spiritual discipline. A better man emerges. It leads to life.

So in every happening that comes to you there is life or death. The common places of life make us common—or Christian! A man's wife called his attention to a wonderful sunset—the sky was streaked with fleecy clouds. "Yes," he said. "It reminds me. Please have the cook see that my bacon is streaked with more lean." He turned a radiant sunset into a reminder of bacon! Thus do some make the glorious into the commonplace. But some make glorious the commonplace. It is all according to what it finds within us. To the woman the sunset became aesthetic life, and to the man aesthetic death.

The pain itself from which we are suffering may have come from some evil source, but the question is not where it came from, but where it is going! Where it goes is determined by whether we allow it to be guided to life or guided to death. And that is determined by whether we put God into the pain, and offer it to Him as we offer everything else, and make it a part of His redemptive purpose for us. The cross is an example of God-guided pain. It issued in salvation. So may our crosses issue in salvation, if God is allowed to guide the pain involved in them.

———

O Christ, who didst turn Thy cross into a throne, help me this day to wear my sorrows and sufferings with regal dignity. Amen.

## WILL LIFE ALWAYS BE JUST?

Yesterday we ended by suggesting that our sufferings might come from an evil source outside our own will. "This is unjust," you reply. Yes, it is. But you must not expect life to be just. It isn't. Christianity never taught it would be. On the contrary, it has a cross at its heart—and that is the world's supreme injustice. Don't ask for justice from life— ask for power to turn injustice into fuller life. Then you have more than justice, you have life itself.

Life wasn't just to Paul. He found life coming to him in the form of imprisonments, of floggings, of desertions, of anxiety and care. It wasn't just. But he made it into something better than justice. "All things work together for good to them that love God," he exclaims. The thing itself may not be good; it may have come from the very devil himself, but God throws in enough good to make it work together for good. Like two cogwheels that work together, God actually uses evil for the destruction of evil. He uses devil-sourced evil for the making of God-inspired men. If you work together with God, you can turn your very defeats into victories. That is what the cross itself is.

Here is an Indian Christian lady who has served others for many years, a beautiful character, but now she is blind. Life wasn't just to her. No, but she made it more than just, she made it beautiful. "It's all dark," she said to me, "but then it's all very lovely," she added, thoughtfully, with a quiet heavenly smile. Don't offer that woman justice; she has grace and that is more than justice.

So this day I shall not ask that life be just, I shall ask that power be given me to make its injustices into opportunities, its very impediments into instruments.

----

O Christ, to whom life was supremely unjust, make me to know Thy secret this day so that I shall not whine for justice, but boldly turn the worst into the best. Amen.

## SEIZING FATE BY THE THROAT

Doctor Vail was performing more operations, I suppose, than any other man in India, among them thousands of cancer operations. And yet he himself developed cancer and has just died of it. Unjust! Yes, but—he flew to Germany, and while not cured, came back to India with a new treatment for cancer which will relieve thousands. Cancer struck him and he strikes back with a cancer remedy. And he struck back even while he himself was hopelessly stricken. He seized fate by the throat!

So did Beethoven. He had gone stone-deaf. "Oh, if I were only rid of this affliction, I could embrace the world." . . . But "I will seize fate by the throat; most assuredly it shall not get me wholly down—oh, it is so beautiful to live life a thousandfold." Fosdick quotes a biographer of Beethoven, himself a musician, who comments on the above: "We are eternal debtors to his deafness. It is doubtful if such lofty music could have been created except as self-compensation for some affliction, and in the utter isolation which the affliction brought about." He seized fate by the throat!

The first Sunday-school pupil I ever had became an engineer. An explosion left him totally deaf and totally blind. There is no way to communicate with him, except to spell out the letters with your finger on the back of his hand. He is shut off from the world. Not at all! He has gained more information and knowledge through other people's fingertips and through his own inner meditations than ninety-nine per cent of those who have eyes and ears. Moreover, he has established a far-flung business for the blind. He seized fate by the throat!

When Denmark was shorn of a part of her territory, her leaders decided that, since they were a smaller country, they would make up in quality what they lacked in quantity. They have! They have produced a co-operative order from which the world is learning. They seized fate by the throat!

---

O Christ, help me this day to seize fate by the throat and make it serve Thy purposes—and mine. Amen.

## LIGHT ON LIFE'S DARKEST PROBLEM

Jesus said He was "the light of the world" on two different occasions. Once when He stood in the Temple in the Treasury, which was the "Court of Women." He was the light of the world at the place of Religion (the Temple), of Money (the Treasury), of Sex (the Court of the Women). At these three places He *is* the light of the world. And how deeply we need light at these three places! But there was another place where He said He was the light of the world—at the place of the man born blind, when the disciples asked, "Who did sin, this man, or his parents, that he should be born blind?" At the place of this problem of unmerited suffering He is the light of the world.

He was and is! The more I have listened to the various proposals of philosophy and religion about this problem of unmerited suffering, the more I am convinced that He is the light of the world at the place of the world's darkest problem. Marx said concerning the world as a whole, "Philosophers have explained the world, we must now change it." Christ, in substance, said that very thing about this problem of unmerited suffering: "Philosophers have tried to explain it, or explain it away, we must now change it—change it into something else, we must use it for the very purpose of the Kingdom of God." He then showed us what He meant. He turned every single adverse circumstance, every single injustice, every single disappointment, every single betrayal and desertion, every single cross and made it contribute to the ends He had in view, the Kingdom of God. To be able to use pain and sorrow—this is light, and the Man who can give us power to do this very thing is the light of the world.

––––––

O Christ, who didst speak the word of light when life seemed dark and mysterious, help me this day to take that light, and live by it, and become light to others at this place of suffering. Amen.

## LIFE FOR THE MASTERY OF LIFE

The world needs nothing so deeply as it needs two things: light on the mystery of life, and life for the mastery of life. Jesus gives both, for He was both. Peep through this open door which leads off from the street and see if you see any light.

A Pharisee had asked Him to dine with him, and then to show his own superiority and semicontempt for this Man, he omitted all of the courtesies he would customarily give to a guest. He gave Him no kiss of greeting, no water for His feet and no oil for His hair. It was a social snub. It is one of those things that send some people writhing to their rooms with a permanent wound and a permanent hatred. Instead of it doing that to Jesus, something else happened. The discourtesy of the Pharisee gave the opportunity to a poor, stricken sinful woman to make up what the host had left undone. And never was there such courtesy—tears to wash His feet, her hair in the place of a towel, and precious ointment for His head—and all this came from the depths of the heart and not from mere customary courtesy. The Pharisee hardens and inwardly criticizes Him bitterly.

Then Jesus assumes moral control of the situation. He points out to the Pharisee the discourtesy, and then proceeds to forgive him and the woman. He bracketed them both in the same category of needy sinners and forgave them both. He, who lacked the gifts that courtesy should have brought, turned and gave the gift of forgiveness. And by doing so was in moral control, so instead of being a snubbed guest, He became the dispenser of a bounty. He did not bear that snub, He used it. And the world sits at the feet of such moral mastery and learns how to live.

———

O Christ, when I am socially hurt and snubbed, help me not to be resentful and bitter, but big and forgiving, and through it masterful. Amen.

241

## LET THE GLORY OUT!

Hard circumstances often make people. Who has not seen a frail, clinging-vine type of woman, who upon the death of her husband straightens up and becomes oak, around which the growing children twine their lives, and are forever grateful for such a mother? But this strength would never have come out and developed had it not been for the tears that watered the vine and made it into an oak.

Says Edwin Markham:

> "Defeat may serve as well as victory
> To shake the soul and let the glory out.
> When the great oak is straining in the wind,
> The boughs drink in new beauty, and the trunk
> Sends down a deeper root on the windward side.
> Only the soul that knows the mighty grief
> Can know the mighty rapture. Sorrows come
> To stretch our spaces in the heart of joy."[1]

Hudson Taylor was seated in an inn with a new missionary in China. He filled a glass full of water, and then struck the table with his fist. As the water splashed out he said to the young missionary, "You will be struck by the blows of many sorrows and troubles in China, but remember, they will only splash out of you what is in you." Out of some of the blows of circumstance and trouble splash complaint and bitterness, but out of others joy and victory. It brings out what is in you. An aged saint was on the platform of a moving train as it was coming into a station. The train lurched and threw him from one side of the train to the other. When he hit one side, those near him heard him quietly say, "Glory," and when he hit the other side, "Hallelujah." The jolting brought out what was in him!

Will trouble serve to shake the glory out? Then you have victory.

———

O Christ, I thank Thee that this is what trouble did to Thee. It shook Thee to death and scattered grace across the world. Help me this day to have such victory that trouble will only scatter peace and joy to those around me. Amen.

[1] Reprinted by permission.

Luke 13. 1–5
Habakkuk 3. 17–19
Hebrews 2. 10

## IS TROUBLE GOD'S PUNISHMENT?

Many feel that when trouble comes, it is God's punishment upon them for some sin. This attitude makes victory impossible.

We must admit that this is a world of moral consequence and that sin does bring trouble. But Jesus repudiated the idea that calamity and sin were always connected. In his comment on the fall of the Tower of Siloam and on those whose blood Pilate had mingled with their sacrifices, the sufferers "were not sinners above the rest," He said.

No, look on this trouble as opportunity for you to show what stuff there is in you.

"Why do I creep along the heavenly way
By inches in the garish day?
Last night, when darkening clouds did round me lower,
I strode whole leagues in one short hour!"

The darkening clouds may only serve to quicken your pace toward Home. An Indian proverb says, "The bursting of the petals says the flowers are coming." So when your heart bursts with pain and grief, the bursting is only the bursting of the cramping sheath-petals to let the flowers out. The heartbreak of Gethsemane was the bursting of the sheath that let the Passion Flower out. And the world is filled with its perfume. As someone has said, "It is wonderful what God can do with a broken heart if He can get all the pieces." Let Him put your broken life together again, perhaps in a new glorious pattern. He had to break it to make it.

In the Mission Agricultural Farm at Allahabad they found that when the tops of the eggplants were withered by the frost, the plants gave a second crop. The frost made them discover something. Now, after the plants have given one crop they cut them back and they give a second. So the cuts that you receive from life may not be God's punishments, but may be God's prunings in order to greater fruitfulness.

———

O Christ, we know that every branch in Thee that beareth fruit Thou prunest it that it might bear more fruit. Prune me this day for I would be fruitful. Amen.

## LIFE STRIKES AWAY OUR CRUTCHES

We must pursue the thought that our troubles may not be God's punishments, but God's pruning. A Christian lady, living near where I am writing, was afflicted for some years with a spinal trouble and could not walk without crutches. One day as she was coming down the stairs she slipped and fell to the bottom of the stairs, her crutches being lost on the way. She lay there calling for help, but no servants were near. With a great effort she drew herself up by the bannister, began to walk and has been walking ever since—without the crutches! The fall and the loss of those crutches was the best thing that ever happened to her.

There are many things in your life and mine upon which we lean heavily—family relationships, money, position. They may not be wrong, but they become crutches which weaken our moral fiber. We depend on them too much. Then calamity strikes them away. At first we are stunned and crushed. Our crutches are gone—what is left? Why, our feet, our own backbones and the grace of God! That is enough upon which to begin life anew. Doctor Worcester tells of a famous physician who lost everything in the San Francisco earthquake—his home, his hospital, his medical records, the very tools of his trade; and he was left practically penniless. When a friend began to condole with him, he said: "Pooh! It will be good fun to start all over again. I feel younger already, and now the people will need a physician for their souls." The old routine broken up he started a new routine—and wider!

Then do not weep over lost crutches. God wishes to make a man of you. Your backbone has been weakened by too much dependence on things—the tragedy of a material civilization. Stand up and be men! That is the word of God to a civilization that has had its material crutches taken away. And perhaps to you.

———

O God, I pray Thee help me not to whimper and whine, but to stand on my feet, when Thou dost take away my crutches. Amen.

## GOD'S INSULATIONS

There are two ways that men try to meet pain and calamity—one by isolation, the other by insulation. Some try to win by flight. They lose their nerve and want to run away.

A man said to me, "I am praying that either I shall die or my wife shall die." I am not sure that he put himself first! Perhaps not. "What else can I do?" he added, "for we cannot get along together." I told him that I thought that he was a moral coward, and that a Christian had another way out. I suggested that he might do what an oyster does when it gets an irritating grain of sand in its shell—it grows a pearl around it. It turns irritations into iridescence. There are many who turn their daily naggings into character, into patience, into beauty. And having stood that lesser thing in the home, they are ready for the bigger troubles on the outside. They are insulated. Troubles become the process by which we put on insulations against greater troubles. It is nature hardening us for bigger strains. Milo of Crotona, an athlete, wagered that he could lift a bull into the air. He bought a calf and lifted that, and each day as the calf grew bigger he lifted it, so when it became a full-grown bull he could lift it even then. So God increases our strength by helping us conquer our daily trials, until one day we shall lift more than a man's load.

At one place in the process of making tin plates the thin steel plates are put through a pickling bath, where the steel is corroded by the acid, so it will take and retain the insulating tin bath, next to come. Without the corroding acid the tin would not stick and rust would set in. So God lets us go through acid sorrows that we may hold the insulations of His grace lest life rust and destroy us.

---

O God, if today some acid sorrow eats into me, help me to remember Thy insulations—and rejoice! Amen.

## SUMMING UP

Life will bring sorrow to us all. "Affliction does so color life," said a sympathizing friend to a sufferer. "Yes," said the sufferer, "and I propose to choose the color."

I once went to see an invalid who had been on her bed for fifty straight years. Struck by a lightning flash during young womanhood, she was left paralyzed. No, she wasn't paralyzed! Only her body was. That room became the center of spiritual power in that city. I think I have never seen a more beautiful face—chiseled into beauty and dignity. She was choosing the color. Father Damien living among his lepers stood up one day to address them and began, "We lepers." This was his announcement that he too was a leper. But it made no difference. He went straight on—and went deeper. He too was choosing the colors! A Moslem teacher wrote me of his decision to become a Christian and also of the loss of his son. "I was standing at the door, and God whipped me in." Affliction might have whipped him in or out. He decided it should whip him in. He chose the color!

The cry of man's anguish went up to God,
  "Lord, take away pain!
The shadow that darkens the world Thou hast made;
  The close-coiling chain
That strangles the heart; the burden that weighs on the wings
  That would soar.
Lord, take away pain from the world Thou hast made,
  That it love Thee the more!"
Then the Lord answered to the cry of His world:
  "Shall I take away pain;
And with it the power of the soul to endure,
  Made strong by the strain?
Shall I take away pity, that knits heart to heart,
  And sacrifice high?
Will you lose all the heroes that lift from the fire
  White brows to the sky?
Shall I take away love that redeems with a price,
  And smiles at its loss?
Can ye spare from your lives that would climb into mine,
  The Christ on His cross?"

O God, we will fight alongside of Thee to take away suffering, for it is not Thy will; but where we cannot banish it, help us to use it. Amen.

Galatians 1. 15–17
Acts 1. 3, 4
Mark 6. 30–32

AUGUST 26

## MUSIC IN THE MAKING

We have been discussing positive pain and suffering, but there are other troubles in which there is no positive pain and suffering, but which arise out of being laid aside, rendered inactive, shelved. Some of these come from temporary indispositions, some through unemployment, and some through approaching old age. In all of these our tasks are suspended and we have to face life inactive. This is sometimes harder to meet than positive suffering.

Someone has said that in music "pauses are music in the making." There is a momentary suspense only to produce music more lovely than before. The pause prepares those who produce and those who listen for the finer music.

Is it possible that these pauses in our lives—these suspensions from activity—may become music in the making? I grant that continued unemployment of healthy, active persons may and does cause deterioration. The only remedy for them is employment, and society must provide it, or it isn't worthy the name of society. But apart from this extreme case, cannot the temporary periods of being laid aside, or of being blocked from our real lifework, be made into periods which become in literal fact, music in the making?

It was so in the life of Jesus. The call to give His message must have burned in His soul like fire during those silent years at Nazareth. Making yokes—when He was commissioned to strike off the yoke of sin and misery from the neck of the world! But He did not chafe. He could wait—yes, for thirty long years. We are glad He waited—the music is sweeter for the waiting. Those silent years are a pause which became music in the making. Thirty years of silence, three years of song. But what a song! It is richer because of the undertones of patient silences in it.

Thus it may be in your life and mine—silences that enrich the ultimate music.

O Christ, make me patient under restriction, that I may be richer under release. And help me not to chafe, but trust. Amen.

## SOME PAUSES

Youth often chafes under the years of disciplined schooling. Many throw away the opportunity for study and it never returns and they wear a lifelong regret within the heart. They refuse the pause, so there is no music in the making.

Many a missionary eager to get to work chafes under the drudgery of months of digging at language roots, passes it by, or slurs it over, and all through his missionary life he sings very broken music, in very broken language. And then lives to regret that his message is ineffective.

Perhaps one of the most distressing of pauses we have to meet is the fact of interruptions during the day. We plan our work and then people upset those plans—and us. And we say our work is spoiled. But it may be that those very interruptions are our work. Jesus made them so. Trace through His life and you will find that almost everything glorious came out of an interruption. Some of His finest teaching, His finest deeds, the revelation of His finest spirit came out of some person, or some circumstance, upsetting His plans. These interruptions did not upset His plans, they only sent His grace off at new angles. He looked upon them as God thrusting human need across His path. Those interruptions were opportunities. Once when He was so pressed that He and His disciples hadn't even leisure to eat, He withdrew them to a desert place apart. But the multitudes, perceiving it, followed Him; and He welcomed them, and spoke to them of the Kingdom of God, and them that had need of healing healed. And then He fed the multitude. Taught, healed, and fed the breakers of His plans and interrupters of His quiet! But those three words, "He welcomed them," are worth to us more than multitudes of books on patience and love. They throw open a window into the heart of goodness. That pause was music in the making. And what music!

———

O Christ, this day I shall meet with many interruptions, sometimes by very trying people. Help me to make those very interruptions a revelation of Thy Spirit within me. Amen.

## THE MOST SOLEMN PAUSE OF ALL—DEATH

None of these pauses we have mentioned can be compared with the awful solemn pause of death. Our work is stopped, our plans are broken off, our ties with others are snapped, the pitcher is broken at the well—at the well, just when it was going to draw water for someone. This is the most devastating pause of all. But is it? It may be the pause which will turn out to be only life's sweetest, gladdest music in the making.

It was so with Alice Means, one of the rarest missionaries we have ever had in India. What an amazing life she was living—building, teaching, making leaders! And then cancer struck her. She thought she might get to America before she died, but was stopped in Bombay by the doctors, knowing she would never reach America. This is the letter she wrote me from the Bombay hospital, after knowing she would be denied even the privilege of going to her homeland to die:

Use me as an illustration in your book, "Sure—but what?" I haven't suffered much yet, and when I do, I may not be able to tell you how it goes. How thankful I am for all these years of perfect, abounding health! What a happy life I have had! Let me tell you of the experience of these last two months. With a host of others I am working along in a great field, digging, sowing, weeding, watering, never noticing I had reached the edge, till I heard, "Alice, that's enough, come over here and sit down a bit." I looked up and there stood Jesus smiling at me. I went over and sat down on the grass by Him, and He said—"You have been busy working and have not had time for all those intimacies that go with a great friendship, such as I want with you. Come along and let us walk together here." He put His arm through mine and we walked along an avenue all covered with grass and flowers, and the birds were singing. Oh, it is beautiful! As I look down toward the river it is a little misty. But I know He will see me through that. Even now I am forever with my Lord. His peace within me is wonderful. Nothing can separate us now. It is heaven. That's all. The doctors and the nurses cannot understand how I can calmly discuss my condition and outlook.

Who can say that this pause of death to her was not music in the making? And vaster.

———

O Christ, we know that even death is but vaster music in the making. Help us to welcome it with joy. Amen.

249

## LIFE'S MOST FRUITFUL PAUSE

Perhaps the most fruitful pause of all is the pause of prayer. It has more music in the making in it than anything I know, and yet how few really use it! "Prayer is the most talked about and the least used force in the world."

I do not mean by using prayer the gaining of a benefit from the reflex influence that comes to us from quiet thought and meditation. I mean something more. I mean that my lesser spirit can come into intimate, personal contact with the Spirit called God, that I can come to a common understanding with Him, can adjust my will to His will, and through the contact can find my personality heightened, enlightened, re-enforced, used. Only a reflex influence? Humbly I say it, I know better! Experience shows that those who think of prayer as only a reflex influence soon give up prayer. For "it is not possible to project one's spirit continuously to that which is not responsive."

Bosworth says, "We could explain any reply to prayer provided we believe that it is possible for God to put a thought into the heart of man." Can God put a thought into the heart of a man? A thought? Why, His very Life! He can re-enforce the very foundations of a man's being by the impartation of His own Life. Life flows into life, Will into will, Love into love—that is what prayer means. It all comes when we are attuned, and prayer attunes us to the Eternal God.

Ethel Roming Fuller says:

"If radio's slim fingers can pluck a melody
From night—and toss it over a continent or sea;
If the petaled white notes of a violin
Are blown across the mountains or the city din;
If songs, like crimsoned roses, are culled from thin blue air—
Why should mortals wonder if God hears prayer?"

I do not. For I have gone to my knees broken, all in, defeated, and have arisen re-enforced, new and victorious. Everything within me said I had met God. And I had.

----

O Christ, this pause of prayer—what music in the making there is in it! Help me to use it this day as a working way to live. Amen.

## WE PAUSE TO CONSIDER PRAYER

Let us get rid of certain notions about prayer. Prayer is not a lightning rod to save us from the lightnings of God's wrath. Many think it is—if they don't pray, something will happen to them. "We don't have prayer or grace in our house, and nothing has happened yet," said a little girl in awed tones. No, dear, nothing has happened yet—nothing except deterioration. And perhaps nothing ever will. But that's enough. However, deterioration is such a slow process that we scarcely see it taking place and so we are not alarmed. Prayerlessness means slow rot, not sudden calamity.

Again, prayer is not bending God to our wills—it is the bringing of our wills to God's. When we throw out a boat hook and catch hold of the shore, do we pull the shore to ourselves? Rather we pull ourselves to the shore. Prayer does not pull God to us, it pulls us to God. It aligns our wills with His will, so that He can do things through us that He would not otherwise have been able to do. An almighty Will works through our weak wills, and we can do things all out of proportion to our ability. Prayer is, therefore, not overcoming God's reluctance; it is laying hold of His highest willingness. Those who pray link up with that willingness. If God has left certain things open in the universe around us to the contingency of man's will—things which will not be done unless man acts—is it strange that He has left certain things open, contingent upon prayer—things which will never be done unless we do them through prayer?

In real prayer our will coincides with His. That is what we mean when we pray "in Jesus' name"—that is, we pray the kind of prayer He would pray. But "it is the forging of Jesus' name to a prayer to pray out of His will."

---

O God, help me this day to make my will coincide with Thy will, that Thy power may coincide with mine. Amen.

## WE FURTHER CONSIDER PRAYER

In prayer I seldom ask for things; more and more I ask God for Himself, for the assurance that my will and His are not at cross-purposes, that we are agreed on all major and minor matters. I know, then, if this is so, I shall get all the things I need. If I seek first the Kingdom of God, then all these things will be added unto me. God is interested in things. But I do not want the reality of prayer to depend on whether I get this thing or that thing. If I get Him in loving communion, then the prayer is answered and is effective. Things are a side issue. But with many Christians they are central, like the little boy who said to me: "I love my daddy. He gives me pennies every day." Penny-praying, like penny-loving, belongs to immature childhood.

A Sufi woman saint was seen running with a pail of water in one hand and a torch in the other. When asked what she was doing, she replied, "I want to burn up heaven with the torch and put out the fires of hell with the water, so people will not love God for fear of punishment or for hope of reward, but will love Him just for Himself." Many Christians might do well to learn from that Sufi saint.

Prayer is the power to get through difficulties, to be at your best, to become effective. A raja ruthlessly took away a bridge across a river in Bengal. A Moslem saint sat upon his prayer mat and sailed across the unbridged river. One can cross uncrossable rivers, scale impassable mountains, and do impossible things through prayer. For God—the Eternal God works with us and in us. Prayer, then, "is the kind of a burden sails are to a ship and wings to a bird." Then pray, my brother, pray, if you want to live—and live victoriously.

———

O Christ, we thank Thee for what prayer did for Thee and through Thee—"power went forth." Help me this day to pray that power may go forth. Amen.

## MAKING THE PRAYER HOUR EFFECTIVE

First of all, have the prayer hour. Sacredly keep it. Build the habits of your life around that prayer hour. Make things fit into it, not it into things. Anyone who, neglecting the fixed hour of prayer, says he can pray all the time, will probably end in praying none of the time. But if you do keep the fixed hour, it will probably project its spirit through the whole day.

In the beginning of the prayer hour be silent. Let your mind relax and let it roam across your life to see whether it stops at anything wrong. If so, tell God you will right it. Let the first moment be a sincere moral search. If nothing is shown to be wrong, then, "Beloved, if our heart condemn us not, we have boldness toward God." We are ready for bold praying.

Then bathe your thought in His Word. It will wash the dust from your eyes. Then you will see, have insight. You will get right attitudes through the Word, so you will pray right prayers. You are pulling your thought up alongside of His thought, your purposes up to His purposes.

Take a pen or pencil with you and write down what comes to you as you pore over His Word. That pen is the sign of your faith that something will come. And it will. Don't hurry through that Word. Every word is precious. Pause, assimilate. When a man hurries through a wood, he sees few birds or animals. They hide. But if he sits down and waits, then they come out. It will be so with you. "Prayer is a time exposure of the soul to God." Expose your inmost being to His Word.

Take obedience with you into that hour, for you will know as much of God, and only as much of God, as you are willing to put into practice! For God will answer many of your prayers—through you.

---

O Christ, I come to Thee to help me make this hour of prayer effective, that I may make through this hour the whole of today effective. Amen.

Luke 24. 15, 32
John 20. 19, 20
Acts 1. 4, 8

## COMMUNION AND COMMISSION

Prayer seems many-sided, but really there are only two sides—communion and commission. The rest are phases of these two. These are the two heartbeats of the prayer life. And a heart has to keep beating in two directions, or death ensues. All communion without commission—death. All commission without communion—death. The two together—life.

First there is communion. As I have looked at the rubber trees, freshly tapped, with the cup nestling up against the wound and taking the sap from the heart of the tree, I have thought of prayer as being just that. We press our empty lives like cups up against the wounds of the Eternal God and take from Him life and power and redemption. Every day let me nestle up against His wounded side, for I am empty without it. And every day let my cup be emptied in loving help to others.

In the call of the disciples there were three things: "He appointed twelve that they might be with Him, and that he might send them forth to preach, and to have authority to cast out devils." (1) To be with Him. (2) Sent forth to preach. (3) To have moral authority. The first item in the call is the call to be with Him—hold that intact and everything else follows. Anyone who neglects communion will find the last two fading out. Also neglect commission and the first and the last will die. And moral authority depends upon the other two. Dim either the communion or the commission and moral authority is dimmed with them. But the one who keeps these two things intact does have moral authority. Empty closet, empty heart, empty hands—this is the spiritual history of many. "He withdrew himself into the deserts and prayed. . . . the power of the Lord was with him to heal"—cause and effect (Luke 5. 16, 17).

———

O Christ, who didst by Thy example show us the Source of power, give to us the will to tap that power and to channel it to other lives. Amen.

## DOES GOD GUIDE OUR LIVES?

Out of communion commission follows. In communion you feel the hand of God upon your life guiding you to do certain things. We have organized our religious lives around certain services in the Church, one on Sunday, one on Wednesday, and so on. If we attend these services, we think we are very good, faithful Christians. But between these services there are great gaps where God functions very feebly or not at all. Guidance fills up these gaps, and makes us every moment responsible to God. He is no longer in the interstices of life. He is in the very fiber of the whole structure. Guidance, therefore, brings God in from the occasional to the continuous. Every Christian should live a God-guided life. For if God is, He should be in everything that concerns us —directing, controlling, inspiring. The Christian that doesn't know this sense of guidance in his life is missing something vital. For, mind you, if you are not guided by God, you are guided by something else. Perhaps yourself. But we all know that to be self-managed is to be self-damaged. And we are not good enough and we don't know enough to guide our lives. God must guide them.

> "Have you and I
> Stood silent, as with Christ, apart from joy and fear
> Of life, to see by faith His face;
> To look, if but for a moment, at its grace,
> And grow by brief companionship, more true,
> More nerved to lead, to dare, to do
> For Him at any cost? Have we today
> Found time, in thought our hand to lay
> In His and thus compare
> His will and ours, and wear
> The impress of His wish? Be sure
> Such contact will endure
> Throughout the day; will help us walk erect
> Through storm and flood; detect
> Within the hidden life, sin's dross, its strain;
> Revive a thought of love for Him again;
> Steady the steps that waver; help us see
> The footpath meant for you and me."

**O God, help me to discern Thy touch upon my life and to obey it. Amen.**

255

## HOW DOES GOD GUIDE US?

God guides us in many ways—not one, but many. Among these are six outstanding ways: Circumstances, by Enlightened Christian Intelligence, by the Spoken or Written Words of Others, by an Intimate Group, by the Scriptures, by the Inner Voice.

Sometimes He guides by circumstances, or shall we call them Providences? Something opens before us, perhaps unexpectedly, just when we are in perplexity. That open door is matched against our perplexity, we walk through it and find it has been God's way. Or He may close something before us, and that closing of the door proves to be God's preventive guidance. Many a time God lets us fail in a secondary thing that we may succeed in a primary thing. For many people are ruined by secondary successes. They get tangled up in them and never get to the really worth-while things. I am sure God prevented me from becoming fond of game-hunting in India. As a young missionary I found my district filled with black buck. What more natural than to take a gun along while visiting these villages for evangelistic purposes? I did. I shot eighteen times at them and never hit one! Bad marksman? No, as a youth I was the best marksman in our crowd. But I had the feeling that God was making me miss. So I took the gun home and sold it, concluding that God had not called me to be a hunter, but an evangelist. My conclusion was right. I might have been crippled by a secondary success. Many a woman, finding she has beauty, soon finds she has nothing else. The secondary success of beauty makes her neglect the primary facts of intelligence and soul and usefulness. God's preventive grace has saved most of us at that point! So be it! Now for the open doors of intelligence, soul—and usefulness! God shuts lesser doors to open bigger ones.

---

O God, sometimes Thou dost save us by hard refusals and sometimes by opening doors. Help us to see Thee in both. And to obey without murmuring before hard refusals, or without hesitation before open doors. Amen.

## GUIDANCE THROUGH ENLIGHTENED INTELLI-GENCE

God guides through Enlightened Christian Intelligence. The development of Christian discernment is a necessary part of Christian development. Hebrews 5. 14 says, "But solid food is for adults—that is, for those who through constant practice have their spiritual faculties carefully trained to distinguish good from evil" (Weymouth).

God wants us to love Him with the whole of our being, including the mind—"Thou shalt love the Lord thy God with . . . all thy mind." Any scheme of guidance which neglects the mind by underemphasis is to that degree not Christian. For the whole man is to be perfected. God's problem is how to guide us, but not override us. For in the guidance He must not merely make us do a certain thing—He must make us—make us free, upstanding, discerning. I question any scheme of guidance which insists that guidance should be only or largely by the blank-sheet method—God is to write on it, as it were, what He wants us to do. Now, I believe that God does guide us by the Inner Voice, but to make that practically the only method and to depend on that Inner Voice to dictate the minute details of our lives would be to weaken us. Suppose a father or mother should undertake to dictate the minute things in the child's life, asking only for implicit obedience, leaving little room for intelligent weighing of moral issues and free decision, would that be guiding or over-riding? Wouldn't the child's personality remain undeveloped under it? Moreover, if we ask for dictated guidance in every little thing, we shall be tempted to manufacture it if we don't get it. This makes for unreality. No, we must not take one method alone and practically exclude others.

God will guide our mental processes if we are inwardly honest with ourselves and all the facts.

---

O Christ, we need the impact of Thy mind upon our minds, for without it our minds are confused and perplexed. And help us to obey our highest light. Amen.

## GOD'S GUIDANCE THROUGH OTHERS

Sometimes God guides us through the Written or Spoken Word of Others. Some passage in a book becomes luminous, speaks directly to our need. It is the very voice of God to us. Some word in a sermon seems to have in it more than the word of the speaker—it is God speaking. Or it may be a quiet word with a friend that opens the door to the solution of the problem, or relief from a grief.

Everyone should have such a friend, a confidant, "a sharing partner," the Groups call him; someone to whom you can open your heart to the depths, so that he really knows you for all you are; someone to whom you can "exteriorate your rottenness," if necessary, or to whom you can share your deepest perplexity. Bacon says, "This communicating of a man's self to his friend cutteth the grief in half." For "a grief shared is a grief halved." Shakespeare puts it this way: "Give sorrow words: the grief that does not speak whispers the o'er-fraught heart and bids it break."

What is a friend for except to share our problems and our sins as well as our joy and our goodness? The friend, freed from your inner emotions, may see the thing in just that detached way so necessary to give needed light. But even your friend's word must be tested by the other tests of guidance. Don't depend on it too implicitly. A student once asked me if I thought she should marry either of two men. I told her I didn't think she should. "Thank you," she said, "that settles it. I told God last night that I would take your voice for His voice." I was right in my advice to her, for both men were rotters, but she was wrong in taking my word too implicitly and blindly. Take the word of the friend, but make your own decision in the quietness before God.

---

O Christ, who didst yearn for a human friend in the hour of Gethsemane's darkness—but found him not, help me to find such a friend, for I shall need him. Amen.

## GUIDANCE THROUGH A GROUP

Many Group Movements with varying emphases have sprung up throughout the world—the Oxford Groups, the Cambridge Groups, the Burma Gospel Team Groups, Kagawa's Fellowship of the Friends of Jesus Group, the Christian Ashram Group Movement in India, and various other types. I cannot help but feel that God's Spirit has been raising up these Groups to meet particular needs. Not that I think that any one of them has the complete truth, but each does seem to have some particular phase of truth—partly neglected by others. The difficulty comes when each becomes exclusive and self-righteous. Then the lilies that fester smell worse than common ordinary weeds.

But God is speaking to this generation through groups. He spoke to the first generation through groups. The fact is that Jesus formed a Group Movement when He and His disciples fellowshiped and worked together. It was out of that fellowship that the New Testament came. The play of mind upon mind, of attitude upon attitude, of method upon method, of life upon life brought forth a body of common ideas and attitudes. These became the New Testament. Individual writers wrote them down, but the Christian groups produced them in their interaction with the Spirit of God and with each other. When the disciples said, "It seemed good to the Holy Ghost and to us," they could have said it not merely in reference to that particular decision, but in reference to the whole body of truth and attitude which was growing up. That Group had become not merely a collection of men, but an organism of the Holy Spirit. He was expressing His mind and redemptive purposes through that Group.

Today God guides the individual through such closely knit fellowships as the groups. Each individual needs the correction and sustenance of some such group. For the group checks up and tends to keep the individual guidance from going astray. So God often guides through a group.

---

O Christ, I pray Thee to touch me through my fellow men and help me to discern Thy voice when Thou dost speak through their voice. Amen.

259

## GUIDANCE THROUGH THE INNER VOICE

By the Inner Voice I do not mean the voice of conscience, for the Inner Voice gives guidance, not merely where a matter of right and wrong is involved as in conscience, but where one is taking life directions, deciding perplexities and where one is bidden to take up tasks and assume responsibilities. The Inner Voice is not contradictory to an enlightened conscience, but is in addition to it and beyond it. It is the Spirit of God speaking to one directly and authentically.

When we turn to the early records of the Christian Movement, the New Testament, we find that guidance was moving directly from the external to the internal. The Gospels open with guidance through dreams and visions and the voices of angels, as in the cases of Zechariah and Joseph. With Jesus it was different: He went off into no visions or dreams, He got His guidance through insight that comes through prayer and the direct voice of the Spirit within. In the beginning of the Acts of the Apostles we find the disciples fumbling badly—casting lots as to which one would become a disciple in place of Judas, and giving God the choice between only two at that! How often we narrow God's choices for Him! God didn't want either of them—He wanted Paul! But they did not repeat this initial mistake of depending on outer signs. The guidance became more and more inward. This was in line with higher evolution, for Professor Simpson says, "The higher organisms gradually substitute internal for external stimuli." The whole movement seems to be Inward—Ho!   Not entirely, but the tendency was distinctly there. And this was in the direction of a deeper Christianizing, for the gospel is producing a man who is not compelled by an external sign, but impelled by an internal Spirit—the Spirit and our spirit working harmoniously and therefore effectively.

---

O Christ, who didst so live in the Father that the gentlest whisper was like thunder to Thee, help us to have that same responsiveness—this day and all the days. Amen.

Exodus 33. 13–15        Isaiah 40. 11
Acts 8. 31              Isaiah 30. 21
Psalm 25. 5, 9

## GUIDANCE THEN AND NOW

We said that the whole tendency of guidance in Acts is to become less dependent on outer signs and more upon the gentle pressures of the Spirit within. A personality is being produced that will naturally and normally take the Christian attitude—from within, just as a well-trained horse doesn't need flogging, the slightest suggestion will do.

But in the Acts there are methods of guidance other than the direct voice of the Spirit: there was the exercise of Christian common sense—"It does not seem fitting" (Acts 6. 2, Weymouth). They were led by the facts—"On hearing this" (Acts 11. 18, Moffatt). They came to group conclusions by vote—"And in every Church, after prayer and fasting, they selected Elders by a show of hands" (Acts 14. 23, Weymouth). In the exercise of thought—"the Spirit said to Peter, who was pondering over the vision" (Acts 10. 19, Moffatt).

God will not guide us in one way only, but in many ways. Perhaps the highest guidance is in the verse, "It seemed good to the Holy Spirit and to us"—we were thinking His thoughts and coming to the same conclusions. That is co-operative spiritual living.

Once it was said, "Having been forbidden by the Holy Spirit to proclaim the Message in the province of Asia, . . . they were about to enter Bithynia, but the Spirit of Jesus would not permit this" (Acts 16. 6, 7, Weymouth). The "Holy Spirit" and "the Spirit of Jesus" were used interchangeably, for they felt that the universalized Jesus and the Holy Spirit were one, the accents of the mind of Jesus were heard in the voice of the Holy Spirit, He was acting as Jesus would act. This gives the key by which we can discern the Voice of the Spirit—does that Voice appeal according to what we have seen in Christ? If so, I accept it. If not, I question it.

O Christ, we thank Thee that we can belong to the sheep that hear Thy voice and know it and follow it. Help us to be keen to catch Thy accents this day. Amen.

261

## THE SCRIPTURES AND THE POWER OF GOD

The key to discerning the Voice of the Spirit is this: Does that Voice speak according to the revelation in Jesus? If so, it is authentic, if not, we should question it. For instance, when Peter says, "The Spirit bade me go with them making no distinction," I feel that this is an authentic voice of the Spirit, for this is just what we see revealed in Christ—a mind that made no distinction between man and man. But if Peter, when he drew back and refused before Paul to eat with the Gentiles, had said, "The Spirit bade me make that distinction," we should have said: "Peter, you are wrong. That was not the voice of the Spirit. It was the voice of prejudice and fears. Your wires are crossed."

Jesus said this penetrating word, "Ye do err, not knowing the Scriptures, nor the power of God." The way to keep from erring is to know those two things: the Scriptures—the past revelations; and the power of God—the present continuous activity of God. Some know only the Scriptures—they do not link themselves with the creative activity of God here and now in themselves and the present age. They err. For they echo only the past. Some know only the power of God now—they do not know in any real sense the Scriptures. They too err. For we cannot correctly discern God at work now unless we continuously check it up by that revelation we have seen in Christ. But that man will not go astray who is in constant fellowship with the power of God now working, and who constantly tests that working with the revelation through the historic Jesus. Revelation issuing in experience, and experience inspired and checked by revelation— these are the two things that keep life from erring. These are the two rails that keep us going safely ahead; but take off one rail or the other, and we land in the ditch.

———

O Christ, help us to know Thee in history and in ourselves, and help us to find no difference. Amen.

## A FURTHER CHECK

A further check in regard to guidance is to remind ourselves that the guidance may be narrowed, or even controlled, by the framework of society in which we find ourselves. The guidance often conforms to the established order.

One of the things that makes me feel the guidance in the Acts was authentic is the fact that it did not conform to the established order. In a framework of Jewish exclusiveness they broke over and founded a fellowship based on brotherhood beyond race and class. In a competitive order they founded a society based on co-operation and economic sharing and equality. They broke the patterns of society in which they lived and formed new ones.

Now, much of our guidance doesn't do that. It conforms to the pattern of society in which we live and we get our guidance within the framework of it. Kagawa's guidance makes him strive to break the pattern of a competitive order. It therefore commends itself to me. But where a man gets guidance, for instance, that makes him take attitudes that lean toward Fascism, which means in essence an attempt to hold the present order by force, I am compelled to suspect that guidance. Why aren't more people now "guided," not merely to modify this order, but to change its very foundations from competition to co-operation? One would think that would be the normal Christian happening.

A lady, with fingers full of sparkling diamonds, told how she was guided to pay back two-penny worth of stuff. The reason she was sensitive at that point was that she belonged to a society which had been built around the sacredness of property, hence stealing was very wrong. But she apparently had no guidance about sharing the worth of useless diamonds with the poor and underfed around her. For she was of a class which tacitly approved these economic disparities. She got her guidance within the framework of a class. It, therefore, was only faintly Christian. It was not insincere—it was limited.

---

O Christ, open my eyes to my narrowing framework and help me to catch the breadth of Thy mind. Amen.

## THE INNER VOICE DEPENDABLE

Sometimes our guidance will be like the voice to Philip, "Arise, and go unto . . . Gaza; the same desert." God often sends us seemingly into a desert. But if He guides us into a desert, He works at the other end, and makes us meet someone there who needs us.

As I look back across the years I am impressed that whenever I have sincerely listened to and have followed that Voice, it has never let me down. It has always proved right. Whenever I have doubted it and followed the voice of my own desires, my choice has always proved wrong. Not that the Voice is always against my desires—God's will is not always the unpleasant. But whether across or with the desires the Voice has always proven right. Sometimes I have misinterpreted the Voice; but when it has been clear, it has always been consistent. Sometimes, however, we have to go to the utmost limit before it is fulfilled. Take one instance out of many: I lost my only pair of glasses on a mountainside in India. I tried to find them that night but couldn't. The Voice was unmistakable: "It's all right. Don't worry, you will find them." I arose at dawn to search before anyone else came out. No glasses. Thus the search went on till well into the day. I was helpless without my glasses. So I said, "Well, I must be mistaken about the Voice." So I started toward the city to order another pair. Noticing my shoestring untied, I put my foot on the railing of a fence to tie it, looked past my foot and there, down in the gully ten feet below, were my glasses. Coincidence? Perhaps. But you cannot convince me of anything but that my Father, seeing I needed the glasses, helped me to find them. If His care extends to the little, why not to the big? Both the sparrow and the star are in His care—and so am I, and you.

---

O Father, I thank Thee that Thou hast never let me down. Help me not to let Thee down. Amen.

## MORE THOUGHTS ON GUIDANCE

"He went in and stood before the Lord"—that is prayer, standing at attention before God to get His orders for the day. You may not get any suggestions then. If you don't, that means you should carry on as you have been. You can trust His silence. If He doesn't answer you at once, don't be discouraged. Jesus did not answer the Gentile woman at once, but He did answer her finally, and more—He filled the Gentile world with His voice and power. He answered her—plus!

But in regard to some important decision if you are uncertain—don't. Wait till the guidance is clear. Don't act on half light.

Have particular times to wait for guidance, but fill in the gaps with spare-moment praying. Peter got the vision that changed his whole life in spare-moment praying. "As they were on their journey, . . . Peter went up upon the housetop to pray." There he saw the essential unity of man and acted on it and was forever changed. The difference in the spiritual lives of people is what they do with the spare moment. Some waste it—and themselves with it. Others gather it up and make it contribute.

Through a spare-moment prayer I became a missionary. In college I had to give a talk on missions, became burdened that something be done about it, and as I had a few moments before the beginning of the meeting, I stepped into a room and prayed, "O God, give me a missionary from this meeting. I'll not go in until I am assured that someone will go." The answer came, "Take one, according to your faith be it unto you." "I will," I replied, and went into the room with an inner assurance. From that moment I was gripped. I was the missionary! I had prayed myself into it. Pray and then put yourself in the way of being guided to answer that prayer.

———

O Christ, help me to have my heart open every moment, for I must be Thy minute-man, ready at any time to do Thy bidding. Amen.

## YOUR COMMISSION FREE FROM STAIN

Cultivate the listening attitude in prayer. And as you listen you will get your commission. And when you get that commission, keep it free from stain. Paul, speaking to a young man, said, "In the presence of God who is the Life of all, and of Christ Jesus who testified to the good confession before Pontius Pilate, I charge you to keep your commission free from stain" (1 Timothy 6. 13, Moffatt). In the light of two things: in the presence of the adequate life of Him who is the Life of all, and in the presence of this Life poured out in sacrifice before Pilate, keep your commission free from stain. The stain of what? Obviously, the stain of emptiness, and the stain of a lack of self-giving.

Here is this Life of God throbbing in every fiber of the universe: in the light of that fact keep from the stain of emptiness. If God commissions you, guides you to take up a task, however small, or however large, He will provide resources. Commission and equipment go together. If God commissions you to speak to a person, or to fight for social justice, He will equip you for that work. Draw heavily on them. Don't be like this bird that is now calling out in wild notes, so the Indians say, "Pilao, Pilao"—"Give me to drink," when it is right here in "Sat Tal" (Seven Lakes) and could have all it wants! Don't cry to God for spiritual equipment. Take it. Emptiness is now sin, for fullness is now your privilege. Keep saying to yourself, "I can do anything I ought to do—through Him who strengthens me." You will be astonished at your ability to do things. Nothing now can make you afraid—nothing. God is your life, and God is your life-equipment.

---

O God, who art the life of my very life, help me to keep the channels open, that this Life may not only be there, but be operative. Amen.

## THE STAIN OF PARTIAL FULFILLMENT

Yesterday we saw that we were to keep our commissions free from the stain of emptiness and the stain of a lack of self-giving. Jesus witnessed His confession before Pontius Pilate at the place where witnessing meant a cross. His commission had in it orders to go clear through, and clear through He would go—and did. These were no half-way completions, no feints at doing it and then drawing back— He put His commission into the concrete.

Carrying out the will of God is not always a pleasant thing in a tangled world like this. Often we shall have to wipe the blood from our lips as we close them upon the set teeth of our determinations. The commission often means a cross. Our friends will misunderstand us and fall away, and we shall be left to witness our confession—alone. So be it. We shall ask for strong inner fiber to be able to endure and to see the thing through.

Wrote a prominent man to another during the French Revolution: "There is a terrific struggle going on here. Our heads are in danger. Come and offer yours." He did. If men can do that when a friend and a cause call, why cannot we do it when a Friend and a Cause call—that Friend, God, that Cause, the Kingdom?

But we shall be tempted in compromise and call it a day— just short of putting it into operation. We become compromised Christians—refusers of the cross.

To try to put justice at the heart of human society will cause a cross, so we decide that our commission reads to change individuals and leave it at that. We refuse our witness before Pontius Pilate. Jesus did not. He witnessed to His kingship before His individual disciples, He also witnessed it before the Roman Empire in the person of the governor and said He was King there too in the corporate relationships of men. That cost Him a cross. But He wit, nessed it.

---

O Christ, I thank Thee, I thank Thee, that nowhere didst Thou draw back. Help me not to draw back. Amen.

## INWARDLY BOUND UP

When we think about carrying out God's guidance in our lives, we suffer from inhibitions. We are not free to express the will of God in our lives. We are inwardly bound up. We must get victory over that sense of inward self-consciousness and shyness, or we shall never be useful for the Kingdom of God.

Ligon quotes a group of mental hygienists who were asked by questionnaire as to what, in their view, were the most serious items in a list of behavior items found in young children. They included these: excessive modesty, suspiciousness, bashfulness, withdrawing, desire to play alone, constant whining, fears, depression, daydreaming, shyness, uninterestedness, overactivity, demands for attention, sensitiveness, sulkiness. These hinder the development of the child. Now note that out of the fifteen items probably ten or eleven of them refer to an inverted self, a tendency to close in and become wrapped up with oneself. Obviously, this inhibited self must be loosed and freed. It is unnatural and therefore unchristian. All crippling inhibitions should be taken out of our lives. When Peter and John were before the Sanhedrin, it was said, "As they looked on Peter and John so fearlessly outspoken—and also discovered that they were illiterate persons, untrained in the schools—they were surprised; and now they recognized them as having been with Jesus" (Acts 4. 13, Weymouth). Their outspoken fearlessness was a sign that they had been with Jesus. It was so then—it is so now. One in company with Jesus is freed from cramping inhibitions and self-consciousness. He has power to impart. "I will give you a mouth and wisdom," said Jesus. Some have a mouth and no wisdom, and some have wisdom and no mouth. Jesus said, "I will give you both—I will give you something to talk about, and I will help you to talk about it."

Tied up lives can be untied and loosed and made victorious.

---

**O Christ, we thank Thee that no cramping fears and inhibitions crippled Thee—freely Thou didst receive and freely didst Thou give. Help me to be like that. Amen.**

## THROWING OFF ALL RESERVE

A crisis had come in early Christianity. The apostles had gone to the Jews alone and had acted as though this were a Jewish gospel, from Jews to Jews. But the crisis came: "Seeing the crowds, the Jews, filled with angry jealousy, opposed Paul's statements and abused him. Then, throwing off all reserve, Paul and Barnabas said, 'We were bound to proclaim God's message to you first. But since you spurn it and judge yourselves to be unworthy of the Life of the Ages—well, we turn to the Gentiles. For such is the Lord's command to us'" (Acts 13. 45–47, Weymouth). They threw off all reserve and saved themselves and their gospel.

They had a larger gospel in their hearts than they were actually proclaiming. They were proclaiming a gospel for Jews when it was a gospel for man as man. Today a similar crisis has arisen in Christianity. We have a larger gospel in our hearts than we are actually proclaiming. We have a gospel which will cure our individual sickness and our social sickness. We have had our reserves about one or the other. We have acted on less than the whole. Now, this world-shaking crisis is forcing us to throw off all reserve. We must act upon the larger implications of our gospel. It is always safe to do so. It is always dangerous to minimize Christ, for there we are always wrong. It is always safe to act upon the larger Christ, for there we are always right. The smaller view of Christ has always proven wrong, the larger always right.

Now, some of us have reserves about giving this gospel to the individual—we are tongue-tied. We cannot impart the vital spark. We are not spiritually contagious. We either haven't anything to give or we can't give what we have.

Others are tied up at the place of giving this gospel to the collective order. They either haven't anything to give, or else they fear to give it.

---

O Christ, deliver us from both paralyses, and help us to throw off all our reserves and be out and out for Thee and Thy Kingdom. Amen.

## MAGNIFICENT OBSESSION

Yesterday we said that we must throw off all reserve in regard to proclaiming a gospel for the total order, for a world crisis is upon us. Life is running into new molds. Shall we allow greed to set those molds as it has done in the past, or shall we set the Kingdom of God on earth as the mold for the future? I choose the Kingdom.

A bishop, criticizing my last book, said that I seemed to be "obsessed with the idea of the Kingdom of God on earth." I wish I could plead guilty to that charge, for it would be a magnificent obsession. But I do confess to an obsession (I only wish it more ablaze) with the idea of a new order on earth, the Kingdom of God.

I *am* obsessed with the idea that poverty could end for all, for we have both the knowledge and the instruments of science to do it. We have everything to do it—everything except the collective will. The Kingdom of God would mean that that collective will would be turned toward abolishing that poverty. I am therefore obsessed with that Kingdom. I *am* obsessed with the idea that race hatred and social clashes could cease and that man could be formed into a brotherhood. The Kingdom of God would mean just that. So I am obsessed with that Kingdom. I *am* obsessed with the thought that these preparations for war are so stupid, so thoroughly devilish, so unnecessary, and so futile. The Kingdom of God would mean an end of war. Therefore I am obsessed with that Kingdom. I *am* obsessed with the idea that the Kingdom of God is the only workable order, and that this Kingdom is at our doors.

I shall therefore throw off all reserve and say so. Someone reported that certain Christians "fairly shouted their answer to the world." I wish we could do that! Magnificent obsession!

O Christ, we pray Thee to help us fairly to shout our answer to the world's need. For we know it is an answer—and the only one. Amen.

## THE KINGDOM OF OUR FATHER DAVID

Note two attempts to reduce the Kingdom. The disciples said, "Lord, dost thou at this time restore the kingdom to Israel?" After three years of teaching they saw in the Kingdom of God only the restoration of the Kingdom to Israel. They did not reject the Kingdom—they reduced it. They made it into something less than it really was. Again, when He came into Jerusalem in triumphal entry, the multitudes cried, "Blessed is the kingdom that cometh, the kingdom of our father David." The Kingdom of God—the Kingdom of our father David.

This has been the bane of the gospel of Christ: He inaugurates something big and challenging and we interpret it in terms of "our father David." Denominationalism is taking the Kingdom of God—a worldwide, universal Kingdom—and turning it into the Kingdom of our father David—the Church of England, Wesleyans, Lutherans, Baptists, Presbyterians, Congregationalists, Pentecostalists—as if the Kingdom of God weren't larger than England, than John Wesley, than Martin Luther, than a mode of baptism, an emphasis on Presbyters, on the Congregation, on Pentecost! All of these and others, are a narrowing of a universal conception—the Kingdom of God—into a local one—the Kingdom of our father David. Luther announces the Kingdom of God; his followers announce the Kingdom of our father Luther! Reducing the Kingdom!

And when I make the Kingdom of God, which is to take in the whole of life, into a means of my individual salvation alone, leaving untouched the social order, am I not making the Kingdom of God into the Kingdom of self?

I repeat, the crisis is on us. We Christians must throw off all reserve and give our answer to the world's need—without hesitation, without compromise. For the world is sick nigh unto death for the lack of it. Our silence now becomes a guilty silence—and deadly.

---

O Christ, forgive us that we have made Thy Kingdom into the small and irrelevant, help us now to make it into the big and adequate. Amen.

## PERSONAL RESERVES IN PERSONAL CONTACTS

Many of us are free and frank until we come to the really important things, the inner things, and then we close up. At the close of a Round Table conference of college professors one remarked, "I have learned more about my colleagues' real inner life during these two hours than I have in years of living together." They were not imparting to each other at the deepest level. We need to be freed from binding reserves.

You say, "I am shy and self-conscious; I cannot do it." True, but you can become strongest in that weakest place. John R. Mott says that the phrase he has repeated most in his life is, "You can become strongest in your weakest place." Jeremiah pleaded, when the call of God came to him, "I am a child, I cannot speak." But he offered that trembling hesitation to God, and when he did speak, how mightily he spoke! When the call of God came to Moses he pleaded that he was unable, for he was "slow of speech." But God loosed him, and when he did get started, he made a speech that covered the whole book of Deuteronomy! He became strongest at his weakest place.

Some people look on religion as something so sacred that it becomes secret. Suppose a mother should say to her children, "Now, children, food is such a sacred thing I cannot talk to you about it, nor can I invite you to partake of it." Suppose the teacher should say: "Now, pupils, knowledge is such a sacred thing I cannot talk to you about it. There will be no classes today." Absurd! But not more absurd than the unnatural attitudes we assume about the deepest thing we have got—the good news about the power of Christ. There we should be natural and contagious.

Someone has defined a Christian as one who says by word and by life, "I commend my Saviour to you." No better definition. No greater need.

--------

O Christ, I pray Thee to loose me from these inhibiting fetters, and help me to be free—free to impart. Amen.

2 Corinthians 3. 17, 18
John 4. 14
Acts 1. 8

## THE POWER THAT GIVES RELEASE

The only way to get rid of self-consciousness is through God-consciousness. We become so conscious of another Self within us that we lose sight of our self. "Where the Spirit of the Lord is there is liberty"—liberty from cramping bondages and inhibitions and paralyzing sins.

But this age has lost grip upon the Holy Spirit. We have taught this age to follow Jesus as an example, and it has produced a pale, colorless Christianity. For the gospel does not ask you to follow Jesus as an example—it offers you the resources of the Holy Spirit in the inner life and then you follow Jesus because of an impulsion. This kind of Christianity becomes colorful and red-blooded. It has resources, therefore power.

A modern translation of the Gospels spells the "holy spirit" thus, without capitals. That is symbolic of what has happened to this age. It has turned the Holy Spirit into a "holy spirit," a vague, impersonal influence, to our impoverishment. That is not the Holy Spirit of the Acts of the Apostles. There the Holy Spirit was no mere vague, impersonal influence—He was God meeting them inwardly, re-enforcing, cleansing, fusing the soul forces into a loving unity, and setting them ablaze with God. Weymouth was right when he translated the passage in reference to Stephen thus, "They were quite unable, however, to resist the wisdom and the Spirit with which he spoke." Note the capital "S." You couldn't tell where Stephen's spirit ended and the Spirit began, for the Spirit lived in his spirit, was the Wisdom of his wisdom. When the disciples got hold of that secret at Pentecost, they were immediately and decisively freed from cramping inhibitions and spiritual bondages and became flaming evangels of the Good News. We need to rediscover the actual resources of the Holy Spirit. Or else bondage.

---

O Christ, we pray Thee to help us to rediscover Thy offer to us and to live by its resources, rejoice in its liberties, and become effective by its power. Amen.

## FREEDOM FOR DAMMED-UP SOULS

Jesus said these remarkable words, "He that believeth on me . . . out of . . . [him] shall flow rivers of living waters. But this spake he of the Spirit." The words "out of him" have usually been translated "out of his belly." We have shied off from the word and from the fact—to our loss. For the "belly" was considered the seat of life, the deepest portion of one's nature. We would say today, "From the depths of the subconscious shall flow rivers of living waters." The Spirit in the depths of the subconscious, cleansing, controlling, empowering. This brings the whole of life into a living unity, and in the flood of this new Life all compartmentalizing, inhibiting dams are broken down. Rivers of living water flow! That is not mere doctrine, it is a fact. The disciples knew it and it turned timid believers into irresistible apostles.

A highly cultured lady said with beaming joy, "I have just stumbled across the meaning of the Holy Ghost. All my life I have tried to find out its meaning. Now I know." And the "rivers" attested the fact.

There are nine "rivers" that flow out of a life Spirit-controlled: "love, joy, peace; patience toward others, kindness, benevolence; good faith, meekness, self-restraint" (Galatians 5. 22, 23, Weymouth). It adds, "Against such things as these there is no law." Have those things at the center of your life and you can act as you please, for you are not constrained by a law to do them, but impelled by an inner Life. You can act naturally because you act supernaturally. But note the first one is "love" and the last "self-restraint"—you begin with love and you end with self-restraint. You restrain your lower self because you love the higher Self. Also note that each one of these fruits of the Spirit is a quality of moral character, not one of them an extraneous sign, and every one of them valid and vital today.

———

O Spirit of the Living God, break down the dams in our lives and make us free. Take over the depths, and we shall not worry about the surface. Amen.

## INTERPRETERS OR INTERFERERS?

We are to interpret through our lives the meaning of God in terms of today. We are to extend the Incarnation. "I know who you are talking about," interrupted a Persian villager as the missionary was speaking of Christ, "Dr. ——. He comes to our village." The doctor had interpreted Christ to them. Once, while on an errand of mercy, bandits stripped the doctor of everything, including his clothes, but, strange to say, they left him with his camera, and he snapped them. Later, one of these bandits came to his hospital for an operation. They recognized each other. He was in the doctor's power—and helpless. The doctor used that power to forgive him and heal him, and, while doing so, interpreted the meaning of Christ.

But some of us interfere with that meaning. "But the disciples interfered" (Mark 10. 13, Weymouth). They tried to keep the little children away and in doing so interfered with the spirit and purpose of Christ. You and I are interpreters of Christ or interferers with Christ. We represent either the cure or the disease.

Jesus interpreted the Father. "The only begotten Son, which is in the bosom of the Father, he hath declared him"— literally, "He hath interpreted Him." And what an interpretation! As I listen to His words and watch His acts and see His spirit, God grows tenderly beautiful before me. And I fall in love with such a God. Mark says, "Jesus walked in the temple," and Luke says in the parallel passage that Jesus "taught daily in the temple." They were both right— His walking was teaching. His very walk interpreted God. Once it was said of Him that He was "teaching, and journeying" on the way to Jerusalem, where the cross awaited Him. Many of us would have nursed our coming pain. But He had inward leisure to teach the love of God to others—on the way to die! But even through that death He gave us a deathless interpretation of the Father. What an interpreter He was!

---

O Christ, as Thou didst interpret the Father, help me this day to interpret Thee. Amen.

## HEIGHTENING THE MESSAGE

I have used a good many interpreters through the years, and some have heightened my message, and some, alas, have subtracted from it. Once they said to me in China, "This man is such a wonderful interpreter that no matter what you say, he will make a good address out of it." He did! He would take a commonplace statement and make it live.

But some have used the opportunity for self-display. I once had to stop an interpreter who was doing this so obviously that he was spoiling everything. And when I did so, I felt that I was rebuking myself, for often I have used the opportunity to interpret Christ into an opportunity to display myself. I thus became an interferer instead of an interpreter. Much of modern preaching is interfering with Christ, instead of interpreting Him. Self-display instead of Christ-interpretation.

Sometimes we block the message because we are in it too much, and sometimes because we are in it not at all. We are perfunctory. It doesn't consume us. We do not burn with it. When asked to become the mayor of a certain French city, a man replied, "I will take the affairs of the city into my hands, but not on my heart and liver." Thus we take the affairs of the Kingdom into our hands, but will not let them reach our heart and liver. We are dead channels of a living Christ. "When I came to this Ashram I was a flickering torch, now I have become a flaming torch," said a radiant youth to me. And he had! If Christ doesn't get into your blood and raise your temperature, I wonder why? Such a Christ, such a message, such a need! We flatten out by our inner deadness what should live and challenge and redeem.

Do we interfere with the message because the self is too much in it, or because we are not truly in it at all? Or do we truly interpret Him?

---

O Christ, forgive me that I have again and again become like static of the radio breaking up clear reception. Help me to become a heightener of Thy redemptive message. Amen.

## GETTING THE MESSAGE THROUGH

We must now study how to get the message through to human need, for it is not enough for us to live victoriously—we must help others to do so. Nothing is really ours until we can pass it on. Someone has defined a Christian as "one who makes it easy for others to believe in God." Jesus did that. He did not prove God. He brought Him. In Korea they do not baptize a new convert until he has brought another to Christ. Then they know he is Christian, for he is Christianizing.

Let us study how Jesus got His message through to an exceedingly difficult case, the Samaritan woman. Not that Jesus ever looked on a person as a "case"; if He had, He would never have won that person. You have to love people to influence them. There were no "cases" with Him, there were persons. Let us study His method, for He was not only our example of how to live, but our example in helping other people to live. We shall take His delicate dealings with the woman step by step and learn as we go.

First, the account says, "He must needs go through Samaria." It was an inevitable thing, so He "evangelized the inevitable." He found His opportunity of getting His message across in the everyday inevitabilities of life. There are certain things in your life and mine which are inevitable—we have to go to office, to school, to workshop, to home duties, or we may be compelled by circumstance to sit on a park bench, unemployed. Evangelize that inevitable thing—find your opportunity in the ordinary contacts of the day. Then that day will no longer be ordinary, for the contacts are redemptive. You are turning the commonplace into the consequential. The little things of life become the big things—big with destiny. Life-contacts become life-changing. Nothing—absolutely nothing bigger under heaven than just that.

---

O Christ, help us to gather up these contacts so drab and commonplace and make them live with meaning and destiny —as Thou didst do. Amen.

## THE FIRST APPROACH

The first step in opening the conversation is the most difficult. Many hesitate to take it for fear of being snubbed. But I cannot remember where through the years I have had a real snub in approaching people about Christ. Even if they should snub you, what of it? Be so spiritually gay that you don't know when you are snubbed!

There were a great many reasons why He should not have spoken to this woman—He was tired and hungry; to talk to a woman in public was to risk His reputation; she was a woman of loose character; "Sychar" means "drunken," probably taken from the character of the inhabitants—nothing could be done with such a lot; it was noontime and at noontime in hot countries everyone rests. These were the reasons against His speaking to her. There was one reason in favor—she needed it! That one reason outweighed all the others. You will find many reasons why you should not share what you have found. I never speak to a person without having to fight past those reasons. But the one reason always persists—people need it, need it as they need absolutely nothing else. Let that be the determining factor.

Jesus began at the place of her dominant interest—water. He began at water and then went from water to living water, and then to fountains of living water in the heart. *Try to find out the dominant interest in people and lead them along the line of that dominant interest.* Is a youth's interest in athletics? Talk to him about a strong body, and the necessity of purity if that body is to be strong, and the dynamic in Christ to keep one pure. Is a parent wrapped up in his or her children? Then the suggestion is simple that they want to give the child the best, but they cannot do it unless they have it themselves.

———

O Christ, help me this day to find someone's dominant interest and to lead him through that interest to Thee. For all real roads run to Thee. Amen.

## BARRIERS AND THE WAY ROUND THEM

The woman threw up a barrier: "How is it that thou, being a Jew, asketh drink of me, which am a Samaritan woman?" The first tendency of the human heart is to close up at the approach of an intruder. It is the instinct of self-preservation. We do not easily let people into our lives. So many workers stop right here, and say it is of no use. The casualties among personal workers are very great at this point. They stop before they begin—discouraged. For there are today many counterparts of the Jew-Samaritan barrier.

But if the first instinct is to close, the second is to reveal. Everyone wants to share his inmost self, provided he can get the one in whom he has confidence. If confidence is given, it should be kept—absolutely. Or else there will be no further confidences. But do not be abashed at the first barrier, wait for the working of that deeper instinct of self-revelation.

How did Jesus get rid of the issue between Jew and Samaritan? He might have been drawn off into that controversy and might never have got beyond it. Instead, He got rid of the lesser issue by raising a higher one—He talked about "living water," and as He did so she forgot about the issue she had raised. That is the principle: *When people raise lesser issues, get rid of them by fastening their attention on higher issues.* Don't get tangled up in irrelevancies; drive on the main business in hand.

Jesus showed an amazing confidence in the woman: "If thou knewest the gift of God, and who it is that saith to thee, Give me to drink; thou wouldest have asked"—if you see the good you will want it! That was an amazing assumption to make in regard to such a woman. Everybody else had probably suggested the opposite. To influence people you must believe in people in spite of what they are.

---

O Christ, Thou great believer in man, Thou who dost believe in me when I cannot believe in myself, help me this day to believe in people, that they may believe in Thee. Amen.

## FURTHER BARRIERS AND THE WAY ROUND THEM

Jesus had an amazing confidence in the woman—she would want the good when she saw it. This leads to the third principle: *To influence people you must believe in them— sometimes in spite of.* The people who influence you for good are not the people who tell you how bad you are, but who tell you how good you may become. Nag people and they sag, believe in people and they bloom.

But the woman was not yet through with barriers. She said, "Art Thou greater than our father Jacob?" She was ready for a comparison. Now, Jesus might have said, "Woman, your father Jacob was a scheming liar who stole his brother's birthright." And it would have been perfectly true! She would have gone away angry and hurt. You and I must not strive to win arguments, but to win people. To win the argument you need only to be clever, but to win the person you need to be Christian.

But Jesus did get rid of Jacob. He slides out of the picture so gently that we scarcely notice that he is gone. How did He get rid of him? Again, by raising a higher issue. He replied in this most wonderful passage, "Whoever drinks any of the water that I shall give him will never, never thirst. But the water that I shall give him will become a fountain within him of water springing up for the Life of the Ages" (John 4. 13, Weymouth). As the woman's thought became fastened on that fountain of water in the heart she forgot Jacob and the controversy. The higher issue pushed out the lower.

This verse, one of the most beautiful in Scripture, was given to an outcaste woman. He did not hesitate to give His best to the worst. Personality was sacred. Your best is none too good for the worst. Then lavish it—as He did. And the worst will become the best—as she did.

---

O Christ, Thy best is offered at the shrine of my worst. Help me to exchange my worst for Thy best. And help me to help others to do the same. Amen.

## THE MOST DELICATE MOMENT

When Jesus spoke about "the well of water springing up into eternal life," the woman said she wanted it, for one thing that she might not come all the way hither to draw. Her motives were mixed—she wanted spiritual satisfaction and to be saved trouble.

People not only have mixed minds, but also mixed motives. Many of us would have dismissed the woman right there. Why bother with her with such mixed motives? But Jesus was infinite patience—He would purify the motives as well. A youth told me he went to the Communion as a semi-joke. But having taken that Communion he felt that he must stand by it—and did. He became a wonderful Christian. Christ took the hand held out in semi-jest, and forever gripped it.

But, in order to purify the motive He must purify her. So He must get to her moral problem. Take it as an axiom: *There is a moral problem in every life.* Get to that problem, or you will miss the point on which everything else hinges. For if we are not saved from sin, we are saved from nothing. How did He get to her sin? He might have said, "Woman, you are living a bad, adulterous life." But had He done so, she would have recoiled at the shock. Besides, it would not have been effective, for it is not enough to point out other people's sins, they must be led to point them out themselves. Then, and then only, are they on the road to get rid of them. So He led the woman to acknowledge her sin by making a delicate request, "Go, call thy husband, and come hither." At the word "husband" her eyes dropped, a guilty flush went across the soul. "I have no husband," she said, simply, and the words meant more than they seem. The guilt was exposed. She was inwardly crumpled before her newly aroused self—and Him.

O Christ, when we get people to that awful hour of sin exposure, give us the sure word to offer, that we may point to a sin exit—through Thee. Amen.

Acts 19. 18, 19    2 Timothy 4. 3, 4
Titus 3. 9       John 4. 19–24

## FACING UP

We left the woman face to face with her sins. We must get people to this place, for no matter what this sophisticated age may say, this is our personal problem. How can I get rid of sin? The first step is to expose it. For sin is like a seed: cover it and you cultivate it. But you ask, "How can I get people to uncover their moral need?" First, be free to talk about your own moral needs and your victory over them. Second, don't be shocked at disclosures. Third, establish confidence that you are a doctor that knows the way through.

To get people to face up to their moral need I find it effective to remind the person of my friend who examines his life in the light of the five tests: "Am I truthful? Am I honest? Am I pure? Am I quarrelsome or am I loving? Am I selfish or am I consecrated?" Repeat them over again, very slowly, and ask the person where he comes out as he thus examines his life. Many will tell you where they break down, glad to get out the whole wretched business. Others to save their face will wriggle and excuse. Or they may try to go off on another subject.

The woman did. She said: "I see you are a prophet. Now tell me where is the place to worship, Jerusalem or this mountain?" Why did she ask this question at this particular place? Because she found the conversation very uncomfortable, and preferred to draw it off to a more abstract religious question. It is easier to discuss abstract religious questions than it is to face one's own sin—easier and more deadly. Beware of the attempt to pull you off of the real thing by drawing the red herring of abstract religious questions across the path. Hold to the moral problem. For life and death lie in this issue. But they do not lie in the question of where to worship.

---

**O Christ, Thy restlessness saves us, for we would go off on tangents—from salvation. Save us from ourselves. Amen.**

## RELIGIOUS BUT ROTTEN

This Samaritan woman was apparently a religious woman —she was interested in the proper place to worship and in the coming Messiah who would tell them everything. Don't be put off the track when people talk religion to you, for we may be very religious—and very rotten. She was. Or we may be religious in spots and rotten in spots. As Streeter puts it: "Some people are only half-awake. They feel paroxysms of contrition because haunted by impure dreams, and yet are perfectly unconscious that their lives are one long expression of envy, malice, hatred, and uncharitableness. Others are sexually impure and yet haunted with remorse for an unkind word." "We compound for sins we are inclined to by damning the sins we have no mind to." Or as Niebuhr says, "We have two motives: the one we publish and the real one. Good people want to do the selfish thing, but they don't until they find an unselfish reason for doing it." We insist then, take nothing and nobody for granted.

Did Jesus answer this abstract religious question about the proper place to worship? Yes, but note how He did it. "God is a spirit"—that rendered Jerusalem and this mountain irrelevant. God desires people to "worship Him in spirit and in truth"—that rendered the moral life relevant in worship—"in truth," by true living. He went off to Jerusalem and to this mountain, but He was back again at the place He left off—the need of worship through truth, through right living.

The moral problem was still central. No matter how far you go off the point momentarily, bring the conversation back to the central issue. You yourself must guide the conversation—not the other person, nor circumstances. As you are leading toward liberty, toward release, so you must be in moral control of the situation. At every point Jesus guided the conversation. And in the end He guided her to release.

---

O Christ, we thank Thee that Thou dost point us to the wicket gate that leads to release. Help us to do that same thing with someone today. Amen.

John 1. 35–37    Matthew 10. 8
Colossians 1. 18   Mark 5. 19
John 20. 28, 31

## THE GOAL

What was the goal of the conversation, the end toward which everything was being led? It was in those words: "I that speak unto thee am he." The goal of the whole conversation was the revelation of Himself. He got her to see herself, that she might then see Himself—savingly.

The end of our work and conversation is just one simple thing—to get people to see Jesus. If we have failed in that, we have failed in our task. Our business is not to be clever, but to be Christian, and we can only be Christian as we show people Christ. But it must not be an intellectual apprehension of Him—it must be a moral apprehension, a taking hold of Christ as the power that shall change and transform life. The person must not merely survey Christ, but surrender to Him. That is what we mean by seeing Christ. Then the person has "root in himself"—and that root is Christ.

There is one step further. The real end was not to get the woman to see Christ, it was to get her so full of that vision that she would go off and give it to somebody else. The woman left her waterpot and ran off to the village and told what had happened. The end of evangelism is to produce an evangelist. We must not be satisfied to get somebody "in"—we must only be satisfied when they are getting someone else "in." Then we have really started something that knows no end. For we repeat, "You belong either to the cure or to the disease;" and if you are not curing, you are causing disease. And as you cure you will be more deeply cured. The account says "as they went to tell his disciples, behold, Jesus met them." On the way to tell others, Jesus met them—He always does. On the way to tell others you will sense a warm, living Presence.

––––––––

O Christ, help us not to feel that we are changed till we are changing, and help us to begin today. Amen.

## SOCIAL RESTRAINT—INDIVIDUAL CHANGE

When the disciples returned, they found Jesus in a very exalted state. He did not care to eat. When they urged He replied, "I have meat to eat that ye know not of . . . my meat is to do the will of him that sent me." Why should He be so abstracted and exalted over such a small incident? Small? In that simple changing of an individual He saw the biggest thing on earth, something which He identified with the will of God. And that will, He said, fed Him like meat.

If Jesus felt that way about changing the individual, why should it be sneered at as of little consequence, as some socially-minded people are now doing? Are we too small to hold two great emphases? Must we swing back from one to the other? Can we not hold both in a living blend? The Kingdom of God does mean the changing of the social order, but it also means just what happened to this woman—a changed individual life.

Some grafted peach trees were planted here in our mountain garden ten years ago, but today they are not over two feet high. The reason is that deer came in from the forest at night and ate off the growing tips as fast as they came out. They have life and it is a good quality of life, but growth has been impossible. Now that we have surrounded the garden with a barbed-wire fence the trees are growing. A barbed-wire fence —a social restraint, and a good quality of grafted-life, an individual change, are necessary for fruitfulness. But a barbed-wire fence around ungrafted wild peach trees will not bring fruitfulness. Nor will a grafted tree without that fence be fruitful. Individual change without social restraint won't do. Both are needed.

And Jesus rejoiced that day that He had put the graft of a higher life into a human soul. That was the will of God for Him—it must be for us.

---

O Christ, keep my life up against this central necessity, and give me power to put the graft of Thy life into other lives. Amen.

## HIS WILL—MY MEAT

Nothing exalts the soul, gives it a sheer sense of buoyancy and victory so much as the fact that we are being used to change the lives of other people. This is a necessary and integral part of victorious living. Without it victorious living will remain an unfulfilled dream. The battle of life is won not by the defensive, but by the offensive. The will of God is redemptive, and when we feed upon that will, we too shall become redemptive.

Jesus said that to Him the will of God was meat, it was something that fed Him, sustained Him, something that He lived by. Now, to some of us the will of God is medicine. It is something to be taken now and again to straighten us out. It is bitter, but it is needed to get rid of our ills. This view of the will of God is very common—it is something to be accepted, with a sigh. The will of God is to be borne. When death and calamity visit us, we say, "Thy will be done"—it is a medicine, and bitter too.

To some the will of God is more like sweets at the end of a meal—something to round off life, and give it taste. But you don't live by sweets. Nor do such people live by the will of God—the will of God is the occasional. It gives life its flavor, but not its food.

But to Jesus the will of God was neither medicine nor sweets, it was meat—the thing that sustained Him. This implies that we are made for the will of God as the body is made for food. It fits our moral and spiritual make up. Everything else is poison—this is food. I live as I live by the will of God—I wither and die as I live by some other will, particularly my own.

————

Help me, O Christ, to feed upon the will of God as my very meat. May that will within me turn to moral strength and spiritual victory. May it be life to me. Amen.

## MY WILL—MY POISON

Yesterday we said that we are made for the will of God as the body is made for food, that the will of God feeds us while everything else outside that will poison us.

H. G. Wells has fed upon as fine a thing as his Utopias, and yet it has left him dissatisfied, unfed. He confesses: "I cannot adjust myself to secure any fruitful peace. Here I am at sixty-five still seeking for peace." Brilliant, modern, and far-seeing, but—agnostic, and therefore feeding on some will other than that of God. And still hungry!

If Wells could not find sustenance in his Utopias, how about some of us who try to live by the will of the flesh? Paul says, "Thoughts shaped by the lower nature mean death; thoughts shaped by the spiritual mean life and peace" (Romans 8. 6, Weymouth)—they are poison to us. Everyone who has tried it knows it to be true. We are not made to live by our lower nature, but by our higher, as that higher is led by the will of God. In South America there are leaves of a tree which, if eaten, take away all appetite; one no longer cares for food; but it is a drug and not a food. Anything that apparently satisfies you, outside the will of God, is a drug.

But the will of God is food—real food. When a man is feeding on that, he is adequate for anything, afraid of nothing. He feels that at the center of his being he has resources, sustenance, a re-enforcement, Life not his own, and he lives by that very Life. Victorious living is the natural, normal outcome of that Fact. He is immovably fixed in God, and immeasurably fed by God.

There is nothing that sustains a man like the fact that he knows that the universe backs his will when he acts. Is it any wonder that we share that same sense of exalted joy Jesus had on this occasion?

---

O Father, I come to Thee to put my life alongside of Thine, to be guided and fed by Thee this day. Amen.

## "HIM UNTO HIM"

We cannot close this phase of victorious living in which we impart our lives to others without summing up the whole in the words, "him unto Him." This phrase sums up the very meaning of our gospel. The whole sentence reads, "They brought him unto him." The first "him" was a youth in need, and the second "Him"—Christ, the "unto" connected the two.

At one end is the "him" of human need, at the other end the "Him" that can meet that need. Never was this "him" of human need more needy than at the present time. Torn from old moorings, adrift, distracted, and desperately wanting something is this modern "him." Going—but he doesn't know where! Feeling—but after what he doesn't know! Thinking —but with no great certainties! This modern "him" is in the deepest need.

This "Him" that can meet that need stands ready, available, adequate. But He cannot reach that human need without a human connection. That connection is the "unto," and the "unto" is the Christian. He touches the "him" of human need on one side and the "Him," the Saviour, on the other and brings them together. To do so he has to be in living touch with both. But some are in touch with the "him," and out of touch with "Him"—the humanists. Others are in touch with "Him," and out of touch with "him"—isolated religionists. But some are in touch with both—the real Christian. The king of England was making a speech over the radio to the whole empire when the connection broke. An attendant grabbed the two broken ends of the wire and held them together throughout the speech and the message got across. He was the vital connecting link between king and people. You and I are to be in such close touch with Christ and human need that we mediate His very life to that need. What a place to occupy!

---

O Christ, we know that if we fail, the message will not get across. Help us not to fail Thee—and them, today. Amen.

## VICTORIOUS LIVING AND TEMPTATION

We have just been studying the fact that victorious living means to say "Yes" to something—the will of God; but that implies that we are to say "No" to something—temptation. Christianity is not a prohibition, it is a privilege, but it does have a prohibition in it.

Jesus said, if either thy "hand," or thy "foot," or thy "eye," offend thee, cause thee to stumble, cut it off (Mark 9. 43-47). In other words, do not tolerate anything from head to foot that cuts across the central purposes of your life. From head to foot you are to belong to Christ.

Now, note the order of these three—hand, foot, eye. The "hand," the doing of the evil; the "foot," approaching toward evil, going up to evil, but not actually doing it; the "eye," the seeing of evil with desire from afar. Cut it out *in any stage*, cut out sin, whether it be hand-sin, foot-sin, or eye-sin. The place to cut it out most effectively is at the place of the eye, the thought. But some live a great deal in that intermediate stage between "eye" and "hand"; they dally with sin at the "foot" stage.

They go beyond thinking about it, they actually approach toward it, come to the brink of it and expect to pull back this side of the deed. In this way they get the semipleasure of getting up close to evil, feeling its burning warmth, but they also get the semipleasure of being good enough to restrain finally. It is an attempt to get the best out of both worlds. A foolish attempt, for it leaves you homeless. You are not at home in Christ and not at home in evil. Dissatisfaction is the end of this attempt at double satisfaction. Watch your feet. Don't let them take you to any brink, for there is such a thing as "the appeal of the abyss." You might go over.

---

O Christ, we thank Thee for Thy decisiveness. We pray Thee to save us from all double-mindedness—help us to be decisive. Amen.

## EYE-SIN

The most effective place to kill sin is in the "eye" stage. That may mean the actual seeing of evil with the physical eye, or seeing it in imagination with the mental eye. The best place to kill a cobra is in its egg.

I pass on a little plan of my own: When an evil thought comes, I find that by batting my eyes very rapidly, the thought is broken up. It is a voluntary act demanding voluntary attention, and thus draws the attention away from the thought. I thus catch my equilibrium, and in that moment I pray, "O Christ, save me." It is the best working plan I know, for it is always available.

But we might offer other suggestions: (1) Change your occupation at once in order to get your attention elsewhere. I know of a man, that man myself, while going through a forest was troubled with an evil thought. He deliberately picked up a very heavy log and carried it back to the Ashram. The attention necessary to carry such a load made him forget the thought. Take on yourself such a heavy task that it demands your whole attention. I find that the greatest battles take place, not when one is absorbed in a task, but when one is on a vacation, where you let down and have nothing particular to absorb you. (2) If you are alone when an evil thought assails you, deliberately go, if possible, to a group of people. We sometimes talk of the temptation of crowds. On the other hand, we can thank God for crowds. They often save us from ourselves and our evil thoughts. We are shamed to harbor them when we are in the company of some people. Moreover, they draw off our minds to other interests. (3) Change the mental picture to a religious one. Train your mind to run at once to the thought of the Crucified. It is hard to think of evil and of Him at the same time. They are incompatibles.

---

O Christ, give me purity in mind, for I want the kind of mind in which Thou canst be at home. Amen.

## OVERCOMING TEMPTATION

We continue to look at the way evil thoughts may be overcome: (4) Put your mind under a rigid discipline. The mind is the servant of the personality and can be made to obey. You can turn off your thoughts as you turn off a radio. The mind soon begins to understand who is master. Paul speaks of "bringing every thought into captivity to the obedience of Christ." But the mind will play tricks on you if it knows that in the end you give in. Be unbending in your discipline of yourself. (5) In order to determine your waking thoughts, think of the purest, finest thoughts just before going to sleep. Those last thoughts before dropping into unconsciousness are very determinative, for the door into the subconscious is opening and they drop into it to work good or ill.

The dream life can be largely controlled by your waking life. Psychologists tell us that you do dream only of things that have occupied consciousness in the last three or four days. Of course these things of recent occurrence may touch off older memories by association, but the dream life of the next three or four days can be controlled in great measure by the waking life of today. Remember you are fighting the battle of the waking and dream life of today and tomorrow when you are fighting that evil thought. Give it no quarter. Do not let your last waking thought be an impure thought, for it will fasten itself upon the mind like a burr. Crowd it out by making your last thought the horizon-filling Christ. (6) Take plenty of exercise. Take up games and become interested in them. (7) Undertake to help someone else in his battle. The very sense of your responsibility for the other will help you in yours, for the thought will persist, "I must not let him down. For his sake I sanctify myself." (8) Breathe an ejaculatory prayer the moment an impure thought is presented.

----

O Christ of the pure mind, make me pure in mind this day—and always. Amen.

Hebrews 2. 1     Matthew 13. 23
James 1. 19     Revelation 2. 7, 11, 17

## TAKE HEED WHAT YE HEAR

In our study of the control of the mind, it will help us to look at a most important verse: "Take heed what ye hear; with what measure ye mete it shall be measured unto you; and more shall be given unto you" (Mark 4. 24). Here Jesus says, "Be careful of what you hear, for with what measure of attention you mete out to anything it will come back to you in impression." The degree of attention is the degree of impression.

After taking a course in Pelmanism on memory training, the only thing I remember (!) of the course is this: It is not a matter of memory, it is a matter of attention. A bad memory is the result of bad attention. So one should not really say, "I have a bad memory;" one should say, "I have bad attention." Someone has said there are just three laws of learning: concentrate, concentrate, concentrate. So, Jesus said, be careful of the thing you attend to. For that part of your environment to which you attend influences you.

This age is thinking about sex—which is to the good. But it is thinking too much about sex—which is to the bad. If you concentrate your attention upon sex, don't be surprised if it comes back to you in sex-impression. And then don't be surprised if you lose your sex battle. Be frank about sex, by all means, but after taking a frank view of the fact of sex, dismiss it from the center of consciousness. But if you are constantly wading through sex-books in the name of frankness, you will soon be wading through filth, at least, in mind. For you follow your attention. Glance at the fact of sex, but gaze at the fact of Christ. But some gaze at sex, and then wonder that sex, and not Christ, has such hold on them.

So take heed what you hear and see, for that attention determines your spiritual destiny.

---

O Christ, we thank Thee that Thou hast spoken this law so plainly. Help us to obey it just as plainly. Amen.

## THE TEMPTATION TO LOOK AT OTHERS

We said that we must be careful of what we give our attention to, for the measure of attention determines the measure of impression. Some of us pay too much attention to what other people say and do. Our eyes are on people instead of on Christ. And then we wonder why we are so weak.

Peter once turned to Jesus and said, "Lord, and what shall this man do?" Jesus' reply was penetrating: "What is that to thee? follow thou me." Many of us get our eyes on people, on their weaknesses in particular, and soon find we are stumbling—over people. A great many of our spiritual problems come from the fact of hurts from stumbling over this insincere Christian, over that weak brother. One of the outstanding Christians of the world became bitter and soured. As he recounted his grievances against this one and that one, I quietly quoted this passage, "What is that to thee? follow thou me." He was startled, but resumed his criticisms. In one of the pauses I again quoted this passage, "What is that to thee? follow thou me." He was great enough to say, "Good, you've got me." He was on the wrong track and knew it. He had starved himself gnawing on these bones. One of the most pathetic sights in India is a lean dog on a dry bone pile gnawing on a dry bone. But not more pathetic than a Christian gnawing on some dry bone of grievance against others. Poor diet—the soul grows lean on it.

You are not following that person—you are following Christ. To his own Master he stands or falls. Christ is the only one who is always the same, dependable, sure, adequate. Follow Him! He will never let you down. People do.

So, if you are tempted to go up or down according to the way people treat you, resist it.

----

O Christ, I pray Thee to help me to get my eyes on Thee and Thee alone, so that, no matter what people may do or not do, I may be fixed. Amen.

293

## THE TEMPTATION TO LOOK AT YOUR FEELINGS

Many stumble by getting their eyes on people, others stumble by getting their eyes on their emotional states. They go up or down as their feelings go up or down. I do not minimize the place of emotion, for it is the driving force of the soul. Only those ideals that have an emotional tone about them get us. But if you pay too much attention to emotion, you won't have any. Emotion is the by-product of a great driving conviction—the waves cast up as the ship pushes forward. Think about your directions and the adequacy of your power to go ahead and your emotions—the waves—will take care of themselves.

Besides, our feelings are often largely determined by our physical condition. It is hard to feel religious with a tooth aching! As someone has put it, The light is still burning, but the lamp chimney has become smoked by some physical ailment. You throw a stone into the water and destroy the moon reflected there. Do you? The moon sails sublimely on in the sky. Your feelings are like the reflection on the surface of the water—subject to calm and storm and many changes. But your faith in Christ is like the moon in the sky, unchanged by what happens to the reflections in the water.

A lady who was up and down with feelings once dreamed that she was in a long tube. When she looked up, she was up, and when she looked down, she was down. She awoke to determine to keep looking up at Jesus, and not down at herself and her feelings. For looking at her feelings was a species of self-centeredness.

Mazzini once said, "Whether the sun shine with the serene splendor of an Italian noon, or the leaden corpselike hue of the northern mist be above us, I cannot see that this changes our duty"—great words and applicable to every Christian!

———

O Christ, save me when I, like Peter, get my eyes on myself and the waves around me instead of on Thee. For amid the flux of things Thou remainest the same. Amen.

## OUTGROWING TEMPTATION

Temptation has its uses. As we grapple, we grow. Goethe says, "Difficulties prove men." When Jesus went into the wilderness, it was said that He went in "full of the Holy Spirit," but He came out "in the power of the Spirit" (Luke 4. 1, 14). Mere fullness had turned to power under temptation. His spiritual tissues had been hardened in the struggle. So it is with us. Two things happen as we grow spiritually: (1) Our temptations move on up to a higher plane, and (2) we outgrow many of them.

The temptations of Jesus were on a very high plane indeed. In the wilderness He did not struggle with lust and passion, but with the subtle questions of how to bring in the Kingdom, and here light could very easily become darkness. It is a compliment to be tempted on that plane. As you grow spiritually you find your temptations less gross and more subtle. The battle with things like spiritual pride takes the place of the battle with dishonesty and lies. And then there comes the time when you outgrow your temptations entirely. This is the highest state of all—to be on a spiritual level where these things no longer touch you, or incite you. You have gone beyond them.

The last petition in the Lord's Prayer is, "And lead us not into temptation." I used to think it an anticlimax, but I now see that it was the highest petition of all and is the very climax of all: Lead me to the place where temptation has lost its grip, where there is literally no temptation. We do that in many things. We say, "He can't be tempted by bribery." His character now automatically spurns it. It will be so with us in thing after thing. We will get the habit of victory. The unconscious effort will more and more take over the functions of the conscious effort. We become fixed in goodness. Habit is working with us now, not against us.

———

O Christ, I thank Thee that every battle now makes the next one easier. Help me to win every one today. Amen.

Acts 2. 41–47
Acts 4. 32

## PRINCIPLES OF CORPORATE LIVING

We have been studying the difficulties that come out of temptations which largely arise from within ourselves. But many of our spiritual problems do not arise from ourselves—they arise from our relations with others. It is not an easy thing to adjust oneself to other people and their wills. Christianity should teach us that very thing, for Christianity is the science of living well with others according to Jesus Christ. Many of our attempts to live together with others are haphazard; they do not obey the underlying principles of corporate living, for there are principles or laws of corporate living as well defined as those that underlie nature. We must attempt to discover them and live by them. All of us have to live in relationship with others. Many try to do it without any underlying principles, and it ends in disaster with its resultant bitterness and strife. If we depend too much on emotion, and not enough on intelligent planning, the result will be disaster.

John Wesley said that he was "a man sent from God to persuade people to put Christ at the center of their relationships." It would be difficult to give a better definition of what our Christian task is than just those words. What are some of the principles which we should embody if we are to live together well?

(1) We should recognize that life is corporate. Many do not recognize this. They still look on life as an individual thing. The consequence is that they are continually in trouble with other people. They want to turn whole situations to themselves, instead of relating themselves to the whole. A cancer cell is one that demands that it be ministered unto instead of ministering to the rest of the body. It is therefore cancerous instead of contributive. There are many who are cancerous in society. They look at what they can get from the whole instead of what they can give it.

---

O Christ, teach me how to live well with others, for I shall want others to live well with me. Amen.

## PRINCIPLES OF CORPORATE LIVING—Continued

(2) After we recognize that we are corporate we must proceed to fix our loyalty to the group in which we are in immediate contact. There are degrees of loyalty of course. There is the loyalty to oneself, to one's family, to one's group, to one's nation, to the Kingdom of God. Our final loyalty should be to the Kingdom of God. Where loyalty to that conflicts with any of the lesser loyalties then the lesser must give way and the Kingdom must remain supreme and final. While this is true, there must be a loyalty to a group in which we work out the principles of that Kingdom and make them operative. If we do not work them out in the smaller, we shall never work them out in the larger.

(3) Loyalty to that group should mean that we will never criticize any member behind his or her back. There is bound to be criticism, for this is an imperfect world of imperfect persons. But the criticism should always be open and frank and always redemptive. One of the mottoes on our Ashram walls is this: "Fellowship is based on confidence, secret criticism undermines that confidence, therefore we renounce all secret criticism." You cannot have fellowship, if you know or suspect that secret criticism is taking place. But when you know that since there is no open criticism, there is no secret criticism, then the situation is filled with confidence and freedom and therefore with fellowship. Another motto on our Ashram walls is this: "When about to criticize another, ask three questions: (1) Is it true? (2) Is it necessary? (3) Is it kind?" If it can pass these three tests, then the criticism should be given openly and frankly.

Religious people are in the business of endeavoring to be good, they are therefore tempted to point out the faults of others, so that by implication they themselves may appear better. It is a miserable business.

---

O Christ, save me this day and every day from the disloyalty of secret criticism. May the words die upon my lips and in my heart because of Thy love. Amen.

Hebrews 12. 5–11　　James 4. 11, 12
1 Corinthians 13. 4–6　Proverbs 17. 9

## CORPORATE LIVING FURTHER EXAMINED

We continue our study of corporate living: (4) We should not only be willing to criticize another for his or her good, we should also be willing to take it for ourselves. And rejoice in it. Many of us are willing to give it, but we hesitate or refuse to take it for ourselves. No one has earned the right to criticize another unless he welcomes the possibility of criticism of himself by others. The principle of give-and-take must be in operation within the group.

(5) But we should be on our guard that we do not thus become petty, always seeking for something to correct in our brother. We should perhaps be more inclined to compliment and encourage than correct. We need not be afraid that we will make people proud, for sincere souls are often more humbled by compliments than by criticism. If we are always looking for things to correct, we become dangerously near to mote-picking.

Two prominent Indians went to England, one came back enthused with ideas which he put into practice, and is now a great spiritual leader. The other came back and could scarcely talk of anything except the signs he saw in an elevator or lift, "Beware of pickpockets." The idea of such a sign being necessary in a Christian country! He fed his soul on mote-picking and withered into insignificance. This has its counterpart in an American business man who on his return from England was constantly talking of a window in the hotel that could not be fastened. It loomed beyond cathedrals and beyond a great people. His message was defective window fastenings! He withered with his message.

Our attitude should be that of finding fine things, but now and then faced with the necessity of pointing out weakness. But the emphasis should be on the search for the good, for people are made more by compliments than by corrections.

————

O Christ, Thou who dost find fine things in me when I cannot find them in myself, help me this day to find the good in my fellow men, and to say so. Amen.

OCTOBER 17

Philippians 4. 5
1 Corinthians 13. 5
(Weymouth)

Matthew 5. 25
Romans 14. 13, **15, 16**

## GIVING WAY IN SMALL THINGS

We go on from where we left off yesterday: (6) There must be willingness to give way in small things that do not involve principles. There are many tiny things that become mountains because we insist on making them issues. It is far better to give way in small matters, that we might stand on the big ones. The bigness of a person can be judged by the size of the thing upon which he takes his stand. One of the great things in life is to learn to keep small things small and great things great. We often reverse these things in our relationship to each other.

(7) Another principle is to refuse to look for slights regarding ourselves. There is no more difficult person than the "touchy" person—always looking for slights and always getting his feelings hurt. If we look for slights, we shall find them. When we look for slights, it shows that we are on the defensive, and to be on the defensive shows we are dominated by fear. The defensive attitude shows that either the inferiority complex or the fear complex is at work.

(8) We should look more to our duties than to our rights. If we are always looking to our rights, we shall throw the emphasis on the wrong side of things. Think about privileges of service and you will have more rights than you will know what to do with.

(9) Meet issues before they get cold. If you harbor a thing in the heart, it will fester. Get it up and out at once. The time element is important. Don't put it off through cowardice. Jesus says, "Agree with thine adversary quickly, *while thou art in the way with him.*" Don't separate and let the thing get cold. Cultivate the *habit of spiritual decisiveness.* I find it a good habit when I pick up a bunch of letters to open first the one that looks unpleasant!

———

O Christ, we thank Thee that in meeting issues Thou didst not hesitate. Give me that same nerve. Amen.

299

## SIDING AGAINST YOURSELF

We pursue our study of the Christian way to live together: (10) We shall often have to side with the group against ourselves. A mother was bringing up her little boy on the principle of getting guidance in life. He had taken the scissors, cut off one side of his hair and left the pillowcase in shreds. When his mother returned, instead of losing her temper, she suggested a "quiet time" in which they could get guidance as to what should be done about it. After the "quiet time" she asked him if he had got any light. "Yes," he said, "I think that we had better not let me have the scissors again!" Sound guidance! He had sided with his mother against himself! This is something that will have to be done very often—we will decide that the group-claim is stronger than our personal claim.

(11) Keep the power of laughing at yourself. Stand before the mirror and burst into laughter! It will keep you from taking yourself too seriously. The capacity of a man to laugh at himself determines how high he has risen. There are these stages: the lowest—the man who doesn't laugh at all; then the man who laughs only at his own jokes; then the one who laughs at the jokes of others; and highest of all the man who can laugh at himself. For the power to laugh at oneself shows the power to look at oneself objectively.

(12) If you find that there is a basic inequality or injustice at the heart of your relationships in reference to anyone in the group, don't counsel patience unless and until you are doing your best to right that basic injustice or inequality. For that basic wrong will poison relationships and will break out again and again until righted. No surface kindness can atone for that central wrong. Build your fundamental relationships on justice and equality and everything else becomes easier.

O Christ, I pray Thee to help us to put Thy mind into all our relationships, and then we shall know how to live together. Amen.

## "ORGANS ONE OF ANOTHER"

We come to an important principle in corporate living: (13) Remember what Paul says in Weymouth's Translation, "We serve as organs one of another." This thought should keep us from jealousy. If a member of your group excels you, say in singing, then he becomes the organ of song for you. You should therefore rejoice that your organ of song is thus so beautifully efficient. Another may excel you in executive ability. You should rejoice that your organ of executive power is functioning. For the point is, you are striving to get a corporate job done, and the strength of any is the strength of all. You will have something in you which will be the organ of the other, something in which you are strong and he is weak. None of us has everything, but we all have something. Take an inventory of your strong and weak points, and see how your weakness can be supplemented by the strength of someone.

(14) Keep up the prayer life, and underneath that prayer life keep a surrendered heart. When we are inwardly surrendered, we don't expect anything, and if anything comes to us, it is sheer gain. Moreover, when we are inwardly surrendered, we become immune to many of the slights and clashes that come in ordinary contacts. In that prayer life let your thought of each other turn to prayer for each other. A lady rather dreaded the coming of a person who was a "critical Christian," and a great trial to her, and she was to stay a week! She felt a night of prayer alone would fortify her against the trial. No sooner had she knelt than the promise came, "God shall supply all your needs!" Her fears vanished. She jumped into bed and slept the night through. The guest came the next day and her hostess quite enjoyed the visit. Prayer had tapped the power of Christ. It will do it for you.

O Christ, Thy power, and Thy power alone can sweeten relationships and make impossible situations not only possible but glorious. Give me that power this day. Amen.

## A CROSS SECTION OF A CHRISTIAN SOCIETY

We have been studying the principles of corporate living and now we must look at a cross section of a Christian society in the first century. "Fear came upon everyone. . . . And all the believers kept together, and had everything in common. They sold their lands and other property, and distributed the proceeds among all, according to everyone's necessities. . . . They took their meals with great happiness and single-heartedness, praising God and being regarded with favor by all the people. Also, day by day, the Lord added to their number those whom He was saving" (Acts 2. 43–47, Weymouth). Let us see what was there: (1) *Fear.* The supernatural was working down through human relationships and was being embodied in a new society. God became an incarnate fact. (2) *Unity*—"all the believers kept together." Many shades of belief and class and color among them, but they had a living unity that transcended difference. (3) *That Unity included the social and economic life.* They were not merely one in spirit, apart from and above the economic and social life—the whole of life was one. They held no difference between the sacred and the secular. (4) *Need was abolished.* Good news to the poor—the first item in Christ's program was fulfilled. (5) *Community, family, and individual life were preserved.* They were "in the Temple with one accord"—the community was preserved; they ate bread at home—the family life was intact; the individual was filled with a great "happiness," therefore preserved and heightened. (6) *Single-heartedness.* The divisions were gone on the inside, and on the outside in their relationships with each other. Life was reduced from complexity to simplicity. (7) *Life became winsome and contagious.* "Regarded with favor" —winsome; "day by day the Lord added"—contagious.

These are the seven colors into which the white light of God's society breaks up. We must rediscover this light for this darkened age and put it not merely into the small group, but into society as a whole. For God wills it!

———

O God, we cannot be fully victorious until everyone shares that victory. Help us to embody that victory in our total life. Amen.

## DANGERS TO THE NEW SOCIETY

The two greatest dangers to this new emerging Society, the Kingdom of God, came from two directions: money and power.

The new society was threatened when Judas gave way to the love of money, and again when Ananias gave way to the same impulse. It was also threatened from within when the disciples began to quarrel over the places of power, and it was more than threatened from without when the authority of the Kingdom of God, as represented in Jesus, came into conflict with the Jewish religious authorities and the Roman secular power. They saw their power challenged and threatened and they struck back with a cross. Money and power crucified Christ. It is strange that sex apparently had nothing to do with it, though we usually think of sex as the greatest center of moral danger. "Hunt for the woman in the case" would be to go astray in hunting for causes in the crucifixion of Jesus. Money and power held the field of causes. They did then and they do today.

It is said that Jesus "sat over against the treasury, and beheld how . . ." It is a serious and awful moment when Jesus surveys the money side of our religion and our civilization. He sees how we make money, how we keep it, how we spend it, and the hypocrisies and strife that have grown up around it all. We feel that He is searching that side of our civilization as never before. He is probing to the roots and is laying bare the fact of the utterly unchristian basis of the money side of our civilization. His awful eye of judgment is upon that central moral fact. We will not be able to get complete victory in human living individually and collectively until we get it at the place of money.

---

O Christ, we pray Thee to become the Conscience of our conscience at this point, for here we need light to show us the way out, and we need power that will deliver us from the love of money. Amen.

OCTOBER 22

Mark 12. 15
Acts 2. 6
Acts 4. 36, 37

1 Corinthians 6. 12
Philippians 4. 11, 12

## VICTORY AT THE PLACE OF MONEY

We saw that money and power are the two sources of greatest temptation in modern life. How can we get victory at the place of money?

There are the individual and the social aspects. We must apply self-surrender to both of these aspects. Money must be individually surrendered. That is, we will say something like this: "I know I need money in a world of this kind, but I don't need more than I need. I will draw a line at the place where my needs end, for at that place other people's needs begin, and to go beyond that line is to steal from them, and I cannot do that and be Christian. In prayer and counsel with others I will find that line, and put the surplus at the disposal of other people's needs." I master money by making it minister to my need and to the needs of others. If money makes me more mentally, morally, physically, and spiritually fit for the purposes of the Kingdom of God, it is legitimate and right—a servant of the Kingdom.

In the social aspect we should inwardly renounce, and get as many other people as possible to do the same, a system of money use based on competition which turns society into "a scramble of pursuers and pursued." We should renounce this order based on the unchristian principle of selfish competition and give ourselves to the producing of an order based on the Christian principle of co-operation. We shall not be able to effect this fully at once. Society is not prepared for it. We must blunder on and suffer more until we are beaten to our knees by the chastening rod of God, and then we try God's way. But in the meantime we have renounced the old order and are working for a new one. On that basis we can live victoriously both individually and collectively, because we are acting as though the victory were already here. It is, as far as we are concerned.

---

**O Christ, help me this day to renounce money as master and to realize it as servant by Thy power. Amen.**

Matthew 20. 26–28
John 9. 14
Philippians 2. 5–9

## VICTORY AT THE PLACE OF POWER

We must now see how power, which usually corrupts people, may serve people. Power is the expression or projection of personality. When the personality is converted, power must be converted along with it. But the matter of power has its individual and its social aspects. So it must be doubly converted.

Jesus "sat on the mount of Olives over against the Temple" and surveyed it and judged it. The power represented in that Temple had turned from service to exploitation. Given to serve the people, it now made the people serve it. It must therefore be cleansed, and if it does not respond, then it must come down. Jesus is surveying the power side of our civilization today. His searching eye rests on the exploitations taking place through power. And we feel His burning condemnations.

Again, we must get the victory by surrender. Jesus said: "Ye know that they which are accounted to rule over the Gentiles exercise lordship over them; . . . But so shall it not be among you; but whosoever will be great among you, shall be your minister: And whosoever of you will be the chiefest, shall be servant of all." I must therefore renounce all power over others in my life that is not gained by service to others. All power based on money, prestige, class, race, or sex must go, and only that retained which is gained by actual self-giving service. This is personal. In regard to the social we must do the same. We must inwardly renounce all power in the social and political order that does not serve the people in their total needs, and we must influence as many others as possible to do the same. Society is not ready to make that the criterion and test of power. Here too we must blunder on and suffer more before we are beaten to our knees under God's chastening rod. Meanwhile we renounce all exploiting power and are willing to suffer through that renunciation. We are living victoriously as far as it depends on us, for we have anticipated the victory.

----

O God, help me not to bend the knee to insolent might, but may I know no sovereignty but Thine. Amen.

305

## THE CROSS BECOMES INEVITABLE

Out of these social contacts a cross arises. If we are in sympathetic contact with people and situations around us, we react in suffering to what is happening. The effect of the gospel is to deepen and widen one's sympathies. This means that your sympathies have been so widened that life will touch you on a wider front. So the process of your Christianization is the deepening of your capacity for suffering. Each new friendship you form, each new convert you win, each new injustice in the social order you come in contact with, each new sin in others to which you expose yourself, each new task you take on yourself, will become a possible suffering point. Through the gospel there is a sensitizing of the soul and a universalizing of the sympathies of that sensitized soul. The cross thus becomes inevitable.

In the case of Jesus, His sympathies were universal in range and infinite in depth. He was the Son of man, so that the cross that came as a result of that fact was universal and infinite. It had cosmic significance. He touched all life in love and out of that love contact all His being reacted in suffering. The cross is the focal point of that suffering. But that suffering was there before and is still there and will be there till evil is banished. The actors in that terrible drama unwittingly bore witness of this universal cross when they put up the inscription upon the cross in Latin, Greek, and Hebrew. That was unusual. Did they dimly sense the fact that here was suffering breaking out into all languages? Or was it that they expressed His guilt in all these languages? It doesn't matter, for it was the same—His guilt was His love—the guilt of loving universally, and therefore suffering universally.

As you become personally and socially Christianized, a cross awaits you. It is inevitable.

———

O Christ, we see Thy cross is not an isolated thing—it continues in us. May I this day be in the succession of Thy cross-bearers. Amen.

## THE CROSS IN ACTION

We said yesterday that our Christianized sympathies become our Christianized crosses. Tyndale-Biscoe devotedly loves his boys in Kashmir and is striving to make men out of them. One day he had a pit dug in the school yard, and then to the astonishment of his boys stepped into it and said: "Now cover me up and bury me. I cannot bear to live as long as you do these things. I would rather die. You must bury me, or you must bury your sins." The boys decided to bury their sins.

You will thus go out into life as a Christian, not to face evil so dramatically as that perhaps, but your contact with evil will turn into a cross for you. Someone has said that he wanted to build a house with no windows and no doors save the slits of a cross as the only opening, so that he could look out upon the world through a cross alone. Beautiful. But we must not only look out on life through a cross—we must touch life through a cross. Our very contacts must become vicarious. We must deliberately take on ourselves what really doesn't belong to us, save as Christ makes us belong to everybody, and, therefore, everyone's sorrows belong to us. When anyone is called a "Sheeny," we wince; when one is an outcaste, we are lonely and degraded in him; when one is hungry, we suffer his pangs; when children are exploited by industry, they become our own children; when a Negro suffers disabilities on account of his color, we become whiter—with pain; when war takes hold of youth and binds him to its nefarious purposes, how can we be free unless we are bound with him —perhaps in prison, as a result of our protest? Our love crimsons into sacrifice as it meets the world's sin. In a world of this kind a crossless Christian is a Christless Christian.

---

O Christ, make me willing to open my heart to its deepest depths to the world's anguish and woe, and may my heart become a place of healing. Amen.

1 Corinthians 2. 1, 12
Galatians 2. 20
Colossians 1. 20

## LIFE LOOKED AT THROUGH A CROSS

I had to leave my Himalayan retreat at this place in my writing and face tragedy within our family circle at the Lucknow Ashram. The wife of our doctor, a nurse, cultured, devoted, beautiful, just married six months, now faces death from a painful incurable disease, and has only a week or so to live. She will not be able to get back to her home in Holland to die there among her loved ones. Cut off at the end of five months of devoted service in India! My God, why?

No one can look in the face of this kind of a tragedy without raising ultimate questions about the universe—is there meaning and purpose in the universe? If there is a God, does He care? I have no answer—except as I look at life through the cross. There I see a God who comes into the very struggle and suffers all I suffer—and more. "Pray that I may get back safely," said an officer to the chaplain as he was about to start out on a dangerous duty to cut wires at night in No Man's Land. "No," replied the chaplain, "I will not do that. But I will go with you." The cross means just that—God goes with us and lets everything that falls on us fall upon His own heart. I can love a God like that. When I stand beside the bedside of "Sister Winnie"—at the bedside of her who would have stood at the bedside of thousands in tender ministry had she lived, I see light only in a cross. My universe holds steady. "The cross saves me from pessimism and saves the truth at the heart of pessimism," said a Christian Indian professor. The truth in pessimism is this: this is a world of pain and sorrow and tragedy. The cross saves us from pessimism by using that pain and sorrow and tragedy for redemptive purposes. Through it all it shows the very love of God seeking, redeeming, healing, saving. The cross is light—the only light.

---

O Christ, we come to Thee thanking Thee that we can see life through Thy wound prints and that through them we can see light—the very light of life. Amen.

1 Peter 2. 19–24
1 Peter 3. 14, 17, 18
Mark 14. 41, 42

## THE FOUR WHO BORE CROSSES

That Day there were four who bore crosses. They represent four attitudes. The first was the impenitent thief—it was a cross of unrelieved gloom. He blamed Christ for not saving Himself and them. He died blaming everybody but himself, and therefore bore a cross that had no light in it. Some bear that kind of a cross to the very end. No repentance, no reconciliation, no release.

The other thief looked through and beyond the shame of it all and saw that Jesus really was a King, and asked to be remembered when He came in His Kingdom. That was the cross that had light in it. It had thrown him in contact with Jesus. That cross lifted up his head and he saw the gates of forgiveness open to him, for his heart was penitent. That was the cross that opened in gloom and ended in gladness.

The third cross was laid upon the shoulders of Simon, the Cyrenian, "a man out of the country." They laid on him an undeserved cross—"him they compelled to bear the cross." Life does that with us—it lays hold on us and puts on our unwilling shoulders a cross. It changed the whole course of life for him and his family, for his two sons, Alexander and Rufus, became well-known Christians. Simon did not bear his cross—he used it. When Life lays its cross on us, we can make that cross throw us in company with Christ—and that contact will forever change us. "It is not suffering that ennobles, it is the way it is borne." Simon bore it well and it made him.

The last cross was that of Jesus—a chosen cross. The rest were involuntary—this was chosen. He put Himself in such deep contact with men that the cross became inevitable. He chose it. That is the highest attitude of all. Since life is bound to give you a cross it is better to anticipate it, to accept it and through it to lift others. The chosen cross is Christ's and the Christian's cross.

---

O Christ, help me to take that chosen cross and to make it redemptive for myself and others. Amen.

309

OCTOBER 28

Exodus 16. 20, 21
1 Samuel 2. 1
Isaiah 55. 12

## THE CHRISTIAN'S JOY

Now that we have spoken of the cross, we can speak of the Christian's joy. For the Christian's joy is a joy won out of the heart of pain. It has a certain quality that distinguishes it from lesser joys. Revelation speaks of those who sing "the song of Moses and the Lamb." There are really three great songs: the song of Nature, the song of Moses, the song of the Lamb.

The song of Nature is the song of the triumph of the strong over the weak. I heard a bird singing gaily with a quivering dragon fly in its mouth. It beat it from this side to that and interspersed the ghastly killing with gay singing. That is the song that comes out of lower nature—it is a song that is mingled with the pains of others. Hunger and power are satisfied even though it costs the lives of others.

Many sing that song. Their joy is the joy of personal advantage, no matter what it may cost others. They rejoice that they have gained in the stock market, even though their gain was somebody's loss. They rejoice in success in business, even though they know that by ruthless competition they have pushed somebody to the wall. It is the joy of knowing that the head of John the Baptist is off, even though they do not like the sight of it on a platter in front of them. They have won. That is enough. It is the song of unlimited rights over the weaker.

There is a slightly higher joy—the song of Moses. It is the song of limited rights, an eye for an eye, and a tooth for a tooth. We rejoice that we got even with someone. Our sense of rough justice is satisfied. We sing the song of Moses. We go through life getting satisfactions out of strict justice. That too is a superficial and precarious joy.

---

O Christ, save us from the satisfactions of the lesser joys that leave their sting, and help us to know Thy joy, because we know Thy cross. Amen.

## THE SONG OF THE LAMB

We saw yesterday the song of Nature—the song of unlimited rights over the weak—and the song of Moses—the song of limited rights. We must now look at the song of the Lamb—the song of unlimited love, the song of doing good to those who despitefully use you, the song of One who dies for His crucifiers. This is life's deepest song. Anyone who can sing this song is in the highest stage of spiritual evolution. He really has victory.

That widow of a murdered prime minister had it when she gathered her children around the coffin of her husband, and prayed for the forgiveness of his murderer, and gave it from herself and family. It was the song of the Lamb. Our young Ashram doctor has it when cruel nature snatches his young wife away and he carries on helping to save others and rejoices in the opportunity.

I had a canary that would not sing until after it had taken its bath. Then it would sing deliriously. I have a heart like that—and so have you. It will not sing until it is washed from all bitterness, all revenge, all hate. When it is cleansed from these, then it really sings—with all the stops out. A Brahmin convert suffered because of his stand for Christ, but this is what he writes: "I am always bubbling over with joy to the bursting point. My Lord is always with me to save, to comfort, to guide and to cheer. May He be with you similarly." That is the Christian note. Don't make light of that joy in the name of modern sophistication, for this joy is the most cleansing, the most energizing, the most service-inspiring and the most rhythm-producing fact on earth. It is salvation by joy. One drop of that puts more oil into the machinery of life than any other known thing.

———

O Christ, we thank Thee for this exquisite joy. When we have tasted it, we know that we have tasted life itself. Help us to share it. Amen.

311

## THE POWER OF THE RESURRECTION

We spoke of the exquisite joy of the Cross—the song of the Lamb. But there is a step further. There is the joy of realizing "the power of His resurrection."

The resurrection means that the worst has been met and has been conquered. This puts an ultimate optimism at the heart of things. The resurrection says that no matter how life may seem to go to pieces around you, nevertheless, the last word is with love. And that on the plane of the physical, in the here and now. Had it been a spiritual resurrection only, it would have meant that the victory is beyond matter, not in the midst of it. But as the battle was an embodied battle, so the victory is an embodied victory. This sweeps the whole horizon, and says that here and now man can meet and conquer anything—everything. No wonder the Christian in the midst of a decaying order is no pessimist. He has solid grounds for his optimism. He has got hold of unconquered and unconquerable Life.

When Paul came to the Athenians and preached "Jesus and the resurrection," they said he was proclaiming "foreign gods"—they thought the "resurrection" to be a separate "god," because of Paul's emphasis. There is no danger of that happening to this age, for the resurrection has been dimmed, and with it an infinite sadness has come over us. We shall not deify the resurrection, neither shall we dim it, but we shall declare it as the most amazing and transforming fact of human history. Nothing really matters now—except this one thing: He is alive forevermore! Related to Him, realizing Him, drawing life from Him we are fellowshiping with ultimate Life, and nothing again can dismay us or make us afraid. If in the end everything will come out all right, then what does it matter what happens to us on the way? He is risen!

---

O Christ, I thank Thee for the joy of knowing that nothing need now defeat me, since nothing defeated Thee. Help me to take hold of that fact and live by it. Amen.

## THE JOY OF HIS PRESENCE

Each morning at the close of our morning prayers at our Ashram the leader says, "The Lord is risen!" and the group answers, "He is risen indeed." In that strength we go forward into the day knowing the power of His resurrection. But we must not depend on the resurrection, but on the resurrected Christ, and not on a resurrected Christ of the past, but on the actual, living, present Christ through whom and in whom we meet God now.

The deepest joy is the communion of Person with person. Sometimes our earthly vessels can scarcely contain the weight of this exquisite joy. We are almost tempted to ask Him to stay His hand. But we wouldn't have Him do it for worlds, for this is Life, Life. "I feel so sacred within," wrote a very modern girl after tasting this new Life. And no wonder! In the center of our being we commune with Life—our thoughts are washed in His thoughts, our wills are strengthened by His will, our affections are bathed in His. Harnack, speaking of the mystics, says, "Some perceive the presence of the Spirit with every sense: they see the brilliant light, they hear its voice, they smell the fragrance of immortality, and taste its sweetness." One moment of that, and it is worth the world. Life can never more be the same.

To us it is no longer strange that God speaks to Moses out of a burning bush, for have not our hearts become in living fact a burning bush, out of which God speaks to us in tenderest tones—and directive? For out of this fellowship with the fire comes the call to redeem, to bid my people go. So this communion ends in a commission. And that commission in turn feeds upon the communion.

The wonder is not that we should speak of it, but the wonder is that we should speak of anything else.

———

O God, my Father, I drop into the shrine of my heart and commune with Thee there, and one minute of that is an eternity. For there we become deathless. Amen.

## THE JOY OF CERTAINTY AND THE OPEN ROAD

Is there any joy more wonderful than the joy of being in touch, saving touch with ultimate Fact? Life becomes immovably centered and fixed. It is not subject to the changes of life around it. A certainty that is open-eyed and still remains certain is certainty indeed. The Christian has just that.

A very intelligent lady wrote: "I had spiritual certainty, but it was without an open road. I was afraid of open roads. So I clung to my spiritual certainty, and became blind to everything else. Then I went to a university and took postgraduate work, and there I got the open road, but I lost my certainty. And I groped along the open road for some time. Now I have both certainty and the open road." She had found life's most beautiful combination.

Some have certainty and no open road. Their ideas, their minds, and their theological systems are fixed. It is a certainty gained at the expense of sight! Others have the open road, but they have no certainties. They know the quest, but no rest. They journey and journey and never arrive. And they call this emptiness virtue. They want no certainties, they say. But the heart knows better. It journeys with a new buoyancy when there is certainty within. But it is certainty that is not a dead certainty, but a certainty that sets us on fire to know more. We know that we cannot live on an after-glow of some past experience, just as Renan says, "We cannot go on living on the perfume of a broken vase." There must be fresh discovery every day. And there is! The deepest sign of life is that we want more life. The surest sign that we are on the Road is that we feel it is an Open Road. There is eternal progress before us. The joy of growth is one of the deepest joys of life. Victorious living means certain, but adventurous living. Experience—exploration sum it up.

O Christ, Thou hast touched us, and our hearts are afire to know more. Feed us upon the "more" and we are satisfied. Amen.

## THE SPIRIT'S LAW

We have been looking at certainty and the open road. A passage which sums up this combination of fixedness and freedom is this one, "For the Spirit's law—life in Christ Jesus—has set me free from the law of sin and death" (Romans 8. 2, Weymouth). Here is an amazing combination of apparent opposites: The "Spirit"—how free, untrammeled "Spirit" seems! "Law"—how fixed and unalterable "law" appears! "Life"—how free, unfixed, "life" seems! "Christ Jesus"—how fixed in the historic facts! But Paul puts them together and says, "The Spirit's law is Life in Christ Jesus."

Sabatier divides religions into "religions of the Spirit" and "religions of authority"—one is directed from within, and the other from without; one depends on inner life, the other on outer law. Paul here puts them together. He says the Spirit's law is life—"life in Christ Jesus."

Life in Christ Jesus is the fixed norm. We are not now adrift—we know what life is, for we know what God is. We had to have God transformed so He could become available. As Bell puts it: "Over a wire comes a mighty electric current. I cannot use it. It is too powerful for my motor. It would melt the thing, ruin it. I shunt off the current into a resistance box and transform it into voltage which is usable. My motor is no longer destroyed, but empowered. So Jesus thus transforms God" (*Beyond Agnosticism*, p. 72). The awful God becomes the accessible God. We now see what He is like and what we can be like. We have a fixed point in our universe. No one knows the worth and significance of that until he has seen it in contrast with systems where there is no norm, no fixed point. Whole systems adrift! But God has met us in history and that meeting is Christ. "Life in Christ Jesus"—that gives us a starting Point.

---

O God, we thank Thee that we have seen Thee in a Face. And now we can never be satisfied until we are like that. Our hearts glow with gratitude. Amen.

## THE SPIRIT'S LAW—THE UNFOLDING

The Spirit unfolds what is infolded in Christ. He will not guide us contrary to what we find in the life and teaching and spirit of Christ. This is as fixed as a law. But the range of unfolding is infinite.

In John 14. 26 we see again the combination: "But the Comforter, even the Holy Spirit, . . . he shall teach you all things, and bring to your remembrance all that I said unto you." "He . . . shall bring to your remembrance all that I said unto you"—this is the turning back to the fixed facts. "He shall teach you all things"—this is the Spirit's direct, immediate voice to each age and to each individual. This points to progressive revelation.

And what is the Spirit's voice for this troubled and distracted age searching for a way of life and plans for the future? The Kingdom of God on earth! He is unfolding the possibility of a new world on God's plan. This Plan haunts the councils where all plans are being examined. We are not ready to take the Plan yet, for we are not ready for salvation. We will stumble along until one day we shall fall on our knees and take God's Plan and then—! A new age, a new world, a new brotherhood, new men! I refuse to take my eyes off that possibility and to listen to the cynics, within and without the Christian Church, who tell me it is a dream, and the only reality is force and compulsion. "Force and compulsion"—where they have healed one they have wounded ten! No, I hear the Spirit's voice amid the clamor of voices, bringing to our remembrance the fact that our Master proclaimed the Kingdom as His message, and He does not change. The Kingdom is still at our doors—our one open road, our one hope. "He that hath an ear, let him hear what the Spirit saith."

———

O Spirit of the Living God, Thou art speaking to dulled ears and Thy voice calls us anew to the Kingdom. Help us to listen or we perish. Amen.

2 Peter 3. 18    Luke 22. 32
Ephesians 4. 12—16    Acts 13. 1—3

## PRACTICAL SUGGESTIONS FOR GROWTH

We have seen that we have been put under a Living Mind, under a Law that is an unfolding Life. We must therefore grow in order to remain Christian.

1. Grow by your mistakes, even by your sins. A good many people collapse under a fall and stay down. But the losing of a skirmish does not necessarily mean the losing of the battle. Many have won battles by the very fact that they lost a skirmish, for it made them more watchful, more humble, more determined. "When a good man falls, he falls on his knees"—a good place to fall! Get up at once, and say: "Well, that was a jolt, but I've learned my lesson. I shall ask for re-enforcements and get them for that weak place." You can become strongest at your weakest places. Paul and Wesley were converted Pharisees and they became strongest where they were weakest—they became men of humility and men who depended on grace. If you fall, don't give up—get up.

2. Grow by taking on yourself a task beyond your powers. That will throw you back on God's grace. Don't limit yourself to things that you can do—that won't stretch you. Do something that you can't do, and that will make you grow in the doing. All my life I've done things I couldn't do. I undertake them at His bidding, and, lo, somehow there is the divine re-enforcement. Paul grew with the size of his tasks. The opening of the Gentile world to him meant the opening and the enlarging of his whole nature, including his mind. "Don't ask for tasks suitable to your powers, but for powers suitable to your tasks." And make the tasks big and demanding. When God called to Mary, she did not shrink, nor did she become proud, she simply said, "Behold the handmaiden of the Lord"—I am ready for anything. And she was. And how amazingly she grew under the greatness of her task!

---

O God, my Father, give me this day spiritual tasks which shall be beyond me, so I may draw heavily upon Thy resources. Amen.

## GROW BY TAKING IN MORE TERRITORY

3. We must not only take on greater tasks in order to grow, we must take in more territory. Christendom has now grown up to the limits of many of its conceptions. It needs larger conceptions. It has gone as far as it can under the conception that religion has only to do with personal release and personal culture. It is finding that the roots of the personal run straight into the social, and, in order even to develop the personal, we must Christianize the social. This is the area of growth in the future for many of us, for we have been like potted plants, confined to the cramping conceptions of a personal gospel. We must be transplanted to the garden of larger social conceptions and endeavors. Then we will grow. We have reached the limit of potted growth.

An expert told me that in planting out trees at the Ashram we should dig a very deep pit, put in a layer of manure, then one of ordinary earth, then another layer of manure followed again by a layer of earth, and so on up to the top. This, he said, gives the growing tree something to reach after. Its roots get to one level and then feel the call of the deeper level of richness. The call of the beyond is ever upon it.

Christianity must put its roots into the total life of humanity, or else it will die, pot-bound. Or it will remain a dwarfed, pathetic thing in this modern world. But we must not talk about Christianity in general, we must talk about ourselves. We cannot wait till everybody else is ready to act. It is said in the parable that the man cast the seed "in his own garden"—we must begin there. Jesus announced His own program at Nazareth first before He announced the program for the disciples in the Sermon on the Mount. We must do the same.

---

O Christ, help us today to set forth the stakes of Thy Kingdom and claim new territory for Thy redemptive purposes. Help us to fear not, but begin. Amen.

## DELIBERATELY PLANNING TO GROW

4. We said that we must take in more territory in the social application of this new life in order to further our own growth. This should not be our motive, for we should save the total life of humanity, not in order to cultivate our own souls, but because it is right. Nothing less than all belongs to Christ. But if we do so, it will result in our own enlargement. How shall we claim more territory?

(a) Do it mentally. Renounce in the depths of your heart a system which is based on the unchristian principle of selfish competition and give yourself inwardly to one based on the principle of co-operation. Refuse to sanction by your approval the present world-order which breeds wars, hate, poverty, and disaster. (b) Go out today and see how you can apply that inward renunciation in positive action in your circumstances. If a business man, begin to build a co-operative order within the area of your influence. If a laborer, organize a co-operative endeavor on no matter how small a scale. It will train you and others in co-operative thinking and endeavor. (c) See where your vote can be cast in behalf of a juster order. For this new day must come down through the political, as well as up through co-operatives. This is the conclusion of many of those who are most eager for co-operatives. Co-operatives must be supplemented by political action. (d) Break down some race or class barrier today. Invite to your home someone not of your race or class. Do not patronize them—they will sense it at once. The will to be brotherly is as important as the will to believe. For in the beginning you will have to act brotherly before you can begin to feel brotherly. (e) Get as many others to come with you as possible. Win converts, unashamedly, unblushingly. (f) Become saturated with the Kingdom idea —"the Kingdom which is the republic of socialized personality," and "the rule of Sovereign Love."

---

O God, our Father, help me this day to begin the Kingdom program and to know the Kingdom power in every single one of my relationships. Amen.

## BEWARE OF THE DEVIL'S ATONEMENT

We said that we should act as though the Kingdom were already in operation, we must anticipate its full coming. During the Great War when a youth was brought up before a court to be tried for refusing to sanction war, the judge said, "But the Kingdom of God hasn't come yet." "It has as far as I am concerned," replied the youth. That anticipating of the new day will cost you. It will mean a cross. You will find your cross at the point of tension between the new and the old.

5. But here a temptation will set in: You will be tempted to plan other people's sacrifices rather than your own. That is the devil's atonement. When Caiaphas "gave counsel to the Jews, that it was expedient that one man should die for the people," he was practicing the devil's atonement, for he was not preparing to sacrifice himself, but someone else to save the people. That is the devil's atonement. When patrioteers call for the sacrifice of youth for the sake of the country and sit safe and sound behind their counters and their desks—it is the devil's atonement. When agitators get people to sacrifice for the sake of a cause and they will not sacrifice themselves—again it is the devil's atonement. When ministers bind burdens of moral responsibility upon others and feel that their duty is thereby discharged, not touching the burden with their little finger—is this not the devil's atonement? When we talk about the new day of social justice and thus get the prestige that comes from the renunciation of this order, and at the same time gladly take the comforts and special privileges that belong to it—it is the devil's atonement.

If, therefore, we take our cross in order to bring in God's order, let us be sure we do take it and not put it on someone else instead.

———

O Christ, we pray Thee that we may fulfill Thy word this day, that each shall take "his own cross" and come and follow Thee. Show me my cross and help me take it. Amen.

James 1. 5–8
Ephesians 4. 23, 24
1 John 3. 16–18

## BRINGING THE MIND INTO UNITY

For real spiritual growth there must be a unity between the conscious and the subconscious minds. The subconscious can be taught the purposes of the conscious mind. It is educable. But it will not listen to what you say—only at what you do. As Streeter says: "The subconscious is always learning from the conscious, but it both learns and forgets more slowly. And the lessons it takes to heart most deeply are not the purely intellectual notions of the conscious mind, but the values and emotions associated with them. A man, for instance, may believe with his conscious mind that God is good and that all men are brothers, but only if he plans and acts toward the universe and man as if these things were true will his subconscious mind believe them also. If his conscious mind affirms the principle of love, but he schemes injury to his brother, it is the attitude of hate that the subconscious mind will learn" (*Reality*).

You cannot therefore teach the subconscious mind any unreality. It will not learn it. Jesus put His finger on this when He said, "Take no extra inner garment" (Weymouth). Here is the man who takes only one cloak, the sign of his renunciation, but he puts on an extra, secret, inner garment. The subconscious mind will learn from the secret inner garment of comfort rather than from the one outer garment of ostensible renunciation. Saint Francis, when induced to wear a woolen inner garment, insisted on wearing a piece of wool pinned on the outside, so there would be no taking of him for more than what he was. Many of our renunciations are of the kind Jesus warned against—we give up outwardly, but hold extra inner garments of comfort, so that we try to get the prestige of renunciation and the comfort of keeping.

Go over your life and ask whether there are any extra inner garments being held to—special privileges, special securities. Growth is growth in reality.

---

O Christ, help me this day to tolerate no unreality, no make-believe. Help me to be real. Amen.

## LIVE TODAY!

6. In your spiritual growth you must learn to live today. One of the most important things Jesus said was, "Do not be overanxious, about tomorrow. . . . Enough for each day are its own troubles" (Weymouth).

Many of us spoil today by bringing the troubles of tomorrow into it. Worry is the advance interest we pay on tomorrow's troubles. Many of us go bankrupt paying interest troubles that never come. So worry becomes sin—sin against the goodness and love of God. Doctor Worcester says, "You could pack all the actual misfortunes of your life into a moderate-sized closet, while your whole house, no matter how big it is, would scarcely hold all the unrealized evils and misfortunes you have feared and looked forward to." While writing on this book a telegram was handed to me. A series of calamities flashed through my mind: "Eunice is ill, come home at once." In a flash I saw all the implications of what that would mean—all plans tumbling to pieces. I opened the telegram and it read, "Jacob fully reconciled"—the good news of the healing of a misunderstanding. Life is like that! Nine tenths of our troubles never come, and we can stand the one tenth. Charles Kingsley says, "Do today's duty, fight today's temptation, and do not weaken and distract yourself by looking forward to things which you cannot see and could not understand if you saw them." Live today! Let Tagore's words become true for you, "Thou dost press the signet of eternity upon many a fleeting moment of my life." You do not have to win tomorrow's battles today. Win these that you face today and tomorrow will take care of itself. His power keeps you this present moment; that keeping will extend to the next, and to the next, and at the end of the day you will whisper to yourself, "Victory."

O Christ, we thank Thee that Thou hast called us to the adventure of today. Help me to make today eternal because I have put eternal worth into it. Amen.

## GROW THROUGH OBSTACLES

7. You will learn to grow through the coming of obstacles. When Beethoven, going deaf, said, "I will blunt the sword of Fate," he meant it and did. He grew by that very obstacle.

When the Samaritans refused to receive Jesus and His disciples, the account says that after rebuking the disciples for wanting to retaliate, "They went to another village." Life always has "another village." If you are blocked in this one, pass on to the next. There is always a "next." And that next village was nearer Jesus' final goal. He didn't have so far to go the next day. He advanced toward His goal by the snobbery of that village.

Thank God, life always has another village. Were you disappointed in finding the life-mate whom you had hoped to find? Then pass on to another village. The early impact of Christianity produced this fact: "Philip had four unmarried daughters who were prophetesses." Spinsterhood emerged as the result of Christianity. It is seldom met in the non-Christian faiths. The unmarried feel the call to be wedded to the sorrows and sufferings and ignorance of the world. Like the daughters of Philip, their spinsterhood becomes prophetic. Have you been disappointed in your lifework? Grow by that disappointment. Henry Martyn, after years of patient toil, translated the Bible into Persian and journeyed to present it to the Shah. He went into the court to make his presentation. As he placed it before them they began to realize what book it was, and they went out one by one, including the Shah. Henry Martyn was left alone with his Book, rejected. His comment was, "I refuse to be disappointed." And he passed on to another village. "I refuse to be disappointed," for the disappointment can be a spiritual growing place. It may make me put out new endeavors, jolt me out of old ruts, deepen my sympathy, and altogether make me a better man. Grow by obstacles!

---

O Christ, I thank Thee that Thou didst make Thy frustrations into fruitfulness. Help me to do that this day. Amen.

## GROW THROUGH OBSTACLES BY PRAYER

These illuminating verses say, "But they were filled with madness and began to discuss with one another what they should do to Jesus. About that time he went out on one occasion into the hill country to pray" (Luke 6. 11, 12). Here was an obstacle—the madness of His opponents which drove them to counsel what they would do to Jesus. They felt they had the final say. Over against that Jesus matched prayer. They counseled together as to what they should do to Him, and He counseled as to what the Father should do through Him. Prayer made it possible that He should not be a victim of circumstances. He met His circumstances from above.

What will my circumstances do to me today? Rather, what shall I do today through my circumstances by prayer? Again, here are my limitations, and they conspire to cramp me, to keep me from being effective. Is the last word with them? Not at all. I decide through prayer, and the power that comes through it, what I shall do with my limitations. Many a man spurred on by a limitation has become great through that very limitation. Adler says, "This feeling that the individual has of his own inferiority furnishes the inward impulse to advance." Much more if coupled with prayer which gives power to advance. Bacon says, "Whoever hath anything fixed in his person that doth induce contempt hath also a perpetual spur within himself to rescue and deliver himself."

What shall my enemies do with me? Rather, what shall I do with my enemies through prayer? I shall have power to forgive them. I meet them from above. "I have power to kill you," said a Roman judge to a martyr, who replied, "But I have power to be killed." And that was the greater and the final power.

You grow by the meeting of an obstacle, but not merely through the obstacle, but through prayer induced by that very obstacle.

———

O Christ, I thank Thee that the last word, even upon the cross, was not with Thine enemies, but with Thee. Help me this day to turn every obstacle into opportunity through prayer. Amen.

## GROWTH IN QUALITY OF LIFE

We have seen that our circumstances do not decide our destiny, but prayer does. Spencer says, "Whatever amount of power an organism expends in any shape is correlative or equivalent of a power taken into it from without." Our spiritual lives are determined by the power we take into them through prayer. So when the calamity of blindness struck Milton, he could say, "I argue not against Heaven's hand or will, nor bate a jot of heart or hope; but still bear up and steer right onward." He was not the victim of circumstances, but the victor over circumstances.

So God says to Paul, "Dismiss your fears: go on speaking, and do not give up. I am with you, and no one shall attack you to injure you" (Acts 18. 10, Weymouth). Note that God doesn't say that there shall be no attacks, but there shall be no attacks *to injure you*. No attack from without can injure you. You can only be injured from within by wrong choices. You are absolutely safe as long as you are right with God.

8. Grow in your victory over half-sins, things that may be lawful to you, but are not expedient. Paul suggests that we are to lay aside "every weight and the sin" that besets. Every weight! Things that bring no condemnation, but also no contribution. Do not ask, "Is it wrong?" But ask, "Does it contribute?" Away with every noncontributing thing!

Jesus says to His disciples: "Take ye heed to yourselves." Why? So that you might escape coming calamity? No. But take heed to yourselves so you will be prepared to give your witness (See Mark 13. 9). Be spiritually fit, He says, so that you may not be taken unawares when called on to give your witness before high and low. For that hour depends not on your circumstances but upon you. Therefore let everything go that will not help you in that hour. Grow in quality of spiritual fitness.

---

O Christ, help me this day to let go every weight that might slow up my pace. For I would be spiritually fit. Amen.

## GROWTH IN CREATIVE FAITH

Jesus used that phrase, "Take heed to yourselves," in another connection. "Take heed to yourselves: if thy brother sin . . . seven times in the day, and seven times turn again to thee saying, I repent; thou shalt forgive him. And the apostles said unto the Lord, Increase our faith. And the Lord said, If ye have faith as a grain of mustard seed, ye would say unto this sycamine tree, Be thou rooted up, and be thou planted in the sea; and it would have obeyed you" (Luke 17. 3-6). He suggests that they "take heed" to themselves—about what? About having an undiscouraged, creative faith in people. When the disciples asked that their faith be increased, it wasn't so much faith in God as faith in people, in wobbly people, that needed to be increased.

He says that if you have faith, you can make a sycamine tree to be planted in the most unstable soil of the world—the sea! You can make souls stable by a creative faith. Never did we need men of creative faith so much as now, for a vast cynicism has crept across our spirits. We are going to pieces for lack of men of creative faith. The Epistle of Diognetus says of the Christians, "They hold the world together." This was written at the time when the social order was going to pieces around them. The Christians did not belong to that decaying order—they belonged to the undecaying Kingdom of God. Therefore they held the world together by their faith. They did then, they must now. We must hold society and individuals from going to pieces by our creative faith.

Grow in your belief in people, in their possibilities, in the fact that the worst can become the best. Take heed to yourselves, and let nothing hurt your faith in the weakest. For if you lose your faith in man, your faith in God goes too.

---

O Christ, help me this day to believe in people as Thou didst believe in them. And help me to remake them by that very faith. Amen.

## A PEOPLE PREPARED

9. As we discuss this matter of being spiritually fit to carry out God's purposes we must pause at this remarkable statement: "For he [John] shall be great in the sight of the Lord, and he shall drink no wine nor strong drink; and he shall be filled with the Holy Ghost. . . . And he shall go before his face in the spirit and power of Elijah . . . to make ready . . . a people prepared" (Luke 1. 17).

A people prepared! Did we ever, ever need a people prepared so much as we need them now? A world in change, a world seeking new moorings, a world feeling after a new order! Are we Christians "a people prepared"? What kind of men can be a people prepared? The account tells us: John was sound in three directions—toward God, toward himself, and toward the people. (1) Toward God he was "great." We need men who are great "in the sight of the Lord" and care not a rap if they are great or small in the sight of men. (2) Toward himself he could renounce: he drank no wine or strong drink. But positively: he was filled with the Holy Ghost. We need men who can give up things for a great cause and who are filled with God's Spirit. (3) Toward others: he summed the best and finest in the past—he came in the spirit and power of Elijah. We need men who do not lose sight of God's dealings in history and who will hold to every fine gain in the past. They must be conservative. But they must also be radical: he shall "turn the hearts of the fathers to the children." We should have thought it would have been the other way round. But no, this older generation must turn its heart to the children, must think in terms of making the world safe, just, and brotherly for our children. We must therefore be radical.

Let us be men sound in these three directions, with these emphases, and we shall be a people prepared.

―――――

O Christ, make me this day a person prepared, that I may help to produce a people prepared. Amen.

327

## A PEOPLE PREPARED—IN MIND

10. In our study of growing we must face the necessity of growing in mind. No people can be prepared unless they are growing mentally. Religion today is up against the most complex problems both within man and within society, for our faith is being challenged from the side of psychology and of economics. It will not do to say with Doctor Parkhurst that "skepticism is the friction caused by a small brain trying to absorb a great idea." We must be able to show how the "great idea"—God—is great enough and dynamic enough to meet a world need.

Today Christians are being forced to think because they have come to grips with the making of a new world. Our religion must function there, or it will be discarded as an irrelevancy. The Kingdom conception demands it. We are grateful for what unlettered Christians have done, but this is no time for ignorant piety. For the world suffers almost as much from wrong ideas as from wrong wills. Wrong ideas in history have produced as much havoc as wrong intentions. Christians, therefore, must think straight as well as act straight.

Therefore, grow in mind. Try to read at least fifty pages of some book each day. If your mind ceases to grow, your soul will cease to grow. You will become the victim of set phrases and stereotyped ideas—caught in mental ruts. A new book will help jolt you out. Sell your coat and buy it if you have to. Spinoza spoke of "an intellectual love of God," and Jesus spoke of loving God "with the mind"—a portion He added on His own accord to the Old Testament quotation. It must have been important. It is.

"For the spirit which God has given unto us is not the spirit of fear, but of discipline, and of love and a sound mind." Did He put "the sound mind" last for emphasis?

———

O Christ, we pray Thee to help us this day to conquer some new worthy idea and harness it to the purposes of Thy Kingdom. Save our minds from ruts. Amen.

## GROWTH IN LOVE

11. But in all our growth we must grow in love. Unless we are growing in love we are not growing at all.

"Jesus knowing that his hour was come that he should depart out of this world unto the Father, . . . he loved" (John 13. 1). It was the greatest thing He had done in life and it would be the last thing He would do in death. Nothing greater in life or death, either for Him or for us. Therefore, "make love your quest."

But let it be an intelligent quest. Go over your life and see if there are unloving and, therefore, unlovely spots. Perhaps you will find some tinge of jealousy toward someone. Set yourself to say something nice about that person today. I found a touch of jealousy in my heart toward someone. I set myself to say everything fine I could about him. Today we are the closest of friends, and the jealousy is all gone.

Or perhaps you will find that your service of Christ is becoming mixed with motives other than pure love. Doctor Weigle tells this story: One morning Bradley put beside his mother's plate a little piece of paper. His mother could hardly believe it, but this is what Bradley had written: "Mother owes Bradley: For running errands, $0.25. For being good, $0.10. For taking music lessons, $0.15. Extras, $0.05. Total, $0.55." His mother smiled, but did not say anything, and when lunch time came she placed the bill on Bradley's plate with the fifty-five cents. Bradley's eyes danced. But there was another little bill which read: "Bradley owes mother: For being good, $0.00. For nursing him through a long illness, $0.00. For shoes, clothes, gloves, playthings, $0.00. For all his meals and beautiful room, $0.00. Total: Bradley owes mother $0.00." Tears came into Bradley's eyes, he put his arms around his mother's neck, thrust his little hand with the fifty-five cents into hers, and said: "Take this money all back, mamma, and let me love you and do things for nothing!"

---

O Christ, cleanse from my heart this day all bargaining and help me to serve Thee and others for love alone. Amen.

1 John 3. 17
Ephesians 4. 15
Luke 10. 25–37

## GROWTH IN THE SOCIAL APPLICATION OF LOVE

The real test of spiritual growth is the test of whether we are growing in love. But this test applies to society as well as to individuals. The test of how much of civilization is in any society is the test as to what degree love is being built into the social structure, manifested as social justice and the abundant life for all.

There are two great driving forces in human life—hunger and love: the struggle for life, and the struggle for the life of others. We have organized the collective life largely around the hunger drive with love coming at the edges to soften here and there the grim struggle. This puts disruption and clash at the very center. If we should change the center from hunger to love, then we should organize life co-operatively. In that case hunger would be at the edges and love at the center as the driving force. This would not only be good Christianity but good economics, for we have now discovered the means of supplying all the economic needs of every last man, woman, and child, provided we can co-operate to do it. To get co-operation life must be organized on the basis of love. So that sound economics is pushing us to the Christian solution.

When hunger is at the center, we live a cow's existence, nine tenths of whose time is taken up with eating or rechewing what it has eaten. The supplying of economic needs should be an incident in human life instead of its absorbing passion. When Jesus was hanging on the cross, the account says, "After this Jesus knowing that all things are now finished, saith, I thirst." After He had done all He could for others He thought of His own needs—"I thirst." We have put our thirsts first. This is not civilization—it is chaos. Love must be dominant and individual thirsts subordinate, if we are to be Christian.

---

O Christ, we pray Thee that we may grow in Thy way—the way of love. For only as we love do we live. Amen.

NOVEMBER 18

Ephesians 5. 30
Ephesians 4. 25
1 Corinthians 12. 5, 12, 13, 26, 27

## DEVELOPING THROUGH COLLECTIVE QUEST

We cannot grow unless we fellowship with other questing lives. Hence the Church. How can we get most out of that corporate fellowship? Simeon came into the Temple and saw the Lord's Christ. How did it happen? He brought something to that hour, and seeing the Lord's Christ was the result of what he brought.

The account says, "And he came in the Spirit into the temple." Go to church that way—"in the Spirit"—and you will see something. But many go to church "in the flesh." It is all on that level—to display clothes or oratory. Or it is all "in the mind"—we listen to some new or attractive thing. Or it is "in the emotions"—our aesthetic natures like the music and the stately ritual. But the Lord's Christ does not appear. We do not come "in the Spirit."

What does it mean to come "in the Spirit"? The account tells us. There were four foundation things: He "was righteous and devout, looking for the consolation of Israel: and the Holy Spirit was upon him." He had a fourfold rightness: (1) Rightness toward man—"righteous." (2) Rightness toward God—"devout." (3) Rightness toward the nation—"looking for the consolation of Israel." (4) Rightness toward himself —"the Holy Spirit was upon him." He was a man four-square.

But the looking for the consolation of his own people did not keep him from seeing the possibilities in other people: "He shall be a light for unveiling [margin] the Gentiles." He saw that Christ would not only bring consolation to Israel, his own nation, but would "unveil" the possibilities in others, the Gentiles. This is Christianity—narrow nationalism is not.

Bring with you these four basic things and that will be coming into the Temple "in the Spirit." Then you will see amazing possibilities in yourself, in your nation, in other nations. All through Christ.

---

O Christ, as we prepare to go into Thy temple, help us to take this fourfold rightness with us, and then we shall see Thee, and when we return we can stand four-square to life. Amen.

## DEVELOPING THROUGH UNITY

The next great step in Christendom is Christian unity. In a world seeking unity, Christians have little moral authority unless they can demonstrate unity. Now we do not demonstrate unity—we demonstrate disunity. This is blocking the acceptance of Christianity and blocking the development of Christians themselves.

I believe that we have gone as far as we can in spiritual development under separate denominationalism. We may advance here and there, but with no great burst of collective spirituality until we come together. But you ask, "How can we come together unless we agree in everything?" But we do not make that a prerequisite of fellowship in the home. The home can be a unity in spite of difference in temperament and belief. The one thing that binds together is that all are children of the same parents. So in the family of God the thing that binds us together is not that we all have the same spiritual temperament, nor the same shades of belief, but the fact that we are all children of the same Father. Let that suffice us. We need our differences as possible growing points. The music of the Hindus is based on melody and not on harmony, as is Western music. A Hindu heard the Negroes singing the Negro spirituals in parts, bringing out marvelous harmony. But his comment was, "What a pity they can't all sing the same tune!' Had they done so, it wouldn't have been harmony! The very differences made for richness. We shall never get melody-unity in church unity, for we cannot all sing the same part, but we can have harmony-unity, and that will be far richer. Each denomination will sing its part, and out of it will come the full richness of our gospel.

We shall grow individually and collectively only as we appropriate from each other the distinctive contribution of each. We must grow in unity.

---

O Christ, we thank Thee that Thou art bringing together many differing parts to make one great harmony. Help us to sing our part and to appreciate and to appropriate the parts of others. Amen.

NOVEMBER 20

Psalm 84. 7
Proverbs 4. 18
Philippians 1. 6

2 Peter 3. 18
2 Thessalonians 1. 8

## GROW IN GRACE

Perhaps the most distinctive thing in the gospel is grace, so the most distinctive thing in our growth must be growth in grace. The grace of God is love judging our sins, suffering for our sins, forgiving our sins, removing our sins, and then abiding in unworthy hearts. That is grace.

To grow in acceptance, in living by that very grace is to grow in the deepest thing in our Gospel. But the modern mind is afraid of the doctrine of grace, however much the deepest instincts long for it. We are afraid that to depend on another destroys initiative, weakens one's fiber, and turns the upstanding into the clinging. If this were the result of grace, I should reject it too. But a strange paradox is found in the gospel at this place. His gifts do not weaken personality, they strengthen it. Jesus says, "But the water that I shall give him shall become in him a well of water springing up unto everlasting life." Now, note the gift of water becomes within one a well of water springing up. The gift produces spontaneity! Now, many gifts do not. They weaken. It is hard to give to people and not weaken them. But here is a gift that strengthens in the very act of giving.

For it is not a gift that demands nothing on our part. It is the most expensive gift we shall ever receive—expensive to us. For when we take it, our very all goes out in exchange. Now, having given to God there is a mutuality. We are no longer worms of the dust—we are co-operating persons. At the very moment we bend lowest we stand straightest. Those who depend most on the grace of God develop the strongest personalities. So when we grow in grace, we grow in personal initiative and energy.

No wonder Professor Royce exclaimed: "Arise then, free-man! Stand forth in thy world. It is God's world. It is also thine."

O Christ, may this well of spontaneous life ever spring up within us, since we depend so much upon Thy life. Amen.

## GROW IN HUMILITY

Yesterday we saw that grace strengthens personality. So Overstreet says, "We come to the most authentic in ourselves as we go forth to that which is immeasurably greater than ourselves." But the very strengthening of the personality will bring a danger. As you grow spiritual pride becomes a real danger. Many fall because of it. Yesterday I went out after a storm and found a beautiful branch of a tree broken off and lying on the pathway. Parasites had done it. Great bunches of a parasite, like mistletoe, had weakened it, and when the test of the storm came, it broke and fell. The most dangerous parasite is spiritual pride—many are weakened by it and fall in the time of test.

Phillips Brooks says, "The true way to be humble is not to stoop until you are smaller than yourself, but to stand at your real height against some higher nature that will show you what the real smallness of your greatness is." Stand at your very highest, and then look at Christ, and go away and be forever humble! When we lose sight of Christ, we ourselves begin to loom large. A Hindu said to me: "I used to believe in idols. Now I don't believe in God at all. But I am coming 'round to believe that I myself am God." Gave up his idols and made one of himself! When we lose God, we lose our source of humility.

The account says, "Jesus, knowing that the Father had given all things into his hands, and that he came forth from God, and goeth unto God, . . . took a towel" and washed His disciples' feet. The consciousness of greatness was the secret of humility. The small dare not be humble. But Jesus' greatness was rooted in God. Being in God made Him great—and humble. Great because humble and humble because great.

Remember, only the humble can lead. "For people who parade their virtues seldom lead the procession." They cannot lead, for we simply cannot inwardly respond to the proud however "spiritual" they may seem to be.

————

O Christ, give me Thy mind. For Thou art meek and lowly in heart. And I would be like Thee. Amen.

## DEVELOPMENT IN CREATIVE OBEDIENCE

When the disciples came in from a night-long, but fruitless, endeavor at their trade, Jesus said, "Launch out into the deep, and let down your nets." Peter in half-doubt, half-faith said, "Master, we have toiled all night, and have taken nothing, nevertheless at thy word I will."

"At Thy word I will"—could fewer words sum up the Christian attitude? "At Thy word"! That "word," speaking to men all through the ages, has never let men down. Whenever men have obeyed it, they have found they were upon an open road; where men have disobeyed it, they have found that they are running into roads with dead ends. That "word" has been energy to the living and grace to the dying. Other words let me down—this "word" does not. Nothing has been so utterly tested in history as Jesus' rightness, and nothing has proven itself so utterly right as His rightness.

Then? There is only one thing left: "At Thy word I will!" But many of us do not say that. We say: "At Thy word I think." We are intellectually aroused by Him, but not controlled by Him at the place of volition. We are mere intellectualists in religion. Or some of us say, "At Thy word I feel." We are moved with strong emotional responses to Him—sermons stir us, the reading of the gospel brings a thrill, but it does not get beyond that, it does not work itself into our wills. We are emotionalists in religion. But there are those who say, "At Thy word I will." They are the Christians. I am really growing as I grow at this point. This is the test of whether the gospel is functioning within me.

Many of us are willing to do God's work, but not God's will. If so, the center remains unchristianized. I am Christian to the degree that Christ has my will. When you can say, "At Thy word I will," then you are really growing.

---

O Christ, I can bank on Thee. Help me to do it this day, and may I show that I do, by the way I will. Amen.

## DEVELOPMENT IN CREATIVE COURAGE

To break with the present order, to put into operation your vision, demand courage. But that is what the Christian is here to do—the impossible. When a thing becomes possible, the politicians take it over. Courage!

Two incidents of creative courage spring to mind. An Afghan convert felt the call of Christ to witness to Him in the closed country of Afghanistan. He no sooner began in Khandhar than he was captured and driven to Kabul at the command of the Amir. Literally "driven," for they put a bridle in his mouth and drove him like a donkey the two hundred miles, and along the way men were invited to pluck his beard and spit in his face. Arrived at Kabul, he was asked by the Amir if he would renounce his faith. He refused. One arm went off. He was offered everything. Again he refused and the other arm went off. When he refused even then to deny his Master, his head went off. Courage! A lamp burns perpetually before the "Martyr's Shrine" at Peshawar, and high up on the list is this man's name. We feed upon such creative courage as that.

Look at these two pictures: The Christian commissioner of Peshawar was asked if mission work could be started on that wild frontier. His reply: "What, do you want us all to be killed in our beds?" He wasn't killed in his bed, but a Moslem fanatic did stab him to death on the veranda. What he feared came on him. Mr. Edwards, the next commissioner, when asked the same question, replied, "It is not a matter of our safety, it is a matter of the will of God. Of course we will do it, for we Christians have no other choice." He called the station people together, took a collection of three thousand rupees on the spot and invited the missionaries in. His name is loved and revered by Christian and non-Christian alike. Courage, creative courage. Grow in that and you really grow!

O Christ, give me this gift, for Thou dost have it and I need it—today. Amen.

## GROWTH IN RECONCILIATION

"Be ye reconciled to God!" How familiar that sounds as a text for the unconverted! This text was not written for the unconverted, but for the converted: 'Be ye reconciled to God . . . as God's fellow workers we entreat that God's grace be not received in vain by you" (2 Corinthians 5. 20; 6. 1). It was to "fellow workers" who had received the grace of God that the plea to be reconciled to God was given. It was not for initial reconciliation, but for a continuous reconciliation that the demand is made. Otherwise the grace of God will be received in vain.

Christ is calling to the Church today to be reconciled to God. (1) In regard to our message. Our message has not been His message: The Kingdom of God. We have not preached the Kingdom "as a head-on sweeping answer to the world's needs." We have preached a doctrine here and a doctrine there for individuals, but this full answer to man's total needs, individual and social, has not been single-pointedly proclaimed. We need to be reconciled to God at the place of our message. (2) We need to be reconciled to God at the place of making the contacts of society vicarious. We have made the contacts antagonistic, or legal, but not vicarious. We need to suffer in the sufferings of those who suffer, to be hungry in the hunger of the hungry, and to be guilty in the guilt of every man. (3) We need to go over our lives and see where there are any points not reconciled to God. Has self-will crept in and taken the place of the will of God?

> "The love of Thee flows just as much
> As that of ebbing self subsides;
> Our hearts—their scantiness is such—
> Bear not the conflicts of rival tides."

There is scarcely anything needed in the world today so much as that the Church be reconciled to God in its total life to the total will of God.

---

O God, bring to my remembrance any point of difference between Thy mind and mine and I will be reconciled to Thee this day. Amen.

Genesis 18. 19    Joshua 24. 15
Psalm 10. 2    Deuteronomy 11. 19

## GROWTH IN MAKING THE HOME CHRISTIAN

Jesus finally won His whole family to His cause. There was a time when "his brethren did not believe in him." But at Pentecost they were all there—"His mother and his brethren," waiting for the gift of the Spirit. Apparently, they had all been won. One of the greatest proofs of the resurrection can be found in that simple fact. Something had happened to change them.

But Jesus did not win His family by compromising with them. He won them by making sacrifices that cost both Him and them to make. Many are willing to sacrifice for the Kingdom, but not if it costs suffering to their loved ones. A mistake. Our decisions will involve our loved ones in common suffering with us. It is a part of the price. But it works both ways for as sacrifice will lift us, so it will lift them. We break with them on a lower level in order to meet them on a higher level.

But we win them not merely by a once-and-for-all spectacular sacrifice, but by the constant pressure of a Christian example. "What then shall this child be? For the hand of the Lord was with him" they cried, for they saw "that the hand of the Lord was with him." The question could be asked in many ways. What shall this child be, seeing that the hand of narrow nationalistic propaganda is upon him? To ask it is to answer it: a narrow, partisan hater prepared to fight! And what shall this child be, seeing that the hand of a ruthlessly competitive order is upon him? Again to ask is to answer: either a hard crusher of others, or a man who turns out a beaten soul. And what shall this child be, seeing that the hand of sex-saturated movies is upon him? The modern libertine!

And what shall this child be, seeing that the hand of a consistent and contagious Christian example is upon him? Who can tell? Infinite possibilities of development open up to such a child. Are you that kind of a father or mother?

---

O Christ, we thank Thee that Thou didst win Thy family. Help me to do the same today. Amen.

NOVEMBER 26

1 Corinthians 13. 4–7
Leviticus 19. 18
1 Thessalonians 4. 9

Hebrews 10. 24
Colossians 3. 20, 21

## GROWTH IN APPRECIATION

We cannot change our loved ones nor anyone else by nagging complaints. The Pharisees thought the only way to change people was by disapproval. They tried it and only ended in being themselves disapproved. Once they journeyed all the way from Jerusalem to Galilee, and what did they see? The glorious coming of the long-looked-for kingdom? The wonder of the love of "the Man of the Healing hands"? The gates of life being opened to stricken souls? Oh, no! They saw only the fact that the disciples ate "with unwashen hands"! They passed by the great and saw only the trivial. They became small by what they saw.

The little boy who said his name was "Johnny Don't," for that was what he was always called at home, probably lived in an attitude of resistance and rebellion. On the other hand, when a hungry little boy sat down to the table and began to obey his appetite instead of waiting for grace, which had to be said when his mouth was full, he replied in response to his mother's inquiry, "Well, anyway I didn't chew." His wise mother commended him for that much restraint! Then appealed for the full restraint. The little fellow evidently caught the spirit of appreciation of others, for when I asked him if he wouldn't like to come and travel with me in evangelistic work, he replied, "You take the baby; he's a good Christian!" I think they are both going to turn out very lovely Christians! Bless them!

The one who is hypercritical is usually hypocritical.

Bring into the home a whole lot of appreciation and you will find that the little flowers will open to its genial warmth. Otherwise they close up. A Hindu student who came to a college principal to tell him of his decision, forgot to take off his cap, was rebuked for it by the principal for the lack, was chilled, and never told his heart's decision. And never became a Christian.

---

O Christ, help me to appreciate people not only for what they are, but for what they may be—in Thee. Amen.

Proverbs 31. 28    1 Thessalonians 2. 11
Ephesians 6. 4

## "PUT FORWARD BY HER MOTHER"

It is a solemn fact that the children in the home catch the attitudes of the parents, rather than their sayings. The child is much like the subconscious mind—it learns by what it sees people acting on, rather than by what they say.

Of the daughter of Herodias dancing before Herod, it says: "And she, being put forward by her mother, saith, Give me." What did the daughter desire? Well, that depended on what the mother desired. She wanted what her mother wanted.

We wonder at the undisciplined youth of this generation. Do we not need to look back to the previous generation upon whom rests a great deal of the responsibility? This generation has been "put forward" by the parents of today. The parents are astonished at present-day youth, for did not the parents repeat the old claims of morality and religion? Why didn't youth listen? Well, because this generation of parents repeated the sanctions of morality and religion with less and less conviction and certainty. The generation before these parents, having undergone conversion in the evangelical revivals at the end of the last century and the beginning of this, had some personal living convictions. The next generation lived on that afterglow with little personal experience. This generation of youth learned not what their parents said, which was too remote and faint, but what they did, which was not remote, nor faint. The actions of the generation of parents now living "put forward" this generation—and this is the result.

The story of the daughter of Herodias is the story of "the prodigal daughter," the counterpart of the story of "the prodigal son." They both said, "Give me"—always the first step down. The prodigal son came back, because he had a good father. The prodigal daughter never came back, because she had a bad mother.

———

O God, our Father, help us this day to so live that we will "put forward" this generation of youth in the direction of desiring the noblest and highest because they see it in us. Amen.

## THE LAMP

In an ancient Syrian church of Travancore, India, is a wonderful old brass lamp, with about a hundred arms hanging from the ceiling. At the end of each is a cup with oil and a wick. At the close of the service the young people come up and take one of the wicks from the lamp to guide them home through the night. Standing on a hillock you can see the points of light here and there moving amid the darkness.

That is what a Christian home should be—a place where youth has put within its hands a torch to guide them as they go out amid "the encircling gloom." There are many such torches youth can take from the home circle—the torch of a basic honesty, of good will, of co-operative living, of respect for all races and classes, of a hatred for war, of the spirit of self-giving service, of a rich personal experience of Christ.

Once my mother put a torch of prayer in my hands, though she did not know that she had done so. The shadow of financial and other calamities was upon the home—one of those periods when pain and trouble seem to be breathed in the very atmosphere. Going upstairs at midnight I heard a muffled voice, stopped, and heard my mother in prayer—a heartbreaking prayer. The little crack of the door, the little peep into her heart—for at midnight the reserves which had been kept up so bravely during the day, were all down, and I saw into the depths. What a flame of suffering love was there! I took a wick from that lamp of devotion that night and it has lighted me down the years.

The saddest thing on earth is a spiritually poverty-stricken home, where there is no central lamp from which youth can get a torch. Be victorious in the home and you are victorious everywhere.

———

O Christ, I pray Thee that this day I may bring into the home such a flame of pure living that youth may get from me a torch that will never go out. Amen.

## IN THE CITY AND IN THE HOME

Yesterday we said that the wick of a personal living experience of God is the greatest thing we can put into the hands of youth. Many a youth holds steady when smitten by modern doubt because of the clean living faith of father, of mother. But some are wrecked because of the weakening of a parent's faith and the letting down of a parent's life. Hear the cry of this distressed and disillusioned soul:

"Because I believed God brought him to me,
And because I believed him gifted of God
With honor, truth, and love of the Right
I believed in God and worshiped God;
Then when I found he was just a thief of love,
When I found he was full of treason and prejudices,
All for money and worldly pride,
The wreck of him was the wreck of God;
So I fainted amid the ruin
Of plaster and sticks and sat in the stillness
That followed the fallen bust of God."

If that child looks on you as "the bust of God," do not let him down, lest for him the wreck of you be the wreck of God. If you are in a danger of slipping, remember that this victorious living is possible in the city and in the home. We blame the city and say this life cannot be lived in it. And yet the Master asked them to tarry "in the city" till ye be endued with power from on high. The city! Its temptations, its strains, its greed, its injustices—right there tarry, and right there I will make you adequate and victorious. It was so. Where they had all failed, there He made them a glorious spiritual success. And the home! Pentecost took place in a home—an upper room of a common home, not in a church, not in a temple. Your home, this day, can prove to be a personal Pentecost to you. Then don't run away, tarry right where you are for adequate power.

---

O Christ, who didst give men power in the very place where they had failed, give me the power, this day, in this city, in this home. Amen.

## HOLDING THE HOME TOGETHER

We saw that the Epistle of Diognetus says, "The Christians hold the world together." They do, and they also hold the home together. A homeless unmarried Man becomes the power that sanctifies marriage and holds the home together! His power was never more needed than just at this place. For the home is being assailed from many directions. If it survives—and it will!—the Christians will save it.

For divorce is very seldom seen among earnest members of the Christian Church. The Christian does not fly to pieces under trouble and misunderstanding, and he knows how to hold situations together. He knows how to give forgiveness when wronged—the central characteristics of the Christian—and he knows how to make an apology when he wrongs another. An apology often saves a situation. As someone says,

An apology
Is a friendship preserver,
Is often a debt of honor,
Is never a sign of weakness,
Is an antidote for hatred,
Costs nothing but one's pride,
Always saves more than it costs,
Is a device needed in every home.

Jesus says, "Have salt in yourselves and be at peace one with another." Have salt in yourselves—don't be dependent on your environment for life's taste. Have springs from within. Then the ups and downs of the home will not mean your going up and down. You are fed from within. That very self-contained sense of taste will help you to be at peace with one another. For the greatest cause of breaking peace with others is the sense of tastelessness within ourselves. We feel out of sorts with ourselves and take it out on others. The Christian holds the world together, he holds the home together, for he holds himself together by the fact that life has inward taste no matter what happens on the outside.

O Christ, give us that inward salt that we may give outward peace. Hold us together, that we may hold the home and all situations together. Amen.

343

## "THIS IS A NEW PEOPLE"

The Christian is the emergence of a new type as different from ordinary humanity, as ordinary humanity is different from the animal. This may be seen from the statement of the Athenian orator, Aristides, who in writing to the Emperor Hadrian (117-138 A. D.) said: "The Christians know and trust God. . . . They placate those who oppress them and make them their friends, they do good to their enemies. Their wives are absolutely pure, and their daughters modest. Their men abstain from unlawful marriage and from all impurity. If any of them have bondwomen or children, they persuade them to become Christians for the love they have toward them; and when they become so, they call them without distinction brothers. . . . They love one another. They do not refuse to help the widows. They rescue the orphan from him who does him violence. He who has gives ungrudgingly to him who has not. If they see a stranger, they take him to their dwellings and rejoice over him as over a real brother; for they do not call themselves brothers after the flesh, but after the Spirit and in God. . . . If anyone among them is poor and needy, and they do not have food to spare, they fast for two or three days, that they may supply him with necessary food. They scrupulously obey the commands of their Messiah. Every morning and every hour they thank and praise God for His loving-kindness toward them. . . . Because of them there flows forth all the beauty that there is in the world. But the good deeds they do they do not proclaim in the ears of the multitude, but they take care that no one shall perceive them. Thus they labor to become righteous. . . . Truly, this is a new people and there is something divine in them."

"A new people, . . . something divine in them." This is the spirit that will create a new world. We must rediscover it and embody it.

O Christ, we pray Thee to make us worthy of this inheritance and worthily give it to this age, so desperately in need of just this. Amen.

## COSMIC OPTIMISM

We began this study and quest for victorious living by asking the question of whether life is a bubble or an egg. We have come out, we trust, at the place of a firm belief that life is an egg, with infinite possibilities if we can get hold of the redemptive energies in Jesus Christ.

Tolstoy, in his *My Confessions and My Religion*, says in substance: There are those who say (1) Life is all bad, so get drunk to evade and forget it. (2) Life is bad, but struggle against it, the stoical attitude. (3) Life is bad, so do the logical thing, commit suicide. (4) Life is bad, but live on like myself, illogical, accepting life as it comes. Obviously, this is not the full Christian statement, for in Christ we do not merely accept life as it comes, we make life what it ought to be. There is redemptive energy available to change the quality of life itself and to turn the course of life and give it a moral mastery. It is true that this new life has its limitations under present conditions, for there are other thwarting human wills and there is recalcitrant nature. Jesus "returned in the power of the Spirit unto Galilee," but He had to confess that a prophet was "not without honor save in his own country." He was thwarted. The seed may be sound, but a lot depends on the soil and other conditions if it is to be fruitful. So there are limitations. But we are not finally limited by those limitations. We can turn those very limitations into contributions. When the invited people in the parable refused the invitation to the feast, the servant was told to go out into the highways and hedges and get everybody he could to come in. Thwarted at certain places the invitation broke into universality. It used its very thwartings.

So Christianity has been described as "cosmic optimism." It is. But an optimism with scars on it.

---

**O Christ, I thank Thee that I can now face life with hope and with a solid foundation of that hope—for Thou art my hope. Amen.**

345

## FAILURES

Christianity is "cosmic optimism." As I sit in Round Table conferences and listen to what men are saying about life, I find that the Christian is the only one—the only one who seems to have hope and an open door. He may be streaky and poor material, but he knows that he has got hold of ultimate reality in Christ.

True, there are failures among Christians and among sincere Christians too. The reason? I think I saw it one morning after a storm as I sat on our prayer knoll at Sat Tal. A vine had reached its delicate fingers up and across the void until it had grasped the branch of a pine tree. It had arrived! But the morning after the storm it was a poor drooping thing with its head hanging to the earth—the branch upon which it was clinging had broken in the storm. The vine had fastened itself upon a rotten branch instead of the strong, central healthy trunk. Many Christians are like that—they fasten themselves upon some dead branch of Christianity, a special rite, or doctrine, or custom, or person, but do not get to the central trunk, Christ. The storm comes and they go down along with the dead branch. This has happened during the years of economic depression—people have gone down because fastened to the culture surrounding the Christian Church, but with no living contact with Christ, the central trunk. But where men have hold of the central reality, Christ, they have stood up against things victoriously and have toughened under adversity. In Acts 13. 17 it says the people were made "great during their stay in Egypt." In more ways than one did they become "great." In adversity we do become "great"—provided we have hold of the central trunk, Christ. So Christianity is a cosmic optimism only if it is Christ-optimism.

———

Christ, my Lord, Thou hast become my one steady place amid a world of flux. Help me to catch Thy dependableness so that people fastening upon me may not be let down. Amen.

## DWELLING IN TOMBS

It is said in Scripture that a certain man had his "dwelling in the tombs." The fact is that we all dwell in a tomb—the earth is one vast tomb largely made up of the very carcasses of the dead. We are on our way to become part of that cosmic dust. That is the truth in pessimism. But there are two ways to dwell in tombs—one is the way of the man who raved and cut himself. On his way to death he deals death to himself. The other way to live in a tomb is the way we live in one at the Lucknow Ashram. The building was built as a tomb, the central dome-room contains the grave around which many living rooms have been added. We have made the dome-room into our chapel, transformed the tomb into a temple. Here we live in joyous fellowship and service. We live a deathless life amid the dead.

The man dwelling in the tombs was "a man out of the city." The city with its problems and oppressions had driven him mad. The city is doing that to many people today, for it is the focal point of human problems. It gets on our nerves and defeats us, so we retreat to tombs and live there tormented by devils of depression and gloom and fear.

But Jesus told His disciples, "Tarry ye in the city . . . until ye be endued with power from on high." This man had tarried in the city until he was endued with fears from below. The city can become the place of torment or the place of triumph. It all depends what is on the inside—unholy demoniac fears or the Holy Spirit.

When we have learned the secret of the Holy Spirit's indwelling, then the tomb becomes an Ashram. We have found the secret of cosmic optimism amid cosmic death, for in Christ we are deathless.

————

We thank Thee, O Christ, that Thy tomb was but the gateway to fuller life. Help me this day to make my living in this cosmic tomb the breaking of seals that keep me from abundant living. Amen.

DECEMBER 5

Acts 23. 6
Acts 24. 15
Romans 4. 18

1 Corinthians 15. 19
2 Thessalonians 2. 16

## "THERE IS NO!"

The Sadducees were the people who said, "There is no resurrection." The best they could say was, "There is no." They lived on a negation—poor diet! There are many who are living on denials. They are getting more spiritually lean every day. The whole thing seems so anomalous—denying the fact of God and the fact of meaning in the universe with the very powers that God has given them. The faculties that can weigh values and meaning, even when deciding against them, have value and meaning. I once found myself looking for my glasses with the aid of the very glasses I was looking for! I had them on! Thus do men deny reason in the universe with the very reason God has given them. They deny God by the very God-given life within them.

The Christian does not deny death. He lives in it and then says: "There is a resurrection, because I am resurrected. I live now in victory over all negation, all denials." We do not deny death. For, as Macmurray says, "This is the first and supreme lie of the devil, 'Thou shalt not surely die.'" Many try to get rid of death by denying it. We do not. We acknowledge death—and then proceed to overcome it and use it!

A friend experienced five successive springtimes on one journey as she traveled from the warmer climate of Persia to the colder climate of Russia and Finland. The Christian lives not in five successive springtimes, but in perpetual spring. There is a renewing taking place at every moment of his life. He is under a cosmic Yes, instead of a cosmic No.

But you say, "Hopes may be dupes." Our reply is, "Yes, and fears may be liars." I know them to be. For when I look at Christ I can say with Sir Oliver Lodge, "Nothing is too big to be believed and nothing is too great to be true."

———

O Christ, Thou dost save me and my universe and Thou dost put a "yes" at the heart of both. I thank Thee. Amen.

## KUCHHA OR PUCKHA?

One of the members of our Ashram, a cultured Indian lady of deep spirituality, lost her husband. She went on with her work undismayed and radiant. Some Sikh village women came to her and said: "You astonish us. We go to pieces under sorrow. You do not. Are all Christians like you? Your religion is very puckha, ours is very kuchha." "Kuchha" means unbaked, "puckha" means well-done, but used in various ways: a dirt road is "kuchha," a metaled road is "puckha"; a mud house is "kuchha," a brick house is "puckha"; green fruit is "kuchha," ripe fruit is "puckha."

These simple women put their finger on the central distinction—the Christian way is *puckha*, it is solid, adequate. All other ways of life are *kuchha*—lacking solidity, adequacy. The Christian way stands up under life. It has wearing qualities. It will outlast all other ways.

In Persia I saw only those hills standing up under the wearing of the centuries which had a central ridge of igneous rock in them. All the others had been flattened out by the rains and the gnawing tooth of time, and had become a part of the plains. Only the *puckha* have stood up under the wear of things. I find everywhere men being flattened out by the pressures and the wear and tear of life. Life becomes too much for them. But the Christian has beneath him a central Rock—that Rock is Christ. That Rock being fused in the fires of the cross is igneous, the ultimate granite upon which the universe is built.

When Sir Humphry Davy discovered potassium, he danced around the laboratory in glee. The Christian, finding this central Rock beneath his feet, dances with a deeper joy. One philosopher said that "all philosophers are sad." Why? Well, they deal in ideas—it is all very *kuchha*. The Christian deals in ideas which become facts—the Word made flesh. It is all very *puckha*.

---

**O Christ, the Rock beneath my feet, help me this day to help someone who has been on sinking sand to get their feet on this. Amen.**

## "FROM HENCEFORTH"

We have been asserting that the Christian way is "cosmic optimism." It is. And it asserts that optimism both about men and things when life is darkest. Edward Burroughs says, "Christianity combines the most absolute pessimism about man's unaided powers with an unquenchable optimism as to what in God's hands he may become." Pessimism—optimism. But the last word is optimism.

If there was ever a moment when Jesus should have asserted pessimism, it was when standing before the Council. They had struck Him in the face, blindfolded Him, spat upon Him, and yet in the midst of it all He stood and said, "Henceforth ye shall see the Son of man sitting at the right hand of power." What a victorious soul! With both His hands bound He talks about sitting at the right hand of power. With swollen lips and bloody face He says, "Final power is mine!" And it is! The ages have confirmed it. But the amazing thing is that He asserted it while in abject subjection to brutal authority—"Henceforth." This is an important element in victorious living. He did not say, "I hope that victory will be mine some day," but, "Henceforth." He brought it into the here and now. And that bringing it into the present is a part of the victory, a very large part.

Bertha Conde tells of a young woman seated in the garden writing when she was startled by a shadow that fell across the page. When she looked up she saw that the shadow was cast by her long-absent betrothed standing behind her. When the shadow of the cross fell upon Jesus, He saw in that shadow His Father's face, and amid it all said, "Henceforth."

We too must catch and assert the immediacy of the victory. Then we shall be close to

> "The pierced side of One
> Who died upon an ancient hill,
> And left a singing in men's blood."

And that song is victory from "henceforth."

---

O Christ, Thou hast put within my blood a song. Help me to sing it this day with an immediacy in it. Amen.

## AN INNER CORRECTIVE

As we talk about holding a cosmic optimism there rise up before us the many, many futilities and puerilities within the Christian Church itself, and these would dampen, if not destroy, that optimism. These irrelevancies stand out now against the background of world need. We have built up things about Christ which have now become an embarrassment to Him—and to us.

A pious monk found that a little mouse disturbed his devotions, so he tied a cat to a post near by, that it might frighten away the mouse. After his death his followers wanted to do everything just as the master did, so they tied cats to the posts of the rooms where they meditated. In the course of time the original reason for tying the cat was lost sight of, and they had long discussions on what kind and color of a cat should be used, how far from the worshiper, and so on. Many things which occupy our attention in Christendom are as meaningless as tying cats in devotional hours. This tendency toward irrelevancies within Christendom drives one almost to despair. Except—except for one fact.

There is within the Christian system a corrective and regenerative principle and power in the person of Christ. He has an asceptic influence upon the Christian system. He exerts a constant cleansing impact from within. This inner corrective is our hope. He is today confronting us with the question He asked His disciples, "What were you reasoning in the way?" And we are silent, as they were, for we too have disputed about our own greatness, our denominationalisms and petty irrelevancies in the face of a world crisis. But as He corrected them so He shall correct us. His Spirit is mightily pleading through the voices both within and without the Christian Church. And, above all, it is pleading through the world need itself. Those that hear that voice shall live, those who do not shall perish.

---

O Christ, we pray Thee that Thy call to us may lead us to repentance and obedience and a full following of Thee. Amen.

## STONES WHICH THE BUILDERS REJECTED

As one looks at the world situation one of the things that strikes him with greatest force is the fact that at every place of world need the mind of Christ becomes relevant and not only relevant, but imperative, if that need is to be met. An erratic genius like Bernard Shaw now and again flashes out the truth: "The only man who came out of the World War with an enhanced reputation for common sense was Jesus Christ. Though we crucified Christ on a stick, yet He somehow managed to get hold of the right end of that stick, . . . and if we were better men, we might try His plan."

Never have so many people come to this realization as now. And yet never have we seemed so desperately near abandoning His plan altogether as now. We were never nearer war and yet never nearer getting rid of war than now. The world situation has become dangerously balanced. It may go one way or the other. But I repeat that the clear-sighted of the world see that what Jesus said is true: "The stone which the builders rejected, the same is become the head of the corner."

The builders of civilization have tried to build a civilization without Christ. True, we thought we could put Him in as a decoration to make the building religiously respectable. But we did not put Him in the foundation and build upon Him. We thought He wasn't practicable. And now the structure of civilization is crumbling around us. The foundations are wrong—they are Christless, hence crumbling. "The builders"—the experts—have failed us, because they failed Christ. All their attempts at diplomacy, balances of power, security through armaments, selfish nationalism have broken down. The bankruptcy of these methods is laid bare before us. We must begin again. This time Jesus must be not merely decorative but in the foundation itself. It is our one hope.

----

Thy patience, O Christ, astounds us. Thou hast waited for this hour. We have messed up the world with our Christless planning and now we are in confusion. Save us. Amen.

## WE LOOK AT SOME REJECTED STONES

Yesterday we said that Christ must be put into the foundation if civilization is not to crumble into ruin. The world demand, rightly interpreted, means that Christ must become the corner stone in the structure of collective living. We have not put Him there. The builders rejected Him. Instead they put within the foundation something that was anti-Christ, namely, ruthless selfish competition. I cannot see how these two things can be made compatibles. Either Christ or ruthless selfish competition must go.

Capitalism has been captured by this underlying competitive outlook. We need capital, but we do not need it as we now have it. If labor had hired capital in the collective good, instead of capital hiring labor for the benefit of the few, our world situation would have been different. The game of "Beggar my neighbor," which is the essence of competition, has gone on till we have beggared ourselves as well as our neighbor. Such a mild critic as Professor J. Morgan Rees make these charges against the present capitalistic order: "Without in the least subscribing to the view that this capitalistic order is being attacked, we must face the facts: (1) That it does not secure the maximum production of goods and services for our people; (2) That it does not attain justice in its distribution of wealth; (3) That it has failed to provide a tolerable existence for its producers when there are millions of unemployed and many more millions needy in a world of plenty; (4) That it fails to give the greatest possible freedom and stimulus to personalities and to social progress." This may not be an "attack" upon capitalism, but it is an indictment which no system can survive long without fundamental change. That change must be from competition to co-operation. If so, Christ would be in the Foundation. His principles would mean "the permeation of the whole of society by a regulative love."

---

O Christ, this stone of love rejected by the builders is now so desperately needed that we perish without it. Give it to us, lest we destroy ourselves. Amen.

## THE LOVE MOTIVE—A REJECTED STONE

The demand of present-day life is that love be built into the social structure. Not practicable? Then living is not practicable, for living demands love. We suggested that society must organize itself around one of two motives—the hunger motive or the love motive. We have organized life around the hunger motive, largely for the benefit of the few to the exploitation of the many. This has brought us discontent, disruption, disaster.

Communism has organized life in Russia on the hunger motive, not in behalf of the few, but in behalf of all who co-operate. This is a higher step than organizing life around the hunger motive in behalf of the few, for they have enlarged the range of co-operation. But note that it is the hunger motive still. Such a sympathetic interpreter as Macmurray says: "The whole Communist interpretation rests upon the hunger motives to the exclusion of the love motives. In his criticism of Feuerbach, Marx said that Feuerbach had deified the love life of man. It would be legitimate to reply that Marx deified the hunger life of man" (*Creative Society*, p. 117). This means that ultimately there will be disruption in Communism, for the hunger motive is disruptive. For "in practice, a dominant hunger may maintain co-operation with the help of the love-principle which is subordinated to it, but only at the expense of a mutual tension, breaking out inevitably in the long run into open struggle, between individuals and groups" (*Ibid.*, p. 116). Only love can provide the ultimate motive for society, for it would include within itself the satisfaction of the hunger motive. For people who love one another will, if their love is real—that is to say if it is a motive determining action— co-operate for the satisfaction of one another's distinct and individual needs.

This love motive rejected by the builders has now become the head of the corner. We perish without it.

———

We come to Thee, O living Christ, to give us courage to believe that this love-motive is the only way to live, and help us to act on it. Amen.

354

Matthew 6. 33      Luke 4. 43
Matthew 21. 43, 44   Acts 1. 3

## THE KINGDOM OF GOD—ANOTHER REJECTED
## STONE

When we study the records, we find that the message of Jesus was the Kingdom of God. When we study "church history" (significant phrase, for the history of the Christian centuries is "church history" rather than "Kingdom history"), we find that the message was the Church. Why this supplanting of the Kingdom of God by the Church? Jesus intended that the Church should be subordinated to and a servant of the Kingdom. But we have reversed that. Jesus said, "The Kingdom cometh not by observation," it permeates silently like leaven from within. But we took the Church from without, as coming "by observation"—it could be counted in statistics, in buildings, in outer forms. We were outwardists, so we took the outward, the Church. The Kingdom is more Christian in its conception than the Church, for it obeys the fundamental Christian law of losing oneself and finding it again. Hence the Kingdom has gone further than the Church.

If you doubt this, ask yourself this question. Is the Church a sufficient foundation upon which to build a new world society? To ask it is to answer it. It was tried during the Medieval Ages and failed. But ask, Is the Kingdom of God a sufficient basis for the new society? The answer is, that it is the only foundation. This stone which the builders, both secular and sacred, rejected has now become the head of the corner. It is emerging as the only solid foundation for human society. It is the Kingdom—or chaos. We have hid this Kingdom light under the bushel of ecclesiasticism. We must now put it on top of the bushel as a candlestick. If we do, we save both. The Church can only be revivified as it becomes, no longer an end in itself, but the servant of the Kingdom, which is far larger than the Church. For the world need cries out for the Kingdom.

———

O God, our Father, in rejecting the Kingdom we have rejected Thee. But Thy patience has worn us down. We now see Thy Kingdom as our only light. Help us to take it. Amen.

## THE KINGDOM OF GOD IS NIGH

When Jesus described the coming of the Kingdom, He used four different phrases all connected with the word "nigh."

He said that when the fig tree becomes "tender," you know that "the summer is nigh" (Mark 13. 28). When life becomes sensitive, tender, has within it an urge for fuller life, is ready to branch out, then know that the summer is nigh, the Kingdom is near at hand. Was ever a world situation more tender and sensitive, tired of the old and yearning after a greater fullness of life than just now? We have wanted fuller life for individuals, but we have never yearned like this for a fuller life for everybody, in everything. Does this not mean that the Kingdom is at our doors?

Jesus said that when these things happen, you know that "he is nigh" (Mark 13. 29). The Kingdom is not an impersonal order. It is a personal Presence—universalized. But what an assumption to say that the coming of the Kingdom and His own coming were synonymous! It is breath-taking.

In a parallel passage Luke says, "When these things begin to come to pass, . . . your redemption draweth nigh." So the Kingdom is redemption! We have seen that the "Kingdom of God" and "life" were used synonymously, but here the "Kingdom" and "redemption" are also used synonymously. The Kingdom is life, but it is the redemption of life as well. Many modernists preaching the Kingdom of God as "life" fail to emphasize the fact that it is redemption. We need nothing so much as we need a conception that is synonymous with life, and at the same time which looses a power for the redemption of life, to make life what it ought to be. The Kingdom covers both. The Kingdom, therefore, is the one open door before a confused and morally collapsed world. It is the stone which the builders have rejected, but is now become the head of the corner.

---

O Father God, Thy Kingdom is nigh. It is now within us and yet we yearn that it burst upon the world with redemptive power. Help us to bring it nigh this day. Amen.

Colossians 1. 14    Revelation 5. 9, 10
Titus 2. 14      Psalm 130. 7

## REDEMPTION—A REJECTED STONE

Of all the stones which the builders of civilization have rejected, none has been more tragic in its effects than the rejection of redemption. Of course individuals here and there have known redemption, but we have not called on its resources for the remaking of the world. We thought we could make a changed world without changed men and we have found it will not work. For "you cannot make the golden age out of leaden instincts." Human sin is the real barrier to the new world.

But the Church must also take its responsibility for rejecting this stone of redemption by confining that redemption to a restricted sphere. We rejected it because we reduced it. We entered into a compromise with the world in which we said we would confine ourselves to saving the souls of men while turning over the economic and social life to the forces of the world to manage. In this we have betrayed Christ. I have seen the idols of the temples of China bricked up and immured when the temples were turned into schools. They were not thrown out—that would be sacrilege; they were lovingly preserved—and confined! We have done that with Christ—we have bricked Him up, confined Him to the personal, and have turned over the rest of life to other lords and masters—to our ruin.

Now we see where the issues must be joined: "It is in the arena of the economic that the next battles for Christ must be fought." For this realm belongs to Him. For, as someone has said: "Christianity is the only religion which takes economics seriously. The material bases of human life are of the utmost importance to it." For, "if a man does not master economics, then economics will master man." Christ must master and redeem both.

This stone of redemption of the whole of life is now becoming the head of the corner. We perish without it.

----

Thou Redeemer of the whole of life, redeem us wholly. And help us not to fear to claim all life for Thee. Amen.

357

Matthew 7. 28, 29    John 6. 63
Mark 1. 27    Matthew 11. 4–6

## THE REALISM OF JESUS—A REJECTED STONE

Of all the strange anomalies in history the strangest is this: the Man who was the greatest realist in history has been turned into the greatest idealist. Jesus' realism was so astonishing, so different that men did not know what to do with it. They had to act on it or reject it. But they couldn't bring themselves to do either, so they found a way by which they would both hold Jesus and hold the old order of life—they made Him into an ideal. That ideal would be practiced some day—but not now. They thus satisfied their sense of being loyal to the high while practicing the low. Christ was crucified on the cross of being irrelevant—*now*.

So we adopted Christianity as an idealism, lifted up high above life, inoperative except here and there in small things. Because we could hold high ideals we thought we were thereby spiritual. But "all idealism is a concealed materialism," for it makes a divorce between body and spirit, and refers religion to the spirit, while other ways of life control the material. Hence idealism becomes materialism, for the latter is acted on.

Jesus was astonishingly realistic. So realistic that men thought it idealism. When He said we must love our neigh-bor as ourselves, that is not idealism—it is realism, and we are discovering that it is the only realism, for nothing else will work. Unless you give an equal and fair chance to everybody, you will have none for yourself. Selfishness is suicide, collective and individual.

When Jesus said we must lose ourselves to find ourselves, this is not idealism, it is realism. It is obeying a fundamental law of life. Nothing else will finally work. The demand that religion be realistic is upon us. The world is perishing for the need of just this thing. So the realism of Jesus, rejected by the builders, is made the head of the corner.

----

O Thou realistic Christ, make us realistic. Save us from imperative ideals that have become opium to us. Amen.

Matthew 9. 8    Luke 4. 32
Matthew 28. 18    Romans 1. 4

## OUR CENTRAL NEED MET

The first sermon I preached in India was on this text: "Thou shalt call his name Jesus; for he shall save his people from their sins." I would be happy if it should be my last text to India—and to the world. For in these words, and in the fact that underlies them, man's greatest need is met.

We said that men needed two things: light on the mystery of life, and power for the mastery of life. In Jesus those two things are met. He gives light on the mystery of life by the way He Himself lived. His life becomes a focal point of life's problems—in Him are raised all my problems and all of them find their solution. He is light. But He is more— He is power to master life, and to save from the crookedness of life. He saves His people from their sins.

A university woman of keen mind was telling me of the discovery she had made of Christ as a man—His humanity brought Him so near to us, He was no longer in the heavens, but alongside of us, struggling with our struggles. She had found an example of life. It left her mentally satisfied, but morally defeated. Then I told her that in Jesus we have two things: One who is like us, meeting life as we meet it, calling on no power that you and I cannot have for our moral battle. He met life, not as God, but as a man. Therefore He is my example. But I find something else in Him. He confronts me from the side of God with one offer of redemption. He is thus unlike me, therefore my Redeemer. Had He been only like me, He could have been only my example; had He been only unlike me, He could have been only my Redeemer. But He was both, and therefore meets my dual need, for I need light and I need power. "Say that in every sermon, won't you?" she said, as this truth dawned on her and made her utterly new. She had found Him as power.

---

O Christ, help me not to stop half way, but to enter into my full inheritance of victory. Amen.

359

## THE MODERN MOOD OF DESPAIR—WHY?

H. S. Wood says that if anyone would interpret modern scientific humanism in a sentence these words would suffice: "Put your trust in science and have confidence in yourselves." This is the faith that is supposed to be the faith of all educated persons under forty. And the scientific humanists were very sure about it all. So sure they became dogmatic.

This was accepted as a modern gospel, but it has turned out to be a gospel with no music at its heart. It doesn't sing. The fact is that scientific humanism has grown very weary, its feet are leaden, and its soul is confused and dismayed. It has lost nerve, because it has lost meaning from its universe. Bertrand Russell says that evolution is a long, wearisome story with a poor point. It resembles a tedious anecdote related by a doddering old gentleman. "This very unpleasing universe is like a bottle of very nasty wine." "I think the external world may be an illusion; but if it exists, it consists of events, short, small, and haphazard. Order, unity, and continuity are human inventions."

Scientific humanism, thinking that it needed no Saviour except itself, has found itself disillusioned and full of despair. Wood comments, "Scientific humanism is fundamentally bankrupt. It can sustain neither faith in science, nor our hopes for mankind." If you would see the necessity of man having a Saviour, do not look at the down-and-outs in the gutter, but look at the finest intellectual flower of our race at the end of their resources, sad and dismayed. Christ is necessary for man and not merely for man as degraded.

Jesus Christ saves His people from the sins of despair and gloom because He saves them from themselves. I know nothing of gloom, or dismay, or discouragement, and if you ask us why, I point to Christ. That's all. But that's enough.

---

O Christ, Thou art my antidote for gloom. For in Thee I find a central gladness. I thank Thee. Amen.

# MADE NARROW AND SAVED FROM NARROWNESS

In the course of our study together we have mentioned many things from which we are saved by the power of Christ. In gathering up the loose ends as we near our goal we must look at a great fear in the minds of many—the fear of being considered narrow. To be called "narrow" is to be damned in modern eyes. This holds many back from a complete freedom in Christ.

There is no doubt that Christ does narrow one. "The love of Christ narrows me," says Paul, and this is true. Jesus says that the new patch on the old garment shrinks and tears the old. There is a sense in which the Christian does pull in and does tear relationships and situations by a very definite shrinking tendency. Christ does narrow us and does keep us from doing many things we otherwise would do. But that is only one phase of the truth. Jesus at the very time He mentions the shrinking says the new life within you will be like expanding wine which will constantly need new wine skins.

The Christian is at once the narrowest and the broadest of men. He becomes a man of one Book and one Person. And yet "all things are yours," so he breaks all bonds and barriers. He is a man of one Book, and then of all books; of one Faith, and then of all faiths; of One Person, and then of all persons; of one Interest, and then of all interests; of one Kingdom, and then of all kingdoms. One compass point is on Christ and then the other sweeps the horizon. To sweep the horizon without having a point on Christ turns out to be Theosophy. To hold one point on Christ without sweeping the horizon turns out to be narrow conservatism. To have both a single-pointedness and an all-inclusiveness is to be a Christian. If you belong to Christ, then all things are yours—you are at once the narrowest and the broadest man in the world!

---

O Christ, I cling to Thee, and now I am free to walk the earth. I thank Thee for this bondage-freedom. Amen.

## GIVEN EXPERIENCE AND SAVED FROM EXPERIENCE

As we have talked about experience during our pilgrimage the objection would probably arise from the side of the Barthians, that experience is an unsure foundation, too subjective, too mystical, bound up too much with the historical process. We must depend, they say, upon the objective Word of God, which speaks to us through the written Word. The first is fluctuating, depending too much on emotional states, the latter is abiding, sure.

There is something in this objection and we must listen to it. Barth and his colleagues provide a corrective and a needed one. But it is only a corrective, and not the full truth. It seems that the full truth lies in both experience and revelation. This passage (Luke 24. 35) puts them together: "And they rehearsed the things that happened in the way (Experience), and how he was known of them in the breaking of the bread" (Revelation).

In that experience they told of how the living Christ was with them and how their hearts burned within them as He spoke to them by the way. To discount that is to discount an authentic meeting with Christ which is individual, personal, intimate, life-changing. We therefore make no apology for experience, for Christ is in that experience just as definitely as He is in the objective Revelation. To repudiate experience, or to minimize it, is to minimize and thus to repudiate this living Christ of experience.

At the same time we must not minimize this objective Revelation. He revealed Himself in the breaking of the bread. He does speak through the Word. And that revelation of Himself is redemptive. Experience needs constantly to be corrected by this objective Revelation. To take one or the other is to impoverish each. We need both. When we take both, we become men of the burning heart and of the constantly illuminated and directed soul. Then we are safe—and saved!

---

O living God, live within me day by day in intimate experience, and then may I listen to Thy voice through Thy Word in humble obedience. Amen.

Proverbs 26. 13–16    1 Corinthians 4. 12
2 Thessalonians 3. 10    Colossians 1. 29

## HE SAVES FROM LAZINESS

We need to be saved from laziness, inertia, lack of ambition, and noncreativeness. The soul must be re-energized, enkindled, and made alive and fruitful.

Christ does that very thing. James says that through conversion "the soul is made more energetic." It is. "By his energy and happiness we know he has found God," said some Hindus in regard to a certain Christian. As the soul has now "a clean joy"—a joy which does not produce counter-currents of disquietude as some joys do, there is a sense of rhythm and harmony and therefore of fruitful energy. The soul is not wasted on the lesser issues of life. It is single-pointed.

When the disciples said to Jesus, "Rabbi, the Jews were but now seeking to stone thee; and goest thou thither again?" Jesus answered, "Are there not twelve hours in the day?" It is not a question of what they will do, or not do—there are twelve hours in the day. I must complete my task.

What a sense of inward drive is found in these words! The redemptive life within Him must give vent to itself in spite of threats or obstacles. The life of Christ within one breaks up inertia. "Jesus disturbs my complacency," said a sincere Indian youth. He does. "He becomes the Conscience of my conscience," said another. And because of this there can be no wasting of time in needless rest. A society lady of sixty complained of her lack of ambition, staleness, inertia, and laziness. Christ came into her life, and immediately "the soul was made more energetic," so much so that she wrote a book— her first book—which went into a number of editions and which met the spiritual need of many. Christ gave her "a second wind" in the race of life. There is a sense of abounding energy when we are in fellowship with this renewing, life-giving Christ.

---

O Christ, I pray Thee that today I may be saved from all lethargy, all dodging of responsibility; may I be really alive and alive in worth-while things. Amen.

Galatians 1. 3, 4   Colossians 1. 13, 28
Romans 8. 2   Colossians 2. 10

## HE SHALL SAVE HIS PEOPLE

I can never again be a pessimist. I know there are enough hard, brutal facts to warrant pessimism if you take your eyes off Christ. But with my eyes on Him my pessimism is cured. Here is adequacy—here is power. Of course that power can only be released if we link up with it by a complete abandon to His will. But given that, anything can happen. "He shall save his people from their sins." That covers every need.

I have social hope amid the hopelessness around me. For as we discover the larger meaning of sin—as we discover that the central social sin is the organizing of life on the unchristian principle of selfish competition when co-operation is open to us, when we discover the disloyalty to Christ involved in allowing the means of production to fall into the hands of the few for private personal gain instead of being in the hands of society for the good of all, when we discover all this, as we are slowly doing, with many a set-back, then we shall turn to Him for a larger salvation. Then there will be a larger release of larger power in larger realms. Wishful thinking? So be it! I would rather wishfully think toward faith than toward collapse.

"He is able to save to the uttermost." That "uttermost" we have only begun to explore. In that word I see provision for every one of my personal sins and for every one of the social sins of this, and succeeding ages. We have seen Christ in the cramping, imprisoning framework of a capitalistic order based on competition, and we have wondered why His power is limited. It is bound to be. But put Him in the framework of a co-operative order and there His full power can be loosed. He will then save us to the uttermost because we will allow Him to the uttermost. And that salvation will not be "in our sins," but "from our sins." There is a profound difference.

---

Christ of the Almighty Arm, work today in my life in saving me from my sins, and in helping me to save society from our sins. Amen.

## "YOUR HOUR" . . . "MY TIME"

Reckitt says, "Hence we find conspicuous in the economic sphere that discouragement which is now the characteristic of a civilization dominated by an exhausted humanism." An exhausted humanism! We have put man on the throne and now our hearts refuse to worship him. We don't like the object of our worship. Man has had his day and he has turned it to darkness. Jesus said, "This is your hour and the power of darkness"—you have had "your hour," and the best you could do with it was to turn it into midnight. These words can be used of this day of humanism. Humanism has exhausted itself and us.

But Jesus uses another phrase to the people of His day: "My time." "Your hour" . . . "My time." "Your hour"—and you reveal darkness! "My time"—and I reveal light through your very darkness; I reveal love through your hate, I heal through your wounds; I sacrifice myself through your selfishness; I am universalized through your very narrowness. I create a universal brotherhood through your national rejection; through the death you inflict I bring life to you and to all men. *My* time—I am master even when most passive. I conquer even when most conquered. I save even when I cannot save myself.

Then and now He is the unexhausted Christ. His "time" will yet come. The "hour" of exhausted man is drawing to a close—the "time" of the inexhaustible God-Man will dawn. It is here—at our doors. Some have taken Him, know His power, but exhausted humanity as such must turn to Him for a vital renewal—or perish.

The "hour" of deified, defeated man is brief. The "time" of the undefeated God-Man is eternal. We belong to that eternal and we will not be dismayed at this "hour." This "hour" belongs to man—the next is His!

So we rejoice in a victory that is, and that is to come. We taste, but this is only a foretaste. His touch is our victory—His "time" is our full victory.

----

O Christ, we thank Thee that we belong to the inexhaustible—help us to draw heavily upon it today. Amen.

Philippians 4. 11–13
John 17. 10, 15–18
Acts 26. 28, 29

DECEMBER 23

## "AMID ALL THESE THINGS"

If I were to choose a verse that would sum up what I have been trying to say during this study quest, it would be, "Yet amid all these things we are more than conquerors through Him who has loved us" (Romans 8. 37, Weymouth). This statement combines an intense realism with an amazing assertion of victorious optimism. I say "realism," for there is no blinking of the difficulties confronting such living. Look at the context. This is not moony lotus-eating which says that all is well for there are no problems, but an open-eyed frankness that says, "Yes, I see the difficulties that come from distress, persecution, hunger, nakedness, danger of the sword, from death, from life, from things present, from the future—and yet, and yet amid all these things we are more than conquerors." It takes in all the facts and yet asserts the central fact of victory.

Note that word "amid." The test of any system is not what it does with the spiritual life, but with the material—"all these things." What is its relationship with things? Does its spirituality include the material? That is the test. The Vedantist word is, "Beyond all these things"; the Moslem word is, "Accommodation to all things"; the Buddhist word is, "Disillusionment with all these things"; the ordinary Hindu word is, "Maya of all these things"; the Communist word is, "Through all these things"; the worldling's word is, "By all these things"; the Christian's word is, "Amid all these things." That word "amid" depicts relationship to, and yet not identification with all these things. It shows realistic contact, and yet inward transcendence. And that is exactly the relationship we need. We must not blink "these things," nor must we be blinded by them. For while we are dependent every moment on matter so that the spiritual life must function through matter or fail to function at all, nevertheless "life is more than meat."

———

O Christ, make me more than conqueror amid all these things. May I know how to be at once at home in the world and yet not at home—as Thou wert. Amen.

366

## "CONQUERORS"

Our battle is an embodied battle so the victory must be an embodied victory. Our spirituality must be shown in relationship to material things or fail to be spirituality. That man is more spiritual who is spiritual through matter than the one who tries to be spiritual apart from matter. So "amid all these things" we must be conquerors.

But how can we be conquerors when so many of our social problems have not yet been solved and we cannot solve them personally? We can acknowledge that the full victory is not here, but that it is here, as far as we are concerned, for our faces and our powers are set in the direction of their solution and dedicated to that end.

In the meantime we can start in motion against every evil a counter-good. When evils came upon Jesus, He did not dodge them, nor bear them, but He started a counter-good. Through His crucifixion He started the counter-good of redemption. When evil came upon Him, He loosed forces for the very destruction of that evil. When hate becomes bitter against us, we can start the counter-good of reconciling love. If poverty is our lot, we can start the counter-good of a regal spirit amid rags. If death takes our loved ones, we can start the counter-good of a deathless joy and hope amid it all. We thus help to conquer death in ourselves and the world. If we live amid turmoil and clash, we can start the counter-good of a peaceful mind, an unperturbed calm. If we live in an unbrotherly world, we can start the counter-good of a brotherhood spirit. "Why, these Christians love each other even before they are acquainted," complained an early enemy of Christianity. They had started the counter-good of class-transcending reconciling love. Every evil that comes upon the Christian can thus make him produce a counter-offensive of victorious love.

––––––

O Christ, Thou dost turn our hearts to the mighty offensive. Help us this day in every situation to whisper to ourselves and Thee, "More than conquerors." Amen.

## THE SIGN IS A BABE

On the first Christmas morning the announcement was made: "And this shall be a sign unto you; ye shall find the Babe." The sign was a Babe—a fact; an embodied fact. This is the key to the whole of Christianity: it began as an embodied fact, it must continue as an embodied fact.

India would have said, "Ye shall find a mystic light—that shall be the sign." China would have said, "Ye shall find a correct code of morality." Greece would have said, "Ye shall find a philosophical conception." But the gospel said, "Ye shall find the Babe." The mystic light, the correct code, the philosophical conception, and very much more, have come together in an embodied Person. Religion was now realization.

He became the reconciling place where opposites met. He was the meeting place of God and man. Man the aspiring and God the inspiring meet in Him. Heaven and earth came together and are forever reconciled. The material and the spiritual after their long divorce have in Him found their reconciliation. The natural and the supernatural blend into one in His life—you cannot tell where one ends and the other begins. The passive and the militant are so one in Him that He is militantly passive and passively militant. The gentle qualities of womanhood and the sterner qualities of manhood so mingle that both men and women see in Him their ideal—and the revelation of the Fatherhood and the Motherhood of God. The activism of the West and the meditative passivism of the East come together in Him and are forever reconciled. The new individual, born from above, and the new society—the Kingdom of God on earth—are both offered to us in Him. The sign is a fact. And thus it had to be: The weeping child would not be satisfied with the idea of motherhood—it wants a mother! We cannot be satisfied with the idea of salvation—we need a Saviour!

---

O Christ, since the sign must be an embodied fact, help me this day to embody victorious living, and may this be in my total life. Amen.

## "MORE"

The word "more" stands out of this passage with peculiar force: "More than conquerors." That word is a window-word that lets us see into the inexhaustible nature of our resources and the unlimited development before us. It is the "more" that really counts. It is this "plus" that turns the tide toward victory. This "plus" is characteristic of the gospel. It allowed men to emerge beyond the ordinary level in goodness, in achievement, in joy, in radiant living. It is that which gives "survival value" to the Christian. In the struggle of life in lower nature it is the extra ounce of strength, the extra power of endurance that makes the fit animal survive when the others fall out, beaten in the struggle.

In this higher struggle it is this extra power that the Christian has at his disposal that keeps him from breaking when everything is breaking around him. It keeps him hopeful amid hopelessness, radiant amid the shadows, morally able amid surrounding moral collapse. In the race of life the extra resources that the Christian finds in Christ make him a moral winner. Since these extra resources were at their disposal, Jesus expected His followers to do "more"—"What do you do more than others?" He expected them to *do* more because they *had* more.

The first testimony I ever gave in public after conversion was this: "There is only one thing better than religion, and that is more religion, and I want more." One touch and my soul was afire for more. That inward passion for more should be an eternal thing. Not dissatisfied, but forever unsatisfied!

And just because this inward cry for more is met by God's offer of a perpetual "more" there is no limit to what the Christian might be and do. Professor James says, "The potentialities of the human soul for development are unfathomable." They are if one is in contact with unfathomable Resources.

---

O Christ of the limitless love, take away the limitations from my love. Put me under the spell of the "more." Amen.

## PERPETUAL PARENTAGE

It is well to remember the statement of Professor Hocking that religion "has had a perpetual parentage." It has been "the mother of the arts." "All the arts of common life owe their present status and vitality to some sojourn within the historic body of religion; there is little that we call culture which was not at some time a purely religious function." Van Deusen says: "Christianity has borne one after another of the arts—not only music and painting and sculpture and drama and architecture, but also dancing, legislation, science, philosophy, moral control; has given them birth and matured them through their critical infancy. Then, as they attained maturity and sufficient strength to exist independently, religion has sent them forth to continue their development as secular enterprises—often not without the struggle and hard feeling so characteristic of adolescence's break from home. Hospitals, schools, colleges, institutions for the unfortunate and the outcast, general philanthropy—all had their birth within the life of the Church" (*God in These Times*, p. 145). These and many other things, such as prison reforms, abolition of slavery, improved conditions of labor, movements for world peace, were the result of that perpetual parentage characteristic of Christianity. A spiritual fecundity is within the Gospel of Christ.

And now victorious living is under a new test. Has it enough power to give birth to a new social order? This is the demand for parentage that is now laid on religion. If it can show a spiritual fecundity here, it will become the mother of a new world.

And we who are launching out into victorious living must be so alive that new movements, new initiatives, new impulses, new lives shall follow as a manifestation of the spirit of perpetual parentage within us. We are more than conquerors because we not only conquer in our own battle, but we bring forth movements which help other people to conquer. More than conquerors because conqueror-producing.

————

O Christ, may Thy power produce in me today some life-giving movement, however small. Amen.

## MORE THAN CONQUERORS

It would have been adequate if Paul had said that we are conquerors through Him that loved us, but he put in the added emphasis, "more than conquerors." Exaggeration? No, plain statement of fact.

It is interesting to see how language had to bear a new weight of meaning with the coming of Jesus into the world. It had been adequate to express human meanings, but now it was called on to express Divine-human meanings. The Divine was breaking through into the human; and language, called on to express that fact, sometimes breaks down. The early Christians had to lay hold of superlatives, coin new words, and ofttimes it all became so overwhelming that "the Holy Ghost disorganized their grammar." The rules couldn't bear the pressure of this new, glorious, effervescent life. The new wine had to be put not only into the new wine-skins of new organizations and institutions, but also into the new wine-skins of a new vocabulary. For here was a fresh, new set of facts.

"More than conquerors"—what does it mean? Some of the tribes of Africa believe that when a man conquers another, the strength of the conquered passes into the conqueror. That is what happens spiritually. When you conquer an evil through the power of Christ, the strength of that conquered evil passes into you in two ways. First, it establishes the habit of victory within you and makes the next battle easier. This means that the more you conquer, the more you can conquer. Goodness becomes habituated and hence the normal attitude toward life. The grooves are cut within our nerve tissues so that life flows naturally in the direction of victory. Second, by the conquering you are able to pass on to others that victory. But in passing it on it becomes more fixed within yourself. So in a double way we are more than conquerors.

———

O Christ, we thank Thee that we are bursting into freedom—freedom from fear of failure and from the fear of future contingencies. For Thou art getting into our blood and into our nerve tissue. Amen.

## THE BASIS OF BEING MORE THAN CONQUERORS

The basis of this conquest of life by Life must be examined to see if it is sound and sure. For this purpose 2 Timothy 1. 7 becomes luminous: "For the spirit which God has given us is not a spirit of cowardice, but one of power and of love and of sound judgment" (Weymouth).

Here is the basis of the overcoming—the whole organism is strengthened. The personality made up of will, emotion, and mind is renewed—there is "power" for the will, "love" for the emotion, and "sound judgment" for the mind. By the renewing of the total life the spirit of fear is cast out. You cannot get rid of fear by bidding the fears depart. They will not depart. They will depart only as they are cast out by some positive influence that possesses you, thereby making these fears absurd. This positive influence is the spirit of power, of love, and of sound judgment—in other words, the Spirit of Christ working in the depths of your being.

The reasons for fear are rooted in one or more of these roots. (1) A sense of being weak in the will, a feeling that we are morally inadequate for life. Life is too much for us. It demands more than we have to give. (2) A lack of love. We do not love people, so we are afraid of them; we do not love God supremely, so we are uncomfortable at the thought of Him; we do not love His will, so are afraid of what He will ask us to do; we do not love life, so we are afraid of it. (3) We feel helpless and confused, for our minds lack a sound, unified judgment. We have no key in our hands that fits the problem of human living—so we fear because of intellectual inadequacy.

But now the whole being is brought under a unified control—the Spirit of Christ. That means power for the will, love for the emotions, and sound judgment for the mind. It is the answer of Life to inadequate life.

---

O Christ, I can overcome anything outside of me if Thou dost possess everything inside of me. Take it all. Amen.

## THE BASIS OF OUR CERTAINTY

I trust that there has grown up a deep spiritual certainty as we have gone on day after day in our quest. We must now say a final word about that certainty and its basis. In Hebrews 2. 3, 4 we read, "This, after having first of all been announced by the Lord Himself, had its truth made sure to us by those who heard Him, while God corroborated their testimony by . . . gifts of the Holy Spirit distributed in accordance with His own will" (Weymouth).

There are three things in this passage: (1) the historic— "announced by the Lord Himself"; (2) the experimental— "corroborated by the gifts of the Holy Spirit"; (3) the collective witness—"made sure to us by those who heard." It is interesting that the Christian Church has fastened on one or the other of these factors as the basis of certainty, as the place of authority in Christianity. Many Protestants have said the place of authority is the infallible Bible—the historical. Other Protestants have made the basis of authority an infallible Christian experience—the experimental. Roman Catholics have made the infallible Church the basis of authority—the collective witness.

Each of these taken by itself is inadequate. But all of them coming together contributes to the final certainty. The basis of authority is at the junction of the three. (1) The historical. In Jesus a norm has been established in history which becomes the touchstone of all life. We have seen Life revealed in a life. (2) But that Life passes from the historical into the experimental—the Jesus of history becomes the Christ of experience. We do not merely remember Christ, we realize Him. (3) But that personal experience may be an hallucination if alone. It must be corroborated by the collective witness. It must be tried on a widespread scale and corroborated. It is. Men of all ages and all climes give a unanimity of witness that it works. The coming together of the historical, the experimental and the collective witness, all saying the same thing, gives a certainty far beyond the certainty coming out of one taken alone. The highest certainty the human mind is capable of knowing on any subject is ours!

O Christ, I rejoice in this certainty. Help me to live worthy of it. Amen.

## THE FIXED ABODE

Our last passage must sum up the whole of our studies together: "In whom you also are being built up together to become a fixed abode for God through the Spirit" (Ephesians 2. 22, Weymouth).

A fixed abode! God, not the dim, fugitive unknown, but God the real, the intimate, the permanent. And how can this be? By being "builded together." Finding God, the Spirit, is an individual thing, but it is also deeply collective. We cannot expect the permanent abiding of God unless we "are built up together." Only a brotherhood transcending race and class and color can be the fixed abode of God. But we have asked Him to abide in a compartmentalized society and in a divided heart. It cannot be.

When Moses was about to build the Tabernacle, he was given a vision and the Voice said, "See that thou make them after their pattern which hath been shewed thee in the mount." He did. Then the account says, "So Moses finished the work. Then . . . the glory of the Lord filled the tabernacle." When? When he made all things according to the pattern.

We have seen the pattern—the Kingdom of God on earth. It has spoiled us for any other pattern. This is it. For it we will live and for it we will bleed—and if necessary, die. We will go out and make all things according to that pattern both within ourselves and in society. And God will take up His fixed abode with us as we are builded together. We cannot ask Him again to abide in this ramshackle thing we call society, where some of the children are pinched and starved and some have an unused overplus, where the weaker are exploited by the stronger and injustice is deeply imbedded. No, we will be "builded together," where the sufferings of one are the sufferings of all, and where the gifts of God are shared with all the other children. Into that holy tabernacle of humanity we can ask Him to come—and He will!

---

O God, our Father, we cease our divisions within ourselves and in society and ask Thee to take up Thy fixed abode with us. We will do our part. With our life we say it. Amen.

# INDEX

# INDEX

376

# INDEX

# INDEX

# INDEX